LIFE AND TIMES

OF

STEIN.

KARL FREIHERR VOM STEIN
OBERPRÄSIDENT VON WESTPHALEN

Helioᵍʳ et imp. A. Durand _ Paris.

LIFE AND TIMES

OF

STEIN,

OR

GERMANY AND PRUSSIA

IN THE

NAPOLEONIC AGE.

BY

J. R. SEELEY, M.A.,

REGIUS PROFESSOR OF MODERN HISTORY IN
THE UNIVERSITY OF CAMBRIDGE.

VOLUME I.

GREENWOOD PRESS, PUBLISHERS
NEW YORK   1968

Hoch auf dem alten Thurme steht
Des Helden edler Geist,
Der, wie das Schiff vorübergeht,
Es wohl zu fahren heisst.

'Sieh, diese Senne war so stark,
'Dies Herz so fest und wild,
'Die Knochen voll von Rittermark,
'Der Becher angefüllt.

'Mein halbes Leben stürmt' ich fort,
'Verdehnt' die Hälft' in Ruh',
'Und du, du Menschen-Schifflein dort,
'Fahr' immer, immer zu!'

GOETHE.

LIBRARY OF CONGRESS CATALOGUE CARD NUMBER: 68-23324

To Dr Reinhold Pauli *at Göttingen.*

Dear Dr Pauli,

I dedicate this book to you, first, because I cannot otherwise sufficiently acknowledge the debt I owe to you for the friendly advice, criticism and constant encouragement which I have received from you in writing it.

But if it were not so, I should still wish to inscribe it to the scholar who has thrown so much light from Germany upon English history, not only out of gratitude, but because your authority might protect me from the charge of presumption in treating German affairs from England. I may be asked why I should write the Life of Stein after Pertz, or treat of Germany in the Napoleonic Age after Häusser. If I should answer by pointing to the new materials which have lately been furnished to the historian in the Memoirs of Hardenberg, Schön's Remains, &c., I might be told that it would be wiser to leave the task of working up this new matter to German writers. If in return I point out that you have not adopted this principle, I hope I shall not be supposed to argue that whatever is possible to you is possible to me also, for I only hope to teach my own countrymen, and do not dream of instructing the Germans in their own history as you have instructed the English in theirs. But you certainly had your own countrymen also in view. You doubtless considered that the principle on which the Historical Series of Heeren and Ukert and the Staatengeschichte der neuesten Zeit have been written is a sound one, and that it is not desirable to leave each nation to its own historians. Germany may boast of having put the history of every great European state as much within the reach of her public as her own history. Your countrymen can study the affairs of foreign countries not merely in translations, or hasty magazine-articles, but in elaborate works, written in their own language, with full responsibility and independence of judgment, written also by those who understand clearly the wants of the public for which they write. Among this group of writers you are best known in England, and I shall make my object in writing this book best understood by announcing in this Dedication that I belong to your school.

PREFACE.

It is not to set forth the merits of a great man who has been too little known that I write the life of Stein at such an unusual length, but on account of the intrinsic importance of the revolutions in which he took part. It has been my object to consider the transformation of Germany and Prussia in the Napoleonic age, which has usually been contemplated by us only as a part of the life of Napoleon, in its proper place as a part of German history.

When I first asked myself how this subject might best be treated, I remarked that it was one which especially needed to be gathered up in a person. I soon satisfied myself that the only person who could be taken in this way to represent his nation and his time was Stein.

Hence arose the plan of this work. When it was formed I had no clear opinion as to Stein's claim to be admired or regarded as a great man. It was enough for me that his central position, his important achievements, and his strongly marked character made him more interesting than any of his German contemporaries. As I proceeded with my task I gradually formed an estimate of his merits. It was a very high estimate, as the reader will see, but it was formed in perfect freedom of judgment. I was not influenced by the consideration which so often makes a biographer partial, viz., that if the subject of the biography is not made out to be a very extraordinary man, people will ask why the book was written or why they should read it. The public are invited to read this book simply because they will find in it an account, the clearest the writer could produce, of a great and momentous transition in the history of Germany.

Such an account could not be given in a smaller compass. To set forth the merits of Stein a rapid sketch might have sufficed, but my plan required that the history of Prussia between 1806 and 1822 should be written in some detail, that abundant information about other German states and about Germany in general should be given, and also that biographies of other distinguished men, such as Hardenberg, Scharnhorst and others, should be interwoven with the biography of Stein. I have felt throughout that my explanations and statements must be full because a large proportion of the questions discussed had never been treated before in English. It is the abundance of matter and not, I venture to affirm, any diffuseness or prolixity of style that has made the book so large.

I proceed to give an account of my authorities.

THE SOURCES.

These fall into several classes.

A. Original narratives by leading actors in the history of the time. Of these we have

1. Stein's Autobiography. This is printed at length in Pertz. I have given some account of it below (III. p. 475). It is often vague, and in small details incorrect; but all the important and precise statements it contains are of fundamental importance, and I have taken the greatest care that my narrative should ultimately rest upon them throughout.

2. The Memoirs of Hardenberg. These appeared in two volumes, edited by Ranke, in 1877. They must be carefully distinguished from the spurious Memoirs attributed to Hardenberg which have misled the world for 40 years; of these an account is given below (III. p. 480). The genuine Memoirs are of the utmost importance for the period with which they deal, but this is very short, being only the years 1804 to 1807, in which years, moreover, Stein had not yet become a politician of the first mark. But they have been of much use to me in Part II.

3. Schön's Memoirs. In the work called 'Aus den Papieren Schöns' (4 vols., 1875, 76), are found two autobiographical papers by this important politician. The one covers the whole period of Stein's public life, and speaks freely of him, but seems to have been written in old age, perhaps about 30 years after Stein's Ministry. The second, written in 1844, covers the period from the establishment

of the Central Administration in 1813 to 1840. There
is also a diary of great importance, kept by Schön from
Nov. 29, 1808 to January 6th, 1809. Other short historical
fragments by Schön are contained in this collection. I am
often obliged to controvert Schön's statements; in each
case my objections are given in the text.

4. Arndt, the well-known song-writer, has two books
containing original information about Stein. Some account
is given of these below (II. pp. 489—499). Arndt was not
much initiated into affairs, but gives lively personal de-
scriptions; he is particularly useful for 1812 and 1813,
and for Stein's domestic life in old age. Another work of
his, written in defence of himself against those who accused
him of revolutionary conspiracies, and entitled Noth-
bedrungener Bericht, contains some additional information
about Stein.

5. Count Senfft, Saxon Minister at the beginning of
1813, has left Memoirs, which were published in 1863. He
was married to Stein's niece, and has two or three passages
which are important for Stein's biography.

6. Ludwig v. Ompteda, a Hannoverian politician, has
left a collection of documents connected by a slight thread
of narrative (Politischer Nachlass aus den Jahren 1804 bis
1813). They were published in 3 vols. in 1869. These are
particularly important for the year 1813, and contain some
new papers from Stein's hand.

7. Hans v. Gagern; Mein Antheil an der Politik.
5 vols., 1823—45. A whole volume is devoted to correspondence between Gagern and Stein.

8. Diaries of Sir George Jackson (1872) and Bath
Archives (1873), 4 vols. in all.

9. Gentz; Tagebücher, &c. I may as well class
here all the various writings of Gentz, diaries, letters,
pamphlets, &c., which have appeared at various times.

They lie a little on one side of my subject, but I have kept them in view.

These are the principal writers that fall under this head. Others, such as Rehberg, the Countess Voss, Bishop Eylert, Scheffner, F. v. Raumer, Steffens, Perthes, Varnhagen v. Ense, N. Turgeneff, General Wolzogen, and others, who furnish perhaps one fact or trait apiece, are not worth more particular enumeration.

B. Biographies founded on, distinctly referring to, and reproducing in more or less number, original documents.

1. Das Leben des Ministers Freiherrn vom Stein, von G. H. Pertz. In 6 vols. (the 6th in two divisions). I have had before me the second edition of the first four vols., dated 1850—1. The other three parts, of which there has been only one edition, appeared in 1854—5. This work, in which is included Stein's Autobiography, is by far the most important that has appeared on the subject—more important, indeed, than all others put together. Many imperfect sketches that had appeared earlier (e.g. Rehberg's) are absorbed in it, and many popular delineations that have appeared since (e.g. W. Baur's) are only abridgements of it. It consists of

(a) The Autobiography.

(β) A narrative founded upon information and papers furnished by the family, and in part upon information given orally by Stein.

If I might criticise a work of such inestimable value, I should say that its principal blemish is a sort of confusion, which reigns through it, between the personalities of Stein and Pertz. The reader is frequently left in doubt which of the two is speaking. And this doubt grows upon him as he studies the book. A number of statements, expressions of opinion, &c., which at first he took undoubtingly to come from Pertz, he discovers to be Stein's, and to have been passively copied by Pertz from the Autobiography. In some cases even Stein's errors are thus endorsed by his biographer[1]. This once remarked, it becomes a question whether many other statements, which also seem to be Pertz', are not really Stein's, and in many cases highly probable that they are; but no means are given us of deciding the question.

(γ) A mass of correspondence, partly incorporated in the narrative, partly added in appendices.

(δ) A mass of invaluable official documents, reports of Ministers, diplomatic despatches, political pamphlets reprinted *in toto*, Cabinet Orders, Laws. These are chiefly contained in the rich appendices of the work.

Altogether it seems to me to have continued up to the present time to be the richest source of information not only on the Life of Stein, but on the whole period of German history.

2. Denkwürdigkeiten des Staatskanzlers Fürsten v. Hardenberg. Herausgegeben von Leopold v. Ranke, 1877. These Memoirs consist of two volumes, of which the first is an introduction to Hardenberg's Autobiography, and the second a continuation of it to the end of the war in 1814. A third volume composed entirely of original documents has since been added. The memoirs are founded upon a collection of documents made by Hardenberg himself with a view to the history of his time, and committed by the Prussian Government to Ranke at the end of the 50th year from Hardenberg's death. To me they

---

[1] For example, we read (III. 647) in a report of Stein's to the Czar that he had procured from the merchants of Königsberg an advance of 300,000 thalers for Yorck's army. Yet in his narrative (III. 278) Pertz calls it 500,000. Dr Lehmann (Knesebeck und Schön, p. 190) calls this statement of Pertz 'incomprehensible.' He has not remarked that Pertz is simply transcribing from the Autobiography, and that the error is Stein's own.

have been particularly useful for the commencement of Stein's Ministry, and its connexion with the earlier Ministry of Hardenberg.

3. Das Leben des Generals v. Scharnhorst. Von G. H. Klippel, 1869, &c. This book has generally been found disappointing, but I have drawn from it most of my sketch of Scharnhorst's life, and several of the documents extracted in the chapter on Military Reform.

4. Das Leben des Feldmarschalls Grafen Neithardt v. Gneisenau. Von G. H. Pertz, 1864, 65.

5. Lebensnachrichten über B. G. Niebuhr. I have generally used Miss Winkworth's well-known translation. The book is admitted by its translator to be meagre on the political side. Pertz gives in his Life of Stein a large quantity of Niebuhr's political correspondence which might well have found a place in this work. I have taken some pains to make the present book serve as a political supplement to the Life of Niebuhr.

6. Das Leben des Ober-Präsidenten Freiherrn v. Vincke. Von E. v. Bodelschwingh, 1853. An unfinished work, principally useful for the Westphalian part of Stein's life.

7. Aus den Papieren Schöns. In this collection, besides the biographical fragments, there is a certain amount of correspondence between Schön, Altenstein, Niebuhr, and others, which has been useful.

8. Preussen während der Französischen Occupation. Von Max Duncker. This essay, which originally appeared in the Preussische Jahrbücher, and has since been reprinted in a volume entitled Aus der Zeit Friedrichs des Grossen und Friedrich Wilhelms des Dritten, is entirely founded upon documents preserved in the Prussian Archives, and is of the utmost importance for the period between the Congress of Erfurt and the Treaty of Kalisch.

S. I.

9. Oesterreich und Preussen im Befreiungskriege. Von W. Oncken, 1876. Founded on new documents. Important for the policy of the Czar in the first months of 1813.

10. Das Leben des Feldmarschalls Grafen v. Yorck von Wartenburg. Von G. Droysen, 1851, 52. This very interesting book is a great authority for the Convention of Tauroggen and the important events at Königsberg at the beginning of 1813.

11. Bernhardi's Geschichte Russlands. Useful on the Congress of Vienna.

12. Aus dem Nachlasse F. A. L. v. der Marwitz, 1852. Marwitz is the best literary representative of the feudal opposition to the Stein-Hardenberg reforms.

C. Detached studies on particular historical points have often been useful to me. I may mention particularly: Aegidi, Die Sendung Knesebecks u.s.w. (Sybel's Hist. Zeitschr. 16. 274); Nasse, Die Preussische Finanz- und Ministerkrisis im Jahre 1810 (Sybel's Hist. Zeitschr. 1871); Dilthey, Schleiermachers Politische Gesinnung u. s. w. (Preussische Jahrbücher, Vol. x.); Treitschke, Der Verfassungsstreit, and, Preussen auf dem Wiener Congresse (Preussische Jahrbücher, Vol. XXXVII.). I might place under this head many other less important biographical works, *e.g.* those of Held on Struensee, of Voigt on Dohna, of Schlesier on W. v. Humboldt, &c., and the correspondence of Clausewitz recently published; the controversial papers that were called forth by the publication of Aus den Papieren Schöns, particularly Max Lehmann's Knesebeck und Schön, and the anonymous answer entitled Zu Schutz und Trutz am Grabe Schöns; Quistorp, Die Kaiserliche Russisch-Deutsche Legion; Eichhorn, Die Centralverwaltung; C. Perthes, Das Deutsche Staatsleben von der Revolution and Politische Zustände und Personen in Deutschland zur Zeit der Französischen Herrschaft.

D. From such studies I may distinguish special treatises on whole departments of affairs. Under this head
come Riedel, Der Brandenburgisch-Preussische Staats-
haushalt, a most complete account of Prussian finance
up to the war of 1806, Bassewitz, Die Kurmark Brandenburg im Oct. 1806, v. Rönne, Die Preussischen Städteord-
nungen, and the same author's standard book Das Staats-
recht der Preussischen Monarchie, the statistical works of
Dieterici, the works of Voigt, Baersch and Lehmann on
the Tugendbund, Kaltenborn's Geschichte der Deutschen
Bundesverhältnisse, &c., &c.

E. Lastly, it is needless to remark that the well-
known histories of the period, such as Häusser's Deutsche
Geschichte vom Tode Friedrichs des Grossen, K. A.
Menzel's Zwanzig Jahre Preussischer Geschichte, Gervinus'
Geschichte des xixten Jahrhunderts, Springer's Geschichte
Oesterreichs, and the various writings of v. Sybel on the
period, have always been before me.

The question may be asked: 'In what relation
does the present Life of Stein stand to the great
work of Pertz?' Is it merely an abridgement such
as Pertz himself published in two volumes under the
title Aus dem Leben Steins, or a popular abridgement aiming at a livelier style, such as is the work
of W. Baur? Or does it pretend, on the other
hand, to be in any degree an original work?

In answer I may be allowed first to point out what
a large number of the authorities mentioned in the
above list did not exist when Pertz wrote. It has
seldom happened that I have found myself reduced
simply to abridge Pertz. I have usually found that
later information has enabled me to add or modify

something in his account. Hardenberg and Schön
on the period just before Stein's Ministry and on the
first suggestions of his legislation, the writers on
the Tugendbund and Schön on the course of it,
Düncker on the period from his fall to the War
of Liberation, Ompteda, Ranke and Oncken on
1813, have perceptibly altered the state of our
knowledge on the greater part of his active life.
This is less the case in his old age, but here I
adopt a much more condensed style, so that my
last hundred pages represent about 1400 pages in
Pertz.

It is also possible to use the information given
by Pertz himself so as to produce a narrative by
no means identical with that of Pertz. There is
room sometimes for difference of opinion even in
estimating the evidence, still more in judging the
persons and measures under consideration. It is
possible at times also to apply a different scale of
importance to the same materials. I have tried to
use my own judgment, though with the caution that
beseems a foreigner.

I have also recast the whole narrative in order
to adapt it to a different public. Pertz could assume the whole world in which his hero lived, the
whole scenery and background of his drama, and
the lives of the dramatis personae, to be already
known. I, on the other hand, not only assume all
this to be unknown, so as to bind myself to give
so much of it as to make Stein's life intelligible,
but I am concerned with it for its own sake, and

describe Stein for the sake of his time quite as much as the time for the sake of Stein. I therefore not only reject a prodigious quantity which Pertz gives, but I also insert much which he does not give. In particular I have been anxious to incorporate several companion biographies. Hardenberg and Scharnhorst are described here pretty fully; Schön, Niebuhr, W. v. Humboldt, and some others are painted with much more care than a mere biography of Stein would require. In like manner I have been anxious to disentangle the thread of Prussian history, and to guide the reader as much as possible across the period which separates Frederick the Great from the present day.

In what I have said of making use of Stein's personality to enliven the history of his age I must not be understood to mean that I have not taken a strong interest in his character for its own sake. It was from the outset my intention to describe him with the most conscientious care, and by no means to be content with the slight careless second-hand sketch which is generally considered enough for a foreign statesman. When I was fairly embarked I soon found the character much more interesting than I had anticipated, and before long it had become a labour of love to me to shed the clearest possible light upon it. I certainly wish this biography to be judged by a high standard, and desire no other allowance to be made for me than what may always be claimed by a biographer who is writing of a foreigner, and of one from whom he is separated by a whole age.

In conclusion I have to acknowledge my obligation for kind help received from Dr Pauli, to whom the book is dedicated, and from the Countess v. Kielmansegge for answers kindly given to inquiries made on sundry questions relating to the family, and for the portrait from which the engraving prefixed to the third volume has been executed, and which the Countess certifies to be 'a very good likeness of Stein at about seventy.'

I have also received useful assistance from two Cambridge friends, Professor Sidney Colvin and Mr Oscar Browning.

I cannot refrain at the same time from acknowledging my debt to the Syndicate of the Pitt Press for the invaluable help which they rendered to me unasked at an early stage of my enterprise. Understanding it to be their function to further the production of laborious works for which the book market did not offer sufficient encouragement, they made me an offer which I could not look for from a private publisher, and which has enabled me, as I fully believe, to finish my task sooner than I could have done otherwise by two or three years. This is indeed endowment of research. And to me personally it has made the greatest difference that the agent of their kindness, Mr Clay, has been inspired with all the good will and sympathy of an old friend.

CONTENTS OF VOLUME I.

PART I.

BEFORE THE CATASTROPHE.

CHAPTER I.

STEIN'S EARLY YEARS.

CHAPTER II.

THE PRUSSIAN SERVICE.

CHAPTER III.

PRUSSIA AT WAR WITH THE REVOLUTION.

CHAPTER IV.

WITHIN THE LINE OF DEMARCATION.

CHAPTER V.

STEIN AS MINISTER OF FINANCE.

PART II.

THE CATASTROPHE.

CHAPTER I.

CHARACTER OF THE PRUSSIAN STATE.

CHAPTER II.

FREDERICK WILLIAM II. AND FREDERICK WILLIAM III.

CHAPTER III.

NAPOLEON AND THE EMPIRE.

CHAPTER IV.

NEUTRALITY OF PRUSSIA.

CHAPTER V.

THE CATASTROPHE OF PRUSSIA.

CHAPTER VI.

STEIN DURING THE WAR.

CHAPTER VII.

STEIN IN RETIREMENT.

PART III.

MINISTRY OF STEIN.—FIRST PERIOD.

CHAPTER I.

CONSTITUTION AND TASK OF THE MINISTRY.

CHAPTER II.

STEIN'S COLLEAGUES.

CHAPTER III.

PREPARATION OF THE EMANCIPATING EDICT.

CHAPTER IV.

THE EMANCIPATING EDICT.

CHAPTER V.

STEIN'S POSITION.

CHAPTER VI.

NEGOTIATIONS.

VOLUME I.

PART I.

BEFORE THE CATASTROPHE.

> Tausend Ritter wohlgewappnet
> Hat der Heil'ge Geist erwählt
> Seinen Willen zu erfüllen
> Und Er hat sie muthbeseelt.
>
> HEINE.

at least that turbulent knighthood produced a descendant to whom, as these pages will show, Germany
owes a debt which she has acknowledged but tardily,
and Europe one which has been left unacknow-
ledged.

The scenery of the river Lahn is very like
that of the Rhine.   Its banks are as lofty and as
richly clothed with wood, and the hills confine the
stream as closely.   The railway from Coblenz after
entering the valley brings you first to the Baths
of Ems, so well known to tourists, and since
July, 1870, so well known to history.   After Ems
the next notable station is Nassau.   This is now
a very quiet country town, with a Water-cure
Establishment, and besides that only one conspicuous building.   A handsome family mansion strikes
the eye, built in the latter part of the 17th century,
standing in the midst of outbuildings with a pleasant
garden behind it and approached from the street
through a line of railings and a court adorned with
a few trees.   On the left hand of the old 17th
century façade, as you enter, is a somewhat singular
tower adjoining the house and rising a little above
it.   This is the house which the Minister vom Stein
inherited and in which he spent a good deal of his
life.   The tower was built by him to commemorate
the War of Liberation.

This house stands in the very middle of the
town of Nassau, and though not a palace, is so
much larger and handsomer than any other dwelling
house in the town, that you recognize at once that
the Stein of the day must always have been what
we should call the squire of Nassau.   Here then

we see a specimen of the course pursued by the great knightly families of this region. Their castles stand in ruins on the hill-side; the owners have descended from their eminence and isolation, entered the towns in which common men live, built themselves handsome houses in a more modern style, and taken up a somewhat different social position, which we might describe by saying that the knight has turned into the squire. For before this handsome town-house was built, the family of Stein had lived on the hill-side in the Burg Stein. It was not till this castle, like so many others, had been sacked in the Thirty Years War, that the family abandoned it and came down to live in the valley.

The town of Nassau stands on the right bank of the Lahn, that is to say, the bank which to a tourist coming from Coblenz is on the left hand. The hills behind it are lofty, but do not present a striking appearance as their ascent is gradual, and therefore they recede as fast as they rise. But on the other side of the river stands out commandingly a single hill, towering high above the town and clothed with wood. On the summit of it stands, what in this region is so common, the ruined keep of an old castle. Is this the Burg Stein? No, but it bears another name much more famous in history. It is the Schloss Nassau, the original seat of the family which first checked the ascendancy of Spain, which filled the whole 17th century, the heroic age of Protestantism, with its renown, which gave a king to England and afterwards a royal dynasty to the Netherlands, and which at the same time in its

elder branch maintained an eminent place—though
it did not run altogether an honourable career—
among the sovereign houses of Germany, until the
duchy of Nassau in 1866 was swallowed up by
Prussia. As the family of Stein descended from
the mountain to inhabit the handsome house just
described in Nassau, so did the House of Nassau
itself leave its dismantled keep upon the top of the
hill and go to occupy palaces at Wiesbaden and at
the Hague.

But the traveller whose object is the Burg Stein,
when he has issued from the railway station and
learned that the commanding tower above him is
not that but the Schloss Nassau, is at a loss, for no
other castle is anywhere to be seen. On inquiry
he learns that the Burg Stein is not visible immediately from this point, but that it is quite near and
stands on a projection from the side of the same hill
which the Schloss Nassau crowns. Already where
he stands he can be made to observe lower down on
the hill-side the peaked top of a new erection which
he is informed covers the statue, quite recently set
up there, of the Baron vom Stein. Let the tourist
then, leaving the railway station, cross the river by
the bridge and he will find himself immediately at
the foot of the great hill. A winding path to the
right leads up the side of it through the thick wood.
In a minute or two he will reach the statue, where
it stands upon a bare projection commanding a good
view of the river and the town. This statue was
recently inaugurated by the Emperor in person and
a panegyric upon Stein delivered by the eminent
historian Heinrich v. Sybel. If, after looking at the

statue and the rich view of the river beyond it, you
turn round and look at the hill itself, you will see
high above you, as before, the Schloss Nassau, but
below it and immediately above your station, you
will now see another ruin. Here then at last is
the Burg Stein.

In the Burg Stein itself there is nothing of particular interest. But at first you are puzzled to
account for the name. The name leads you to
expect a rock, and as yet you have seen no rock
but only a large hill covered with trees. Moreover you do not see why the name should have
been appropriated in such a marked manner to
this particular family. And here let the reader
give a moment's attention to the name and title of
our hero. If an Englishman ever had occasion to
speak of Stein, which indeed scarcely ever happens,
he would certainly call him the Baron von Stein,
and even German writers constantly fall into the
same slight inaccuracy. But his name referred in a
more pointed manner to the particular rock on
which the family castle stood. His full title was
Freiherr vom und zum Stein (of and at the rock),
and when this is abbreviated it becomes Freiherr
or Baron *vom* Stein, but not *von* Stein. Where
then is *the rock?* You will find it if you leave the
Burg Stein and pass upward to the Schloss Nassau.
One of the windings of the path brings you to a
point at which you have the Burg Stein directly
below you. And from this point you see at once
the meaning of the name. You see now that the
castle stands upon a projection of the hill, which
on one side is so steep as to be quite perpendicu-

lar, and of course therefore exhibits the naked rock. One side of the castle is indeed quite close to the precipice.

The admirers of Stein have been fond of playing upon his name. I have seen in English books contempt poured upon the well-known description *Des Guten Grundstein, des Bösen Eckstein, der Deutschen Edelstein*, as a specimen of awkward and pointless German wit. To me, I confess, the pun seems as defensible and as natural as a pun can be. But perhaps it is worth noticing how it was partly suggested by the fact that Stein's relation to his name, if I may say so, was particularly intimate. Not only was his family of immemorial antiquity, but the explanation of the name it bore was clear and striking. We might almost say that the massive angularity, which as we shall see in the sequel was his chief characteristic, had really passed to him from the rock on which his family had lived for so many centuries. It was at least plainly connected with the kind of life his ancestors had led, dominating the country from the mountain side. And at any rate the name could never pass into a meaningless appellative, so long as it had an explanation so obvious, so long too as the family continued to live under the very shadow of their name, and looked up continually 'to the rock whence they were hewn.'

Heinrich Friedrich Karl, Freiherr vom und zum Stein, was born Oct. 26th, 1757. That we may look for a moment at his life as a whole, I add here that he died June 29th, 1831. At the time of his birth Germany was convulsed by the Seven

Years War. It was the time of the alliance between Frederick the Great and Chatham. The battle of Rossbach was fought ten days after. Stein was eight years younger than Goethe and Charles Fox, two years older than Schiller and William Pitt. He was twelve years older than the man who was to be his fate, the author of all his misfortunes and all his glory, Napoleon Buonaparte. He was thrown, as we commonly say, upon the Revolutionary Age, but it is to be observed that the period of his great achievements came late; so that whereas William Pitt, though two years his junior, entered upon his later and less glorious period with the outbreak of the Revolution, and died before Napoleon's power culminated, Stein had achieved nothing of historical importance until Napoleon had reached his zenith and Pitt had died. Properly speaking indeed it is not the Revolutionary Age that he belongs to, but another.

The most active and successful period of his life is comprised within the years 1807 and 1815, and this is the period of the insurrection of Europe against the tyranny of Napoleon. It is a period when the controversies excited by the French Revolution were for the moment at an end, when almost all honest men were united against France, when in England Fox in office had found the impossibility of making peace, and when Sheridan declared enthusiastically in favour of the Spanish insurgents. It is the period in fact of a new Revolution which extended itself over all Europe, for as such the movement against Napoleon, which we are too much in the habit of regarding as purely military, ought to be considered.

This Anti-Napoleonic Revolution, its peculiar relation to the earlier Revolution of France, and also
its effect upon the subsequent course of affairs in
Europe, will be a main subject of this book; for it
will be seen that Stein more than any other man
is to be regarded as the statesman of it. He may
almost be said to have commenced it; he saw it
successful in its immediate object of overthrowing
Napoleon; afterwards, in the retirement of his old
age, he saw it gradually change its character, and
before he died, he saw it actually blend itself with
the tide of that French Revolution which it had
originally been called into existence to oppose, for
he saw the Three Days of Paris hailed with emulous
sympathy by the patriots of Germany. After this
glance at his after-life, and the general character
of his work, we must return to Nassau and speak
of his family.

Here are the words in which Stein in his old
age described his parents and the education they
gave him. 'I was born of very honourable parents
and educated in the country under the influence
of their religious and truly German and knightly
example; the ideas of piety, patriotism, the honour
of my family and of my order, the duty of devoting
my life to public ends and of acquiring by industry
and exertion the qualifications necessary for that
purpose were deeply impressed on my young mind
by their example and precept. My view of the
world and of human affairs, I gathered as a boy
and youth in the solitude of a country life, from
ancient and modern history, and in particular I
was attracted by the incidents of the eventful

English history. Though this view was undoubtedly onesided, unpractical, and leading to a certain unfairness in judging of what was near and real, still it removed me at the same time from what was vulgar and from a pitiful frittering away of time, and gave me the habit of observing a great strictness in the choice of my friends, of seeking them only among the better, nobler, really worthy youths, and avoiding the dull, empty and silly. My parents intended me for a place in the Imperial Law Court, and it was to the attainment of the knowledge necessary for this that my education and my academic course were directed.' These few sentences of his short autobiography, and some expressions of gratitude to his mother and sisters for having sown in his mind the principles of duty and faith, convey all the special information we have about Stein's earlier years. Nevertheless, in Stein more than in most men we can trace a character formed by the station and circumstances into which he was born. It is strongly marked on his whole career, that he belonged to the order called the Imperial Knighthood (Reichsritterschaft).

This was a class to which nothing similar has ever been known in England, and which even in Germany was strictly limited to a single region. It was to be found only in Suabia, Franconia and on the Rhine; and it may be possible to describe it sufficiently for the present purpose without entering far into the intricate German constitution of which it made a part. Further on I must indeed ask the reader's attention to that constitution itself,

but for the present it will be enough to remind
him of its capital characteristic, which was the paralysis of the central government, and, consequent
upon that, the assumption by local authorities of
powers properly imperial. A number of municipal
corporations, which in England would have only
had the power of levying rates for local purposes
and appointing local officers with very insignificant powers, had in Germany become practically
independent republics. Magnates, who in England would have wielded a certain administrative
and judicial power as members of Quarter Sessions,
and in France would have been exempt from the
taille and would have exacted corvées from their
peasantry, had risen in Germany to the rank of
sovereigns. In one or two instances they had become almost equal to the greatest sovereigns of
Europe, but in the majority of instances the territory
within which they exercised this peculiar sovereignty
(Landeshoheit) was small, too small in fact to bear
with comfort the burden of an independent government in the midst of the mighty European states.
These sovereigns bore different titles; the highest
were Electors; below these were Dukes, Princes,
Counts. Bearing the humblest title and ruling the
smallest territories, were the Imperial Knights of
whom Stein was one.

Some people hold the opinion that small states
are happier and better governed than large ones.
They cite of course the instances of Athens and
Florence, they even cite from the multitude of
small states we are now considering, the case of
Weimar. They should remember however, that

Athens and Florence were only happy and well governed as long as there were no great states in their neighbourhood, and that they sank into dependence when the power of Macedonia grew up in the neighbourhood of the one and the power of the House of Austria consolidated itself in the neighbourhood of the other. The small states of Germany were very peculiarly situated, and it is impossible to deny that in the last half century of the Empire not Weimar only but several of them enjoyed periods of conscientious and judicious government. German opinion however has certainly on the whole pronounced against them, and even those who assert in general the happiness of small states, would not deny that there is a limit of smallness, beyond which government, at least if it be monarchical, cannot possibly be good. By general admission the little territories of the Imperial Knights were within this limit. Their government on the whole was the worst in Germany, and the very existence of such contemptible potentates in the Empire was regarded as a scandal. 'In many districts,' says Moser, 'you do not need to inquire what is the government of the place, the very look of the village tells you that it belongs to a knight.' 'Almost everywhere,' says Perthes, 'though for the most different reasons, there was intestine discord on the knightly territories between the landholder and the peasants, who made their disaffection known in the Imperial Courts by complaints and accusations that were often well grounded, often however altogether perverse. Not unfrequently were the subjects driven

to rebel against their lords, and to recognize a
neighbouring lord as their ruler, or with sound
of the tocsin to assail their ruler in open insurrection.' Such was the almost inevitable working of a system which entrusted the dangerous
powers of almost irresponsible government to so
large a number of individuals (there were more
than 1000 Imperial Knights!) which combined in
the most invidious manner the characters of proprietor and of ruler, which pampered all the in-
stincts of profligacy and tyranny in so large a
class, and at the same time stimulated in them in
an excessive degree the exclusive spirit of caste.

So far it may not appear to have been fortunate
for Stein that he was born to the position of an
Imperial Knight. He does not seem ever to have
shut his eyes to the anomalous and abusive character of the petty sovereignty that he had inherited. When his powerful neighbour, the Prince
of Nassau, threatened to annex his territories, on
the ground that it was time to abolish as mischievous the sovereignty of the Knighthood, it is
to be observed that Stein, in his spirited protest,
does not say a word in defence of the institution
but carries the war into the enemies' camp, and
asserts that larger but still petty sovereignties like
Nassau would in the long run prove more mischievous still. Still in spite of all that might be
alleged and was loudly alleged against the Order,
these Knights had two merits which appear conspicuously in Stein, and which mainly enabled him
to achieve what he did.

First they retained the spirit of freedom. Often

in times of oppression independence of character survives only in an aristocracy which in the exercise of excessive and invidious privilege acquires the self-confidence and the pride which prompts it to resist oppression from above. The Imperial Knighthood was, just at that time, the body of men in Germany in whom alone this useful pride could be looked for. Through the enormous multiplication of absolute governments the German nation had been practically almost divided into the two classes of despots and slaves. The peasant and the citizen (except in the decaying and corrupt free towns) were the subjects of an absolute master. The old high aristocracy of the Empire on the other hand held these absolute powers. There was wanting in general a class too proud to serve and at the same time not admitted into the caste of absolute princes. The Imperial Knighthood best supplied the place of such a class. For we are to notice that, though they exercised sovereignty, and might often exercise it tyrannously in their petty territories, yet they could not at all feel themselves on a level with the average sovereign Princes of the Empire. From these they were separated not merely by their inferiority in wealth and power but by a more palpable distinction. All the sovereign Princes of Germany above the Knighthood were represented at the Diet (Reichstag). Some indeed had only a share in a collective vote, but either individually or collectively all voted. The Imperial Knights had lost this privilege, and had thus fallen into a sort of middle position between the Princes and the subjects. In consequence of this, I may here take occasion to mention, the descendant of an Imperial Knight is not now reckoned to belong to the high nobility of Germany. That most exclusive caste, into which, as into the patricians of ancient Rome, no power on earth can introduce a new member, consists only of the descendants of those who before 1806 both had sovereignty and a place in the Diet. The Imperial Knights only satisfied the first condition, and therefore had Stein left sons, they would not have been admitted into it.

Not only did the Knights occupy this middle position, but owing sometimes to poverty, sometimes to the dulness of their isolated country life, they were often induced to take service under one of the great princes of Germany, as Stein himself, we shall see, entered the service of Frederick the Great. In such cases of course they voluntarily assumed the character of subjects. Yet they did not cease to have the thoughts and feelings of men accustomed to look up to no superior except the distant and powerless Emperor. This consideration explains much that is most observable in the character of Stein. It is the secret not only in part of the imperious will which enabled him to impose his legislation upon an absolute monarch rather frightened perhaps than convinced, but also of that peculiarity of manner which especially struck his contemporaries. All that generation in Germany had the manner of courtiers, as was natural in a country where there were more than sixty courts. A peculiar tameness and characterlessness both of speech and of political thought marked them.

Nothing distinguished Stein on the other hand so much as the fearless frankness, the rigid definiteness, the combativeness, the unyielding angularity with which he habitually maintained his opinions. In particular, his biographers continually relate shuddering the shockingly plain words he ventured to speak to sovereigns. On one occasion it was the Czarina whom he summarily set down. In the sequel I shall give extracts from some really singular official letters he wrote to his own sovereign. Arndt in describing an interview which he witnessed between Stein and the Duke of Weimar remarks that Stein throughout had the air of a superior and the Duke seemed to play the second part. This assumption, when we consider, was not unnatural in a man who to an originally strong character joined the consciousness of the Imperial Knight, and who in all societies remembered that by the old constitution of the Empire he owned no superior but the Kaiser.

The second merit of the Imperial Knighthood was that they were the only class which still, in a manner, remembered and prized the unity of the Empire. Having no ties except to the Empire itself (reichsunmittelbar), forming a tolerably numerous class and being constantly assailed by their natural enemies, the greater Princes, and by public opinion which they had provoked by their misgovernment, these outlaws of sovereign power were forced to stand shoulder to shoulder and to attach themselves to the only patron they could find, the Emperor. Their attachment to him was a tradition—Götz von Berlichingen, we remember, puts the name of the distant Emperor between those of his closest friends when he complains that 'Selbitz is dead and the good Emperor and my George,' —and the Emperor, for his part, naturally did not repulse the advances of those who could afford him help where he so sorely wanted it, that is in his relations to the Empire. The Knights associated themselves in a number of cantons, each under its Captain (Hauptmann) and its Executive Council. These Cantons again formed themselves into the three Knightly Circles of Swabia, Franconia and the Rhine, and the Circles again formed the Corpus of Knights, over which each of the three Circles presided in turn; on some extraordinary occasions the Executives of all the three Cantons met for common deliberation. Thus organized, they placed themselves in a direct relation to the Emperor; they paid him a tax (Charitätivsubsidien) which not only was the most important subsidy which he received from the Empire but remained absolutely at his free disposal, while at the same time they firmly refused to pay any tax imposed by the Diet. In return the Emperors declared the Knights to be their own personal subjects and not subject to the Diet, assigned them a number of privileges, and always when they could interfered to protect them.

Perhaps no one so early, so clearly and so habitually as Stein contemplated the unity of Germany. And it is unquestionable that he was led to do so partly by his position as a Knight. It was this position which induced his parents, as we have seen, to destine him to an appointment in the Imperial law-court rather than to any career offered by one of the States of which the Empire was composed, and again by this decision of his parents he was led to study particularly the Imperial Constitution. It was his position as a Knight which opened his eyes to see what was mischievous in the Middle States—for these were the standing enemies of the Knighthood —and the necessary alternative to the aggrandisement of the Middle States was the unity or at least the duality of the Empire. Moreover scarcely any German who was not in the peculiar position of an Imperial Knight could have been so free from the ties, so completely unentangled in the web, which local sovereignty had spread over the country, as to be able to think of the Empire as really still existing, to understand its nature and wish for the restoration of its efficiency. In a letter to Count Münster Stein expressly attributes his devotion to the cause of the unity of Germany to the fact that he had been born a subject of the Empire and of the Empire only.

The Knighthood, finding their numbers decay and much territory passing from various causes out of their hands, had taken pains to add to their strength by admitting new members. The Steins however were not among these new members. His ancestors had held the estate at Nassau from immemorial time, 'demonstrably,' says Stein himself, 'for 700 years[1].' They had fought against the French under Edward III. and Charles the Bold, and they can be traced through the period of the Reformation and of the Thirty Years War as consistent Protestants. Their property at Nassau, Schweighausen and Frücht

[1] See below, p. 126.

2—2

(where Stein lies buried), and Landskron on the left bank of the Rhine, had become encumbered with debt—as was frequently the case with knightly estates—when it passed into the hands of our hero's father, Karl Philipp Freiherr vom Stein. His life was passed in the service of the great ecclesiastical Prince Kurmainz, with whose court we shall find more than one of the sons also at times connected. He was a Privy Councillor at Mainz, and he sat on the knightly Council of the Canton of Middle Rhine. The passionate irritability which marked the Minister seems to have been inherited from this parent. In other respects he is described as being simply a respectable and hearty country gentleman, devoted to hunting. At the age of 38 he married Fraülein Langwerth v. Simmern, who had become by a former marriage Frau v. Löw. I have already mentioned the gratitude Stein felt towards his mother.

Stein was the last but one of ten children, of whom seven grew up. Of his three brothers the eldest Johann Friedrich figured for a time in the world and was a well-known name many years before his younger brother was known to the public. He held the post of Landjägermeister at the Prussian Court and was, for some time, a favourite of King Frederick William II. He is described as something of a sensualist. He will appear once but only once in his brother's biography. When Lord Malmesbury in his diary of his embassy of 1793 writes, speaking of the king's favourites, 'Stein is now completely out of favour,' he is referring to Johann Friedrich.

The second son Friedrich Ludwig bade fair to be the glory of the family. He entered the Austrian military service, and in the summer of 1788 all Europe was talking of his defence of the Veterani Cavern against the Turks. Thus speaks our own Annual Register of that year:

About this time the Turks took a town or place called Mitrouski (of which we have no knowledge) after a very brave defence and with an avowed considerable loss of men. A famous cavern, situated in an impracticable defile covered with mountains and called the Veteranihöhle from General Veterani of the last century, by whom it was fortified, was, after a most obstinate resistance made by a handful of men, at length compelled to surrender. The Grand Vizir was so much charmed with their gallantry that besides granting them an honourable capitulation and safe convoy he desired to see *the brave Major who commanded* and his fellow-officers upon their coming out. The Ottoman treated them with the greatest liberality, &c.

The brave Major here mentioned is Major Baron Ludwig vom Stein, Knight of the German Order. But the hero of 1788 died in 1790 of a fever, following his master, the Emperor Joseph, to the grave, and he has no place in this biography.

The third brother, Ludwig Gottfried, was the *mauvais sujet* of the family. He was disowned by his family and *cut* by his brother when they met at Berlin. In the end he fell into great poverty, consented to renounce the family name and lived in retirement upon a pension allowed him by his brother, whom he outlived.

Of the sisters the eldest, Johanne Louise, of remarkable beauty, will be spoken of below; the

second, Marie Charlotte, was married to v. Steinberg, of a Hannoverian family, who in the end rose
to be a Minister in his own State.   Thus by his
sisters' marriage he was connected with the aristocracy
which surrounded the electoral throne of Hannover
on which sat—figuratively, for he never visited the
country—the personage known so well to Englishmen
as George III.   Stein's own marriage, as we shall
find, strengthened his connection with this aristocracy
and even brought him into a certain family relation
to the English royal house.   The youngest sister,
Marianne, remained unmarried and obtained one
of those ecclesiastical appointments in which the
German aristocracy of that period found such
a convenient economical resource.   She became
Dechantin—how shall I translate it?—and later
Abbess of the Foundation of Wallerstein at
Homberg in Hessen.

Of these sisters the eldest—who, we shall see, is
mentioned with much admiration by Goethe—was,
we are told, Stein's favourite.   The affection between
them, writes his college friend Rehberg, was most
interesting and touching to witness.   On the other
hand Marianne was, as it were, his counter-
part.   She had his commanding countenance and
his curt, definite manner of speech.   She had
the honour of sharing with him the hatred of
Napoleon.

This family, almost every member of which seems
to have had both talents and strongly-marked character, had, it seems, to submit to some of the most
deplorable exigencies of rank.   After the eldest
sister had refused many suitors, her brothers, we are

told, gave her warning that she must accept the
next offer. She was forced therefore to marry,
without affection, v. Werthern, an official in the
Saxon service, and the marriage was unhappy.

When we consider the atmosphere in which Stein
grew up, an atmosphere of inordinate privilege and
of marriages of convenience, we might be disposed
to think that it was favourable to energy and independence, in fact to the aristocratic virtues, but
also that it was calculated to foster the aristocratic
vices of waste and sensuality. It was calculated
in fact to form such men as Johann Friedrich, dis-
solute but vigorous, and, as it appears, generous.
It is therefore particularly to be noted that our hero,
with more than all the energy and generous independence of his race, seems to have escaped this
taint altogether. He had something of the fire of a
Fox or a Mirabeau with no trace of their lawlessness.
His stainless virtue, both public and private, in a
lax generation, is indeed a remarkable phenomenon.
In religion he was bred to orthodoxy, and never
showed any sympathy with the scepticism of his
generation. Though not in the least a theologian,
he yet meant much when he called himself a
believer. He meant that he had never quarrelled
with the past; he meant that he worshipped in his
mother what seemed to him to be Christianity, and
that he clung to her religion as he clung to his duty
or his honour.

The superiority of the future Minister to his
brothers was early perceived by an observant eye ;
and a curious incident occurred also characteristic of
an aristocratic family. On the 2nd February, 1774,

that is when our hero, who was called in the family Karl, was in his 17th year, the mother succeeded in bringing about a family agreement according to which (1) the sons renounced in writing the inheritance of their father's property in favour of that one among them whom the parents should choose to marry and to continue the family; (2) the daughters were to renounce all rights of inheritance if they married into any family which was not German and knightly. This agreement was followed by the nomination, also at the instance of the mother, of Karl to the position of maintainer of the family (Stammhalter). The young Jacob, thus invidiously preferred by his mother, had for a time a difficult part to play. Esau, or the wild disinherited elder brother, could not easily put up with the loss of his birthright, but the fortunate supplanter showed both tact and firmness, and in the end the peace of the family was preserved.

Before we bid farewell to the family circle in which Stein's boyhood was passed—for when the course of the narrative brings us again to the house at Nassau, it will be no longer the house of Stein's parents but his own—we may look at it through the eyes of a casual visitor who was there in 1772.

This visitor was one who was to be brought in after life into such close association with Stein, that his name will reappear in this book oftener perhaps than any other except Stein's own and Napoleon's, and that of the King Frederick William III. In consideration of this I must ask the reader to allow me at this point to quit my main subject for a moment and begin another biography. Karl August,

Baron von Hardenberg, was born at Essenrode (Brunswick-Lüneburg) in the year 1750, so that he was seven years older than our hero. He was of an old Hannoverian family, and his father had distinguished himself in those campaigns of the Seven Years War, in which Ferdinand of Brunswick, assisted by English subsidies, had defended Hannover against the French. In 1766 he went to the University of Göttingen, and thence in 1768 to Leipzig. The condition of Leipzig University at that time and the distinguished persons who taught there are known to the readers of Goethe's autobiography. Here Goethe and Hardenberg became acquaintances. He soon returned to Göttingen, where he studied jurisprudence under the great master of that department, Pütter, and at the same time attended Heyne's philological lectures. In 1770 he entered the Hannoverian service in the department of Justice. The greater part of the years 1772 and 1773 he spent in travelling. Setting out on July 15th, 1772, from the Castle of Hardenberg, he passed through Minden to Cassel and then made his way to the Rhine through Ems. He had an introduction to the Frau vom Stein, but had been warned, it seems, by a relative who knew the Stein family, to be on his guard against the handsome daughters. He seems to have stayed some time at the house in Nassau, and even to have made a little tour with the family to Ems and Neuwied. A certain v. Heinitz and his wife, of whom we shall hear more in the sequel, common friends of Hardenberg and the Stein family, were of the party.

The diary is preserved in which Hardenberg records his impression of the family of his hosts. The father struck him as a good old man with more intellect and learning than was at first discernible. Frau vom Stein was a notable housewife, cordial in her manner, and not without a knowledge of books. The daughters struck him in the same way as combining acquired information with force of character. The eldest impressed him most— 'she is lively and says what she thinks.' There was no old-fashioned ceremoniousness between the children and their parents ; Hardenberg heard the youngest (*i.e.*, I suppose, the youngest except our hero, for he was absent) break in upon a conversation between his father and mother which was growing warm, with *Mulier taceat in ecclesia*, 'I suffer not the woman to speak.' He remarks on the girls, 'Nice daughters—Louise the eldest and handsomest—elle est brunette, bien faite et a de beaux yeux noirs—sentimental maids (this in English)—Marianne la seconde pourroit servir de pendant à Esope—Charlotte la troisième bien faite et assez agréable—un peu marquée de la petite vérole.' The reader will see that when Hardenberg wrote this he had not mastered the comparative ages of the ladies concerned.

As the diary goes on we find Hardenberg forgetting the hint he had received from his relative. He is deeply in love with Louise. 'It is all very well to be a philosopher, but how can you help thinking amiable persons amiable, particularly when they are so in such a high degree as Louise Stein ?' and then he breaks out, 'I love her indescribably !'

He adds that he had not courage to tell his love, for he doubted whether Louise would return it, or whether she was free. But he did not conceal it from his own family. Stein and Hardenberg were destined to be united in history, but not by family affinity. His family had found a rich heiress for him, a certain Countess v. Reventlow of a Danish family. After some little resistance he yielded to their wishes, and the marriage ultimately took place on July 8th, 1775.

But we shall see how far from happy it was. Louise's fate seems indeed to have been perverse. As we have seen, she was sacrificed herself, and Hardenberg, to whom she might have been an incalculable blessing, was sacrificed too. He was a man of honour and of ability. If we put Stein and Scharnhorst aside, no man of that generation did or underwent so much for Prussia. But his career was in a great degree spoiled by his domestic unhappiness, which drove him into profligate habits and profligate society, and deprived him of the respect of good men. Stein himself, we shall find, regarded him when he was at the height of his successful career with strong dislike and disrespect; still more so did Niebuhr. They missed in him the gravity and dignity, which it would appear no one would have been more capable of adding to his character than Louise vom Stein.

Louise had another admirer besides Hardenberg, one both more famous and more capable of conferring fame. Her marriage took her to Neunheiligen in the Thuringian district, and here she was visited in 1781 by the Duke of Weimar, in whose

company was Goethe. She renewed her acquaintance with the poet afterwards in Weimar, and how
much she interested him we may read in his letters
to that Frau von Stein who plays so great a part in
his life, and who—as it may be well thus early to
inform the reader—was in no way related or connected with the Steins of Nassau. He finds in
Louise 'a correctness of judgment, an undisturbed
life, and a goodness that fills him daily with new
admiration and pleasure.' 'He has so often,' he
writes, 'heard people speak of knowledge of the
world, of the great world, without attaching any
meaning to the phrase, but this little creature has
enlightened him; she knows how to deal with the
world; secure of her own value and position, she
moves with a delicacy and ease which must be seen
to be imagined. What is genius in Art she has in
the art of life. She knows the greatest part of what
is distinguished, rich, beautiful, intelligent in Europe,
either directly or indirectly, and has present to her
mind, in the highest sense of the word, the life and
actions and relations of so many people.' He dis-
likes her husband, who seems to have been pedantic,
pompous, and absurd, and at times his compassion
for Louise rises into poetry. 'She is lost for this
life, and seems like a beautiful soul just emerging
from the flames of an undeserved Purgatory and
mounting towards heaven on the wings of love.'
Accordingly she has her place in Goethe's picture
gallery, and the reader has met with her before
without knowing it. She is the beautiful Countess
in Wilhelm Meister, who takes an interest in Wilhelm's dramatic compositions, the fact being that

Louise had been allowed to see Wilhelm Meister itself while it was in progress, and had sent back the MS. with a flattering letter. The well-known scene where the Count entering his room sees himself, as he believes, reading at the table, is said to have been suggested by something which happened to Louise's husband in Spain. But it is time to return to my principal subject.

We read nothing of any school to which Stein was sent. The account he gives in his autobiography of his education is as follows :—' In the autumn of 1773 I went with a private tutor to Göttingen, where, in obedience to the wishes of my parents, I studied jurisprudence with much zeal, but at the same time made myself acquainted also with the English history and the English books of statistics, political economy and politics; and in general by confidential intercourse with several like-minded young men, such as Rehberg and Brandes, my predilection for that nation was confirmed. At Easter, 1777, I left Göttingen, paid a visit of three months to Wetzlar in order to learn the procedure of the Kammergericht, passed the winter of 1778 at Mainz, made a tour with a friend, Herr v. Reden, now (*i.e.* in 1823) Hannoverian Ambassador at Rome, to the German courts at Mannheim, Darmstadt, Stuttgard, Munich, stayed two months at Regensburg for the sake of the business of the Diet, and went in the winter of 1779 by Salzburg and Passau to Vienna for the Reichshofrath, where, however, I lived in much distraction and quite devoted to society for nine months, made journeys to Styria and Hungary, and in February, 1780, went by Dresden to Berlin.'

For the English reader this summary account will need some amplification.

Göttingen, the University of Hannover, founded by George II. in 1737, had been the first of the German Universities to attain European celebrity as a seat of learning. It still held the highest rank among them, and occupied a large space in the public mind both by the eminence of its Professors and by the activity of thought among its students. Christian Heyne was the representative of philology, and just at the moment when Stein visited it a literary school was growing up there. I mention this latter fact, not because it is important in Stein's biography, but for the very contrary reason. It is desirable to mark thus early, that between him and the literature or philosophy—not the learning or science—of his time and country there was no connection at all. His age was what we commonly call when we speak of Germany the age of Goethe and Schiller. It was the age of Germany in which literature and philosophy were more zealously pursued than they have perhaps ever been in any country of the modern world. Nevertheless in this biography the reader will find scarcely anything about Goethe and Schiller, or Kant and Hegel. Stein is almost as silent about the great philosophical movement of his time as if no such movement had been going on; the only effect it produces upon him is to excite a keen feeling of alarm lest it should, in any way, extend to practical politics, and lest the management of affairs should in any degree pass into the hands of those whom he calls, with strong contempt, *metapoliticians*, that is of course those who stood in the same rela-

tion to politicians as metaphysicians to the students
of nature. The literary movement he seems to have
regarded with simple indifference. Poetry was to
him, as in fact it is to most men, only a more impressive kind of rhetoric. Accordingly it never
occurs either to Stein himself or to his biographer
Pertz to mention the literary agitation that was
going on at Göttingen during the very years he
spent there. The great light of German literature
was just rising above the horizon. Götz von Berlichingen appeared in this very year 1773, but the
time was still far distant when those who are now
regarded as the leading German poets were to acquire that place in the national estimation. In those
days young lovers of literature occupied themselves
with two names now half forgotten, Klopstock
and Wieland ; and the controversy turned not as
afterwards on the difference between Classicism and
Romanticism, but on the difference between the
French School and the native German School.
Wieland was the great representative of the foreign
taste, and just at this moment the youth of Göttingen were gathering themselves into an organized
opposition to it and him under the influence of
Klopstock. Their organ was the Musenalmanach
set up in 1770, under the editorship of Boie, brother-
in-law of one still remembered in Germany, the best
representative of the Göttingen school, Johann
Heinrich Voss. They formed themselves into the
society called the Hainbund, and in this very year
they held a solemn feast on Klopstock's birthday.
A chair stood empty for Klopstock, and his works
were crowned ; a bust of Wieland with a copy of

his Idris was solemnly burnt; the healths of Hermann, Luther, Klopstock, Herder, Goethe and others
were drunk.   Men of rank equal to Stein's belonged
to this society; for example, the two Counts Stolberg.   But Stein appears to have known nothing
about it; all such displays, indeed all the sentimentalism and mawkishness of his generation, were
completely alien to his character.   Long after, when
there was really need to rouse the German spirit
against a foreign invader, when patriotism became
somewhat more than a pompous word and the
memories of Hermann and Luther were really worth
appealing to, Stein would have nothing to do with
the Tugendbund, which was very similar to this
Hainbund of Göttingen.   And yet if any such
society were formed now by enthusiastic German
students, and the object were to stimulate national
feeling by recalling the national glories, probably
the health of Stein would be drunk along with
those of Hermann and of Luther.

His object at Göttingen was not literature but
political science.   History and law have always formed the basis of the studies of Göttingen.   The fame
of Pütter, the Blackstone of the Empire, attracted
at that time from all parts of Germany the young
men who looked forward to a public life.   Somewhat unaccountably it appears to be certain that
Stein did not attend the lectures of Pütter.   But it is
interesting to notice the emphatic manner in which
Stein declares that his studies, so far as they were
guided by his taste rather than his interest, were
in English history, English politics, statistics and
political economy.   I shall examine later the ques-

tion of the sources from which the political ideas
embodied in his legislation were derived. It is
sufficiently evident that he considered himself
to belong to the English school of statesmen.
But it was not solely by his natural taste that his
studies at Göttingen were drawn in this direction.
He found, he says, other students, among whom
he mentions Rehberg and Brandes, who were also
devoted to the study of English institutions. It
is to be remembered that at Göttingen all these
young men were living under the rule of George
III. of England, and that his grandfather had
founded the University. For a long time the
library was regularly supplied with English books.
The present distinguished Professor of History at
Göttingen, Dr Pauli, tells me that the history of
England can be studied at Göttingen almost as
well as in England itself. It was thus through
our connection with Hannover that English ideas
found entrance in Germany and in the mind of one
who later found an opportunity of realizing some of
them on a grand scale.

The reader will desire to know what was the
extent of the acquirements Stein carried away with
him from Göttingen. He certainly never became
learned in the sense in which his friends Niebuhr
(who however refers expressly to Stein's 'extensive
knowledge') and W. v. Humboldt were learned, but
it would be a great mistake to infer from his indifference to the literary and philosophic controversies
of his time that he was not a reading man at all. It
was in Germany a peculiarly speculative age, and
his disposition was not speculative. Moreover, he

belonged to the noble and official class, which par-
ticipated much less than the middle or citizen class
in the grand intellectual excitement of the time.
But in his own way he was always a reading man,
and no one has more emphatically asserted the
necessity of continuous study to the statesman.
History, as he tells us, was his favourite study, and
he was not so practical that he could not take an
interest in ancient as well as modern history. But
I imagine that the abstruse investigations of the
Wolfs and Niebuhrs, or the attempts of Herder and
the Romanticists to enter into and sympathize with
remote ages, ways of thinking, and forms of society,
were not interesting to him. His studies were those
of a practical politician, and he consulted history
as a great Blue Book containing the expedients
former statesmen had resorted to in difficulties like
those of Prussia. For such purposes the new German literature, which had every merit rather than
that of throwing light upon practical affairs, was of
little service to him.

His colleague Schön has recorded the impression
he received of Stein's culture. So far as it is dis-
paraging the reader must be asked to receive it
with caution, for reasons which will be given later,
reasons connected with the character of the witness.
Stein, we are told, did not read Faust till the year
1808, and then hurried through it in a night, and
sent to ask for the Second Part, which, as the reader
remembers, was not published for twenty years after
that date. His only comment on the poem was
that it was too indecent to stand on a drawing-room
table, and Schön could perceive that he did not

look at it from an aesthetic but altogether from a
historical point of view. I think we need hardly
stop to defend a statesman for not finding much
leisure to read poetry. It is probable that Cromwell
never read his Secretary's verses, while on the other
hand it is known that Charles I. was fond of reading
Shakspeare. Cavour describes in almost ludicrous
language[1] the bondage to reality under which he
had allowed his mind to come. Not that the statesman does not need imagination ; on the contrary,
he wants it so much that he ceases to use it for
pleasure or play, and sets it to stern work. But
we learn at the same time from Schön, and this
we may safely believe, that Stein's knowledge of
the facts of history was such as would not have
misbecome a professor. It is confirmed by
Turgeneff, who says that he had known learned
professors admire the depth and variety of his
knowledge in German history, adding that Charlemagne and Luther were his heroes. We gather
also that his knowledge of modern languages was
considerable, perhaps large. From other evidence
we know that he wrote French with familiar ease, if
not always with correctness, and that he read a great
deal of English. Latin one who was long intended
to be a lawyer of the Imperial Courts could not be
without, but he does not seem to have been a classical

---

[1] 'Do not expect from me any article in which it is necessary
to make any call on the imagination. In my case *la folle du logis*
is a lazy jade who is not to be stirred up. You would hardly
believe it, but I have never been able to invent the simplest tale
to amuse my nephew, though I have tried very often.' De la Rive's
Reminiscences of Cavour.

scholar in the peculiarly English sense of the phrase.
He seems however to have known the Latin historians, and during his stay in Russia in 1812, we find
him taking up those of Greece, and even receiving
lessons in Greek in order to profit better by them.
But throughout his life when we surprise him over
a book, it is in nine cases out of ten a book of
history, or of one of the subjects bordering on history, such as Political Economy.

A young man of family, who was destined to the
service of the Empire proper, was expected first to go
through his course of jurisprudence, and then to
travel a little. After this he might soon expect by
the interest of his family to obtain an appointment;
perhaps to take his seat on the Noble Bench of the
Reichshofrath, or if, as was the case with Stein, his
name was known at the Court of Mainz, to get a
place on the Kammergericht, of which Kurmainz
had the patronage. It was evidently with these
views that Stein, after completing his course at Göttingen, sets out on his travels. His intention, the
reader must carefully observe, was not to enter the
service of any of the German States, not even of
the Austrian States ruled by the Emperor; he was
qualifying himself to become an official of the Empire
itself, of that organization of which the ruler of
Austria was at the same time the titular head. This
organization was in such decay, was so much lost to
view behind the greatness and splendour of Austria
and Prussia, that the English reader finds as much
difficulty in apprehending its true nature as those
who have not been at one of the English Universities find in conceiving what the University can be

as distinguished from the Colleges. But though in
complete decay, and so powerless, that for practical
purposes Germany may almost be regarded as a
number of independent states, united by nothing but
a common language and common traditions, a federal
organization did exist. Young men choosing a profession actually considered the claims of the Imperial
official service among other professions, and weighed
its advantages against those of the Austrian, Prussian, or Bavarian service. A comfortable and dignified livelihood might be made out of it, particularly
if you were well connected, and most particularly if
you were of a knightly family. Now if, having
grasped this fact, the reader will observe what places
Stein visits, he will discover where the principal
organs of this languishing political system were
placed. As in the American Union the federal life
is centred at Washington, and so Washington belongs, as it were, to a different system from Boston
or New York, so in Germany, while state life had its
centres at Vienna, Berlin, Dresden, Munich, &c.,
there were two other towns, Wetzlar and Regensburg (Ratisbon), which belonged, in a peculiar manner, to the Empire ; and Vienna, as the residence of
the Emperor, belonged at the same time to Austria
and to the Empire. These, it will be observed, are
the three towns which Stein has principally in view
in his travels. He goes straight from Göttingen to
Wetzlar, where he passes three months; he spends
two months at Regensburg, and afterwards nine
months at Vienna. The only other place where he
makes any long stay is Mainz, with which his family
was closely connected, and it is to be observed that

after the three towns above-mentioned Mainz had
of all German towns the closest connection with the
Empire, for it was the residence of Kurmainz, the
first Imperial official and, more almost than the
Emperor himself, the depositary of the Imperial tradition.

It will be well for the reader to take this
opportunity of fixing in his memory the principal
features of the system connected with these three
towns. The main organs of a political system are,
of course, the judiciary, the legislative, the executive
bodies. It was the judiciary of the Empire that had
its seat at Wetzlar. The Court was called the
Reichskammergericht, and, we see, it was to study
its procedure that Stein stayed at Wetzlar. But
there was a rival Court at Vienna, the Reichshofrath,
which Stein mentions as the object of his visit to
Vienna. Regensburg was the seat of the Legisla-
ture, the Diet or Reichstag. As it will be seen
immediately that Stein abandoned his design of devoting himself to this career, I have no excuse here
for dwelling at length upon the Imperial institutions.
But we have a letter of Stein's to his friend Reden,
the only letter extant belonging to this early period
of his life, dated Nov. 20[1], 1777, in which he describes the society of Wetzlar. Two or three sentences must be extracted; they will help the reader
to picture to himself the Kammergericht of the old
Empire.

[1] From this date it would seem that Stein's account of his
travels must be either not quite accurate or not quite complete.
He says he left Göttingen at Easter and stayed at Wetzlar three
months; yet we find him still there in November.

A place like this, where important affairs are conducted, must always be divided—there are necessarily parties in it, which, quite independent of each other, carry their feuds even into their amusements. If you know the state of things you can tell beforehand who will be at a particular gathering, who is admitted into a particular society or excluded from it. All this robs the meetings of all unity, makes them less agreeable, banishes cheerfulness and comfort from them, and sometimes embarrasses the stranger, who finds respectable people on both sides, and cannot surrender himself to them as he would wish. Besides, our society consists exclusively of Jurists, whose pursuit, by the mass of conceptions with which it loads the memory, fatigues the mind and stifles all imagination, from which one may readily infer that our men are not altogether of the most attractive. The women, for the most part, are provincial, and by ennobling their husbands the Emperor has not taken from them their little shrill, petty, formal manners. So it is in vain to look here for courteous, entertaining people, ready to give you attention; you either find them in a corner talking law or with the cards in their hand, and any civility you pay them they receive either with offensive rudeness or with ridiculous embarrassment, or else they cannot find any words to answer you with.

But he seems not yet to have conceived any distaste for the career which had been marked out for him, for he says, 'As I have been admitted to work under a well-informed and excellent assessor' (Hofmann, in whose house Stein was living) 'and have the opportunity of enlarging my knowledge by referring in the reports to the most important cases which the Court has decided, my life here is made agreeable and the time I spend valuable.' No record helps us to understand how this feeling of contentment was changed into dissatisfaction. But the next sentence in his autobiography records a complete alteration in his views and plans.

CHAPTER II.

THE PRUSSIAN SERVICE.

'MEANWHILE my disinclination to an appointment in the Imperial Courts had been avowed, and my parents had given way, and my profound regard for Frederick the Unique, who had just then, by rescuing Bavaria, won himself the gratitude of that State and of the whole Fatherland, had kindled in me the desire to serve him and to form myself under him.'

Stein, we see plainly, has already learnt an art, of which he showed himself later a great master, the art of having his own way. His resolution to take service under Frederick was, in his circumstances, remarkable, and assuredly it is a memorable event in German history. We can easily understand his speedily conceiving a distaste[1] for the Imperial Courts, which demanded the most absorbing diligence, the most complete abandonment of other studies, and did not offer in return the prospect of a great career. But if he determined to take service, not in the Empire, but in one of the States, we

[1] See Life of Vincke by Bodelschwingh, p. 22, for the repugnance felt for them by a man whose nature was much less exacting than Stein's.

should have expected him, as an Imperial Knight, to choose Austria. His brother Friedrich entered the Austrian service. Here a knight could indulge the traditional loyalty of his order to the Emperor. One who belonged by birth to the old order of things would feel most at his ease in this service, and, we might think, whatever service he might choose, would avoid that of Frederick. For Frederick was the great enemy of the Imperial house, the most dangerous disturber of the Empire. On the other hand, he had revived the reputation of Germany in Europe by victories over France and Russia, and this may have weighed with Stein; in fact, the words he uses seem to imply it. We know that in later life he remained steadfast to the cause of Prussia, because he recognized that in Prussia rather than in Austria lay the hope of the unity of Germany. But such large views were hardly formed in his youth, or before the fall of the Empire, and his own words suggest a different explanation. In the War of the Bavarian Succession Austria and Prussia had, in fact, exchanged parts. Frederick had appeared on the conservative side, and had defended the old constitution; Austria, under the rash guidance of Joseph II., had appeared as a revolutionary Power. Somewhat later we shall find Frederick forming a conservative league of Princes, and employing Stein himself to procure the adhesion of the natural head of all the conservatism of the empire, Kurmainz himself. Kurmainz did actually join the league against the Emperor. We can understand, therefore, that without abandoning the position of an Imperial Knight, without turning

his back on the politics of his family, Stein might in
1780 take service under the prince who, besides
being the glory of the German name, had just interfered to save the Empire from a revolution deliberately planned and attempted by the Emperor
himself.

The luckless Emperor Joseph—a French Revolution on the throne—who 'failed in everything that
he undertook', may thus, by his *coup d'état* of 1777,
have lost the services of Stein, a man of funda-
mentally conservative views and one of the few
Germans of that age who had the gifts of a statesman.

Stein does not distinctly inform us whether his
new resolution was taken on advice or entirely from
the impulse of his own mind.   It may be that when
in February, 1780, he quitted the Austrian dominions
and went by Dresden to Berlin, his mind was already
made up to offer his services to Frederick.   It is
possible on the other hand that he visited Berlin out
of curiosity and formed his determination in consequence of advice received there.   If so, it will not be
hard to conjecture who the adviser was, but the fact
that Stein, though he gives a remarkably full account
of him and acknowledges an ample debt to him, does
not expressly credit him with such an important suggestion, inclines one rather to think that Stein's
resolution was formed independently.   There was at
this time at Berlin a Minister of State, v. Heinitz,
who was a friend of Stein's parents, and who was, no
doubt, one of the first the youth would visit on his
arrival.   The following is the tribute which Stein
has paid to his memory.

According to the customary order of things I should have had to begin as Referendarius in a War and Domains Department, and perhaps I should have lost myself in formalities (Anglicè, 'been choked with red tape'), and dependence on a mediocre, stiff, pedantic superior would have had a fatal and overwhelming influence upon me.   But thanks to a kind Providence I found in the Minister of State, v. Heinitz, a paternal chief who guided my destiny affectionately, earnestly, wisely, till his death in 1802 (*sic;* it should be 1803).   He was a friend of my parents, as was also his excellent wife: both received me with sympathetic and indulgent kindness.   The Minister v. Heinitz was one of the most excellent men of his time.   Deep religious feeling, earnest persevering effort to elevate his own inner nature, freedom from all selfishness, susceptibility to everything noble and beautiful, inexhaustible goodwill and gentleness, continual carefulness to appoint meritorious, good men, to do justice to their deserts and to form the characters of young people—were the principal features of his excellent character and had the happiest effects in the department entrusted to his administration. At that time it was the Mining Department that he was striving to raise out of its nothingness and in which he proposed to appoint me.

When the reader has made a fuller acquaintance with Stein he will be better able to see the full importance of these sentences than perhaps he can now. Stein is here looking back upon the step which determined the whole course of his life, the step which gave him at the same time a country and a vocation. He is henceforth a statesman, but we are to remember how different a notion attached to this word in Prussia from that which attaches to it now in England. There the only way to become a statesman, the only way to the highest political posts, was to do the very thing which in England excludes a man from the highest political promotion and from almost all that is called politics among us, namely to enter the civil service. To become a politician there

was identical with becoming an official. Now Stein
became in the sequel a most decided enemy of
that form of government which has been called
bureaucracy, that is, government by paid officials.
It is a remarkable fact that this bitter enemy of
officialism and officials should have been himself
an official from his twenty-third year. It is evident
that the singularity of this struck him in writing
these sentences. How is it, he is saying all the
while to himself, that I escaped becoming the
mere *writing-machine* I have so constantly asserted
all paid officials to be? He accounts for it in a
way which shows that there may after all be a
good side to bureaucracy. The precept and example of Heinitz saved him ; Heinitz showed an
admirable devotion to the public service. But then
Heinitz was also an official, and yet he also, it appears, had escaped becoming a writing-machine.

The fact is, it appears likely that the bureaucracy
of Frederick, though it had all the faults which Stein
attributed to it and which helped to bring Prussia to
ruin in 1806, produced also some good effects upon
those who imbibed its influence. It formed many
pedants, many slaves of routine ; it was not founded
upon patriotism and had no tendency to awaken it.
But in the better natures it trained a martial sense of
duty—duty in its most imperious and absolute form
—which was of great value. The Categorical Imperative of Kant was appropriately first named and
described in the age and country of Frederick the
Great. This devotion to duty is what Stein cele-
brates in his patron and what he himself owed to his
patron's example. The language of panegyric is

always apt to sound formal and more or less un-
meaning. When we read that v. Heinitz was one
of 'the most excellent characters of his age' we are
in danger of deducting so much from the statement
on the score of Stein's gratitude for having been
pushed forward in the service by him, that no more
meaning will remain in it except that he was a good
sort of person. But it is quite certain that Stein
means all that he says, and that he owed to v.
Heinitz not merely promotion but much of the
earnestness and energy in duty that distinguished
him. When we see him in 1807 towering above all
the herd of Frederick's officials as the only man with
a soul and a character, we may attribute something,
as I have said above, to his birth and breeding, and
of course we must attribute much to what we may
call his genius, but much also is to be attributed to
this friend, who more than any other man was his
patron and whose memory he has embalmed in this
description. As late as 1826—nearly a quarter of
a century after the death of this patron—when for a
moment it was expected that Stein would return to
office, he wrote—'I have not the smallest desire to
play a part, and have never had it in any relation
of life. All that I have done or could do seemed
to me always so utterly below a certain ideal good
which I had formed to myself; and then the example of my excellent mother and of the venerated
minister Heinitz was constantly before my eyes;
their life was a series of efforts and sacrifices, and
they never took their own comfort into account.'

Stein is not the only great statesman who has
mentioned the name of Heinitz. He is referred to

frequently in Mirabeau's book on Prussia, in which will be found printed a long Memoir on the Prussian Mines written by him and mentioning, as we shall see below, the name of Stein.

The year 1780 is thus the beginning of Stein's political career. Let us for a moment take note of the condition of the political world. Frederick the Great then was in his old age and had but six years more to reign; Maria Theresa died in this year, and Joseph, who had hitherto been only Emperor, that is, almost as powerless as his father had been, now by succeeding to all the Austrian States became the most powerful, as he was known to be the most restless, person in Europe. A period commenced which, if the French Revolution had not almost extinguished the very memory of it, would be remembered by the disturbances created over the whole extent of the Austrian territories and also over Germany by the lawless and senseless though not altogether ill-meant aggressions of the Emperor. The American war was dragging along, and Lord North was gradually sinking under the weight of ill success and under the assaults of Charles Fox. Chatham had been two years dead, and in the same year in which Stein entered the Prussian service William Pitt entered the English House of Commons.

But in little more than three years from this time William Pitt was Prime Minister, and his name was bruited over the world. Twenty-four years, among the most eventful in history, passed before Stein made his way up the official ladder to the post of a Minister of State. During all this time he was exhibiting great qualities, but in a country where there was no political knowledge and no general interest in public affairs the merits of an official could only be known to a small circle. The reader will therefore understand that this biography must pass very rapidly over a long and deeply interesting period. Pertz devotes only one volume out of seven to the first 50 years of his hero's life, and he was writing for those who could naturally take more interest in the concerns and occupations of a Prussian official than we can be expected to do in England. I shall take pains therefore in treating of this period to trouble the reader with nothing which is not either essential to the subject or else interesting by the light it throws on Stein's character or on the general history of Prussia or Germany.

Heinitz was at the head of the Mining Department, and Stein at his own request was appointed by Frederick to be a Referendarius under him, taking the oaths on February 10th, 1780. What was the Mining Department? The English reader thinks naturally of a department exerting some sort of control by means of inspectors over the mining industry of the country, interfering for example to prevent the labourer from being ill-treated by the capitalist, from being overworked or set to tasks likely to injure his health. The truth is very different, and must be explained the more carefully because at this point we enter upon the history of Prussia, and because in a life of Stein, who reformed, among other things, the administrative system of that State, the original character of that system is a matter of capital importance.

The old administration of Prussia, a country in

which the Kings had reared a great army on the basis of the feudal state, centred round this army. Local justice and local police were still in the hands of the feudal lord; trade, manufacture, culture were in their infancy; almost the sole business of the Government was to maintain and regulate its army. This called for great financial arrangements, but finance also was in a primitive phase. The Ways and Means of the Government consisted mainly in the revenues of a great landed Estate or Domain. The old Kings of Prussia were accordingly compounded of the General and the Land-owner. They are concerned with an army and an estate. In the latter part of the Great Elector's reign we find that there are two Finance Ministers, one for the Army, the other for the Domains. War and Domains were the two subjects which occupied that prince. The same was the case with his successor Frederick I., and when Frederick William I. came to the throne there were still two bodies of administration side by side, and usually quarrelling. At the seat of Government the General Finance Directory stood opposed to the General War Commissariat, and over the country War Commissariats were formed by the side of Domain Chambers.

The changes made by Frederick William I. in 1722 and 1723 were intended to remove this doubleness, and they introduced the form of administration which subsisted in Prussia until the Peace of Tilsit. War and Domains are now united. There is a General Supreme Financial War and Domains Directory, and in every district the representative of the Government is the War and Domains

Chamber. The General Directory had the King for its President, but it was divided into five Departments, of which each had a Vice-President. Out of these Vice-Presidents grew by degrees the Prussian Ministry; but originally they did not divide among them the great provinces of Government, but were all alike Ministers of Finance and all alike occupied with applying the revenues of an estate to the maintenance of an army. New Departments had since been added to the original five, particularly when the losses of the Seven Years' War set Frederick the Great upon devising modes of increasing the production of his Domains. Of these was the Mining Department, created in 1768.

Thus it appears how large a part of Prussian politics at this time did not differ from private industrial business. When Stein entered the Mining Department of the State he devoted himself to much such work as would have fallen to him had there been mines on his estate at Nassau. He had to study Mineralogy and Chemistry, and passed his time in travelling from one mine to another and reporting on them to the King.

There is here a certain discrepancy in our accounts. In his Autobiography Stein speaks of this as an occupation which was completely new to him and for which he had no previous preparation. These are his words. 'Thus in February, 1780, I entered upon an entirely new career *for which I wanted all the necessary acquirements;* it was my serious resolution to gain them, and thus I began *entirely new* studies, resorting to the colleges at Berlin, accompanying the minister, v. Heinitz, in his business journeys, in 1780 through East Friesland, Holland, Westphalia, the territory of Mannsfeld, in 1781 through East and West Prussia,—whence I returned with Count v. Reden, later Minister of State, by Warsau, Wilitzka, Krakau, through Silesia to Berlin—in 1782 passing a year at Freiberg, and in 1783 three months at Clausthal.'

This statement is not quite consistent with what is now to be related. Two years after his appointment the Minister was so well pleased with him that he presented his name to the King for promotion in the Department. The King was startled—it is worth while to remember that in the same year, William Pitt, two years his junior and without a single month's experience in office, became with general approbation Chancellor of the Exchequer— and said, What! Oberbergrath at once! surely that is a little too much! (*Gleich Oberbergrath sei doch ein bisgen viel*) What has he done to distinguish himself? The Minister's answer was that in consequence of his industry at the University and his careful examination of mines and metallurgy, particularly of the steel and iron manufacture, in his travels in Hungary, Styria and other parts of Germany, he had been fit for the post of Oberbergrath when he first entered the service, that he had since distinguished himself by his energy, and in short that the Minister repeated his recommendation. The King gave way.

It is impossible quite to reconcile these two accounts; there has probably been a little exaggeration on both sides in opposite directions. Stein may have amused himself at odd hours at Göt-

tingen with metallurgy and may have studied with
interest such mines as came in his way on his
travels; perhaps indeed may have gone to Styria
and Hungary expressly to see the mines; at least
he gives no other reason for visiting those particular
countries.   But he had a great contempt for amateur
knowledge and may have considered all that he had
picked up in this way not worth mentioning.   On
the other hand v. Heinitz, finding, as no doubt
he did, that he had secured in Stein a consummate
administrator, may in his eagerness to push him
up the ladder, have exaggerated the knowledge
Stein brought with him in about the same degree
as Stein himself underestimated it.

Stein has now found his vocation; he found it
easily and at once.   A talent like his, which was
rather general vigour of nature than any special
endowment, and a disposition inclined rather to give
than to take, expecting little from life and bent upon
accomplishing much in it, finds a vocation everywhere.   Whatever task might have been assigned
him he would have performed it as if he had been
sent into the world for no other purpose.   But we
can plainly see that his talents were really best fitted
for what we call 'affairs'.   At Göttingen, when he
was preparing to be a lawyer, we saw that all his
spare time was given to the studies of the statesman and the economist.   His parents had recognized that if the family estate was to be disencum-
bered of debt it must be by placing it in his hands,
and the time was one day to come when he was
to render the same service to the estate of the
whole Prussian nation.   He was now to commence

his apprenticeship; to such qualities, inherited and
inborn, as I have described, he was to add a practical familiarity with manufacture, trade and finance.
He was to make himself master of the problem of
the Wealth of Nations.   Other departments of
statesmanship were to remain comparatively strange
to him.   Diplomacy he tried seldom, and though by
no means unsuccessful in it, yet conceived a strong
dislike to the pursuit.   For parliamentary arts or
management, for *posing* before a public assembly, he
never had the least occasion; he never had to lead
a party, though he may be said to have created one.
His statesmanship was to be of the type of Turgot's,
but it was not to fall upon a peaceful period.   It was
to be displayed in conjunction with heroic constancy
in the critical hour of national transition.   Un-
favoured by fortune, it was to accomplish a work
that cannot be done twice in the history of a state.

When Stein reviews the years he spent in the
Mining Department he makes a highly characteristic
reflection, which must on no account be omitted
here.   'Although I quitted it as early as the year
1793, yet life in an occupation which had to do with
nature and human beings, and at the same time
developed the bodily powers, did me the service of
strengthening my constitution, calling out the practical business talent, and *opening my eyes to the worth-
lessness of the dead letter and of mere paper industry.*'
The sequel will furnish a sufficient commentary to
these remarkable words.

What Frederick thought of the young official who
served him for six years, we can only gather from
the little anecdote I have just related.   Stein pro-

bably learnt from the master he had chosen to give full play to the restless driving energy which was natural to him. As he was always severe and somewhat despotic, we may gather from some words he uses that in these first years his vehemence and irritability brought him into some difficulties. He relates his next promotion as follows : 'After my return in 1784 to Berlin, the direction of the mines and manufactures of Westphalia was entrusted to me, and I devoted myself to it with zeal, but with a somewhat blind intensity; this caused discontents and grievances which I could have avoided with more gentleness, and in the sequel did avoid.' A fragment of a letter written in the same year, 1784, to his sister Marianne, throws light on this : 'I must preach to you patience with my father, though I have little of the quality myself, and grow daily more vehement and irritable on account of the drowsiness and dulness of the majority of the people that work under me. Still by perseverance one comes to the goal at last, and ends one's life not like a vegetable.' And in March, 1785, 'Things do not go altogether as I wish, the right thing is but slowly brought about, and one wastes a part of one's life in correcting the follies of one's predecessors and the misconduct of one's underlings.' I must not linger on this period; what specially deserves notice in it is that the zeal which eats the young man up seems to have little in it of ambition ; promotion seems to be little in his thoughts, and fame not at all; what he wants is simply to get 'the right thing done, and not to end his life like a vegetable.'

In June, 1785, came an interruption of his official duties, which must be briefly described.   It gives us a glimpse of the politics of the old Empire just before it passed under that cloud of war from which it never emerged.   I shall, as usual, first insert Stein's curt narration, and then add such explanations as may seem necessary.

'Quite unexpectedly I received in June, 1785, the commission to go as Prussian Ambassador to Mainz, Zweibrücken and Darmstadt, in order to obtain the adhesion of those courts to the German League of Princes, which Frederick the Great opposed to the ambitious views of Joseph II. upon Bavaria.   I succeeded in inducing the Elector of Mainz, Karl Friedrich, to join it; to see the Imperial Arch-Chancellor and first spiritual Elector separate himself from the Emperor and the House of Austria, and join a league opposed to it, was startling.   The Elector had a strong will; he believed himself specially called upon as Arch-Chancellor to defend the constitution and maintain the laws.   He was disquieted by the aggressions of Joseph II., who had personally affronted him, and he was flattered that the famous old king courted his friendship.'

I shall show in the sequel by what steps the hopeless confusion and feebleness of the Empire led to its fall in 1806.   It fell before a foreign invader, but had France never interfered, it is possible that it would have been brought to an end by some other process from within.   The Emperor Joseph, who by the death of his mother in 1780 had acquired, in addition to the empty title of Emperor, the substantial power of Austria, had evidently in his secret mind pronounced the condition of things intolerable, and had set himself to work a revolutionary change. Perhaps he intended to abolish the Imperial Constitution, but in any case he meant without regard to the interests of the Empire to consolidate, centralise, and extend the Austrian State.   He gained the support of Russia by allowing her to conquer the Crimea; his sister was on the throne of France, and it was believed that the old rivalry of Bourbon and Habsburg was for ever at an end; England had been exhausted by war with her colonies.   In these favourable circumstances Joseph pushed on his scheme with reckless impetuosity.   Much could be accomplished by filling the great ecclesiastical appointments with members of his family, but he depended mainly on what Stein calls 'his ambitious views upon Bavaria.'

The two electorates of Bavaria and the Palatinate had eight years before, by the extinction of the younger branch of the House of Wittelsbach, melted into one.   Instead of the Kurbaier and Kurpfalz, which had existed side by side since the Peace of Westphalia, there was now only a Kurpfalzbaier. The actual Elector, Karl Theodor, was old and childless, and Joseph still hoped with the help of Russia to accomplish, when the next vacancy should occur, what Frederick had prevented by war in 1778.   Bavaria, the Upper Palatinate, Neuburg, Sulzbach, and Leuchtenberg were to pass to Austria in exchange for the greater part of the Austrian Netherlands, which was to be erected into a kingdom of Burgundy.   By this means Austria, from a scattered, would become a consolidated State.   Her

possessions in Suabia, called Hither Austria, would be
united with the main mass of her territories, and she
would be relieved of the responsibility of the Netherlands.   Almost all South Germany would be united in
one powerful State.   Whether this result would have
been beneficial for Austria or Germany or Europe
in general was a question which Frederick and the
other German powers perhaps hardly considered.
They only felt that the formation of such a mighty
new State would be dangerous to them.   Frederick
had lost all his foreign allies, and his only resource
was to revive the scheme of those German princes,
who, in the 16th century, had been so nearly swallowed up in the universal monarchy of Charles V.,
and to form a second Schmalkaldic League.

But this he could the more easily do because
Joseph's plan was evidently and avowedly revolutionary.   It was not framed for the benefit or the
restoration of the Empire.   It sacrificed the Empire
to the interests of Austria.   Accordingly it revolted
all the conservative feeling which was anywhere to
be found, and Frederick, the lawless usurper of Silesia, had the pleasure in his old age of appearing
as the champion of the Germanic Constitution.   He
began by procuring the adhesion of the Elector of
Saxony and the Elector of Hannover (George III.)
to his League of Princes.   Hitherto the Emperor
had been the recognized head of what we should
now call the conservative party, and in that character had always had the support of the Ecclesiastical
Princes, who, as they depended almost entirely upon
the Constitution and had but little military or territorial force to fall back upon, could not but be

devoted Conservatives. Accordingly the effect of Joseph's apostasy was soon perceived by the agitation which spread through the spiritual courts. It was almost as fatal an omen for the Emperor as the opposition of the Bishops to James II., and thus Stein describes it as startling that Kurmainz himself should be disposed to separate himself from the House of Austria and to join a League opposed to it.

In April, 1785, Friedrich Karl, that Elector of Mainz, upon whom seven years later the storm of French invasion broke so suddenly, made a secret application to Frederick, desiring to know whether in case of disturbances or war in the Empire he might count on the King's assistance against Austria. This naturally excited the hopes of the Prussian Court, which before had only contemplated winning at the utmost Kurtrier from the number of the ecclesiastical Electors, and had not looked so high as Kurmainz. It was determined to send an agent to procure the adhesion to the League of Princes, not only of Kurmainz, but at the same time of the Margrave of Baden, the Landgrave of Hessen Darmstadt, and one who, as legally the heir of the territories threatened by Austria, and as known to be firmly opposed to the Austrian scheme, was now of the greatest importance—the Duke of Pfalz-Zweibrücken. A certain v. Seckendorff was chosen for the commission, but just at this moment he died. And now the Minister v. Heinitz, who before had been so convinced of Stein's fitness for promotion in the Mining Department, stepped forward to recommend him, a young man of 27, for a most delicate diplomatic mission to an ecclesiastical Court. It seems

evident that Stein's character had strongly impressed
Heinitz. At the same time his character and
manners were certainly not those of a diplomatist,
and he himself tells us that he had a strong distaste
for diplomacy. But Stein's elder brother[1] had already been employed in negotiation at Mainz, and
we shall see that when the adhesion of Kurmainz
had been secured, and Prussia had determined to
place a resident agent at his Court, the person selected for the post was again this same elder brother.
It thus appears that the *family* of Stein was considered to be specially suitable to furnish persons to
conduct negotiations at the Court of Mainz, and this
is easy to understand when we remember that the
father passed his life at that Court, and therefore
that the very name would be likely to inspire the
Elector with confidence. No doubt this was what
Heinitz urged, and it was this consideration rather
than any praises of the young man which he may
have added, that led cool judges like Herzberg and
Frederick himself to acquiesce in the recommendation.

The commission came to Stein while he was on
one of his mining tours, and he declined it on the
ground that he knew nothing of politics or diplomacy
and would be certain to fail. The appointment was
therefore officially revoked, but in the meanwhile
Heinitz had induced him to change his mind, by
telling him that his refusal was attributed to the fear
of Austria. He now begged that the appointment
might be renewed, declaring that he now felt his

---

[1] See a letter of Dalberg's in Pertz I. 71.

honour to be concerned. The Government acceded so far as Mainz was concerned, but determined to send another agent to the other Courts. This again seems to show that it was his special family connection with Mainz, rather than any credit he enjoyed for general diplomatic ability, which influenced the Government.

Stein performed his task with zeal, and we may judge from this fact, considering his conservative and loyal disposition, how far Joseph had alienated his hereditary followers. The details of the negotiation, important in German history, are not important enough in Stein's life to detain us long here. They present a curious picture of the old Empire,—the Duke of Zweibrücken with his Court on the scandalous model of Louis XV.'s; the Landgrave of Hessen-Darmstadt who could not be negotiated with because he had entirely disappeared, like the Duke in 'Measure for Measure', and no one knew where he was; Kurmainz himself eking out an inadequate revenue by the sale of his patronage, besieged by two rival candidates for the Electoral dignity, the Duke of Württemberg, who offers 500,000 gulden, and the Landgrave of Hessen-Darmstadt, who outbids him with 400,000 thalers; the Elector's niece Frau v. Coudenhofen, whom the Austrian Court tries to win over by offering her *a decision in the Reichshofrath worth* 60,000 *gulden*. We gain an insight into the principal peculiarity of an ecclesiastical Court, namely, the instability of its policy, caused by the irresistible impulse of each Sovereign to show his independence at the beginning of his reign by reversing the policy of his predecessor. It was in consequence of this

well-known peculiarity of an elective Court that
the Prussian negotiators felt that, after all, little
would be gained by merely securing the adhesion of
Kurmainz himself, who was in his 67th year, unless
they could also secure the support of his successor.
And here is introduced to us the man who played
the most prominent part among the ecclesiastical
personages of Germany in the age which was then
about to open, Dalberg, afterwards Prince Primate
in the miserable Confederation of the Rhine. He
had talents and active benevolence, and Stein at this
time had a high opinion of him. Just before the
negotiation (March, 1785) he had remarked in a
letter to his sister, ' It would be very fortunate
for our poor country if Herr v. Dalberg should
become Archbishop of Mainz.' But Dalberg was
to show in the time of trial, like several of his
fellow-countrymen, that character is something different both from ability and from benevolence, and
that in such times only definite and unalterable
convictions can secure the most amiable man
from becoming the instrument of incalculable mischief, and leaving an ignominious name to
history.

Stein reached Mainz on the 3rd of July, and the
object of his mission was attained on the 15th of
October, when the Elector gave his adhesion to the
League. He seems to have shown himself not
wanting in the necessary tact, but his task was
mainly negative. The Elector's inclination to the
League had been expressed before the negotiation
began, and it was not easy for him, had he wished it,
to retract his words. Moreover there was no serious

consideration that could make for Austria.   In Joseph's proceedings there was nothing conciliating, nothing plausible.   It did indeed require a good deal of moral courage on the Elector's part to decide upon a course so contrary to the traditions of the Electoral Court.   Accordingly it was to his fears that the Austrian party appealed.   Trautmannsdorff, the Austrian Ambassador, Romanzow, the Russian Ambassador, and O'Kelly, the French Ambassador, who produced urgent letters from Vergennes, threatened him by turns.   But Stein says the Elector had a strong will; to others he seemed rather a man of restless self-importance, and he felt his own importance the more, the more urgent were the threats of the Great Powers; so that there remained nothing for Stein to do but to flatter his vanity by convincing him of the great Frederick's respect for him and eager desire for his adhesion.   We shall see that in later times Stein's peculiar power lay in inspiring courage; timid men became resolute in his presence and procrastinators suddenly made up their minds.   Perhaps he produced some such effect on the Elector, and the strong will with which he credits him may have been in some degree a reflection of his own.

And here the curtain falls upon the old regime of Europe.   Frederick the Great died on the 17th August, 1786, and within three years from this date the new period opened.   When next we speak of politics they will be the politics of the revolutionary age.

Stein continues his autobiography thus: 'I petitioned for my recall, for I had always a repugnance

to diplomacy on account of the changeableness of
the politics of Courts, the alternation of idleness and
a crafty calculating activity, the constant inquiry for
news and effort to make out secrets, the necessity of
living in the great world and reconciling oneself to
its pleasures and fetters, its littlenesses and tiresome-
nesses, and on account of my inclination to independence and my frankness and irritability—and in
the winter of 1785 I returned to my post, executed
various plans, and in November, 1786, made a
mineralogical and technical journey to England,
whence I returned again in August, 1787. I was
offered an embassy at the Hague, then to Russia,
which I refused. But I was appointed Kammer-
Director in the War and Domains' Chamber at
Cleve and Hamm, charged specially with the direction of manufactures, navigation, and road-making,
and I completed the system of communication in the
County Mark by the construction of twenty (German) miles of artificial roads within four years; in
this hilly, manufacturing, richly productive country,
all the labour was paid for, and no compulsory services exacted; I also effected an alteration of the
Excise or Tax on Consumption in the County
Mark into a payment better suited for an open
industrial region.'

Stein's autobiography has a peculiarity which
anywhere else would be a merit, but is a serious
fault in an autobiography; it is not egotistic enough.
The facts are briefly given, but without any commentary, even where a commentary was almost
necessary to bring out their significance. In this
passage he gives us, indeed, the reasons—and very

characteristic reasons they are—which led him to decline the diplomatic career, but he does not pause for a moment to explain to us what was the magnitude of the prospects he thus renounced. He does not even tell us what were the objects of the mission to the Hague, and of that to Russia, which the Government wished to entrust to him. Nay, he does not leave it quite unquestionable at what date the offers were made. But he says just enough to create a surmise that—no doubt in consequence of his success at Mainz—the greatest value was attached to his diplomatic services, and that he might at this moment have stepped at once into a very prominent position had he not deliberately preferred to remain in comparative obscurity for about fifteen years. For he seems to mean that the embassy at the Hague was offered to him immediately after his return from England in August, 1787, and that on his refusing it, then or soon after, he was tempted with the embassy at St Petersburg. But if we look at the history of the year, we shall see that these two embassies were just then among the most important appointments which the Prussian Government could have to fill. It was in June, 1787, that the disturbances in Holland reached a crisis through the detention of the Princess of Orange, sister of the King of Prussia, by the Patriots on the frontier of the Province of Holland. It was on the 9th of September that the King of Prussia, having demanded satisfaction for the insult to his sister, presented his ultimatum to the States, and in the same month his troops crossed the frontier, and reinstated the Hereditary Stadtholder at the Hague. It is evident that the Government must have had no ordinary opinion of the talents of a young man of thirty, if, just at this moment, they thought of sending him to the Hague. So much for the first offer; and now what of the second? What were the relations of Prussia, just at this moment, with the Court of St Petersburg? On the 24th of August, 1787, the Porte declared war against Russia, and the war began which is remembered by Suworoff's victories and Laudon's capture of Belgrade. Prussia did not actually intervene, but she watched the contest most eagerly, with a view to make her own profit out of it. The four years between Frederick's death and the convention of Reichenbach were the years of Herzberg's influence. This minister's head was full of daring combinations, and his favourite scheme aimed at the acquisition of Dantzic and Thorn as an equivalent for the territories he expected Russia and Austria to acquire by conquest from Turkey. If the Dutch affair may have been for a month or two more urgent, the Eastern question was more difficult, and, in the long run, more important. And it was in this crisis that the Government proposed to send as an ambassador to the Court of Catharine—Stein!

We saw that it was Heinitz who recommended him for the embassy at Mainz. But Herzberg is also mentioned as having favoured him on that occasion. Herzberg was now, after Frederick's death, a much more influential man, and the Eastern question was, at least for some time, almost entirely in his hands. It is natural to conjecture that it was he who had been impressed by Stein's management of the Mainz negotiation, and was now recommending him for the highest posts of diplomacy.

The period just commencing was one of deep disgrace for Prussian foreign policy. No statesmen appeared who had clear views, no diplomatists who had firmness and courage. Speaking of this period long after Stein wrote, 'We lived through that unhappy time, it consumed our best years; one cannot think without deep repugnance of the multitude of narrow, interested, selfish, insincere men in whose hands Providence placed the destiny of the nations —the Duke of Brunswick, Coburg, H. v. Lucchesini, Haugwitz, Colloredo, Thugut, &c.' One is tempted for a moment to think how happy it would have been for Prussia had Stein devoted himself to the task of putting clearness and frankness into her diplomacy. But probably he could not have done this in any position but that of an all-powerful foreign minister, and for such a minister the Prussian system of government left at that time, as we shall see, no place. The paralysis of Prussian policy began in the central organ; it was caused by Frederick William II.'s want of clearness, and Frederick William III.'s want of decision; and nothing could be done for the State until, as after Tilsit, extreme need had forced the King to abandon the reins to a statesman more capable than himself.

Meanwhile, in diplomacy, Stein would have lost his grasp of questions which were then all-important for Prussia. These questions were industrial and administrative; how to support a poor State in the position of one of the great powers of Europe; how to make a uniform administration for provinces loosely united, and some of them recently acquired; how to raise the State above the terrible risks to which the best-intentioned personal despotism cannot but expose it. These questions called for other studies than those of the diplomatist. Scarcely any position could have better enabled him to prosecute them than that which he wisely refused to quit, a position in the midst of the most advanced industry and the freest institutions to be found in the whole country.

Stein's reticence is particularly annoying when he speaks of his journey to England. Not one word does he say of anything that he saw, or any person whose acquaintance he made there. Nor have I found any reference to the journey in any of his letters. And yet, as the reader remembers, he has already spoken most emphatically of the interest he felt in our country and in our literature. To English history he seems to have owed the whole awakening and development of his intellect. In evidence of this I will quote here a letter written in March, 1812, on the subject of the education of his nephews, the sons of Count Arnim, to whom he was guardian. After declaring himself pleased to hear that one of them is fond of the Classics and of Mathematics, he goes on to say that the most important study is history, 'which raises us above the vulgarity of the present, and makes us acquainted with what the noblest and greatest men have accomplished, and what indolence, sensuality, vulgarity, or the perverse application of great powers have marred.' And then he adds, 'English literature among the modern European literatures deserves best to be accurately known, as it has the most good historians to show, who have faithfully represented incidents and characters, rationally and with special knowledge developed causes, and in whom chiefly morality, public spirit, and thorough knowledge of the foundations of civil order reign.   For these reasons is the study of the English language and literature, and particularly the historical part of it, solidly and in every way beneficial.'   And yet not one word about his journey!   Nor does Pertz add anything except that Count Reden was his companion.

Pertz, however, here omits one or two circumstances, which, though of little importance in themselves, might as well have been mentioned in so exhaustive a biography.

I find in a sketch of the eccentric Count Schlabrendorf, by Varnhagen v. Ense, the following sentence.   'After he had travelled through Germany and Switzerland, and taken a first survey of France, he betook himself to England, where he spent six years, and for some time had the Baron vom Stein as companion in his travels in the interior of that country.   Here, too, in the year 1786, he made the acquaintance of the philosopher Friedrich Heinrich Jacobi, and formed an intimate friendship with him.'

As the name of Jacobi has thus been introduced, it is worth remarking that about this time Stein appears to have been much in his society.   Jacobi just then occupied a philosophical position something like that of Coleridge late in George IV.'s reign among ourselves.   Lavater was his Edward Irving, and on the other side Nicolai and the other followers of

Lessing (who had died in 1781) answered to the philosophic Radicals and Westminster Reviewers. At this particular moment he was concerned in an affair which made much noise in Germany. In August, 1786, appeared in the Berlin Monthly an essay by a certain Leuchsenring, a man at that time held in considerable estimation among the savants of Germany, undertaking to prove the existence of a wide-spread Jesuitic conspiracy, in which many leading writers of Germany were implicated. The religious revival, of which Lavater was the prime mover, was interpreted as one of the symptoms of the secret action of this conspiracy, and the writings of Jacobi might naturally be regarded as another. From this paper of Leuchsenring's the Berlin school of writers, Nicolai and the staff of the German Library (Deutsche Bibliothek), at once took the alarm, and the cry of secret Jesuitism, secret Catholicism, was loudly raised. Jacobi's letters at this time are full of the affair, and more than once he mentions conversations he had held on the subject with the Baron vom Stein, who no doubt was often brought by his official occupations into the neighbourhood of Pempelfort, Jacobi's well-known house near Düsseldorf. I am not sorry to notice Stein's few points of contact with philosophy and literature. The agitation against Jesuitism was triumphantly laughed down ; Nicolai and his school had later to encounter a superior antagonist in Fichte, and became a byword of contempt to the next generation. Nevertheless the religious movement of those years had actually for one of its results, like most religious movements since scepticism began to make way, a revival of Catholicism. This first appeared long after by the conversion of Count Friedrich Stolberg in the year 1802, and the great sensation which that event produced probably arose, as among ourselves in the case of Dr Newman, from the decisive confirmation it gave to so many suspicions, and the decisive refutation it gave to so many earnest protests. The bitterness with which Jacobi attacked his old friend Stolberg on that occasion was therefore very natural, though it revolted Stein's feelings. He could look at the matter with more impartiality, and wrote, 'Stolberg I still regard with respect, for his pure love of truth, and the resignation with which he sacrifices so much; the conduct of his literary friends, Jacobi and Voss, I still think harsh, brutal, narrow—they who live with people of all sorts, all opinions, all crazes, why do not they let Stolberg live according to his conviction? He thinks he finds in the Catholic religion rest and definiteness, he finds in it the pure original Christianity; why pursue him with anger and taunts?'

To return to the English tour; it seems probable that he was with Jacobi in England, as it is certain that he was with Schlabrendorf, but what we desire to know is what Englishmen he saw. Did he see Pitt, then in his glory? Did he converse with Burke? I think probably not, as we find no allusion to any such intercourse in his numerous letters. He calls his visit to England a mineralogical and technical tour, and perhaps he means to imply that he was at this time so absorbed in his pursuit that he paid no attention to public affairs.

The promotion which Stein received in November, 1787, was an important step, for it took him out of the Mining Department and placed him at the head of one of those War and Domains Chambers, through which Local Government in Prussia was conducted. I suppose it is this appointment which Heinitz refers to in his Memoir printed in Mirabeau's Book on Prussia where he says, ' It was only last summer that I succeeded in placing the Baron vom Stein, Member of Chamber and Mining Counsellor, in the provinces beyond the Weser. He is intelligent and interested in the subject ; with competent subalterns he will give success to the arrangements which have been made.' The period which follows is in Stein's life what the Administration of the Limousin is in Turgot's, and it seems not unlikely that this comparison had passed through his own mind. Turgot's example had been set before all Europe by Condorcet's Life of him about the time when Stein rose to be a provincial governor, and we observe that Turgot's great innovation of road-making without corvées is precisely what Stein boasts of having introduced into Westphalia. The district entrusted to him was one in which almost everything had still to be done in order to bring out its industrial capabilities. This is now the manufacturing province, the Lancashire, of Germany ; but then it wanted not merely capital and private enterprise, but roads and navigable rivers. Here then Stein worked, not always in the same capacity, and interrupted in his labours by three years' war, but remaining always in this region, and watching over the development of territories which are now included in the Westphalian province of Prussia, until 1804, when he rose to be Trade Minister of the Prussian State.   He identified himself so long with this province, in which more independence of character and more traces of popular institutions were to be found than in other parts of Prussia, that he came at last to regard it as his home, and to have the feelings of a Westphalian.   His Westphalian notions were regarded with some alarm when he became Minister of State.   Eleven years later, when his stormy public career was over, he bought an estate in the province, called Cappenberg, at which, in his old age, he lived more than at Nassau, and at his death his friend v. Vincke (father of the well-known Prussian politician of our own time), who had succeeded him as Superior President of the province, said in an obituary notice, 'The Province of Westphalia deplores in him the irreparable loss of its most distinguished inhabitant, many creations of whose earlier official activity, continued through twenty years, still remain to benefit us, and who later, having retired from a most active public life into this province from love and regard for its inhabitants, never ceased to be animated with a patriotic zeal for all good objects.'

As I wish to treat this period of Stein's life in a summary manner, I shall insert here a list of the appointments successively held by Stein in the Prussian service up to the time when he became a Minister of State.

MINING DEPARTMENT:

Referendarius	1780, Feb. 10th
Oberbergrath	1782, March 8th
Director of Westphalian Mines and of the Minden (additional) Mining Commission	1784, Feb. 16th
Geheimer Oberbergrath	1786, Oct. 31st

WAR AND DOMAINS CHAMBERS:

2nd Director of the Chambers at Cleve and Hamm (principal town of the County Mark)	1787, Nov. 7th
1st ditto	1788, July 27th
President of the Chambers of Mark (retaining the former appointment) .	1793, Feb. 18th
President of the Chamber of Cleve (retaining former appointments and becoming also Royal Commissioner at the Provincial Assembly) . .	1793, Nov. 23rd
President of the Chambers of Minden (do.)	1796, May 10th
Supreme President of all the Westphalian Chambers, Minden, Ravensberg, Tecklenburg, Lingen, Cleve, Meurs, Mark, Geldern	1796, June 21st

MINISTRY OF STATE:

Minister of Trade	1804, Oct. 27th.

There was not yet at this time any Prussian
Province of Westphalia. A Circle of the Empire
was called Westphalian, and some scattered territories
within it belonged to Prussia. The whole list of
these possessions is as follows : the Duchies of Cleve
and Geldern, the Principalities of Minden, Meurs
and Ostfriesland, and the Counties of Mark, Ravens-
berg, Lingen, Tecklenburg, and Sayn-Altenkirchen.
But Ostfriesland lay far to the north. With the exception of this and Sayn-Altenkirchen, Stein, it will

be seen, gathered at last under his government all the Prussian possessions which could then be called Westphalian. But his closest and longest connection was with the particular territory called the County Mark.

In this gradual ascent of the official ladder, in these years devoted to the study of local government, Stein gained an insight into the whole working of government, which he could never have acquired in as many years of official activity in Berlin, much less of diplomacy. Not only did he learn in this period, as I have remarked, the limitations of government and the necessity of a large measure of liberty and individual enterprise; he learnt another lesson of scarcely less importance, he acquired original and most clear views of the manner in which administration should be carried on. It is one of his great merits that, though the great enemy of officialism, he knew better than almost any statesman the difference between good officialism and bad, and thus was able to appear not only as an emancipator of the people from bureaucracy, but also at the same time as the reformer of the bureaucracy itself, increasing its efficiency at the same time that he carefully limited its sphere.

CHAPTER III.

PRUSSIA AT WAR WITH THE REVOLUTION.

WHEN in the biography of a person belonging to this period the narrative reaches the outbreak of the French Revolution, the reader instinctively prepares himself for a complete change both of matter and style. He expects a sudden breach of continuity, a disappearance of all that has hitherto occupied the scene, and in its place a crowd of new personages and new ideas. He expects first a discussion of the first principles of politics, the rights of man and the social contract, and afterwards an Iliad of war and battles; he expects at the same time the quietness and tameness of ordinary life to give place to dramatic incident. But in Stein's life the French Revolution is no such important date, and for many years after the outbreak of it his occupations and thoughts continued to be, except during one short interval, what they would have been had it never taken place. In the end, what may be called the indirect or remote operation of the French Revolution did indeed strike him more overwhelmingly than almost any other German public man, but that was in a later time, and when the Revolution, if we choose to call it so, had gone through the whole series of its changes of form, and was now nothing but a military tyranny of the most pernicious kind. Stein, I remind the reader, does not belong to 1789, but to 1807, not to the French, but to the Anti-Napoleonic Revolution. Our narrative, therefore, need not concern itself much for the present with France. The storm is there, but Stein is not within the eddies of it. For in the first place it produced very little effect upon his mind. Though he was imaginative in a certain sense and had a very vivid way of conceiving whatever interested him, his imagination was altogether practical. He had no *play* of imagination, none of that faculty which is everything to the poet or literary man, or, if he had it, he controlled it as a weakness. He was very busy, and moreover, as a German patriot, he soon began to fear Revolutionary France too much to sympathise with her. The Revolution does not seem to have aroused in him the most transient gleam of enthusiasm. Its magnificent generalities and abstractions, which turned so many heads, only reminded him of the weakest side of his own nation, and what Napoleon branded as ideology he rejected with equal contempt as metapolitics. On the other hand, he was just as far from being blind to what there was of vital force and energy about the Revolution. This appeared plainly, and in such a manner as to puzzle some who knew him best, by his legislation of 1807. But to be seized by the genuine revolutionary enthusiasm Stein should have been about ten years younger and should have never undergone the cooling process of a discipline in practical administration. No doubt also the prepossessions of his caste swayed him in the opposite direction.

There did come a time for Stein when the whole course of his life was altered, a sudden cataclysm, such as the French Revolution brought for so many. But this time was not 1789 but 1806, and the catastrophe was not the fall of monarchy in France, but the fall of the German Empire and of Prussia. When the narrative reaches that point it will indeed change its character, spread wider and flow deeper, but not till then. The fall of Germany, in one word, and not the revolution of France, is the central incident in Stein's life.

Meanwhile he continues his industrial career in Westphalia, giving even less attention than we should have expected to general politics, and scarcely so much disquieted as he ought to have been by the ominous change in Prussian affairs, which began with the death of Frederick, and was revealed to all the world by the Treaty of Reichenbach and the appearance on the stage of a new and most mischievous school of politicians. His energy is always great, but he shows, as yet, few signs of rising out of officialism into statesmanship. I do not intend to linger on his achievements as a local administrator, great as they were, but I shall be detained for a while by the incident which in 1792 interrupted the quiet course of his government, viz. the first war of Prussia with the Revolution, which was terminated by the treaty of Basel in 1795, and I shall also give an account of his marriage, which took place in 1793.

It seems to have been on his appointment in 1784 to the superintendence of Westphalian mines that he received, for the first time, a salary. It amounted at first to 1060 thalers, but was raised soon after to 1260 thalers. To this was added a house at Wetter on the Ruhr. It is said that on first receiving pay the spirit of the Imperial Knight awoke in him, that he shed tears and flung the money on the ground.

He lived at Wetter till 1793, when he was promoted to the post of President of the Chambers of Mark and Cleve. He then obtained a salary of 2500 thalers, and soon after of 3000 thalers, with a residence in Cleve. As this was also the time of his marriage we may consider the year 1793 as the principal subdivision of this part of his life. Bishop Eylert, in his book on the character of Frederick William III., tells us that when he asked Stein where he had been happiest the answer was, 'At Wetter. There I tasted the delight of solitude in a beautiful country. Ever since I have had a longing for it, I yearn towards it with love.' It was during this period that his great works of engineering were accomplished. He mentions with evident pride the system of road communication for the County, which he completed in four years, without exacting any compulsory service.

It is strange that Stein should omit to mention another work of equal magnitude which his biographers attribute to him. We are told that he made the Ruhr navigable, and thus created an outlet by which the coal of that region could be transported to the district of Cleve, to the Rhine, and to Holland. It is evident at once how vast was the importance of such a work, and how the author of it must deserve to be called the founder of the wealth of that province, and, in fact, of the manufacturing prosperity of Prussia. And yet Stein says not a word about it. Throughout this Autobiography we shall see that he claims no credit for anything which was not indubitably and entirely his own work. For instance, in describing the firmness shown by the Czar Alexander in prosecuting the war against Napoleon, he says nothing of the effect which his own advice may have had in producing this firmness, though most of his countrymen believe that the Czar's unaccustomed constancy at this time was simply due to the fact that Stein was at his side. Possibly he may have judged in reviewing his work at Wetter that some one else had a share equal or nearly equal to himself in making the Ruhr navigable, and in order to avoid the danger of claiming too much credit for himself, may have chosen—it was a choice which cost him nothing—to claim no credit at all.

In these years Stein must have acquired a fund of scientific knowledge, which in later life he had little occasion to use. A. v. Humboldt thinks that in knowledge of mining he surpassed both his patron Heinitz and his friend Reden, who succeeded Heinitz at the head of the Department, that he applied science to the subject as it had never been applied before, and in particular that he was the first to apply chemistry in the salt manufacture. But in Stein's biography the most important incident of his earlier career is his financial reform in the County Mark. Nevertheless I cannot expect the reader to interest himself in the finance of a mere corner of the Prussian State. Two points only about it I must ask him to note. The first is that the Reform, which received the royal sanction March 18th, 1791, was not accomplished in the despotic fashion, but by a negotiation with the Estates of the County, and that the success it met with may well be supposed to have inclined Stein favourably towards the parliamentary way of governing. The second is that the Reform was in the spirit of Free-trade. The sporadic character of the Prussian possessions in Westphalia made, it may be imagined, the difficulty of levying a general Excise insurmountable, while the industrial character of the district made the tax oppressive. Stein confined the Excise to the towns, and even there to a few articles. To the country districts he gave almost complete free-trade. In both points the Reformer's first essay was a rehearsal of the grand achievement of his life.

I have said that the French Revolution produced little effect upon Stein's mind, and little change in the course of his life. At the same time the war of France and Prussia, between 1792 and 1795, interrupted his labours for a time, one principal scene of it being Mainz, with which city he was closely connected, and another, the frontier of the Westphalian possessions of Prussia. Few people, indeed, not themselves soldiers, could have seen more of that war than Stein did. Yet when he wrote his Autobiography he judged it scarcely worthy of any mention. He writes, 'In the year 1793 I became President of the Chambers at Cleve and Hamm, in 1794 I was driven from Cleve by the advance of the French, in 1795 charged with the provisioning of the army under Möllendorff, which marched to

Westphalia in May. I succeeded in it in spite of
the bad harvest, of the long stay of the army of
Clairfait on the Lower Rhine, and of the English on
the Weser, and I did it cheaply by dividing the whole
territory, from which the provisions were to be
drawn, into distinct districts, in which the purchases
were made at fixed prices by trustworthy commis-
sioners who had an interest in the saving, by
arranging lines of transport from the principal
magazines into the distribution magazine with power
of pressing vehicles, and by excluding the general
contractor.'

This passage shows that Stein meant his Autobiography rather as a contribution to the history of
his time than as a personal history. This is all he
says about a period, which to himself personally was
very eventful; he has not even a word about his
marriage. Nor would anyone suspect from this
account that he was almost a spectator of the fall of
Mainz in 1792, and actually a spectator of its recovery in July, 1793, and that he was not charged
for the first time in 1795 with the duty of provisioning troops, but had discharged the same duty for the
Duke of Brunswick in 1793, and even at the end of
1792.

Though Stein was not at this time of sufficient importance to allow us to consider the
general history of the first Revolutionary war as
a part of his biography, yet it will be desirable to
insert here some remarks upon it, in order that the
reader may be gradually prepared to look upon
European events from Stein's, that is from the
German and more particularly the Prussian point
of view.

In the history of England the French Revolution leads to a war which beginning in 1793 lasts, with only a year's intermission at the Peace of Amiens and another year's intermission after Napoleon's first abdication, till 1815. But between France and Germany, and still more between France and Prussia, there was no such continuous war. Austria indeed waged war from 1792 to 1801 with the interval only of part of 1797 and the whole of 1798, but after 1801 the wars of Austria with France, though terrible, were short and waged at long intervals. There was one in 1805, another in 1809, another in 1813-14. The case of Prussia in this period was still more different from that of England. Prussia had three wars with France ; the first began in 1792, and ended with the Peace of Basel in April, 1795 ; the second began in 1806 and ended with the Peace of Tilsit in July, 1807 ; the third began in 1813 and ended (for we may be allowed to consider the campaign of Waterloo as a mere supplement to the War of Liberation) at the general peace. The period therefore is for Prussia on the whole rather peaceful than warlike. Three years of war are followed by eleven years of peace and apparent prosperity, and afterwards a war of less than one year is followed by nearly six years of peace, though peace accompanied with humiliation and despair. It is with the second and third of these wars and with the interval between them that this biography will be principally occupied.

How it happened that Prussia was able to enjoy peace and prosperity for so many years, while the rest of Europe was disturbed by war, and that she afterwards fell with such a sudden catastrophe when she could remain at peace no longer, will be a main subject of our inquiry. We shall have to examine the peculiarity of the Prussian State and government, and this it is not convenient to do yet. But without going below the surface we may make some observations on Prussia's war of 1792—1795, which are likely to be new to the English reader who has been used to consider that war always either from the English or the French, and never from the German point of view.

For our purpose then the importance of this war consists not in the triumph it gave to the revolutionary cause and the foundation it laid for the throne of Napoleon, but rather in the fact that it gave the death-blow to the Germanic System. This war, which was the result of a revolution in France, was the cause of a revolution perhaps not less momentous in Germany. The separate Peace which Prussia concluded at Basel, and into which under the shadow of Prussia all other Princes and Estates of the Empire with the exception of Austria were allowed at their pleasure to enter, was in itself a sufficient token of the complete dissolution of German unity; but the principle which the Treaty laid down of indemnification to Prussia for those territories on the Left Bank of the Rhine which she ceded to France involved, as will be seen later, a formal as well as a substantial dissolution of the system. The Holy Roman Empire came to an end in 1806 in consequence of the shock received in this war; and from that time to 1870 the German Question was how to find a substitute for it.

How was it that an institution which had lasted so long and weathered so many storms was destroyed at last? The mortal blow was not given by Napoleon in his might, but by the Revolution when it had scarcely emerged from its first weakness. In few wars has fortune swung so violently round from one side to the other. The Prussian army had penetrated into the heart of France in September 1792. As late as the end of 1793, the Austrian Minister Thugut discusses with Russia a plan of extending the Austrian Netherlands so as to give them a frontier on the Somme and on a line drawn from the sources of the Somme by Sedan and Mezières to the Meuse. Two months later he is carving out a principality for an Austrian Archduke which is to consist of Lorraine and the Three Bishoprics, and the least that will content him is the frontier as it was fixed at the Peace of the Pyrenees. A year later France is in possession of Belgium, and has set up in Holland a government dependent on herself, and the despair of Prussia is such that she concludes a separate Peace on terms which, as we have seen, involved the fall of the Empire.

To Stein, this seemed much less unaccountable than it does to the English reader of the present day, because the internal politics of Germany were not a blank to him. He saw Germany and Prussia struggling not with the Revolution alone, but with other enemies and other difficulties at the same time. In the first place, he saw the Polish Revolution on the East as clearly as the French Revolution on the West. This Polish Revolution occurred May 3rd, 1791, and was of the most pressing importance both to Austria and Prussia. It abolished the whole system of anarchy which had ruined the country, the *liberum veto* and the elective monarchy, making the crown hereditary in the Saxon line. Such a change concerned Prussia much more nearly than the changes which were making at the same time in France. Three days after it had taken place a Report was laid before Frederick William, expressing the views of Herzberg, the statesman who represented the foreign policy of Frederick the Great, in which it was declared that the new Polish constitution was a serious peril for Prussia and that Prussia could have no security but in the continuance of the free elective monarchy. What seemed to Prussia a serious danger appeared altogether intolerable to the Empress Catharine. In April 1792, that is just at the moment when the Revolutionary War began, she occupied Poland with her troops; and the anarchy which there went by the name of freedom was fully restored by July. Meanwhile the three Powers that had made the first Partition renewed their understanding. In January 1793, when the war in the West was in full progress, two months after Dumouriez' victory at Jemappes and occupation of the Netherlands, and a month after the King of Prussia had retaken Frankfurt, his general Möllendorf entered Poland to accomplish the second Partition.

Again in March 1794, or three months before fortune inclined decisively to the French side in

Jourdan's victory at Fleurus, commenced the great Polish rising under Kosciusko, and in the middle of April the insurgents got possession of Warsaw. Soon afterwards Wilna fell into their hands, and in a short time almost the whole country obeyed the national leader. Here was a new burden for Prussia. Frederick William set out in person for Poland on May 14th, and it was evident that he had on his hands a task which might well employ the whole energies of his kingdom. Upon the Rhine Prussia is as if struck with paralysis. It was not till November that the *finis Poloniae* arrived.

These well-known facts, as they relate to a part of Europe distant from the scene of the revolutionary war, are commonly treated as if they belonged to a different period. But Germany, and especially Prussia, was equally affected by the Eastern and by the Western disturbances. When we have looked more closely at the Prussian State, observed the poverty of the country and the difficulty with which even in peace it maintained its overgrown army, we shall cease to be surprised at the exhaustion and despair to which it was reduced at the beginning of 1795, and shall begin rather to wonder how it could have played its part so long in the war with France at the same time that it accomplished the Second Partition of Poland and made everything ready for the Third.

When we compare the struggle of Germany with Louis XIV. to her struggle with the French Revolution, we may be perplexed at first to find her succumbing so soon in the latter, while she came safely out of the former. Her military force was much greater now than it had been a century and a half before. The mighty Prussian army consisting of 250,000 men had grown up in the interval, and Austria had also grown much in vigour and improved greatly in organisation since the accession of Maria Theresa. Flanders, instead of belonging to the inert government of Spain, was now in the strong hand of Austria. Holland and England from the beginning of 1793 lent their help, as they had done in the earlier struggle. But from this estimate of the resources of Germany several deductions are to be made. Holland had been in steady decline since the death of William III. Its main stay, the hereditary capacity and heroism of the House of Orange, had been lost with him, for the collateral branch which had now for half a century held the hereditary Stadtholderate exhibited none of the qualities of the elder line, and the standing conflict between the Orangists and Republicans had led, only five years before the revolutionary war broke out, to civil war and the intervention of Prussia, so that it required but a touch from Pichegru to subvert the government and convert Holland from an enemy into a devoted ally of France. Next the vigour of Austria was just at this moment paralysed by the discontents which had been caused by Joseph's rash innovations. This made the Austrian Netherlands as unsafe a bulwark to Germany as the Dutch. There too the ground was undermined, and France was likely to be welcomed by one party as warmly as she would be opposed by another. And thirdly, the fact that Germany could bring into the field two mighty armies, those of Prussia and Austria, each of which had in the age before seemed capable of matching France, was neutralised by the bitter jealousy which existed, and which during the war grew fiercer than ever, between the Austrian and Prussian governments. What that jealousy had been in Joseph's time, we have seen. Leopold in his short reign of two years (1790—1792) had brought the two Powers into a formal alliance, so that they were able to take the field together against France. But their mutual suspicion was scarcely intermitted for a day, and the Second Partition of Poland in the next year opened the wound again wider than ever, for Austria had supported the changes in the Polish Constitution which by alarming Prussia and Russia led to the Partition, and not only was the Partition a blow to Austrian policy, but Austria was actually excluded from the benefit of it. In that cynical race for territorial acquisition which the two Powers had been running since the accession of Frederick the Great, Austria was now suddenly left behind, and the rage of her Ministers, particularly Thugut, whose ascendancy now begins, knew no bounds.

But the particular weakness of the German system which most evidently led to its destruction in this war, still remains to be noted. The armies were there, and there was no doubt wealth enough in all Germany taken together to have kept them in the field for many years. But there existed no machinery by which the wealth could be appropriated to this purpose. It was absurd to expect of either Prussia or Austria, that they should not only place their armies at the disposal of the Empire, but should also *pay* those armies. Their obligation extended only to the furnishing a certain contingent to the Imperial Army. If they went beyond this obligation it was evident that the Empire, that is the Diet at Regensburg, must find Ways and Means; otherwise Prussia would sooner or later become incapable financially of bearing the burden, and Austria if she continued the contest, would do so in her own interest rather than in that of the Empire. There is a Parliamentary history of Germany during these critical years which has been little noticed. In January 1794, we find Frederick William commissioning Count Görtz, his representative at Regensburg, to propose that the provisioning of his army should be undertaken by the Empire. He declares that in the recapture of Mainz, and in the last campaign of Brunswick, the Prussian army has actually done the work of the Imperial army, but that Prussia is now exhausted, that the fundamental principle of the Prussian State is that the enormous cost of its army shall be made remunerative to the country, and that Prussia had never been capable even in the Great Frederick's time of supporting a long foreign war without subsidies. Pending the decision of the Diet, an attempt is made to induce the particular districts which were most exposed to the French attack, to furnish provisional assistance, and Hardenberg, who now begins to be conspicuous, is entrusted with this negotiation. When the proposal came before the Diet, that body displayed the hopeless inefficiency which had characterised it so long. That the Prussian army should become the Imperial Army, and the Prussian king Germany's commander-in-chief, was a proposal which Austria felt bound in honour to resist. But it was necessary for her to make a counter-proposal. Accordingly she proposed a reform in the Constitution of the Empire, which by strengthening the Executive in military matters, should make the Imperial Army, what it had never been yet, efficient. But since to strengthen the executive meant to strengthen Austria, this counter-proposal was in its turn certain to be opposed by Prussia.

A Resolution was agreed to in the Diet, on May 12th. It thanked the Emperor for the exertions he had made, and expressed the hope that all the Estates would do their duty in the present dangerous war, but rejected the proposal to strengthen the executive Power. At the same time it declared that the Imperial Army must be reinforced, and that the easiest and most convenient way of doing this was by taking into pay a corps of the Prussian army. By this middle course, Prussia gained the honour of furnishing as it were a second Imperial Army, but at the same time the financial difficulty under which she laboured was very imperfectly met. Her ministers seem to have considered that their proposal had practically failed.

Meanwhile, the Treaty of the Hague had been concluded on April 19th, and Prussia's way seemed to be made clear for her by an English subsidy. This is one of the points of contact between English and Prussian history. For a subsidy of £50,000 a month, with certain extra payments to be borne by England and Holland, Prussia was to put in the field an army of 62,400 men, which was to be stationed wherever the maritime Powers thought it could be employed the most usefully, as it should be determined by a military convention between England, Holland and Prussia. Most of us remember to what unfortunate differences this arrangement led. The maritime Powers required the Prussian army to move into the Austrian Netherlands; the Prussians refused to stir from the Rhine. An angry Conference took place at Kirchheim-Bolanden, between Lords Malmesbury and Cornwallis for England, Kinkel for Holland, and General Möllendorf supported by Hardenberg and Schulenburg on the part of Prussia. The result was a breach between Prussia and England, and a declaration from Pitt that the payment of the subsidy for October would be suspended until Prussia should show more active zeal for the protection of Holland. Few German authorities altogether defend the conduct of Prussia in this affair. The latest, Ranke, allows that the conduct of Haugwitz (who negotiated the treaty of the Hague) is 'not free from ambiguity;' indeed, on other and still more important occasions the conduct of Haugwitz is open to precisely the same criticism. Nevertheless we have hardly in England considered sufficiently the King of Prussia's position. Though Haugwitz had committed him to unfortunate language, he had never intended to become a leader of mercenary troops. On the contrary, he had erred on the side of chivalrous generosity. As long as he could, he had fought at his own expense for the Empire; when he accepted the English subsidy he considered himself to be fighting in the common cause of Europe, and he regarded the subsidy not by any means as a price for which he sold the services of his army, but as an indemnity without which he could not afford to give them.

But in the failure of this arrangement was involved the fall of the Empire. Prussia's efforts had already brought her into a financial condition which, as we shall see, was quite unprecedented in her history; and, as we have already seen, she had Poland on her hands. Whether she *could* continue fighting for the Empire was doubtful, and now the question began to be asked, why should she? She had already exceeded her legal obligations in rendering it help, and what was the Empire that she should make unlimited sacrifices for it? It was fresh in memory that a head of the Empire, Joseph, had openly avowed that he considered the Imperial system out of date, and had made violent efforts to disentangle Austria from it; Prussia had opposed him at that time, but not assuredly from any enthusiasm for the Imperial system as such. The French Revolution had since prepared men's minds for great changes. German politicians, for example Hardenberg, were beginning to say that there must be a corresponding revolution in Germany, only that it must be accomplished by peaceful means. Those who held such a view, were not likely to suppose it possible to preserve an institution so evidently effete as that which had its seats in Regensburg and Wetzlar.

Nevertheless such views were not openly avowed.
When the Treaty of Basel was concluded between
Prussia and France in April 1795, a mortal blow
was certainly given to the Imperial system, and
the German public were not slow to recognize the
fact. When a line of demarcation was drawn round
the principal territories of North Germany, which
the French undertook not to cross, and when a
term of three months from the ratification of the
Treaty by France was allowed, within which any
Princes or Estates might be admitted to share in
the neutrality on the mediation of Prussia, it could
not long be concealed that North Germany was
practically separated from South Germany. The
Line of Demarcation marked off substantially the
same territory within which the North German
Confederation of 1866 was established. But all
this the Prussian politicians studiously concealed
from themselves, and represented the Peace of Basel
as a preliminary to a Peace between France and the
Empire, to be concluded on the mediation of Prussia.

During this war Stein does not emerge from
obscurity. Hardenberg on the other hand was
the negotiator who put his name to the Treaty
of Basel, and thus stepped into a prominent position among the politicians of Prussia, which he was
to retain as long after Stein's fall as he gained it
before his rise. It seems also that the policy which
suggested the Treaty of Basel was in an especial
degree the policy of Hardenberg. We may therefore pause here to inquire what has been the course
of his life since we saw him in early youth, visiting
Stein's parents at Nassau.

His unfortunate marriage with the Countess Reventlow had taken place in 1775, that is, while Stein was at Göttingen. He then entered the public service of Hannover. In 1781 he visited England, having apparently fixed his ambition upon the post of Hannoverian Minister resident in London. He was a good deal at court, and at last takes up his residence in the neighbourhood of Windsor. Soon whispers were heard of the attentions which the Prince of Wales was paying to his wife; there were even paragraphs in the newspapers. The Prince declares himself the unhappiest of men; he 'will beg his father to allow him to leave England and drag on a wretched existence which has become a burden to him, in some corner of the world, it does not matter what!' Then we find George III. writing to Hardenberg's father on the subject, and the house near Windsor is given up. In the end, partly on account of this affair, partly on account of dissatisfaction with the system of government by an absentee king, Hardenberg quits the Hannoverian service, and enters in 1782 that of the Duke of Brunswick. The English reader may here require to be reminded that this Duke, who plays so important a part in the history of his age, as commander of the Prussian army both in the revolutionary war and in the war of 1806, was at the same time a Sovereign Prince in Brunswick. Here we find Hardenberg meditating plans of resistance to the encroachments of Joseph and at the same time schemes of educational reform. In 1787 his domestic troubles came to a crisis. He procured a divorce, and in the

next year married again. But by the divorce he
lost much of his property, and his second wife was
not well received at the Brunswick court. He
begins again to think of finding another service.
Through the Duke of York, with whom he was
on confidential terms, he makes a second attempt to realise his original desire of becoming
a Minister at London for German affairs. This
was the time of the famous Regency Controversy
in England, and it might be expected that Hardenberg would hardly desire to become Minister to
the Prince of Wales. Nevertheless he writes to
the Duke of York : 'The obstacles which existed,
and might have hindered me from aspiring to the
favour of His Royal Highness the Prince of Wales,
exist no longer....I could devote all my zeal and
attachment to His Royal Highness the Prince of
Wales if he would deign to accord me his favour
and confidence.' We have before us, it is evident,
a man of the old régime! The Duke's answer is
general ; he is full of indignation at the treatment
of his brother by Pitt, and of disquiet about the
state of English affairs. Again in 1790 Hardenberg applies to George III. himself, remarking that
he has had offers from the Margrave of Ansbach,
but that he still clings to the service of his born
sovereign. To this application it seems that George
III. returned no answer whatever ; and thus it was
that Hardenberg, like Scharnhorst a few years
later, passed out of the service of the Guelphs
into that of the House of Hohenzollern, for Ansbach along with Baireuth was at that time ruled
by a Margrave who belonged to the Prussian family.

This Margrave, under the influence of a certain Englishwoman, Lady Craven, was meditating in 1790 a plan for liberating himself from the tutelage of his leading officials. For this purpose he had appealed to the King of Prussia as the head of his house, and had particularly asked for Ministers from Berlin by whom he might replace those whom he had determined to dismiss. Hardenberg found himself at Berlin in April on Brunswick business, while the nomination of such Ministers was under consideration, and the same eye which ten years before had discerned the merit of Stein was now fixed on Hardenberg. Heinitz pointed him out to Herzberg as the man who was wanted. In October Hardenberg was in Ansbach.

One step more, and he found himself a Prussian Minister. The Principalities were to fall in to Prussia at the death of the Margrave, and Hardenberg had received a promise of being taken into the Prussian service when that event should occur. He did not wait so long. The scrutiny to which he subjected the Ansbach affairs, the abuses he detected, the reforms he set on foot, speedily inspired the Margrave with an impatient desire to be quit of the business of reigning. He determined to abdicate, stipulating only for a life income to be paid to him in his retirement in foreign parts by the King of Prussia. The Treaty was signed in January, 1791. In the course of that year the manner in which the new territories should be incorporated with the Prussian Monarchy was considered and decided. It was determined that the whole administration of them should be united

in the hand of a single Minister specially appointed
for the purpose, and controlled only by the royal
Cabinet. The nomination of Hardenberg to this
exceptional position followed as a matter of course,
and thus he became a Prussian Minister in the
beginning of 1792, or eleven years earlier than
Stein.

In his provincial administration he seems to
have gained not less distinction than Stein was
achieving at the same time in Westphalia. But,
unlike Stein, he soon became known and active in
the general affairs of the Monarchy, and in three
years he had the honour of signing his name at
Basel to the Treaty which forms a landmark in
Prussian history. He thus founded that singular
and ill-omened neutrality of Prussia, which after
procuring for her eleven years of peace caused
her to fall, friendless and unpitied, before Napoleon.
He then, as we shall find, initiated that system of
dictatorial Ministers under which Stein was enabled
soon after to reform the institutions of the State;
after Stein's fall, he took up the work where Stein
had left it and remained at the head of the State
through the war of Liberation; negotiated at Vienna
and Paris, nay later still at Aix-la-Chapelle and
Verona, and died at last in office after a continuous Ministerial reign of twelve years. Let
us now inquire how Stein was occupied during
the troubled years in which his rival in fame was
advancing with such rapid strides.

Stein's share in the war divides itself naturally
into two parts. His connection with Mainz and his
house and estate at Nassau involved him in the dis-

turbance which attended Custine's invasion of this region in October, 1792, and which continued till Mainz was recovered in the following July. Again when the conquest of Belgium by France took place in June, 1794, he was disturbed in his Westphalian province by the advance of the French to the Lower Rhine, by the retreat of the Austrians under Clerfait in this direction, and finally by the arrival of the Prussian army of Möllendorff to protect the province and Prussia's ally, Holland. But the latter half of 1793, and the beginning of 1794, was a quiet interval in this disturbed period of his life. We may call it his honeymoon, for on the 8th of June, 1793, just before the recovery of Mainz, he was married.

It is the distinction of Custine to have first discovered that utter helplessness and defencelessness of the Empire, of which Napoleon afterwards reaped the full advantage, as Xenophon with the Ten Thousand showed the way into Persia to Alexander the Great. It is enough here briefly to indicate in what this defencelessness consisted—the minuteness of the German principalities which were each separately incapable of any considerable military effort and all practically independent of each other, and the fatality which had thrown a large part of the frontier into precisely the weakest hands. Just here lay the possessions of the Imperial Knighthood, the weakest of German sovereigns, and just here those of the Ecclesiastical Electors and several other Ecclesiastical Princes, who were naturally the least military of them. War was uncongenial to these Princes of the Church; they had troops indeed, but we are told that the Bishop of Hildesheim caused to be

inscribed on his soldiers' caps the motto, not calculated to give them an interest in their profession,
'Da pacem, Domine, in diebus nostris,' and Kurmainz
himself, that same Friedrich Karl with whom we
have already made acquaintance, and upon whom
the invasion was about to break, gave by a formal
rescript at the opening of the war permission 'to
all officers, who did not feel themselves vigorous
enough or whose domestic circumstances did not
permit it, to decline without loss of honour to take
the field.'

There was one man in Mainz who saw the defencelessness of the frontier at this point more clearly
than Custine himself. This was Johann Friedrich,
Baron vom Stein, and Colonel in the Prussian army,
the elder brother of our hero. He had been placed
at the Court as Prussian agent to secure the advantage which the younger brother had won when he procured the Elector's adhesion to the League of Princes.
As early as May, 1792, he called the attention of his
Government in energetic language to the danger,
begged for troops and artillery, for permission to
negotiate with the Elector about the fortifying of the
town, pointed out the precariousness of all dependence on neighbouring Powers, for example, the
Palatinate, or on the loyalty of the inhabitants,
among whom there was a revolutionary party ; and
here he named a man still remembered in Germany
as one of the earliest German political thinkers, Georg
Forster. When the danger became imminent, and
Custine had already seized Speyer and Worms,
Colonel vom Stein exhausted himself in applications
to the neighbouring princes, to Darmstadt, Würz-

burg, the Palatinate, &c. Nassau and the city of Frankfurt alone sent help, and at the last moment an Austrian officer threw himself with 1,000 men into the town. But it was too late; Mainz surrendered on Oct. 21st with a garrison of 3,862 men; Colonel vom Stein hurried to his brother's house at Nassau, but found that he had just left; went on to Coblenz, where for safety he sent away the great hospital and part of the magazine to Wesel, and at last met his brother on the 25th at Giessen.

Stein had been at Wetzlar with his elder sister, who had intended to winter at Mainz, when he heard of its fall. He determined to take her to Cassel, but at Giessen he met a friend who will appear again in this biography, Field-Marshal Count Walmoden, head of one of the most influential families of Hannover.

The two brothers and the Marshal held a council of war. The Empire had been invaded in its weakest part just at the moment when the invasion of France from the Netherlands had failed, and the Prussian king and army were at Luxemburg. The question was how to save what still remained of the Middle Rhine. Help must be procured if possible from all the neighbouring princes, from Hessen-Cassel and Hessen-Darmstadt, from Hannover, and what was still more important, the King of Prussia must be induced to come to the rescue. The Steins divided the task between them; the elder received from his brother a loan of 4,000 thalers and departed to Würzburg, whither Kurmainz had retired; the younger undertook the task of securing the two Landgraves of Hessen-Cassel and Hessen-Darmstadt, and of dissuading them, if possible, from concluding a separate peace with Custine.

He was successful in his efforts, and in a few days the prospect brightened when Major v. Rüchel threw himself into Ehrenbreitstein, and the King of Prussia with his army arrived at Coblenz and formally undertook the defence of the Rhine. Stein saw the King at Coblenz, and carried despatches from him to the Landgrave at Cassel. At the end of November he returned to the Prussian camp, and was present at the recapture of Frankfurt on the 2nd of December, and afterwards at the capture of Hochheim.

By the middle of this month Dumouriez had won the battle of Jemappes, overrun the Netherlands, driven the Austrians across the Meuse, and levied requisitions on some Prussian towns, among others Cleve, which a few months after was to become Stein's residence. The French appeared before Wesel just at the time when Stein arrived there on a commission from the king to procure provision for the troops on the Lower Rhine. A story is told, but Pertz declines to vouch for it, that he saved the town by arming his train and recovering the island Büderich, which had been taken by the enemy.

In 1793 he was charged with the provisioning of the army of Brunswick, which in the autumn cooperated with Würmser on the Middle Rhine. In July he was at head-quarters and witnessed the recovery of Mainz. But he was now a married man.

Marriage had been imposed upon Stein as a duty to his family and a condition on which he held his estate. His marriage accordingly was not a marriage of passion, scarcely even at first of strong affection. He determined to marry, and indeed he seems to have determined that his marriage should take place within a given time, before he had made up his mind who the bride should be. But it proved a happy marriage in the end, though the object with which his family had imposed it on him was not attained, for Stein had no sons and his name died with him. About this time he began to correspond with a certain Frau v. Berg, who afterwards became known by her 'Recollections of Queen Louise.' In this correspondence may be traced the history of his marriage; I give the extracts.

April, 1792.—In Hannover I found Frau v. Walmoden so unwell that she could not see me. The spirit of gossip is stronger in Hannover than elsewhere, caused by the want of every other sort of interest, except in society and its petty relations, favoured and intensified by the heaviness of the Lower Saxons. Countess Wilhelmine I found as ever gentle, good, pliable, and clinging to her joys and her parents; I think she has a just understanding and purity of character.

April 30.—I am very fond of my work because I have the habit and in some respects also the talent of work, but I feel very keenly how melancholy is a complete solitude, a total separation from the people one loves, how it makes the temper gloomy and reserved.

June 9th.—Your judgment about Countess Wilhelmine is very just; she is certainly alive to what is good, and in the society of good educated people she will get love of occupation and a greater abundance of notions than she possesses. She is coming with the whole family in June to Ems, a bath which Zimmermann has prescribed to the Countess Walmoden, and in July I shall go to Nassau and see her oftener and nearer than one generally sees one's acquaintance in towns. (The reader remembers that Nassau is within an easy ride from Ems.) The wish to have some one about me that is an object of love and goodwill becomes daily stronger in my mind, and I am tired and disgusted with this empty sort of existence, removed from all people whose society is a pleasure to me.

But it is to be noted that the Countess Wilhelmine was at this time only one of the candidates whose claims to his hand he was weighing in his mind; for he writes thus—

July 23rd.—The Walmoden family is at Ems. You know the bath is only an hour or two from here; the Countess is better, the bath has a good effect, and there is every probability that this pure, noble, loving woman will be preserved to her family and friends. Countess Wilhelmine has no doubt purity of character, feeling and devotion, but I fancy she has some family and provincial pride which is peculiar to the Hannoverians. My sister draws such a flattering picture of Charlotte Diede, that my curiosity and my wish to become acquainted with her is extremely raised, so that I am reluctant to take any further resolution till I have been with my sister this autumn at Ziegenberg.

How little he thought of his future wife as a friend or companion appears from the following, also addressed to the Frau v. Berg :—

Sept. 2nd.—Of all the human beings of this earth with whom I have been brought in connection, there are only three with whom I stand in a perfect relation of agreement of feelings and notions, in whose society I am quite at home—they are my sister Marianne, Rehberg and you. With very little gallantry I put your name last because my friendship for you still wants one quality which is for me of indefinite value, age and length of duration—it is often inexplicable to me why this is so with me who take impressions easily and have a good deal of sensibility, and yet it is so.

In the same letter comes the following sentence :

I do not think I shall go to Berlin this winter, for the following reasons: probably I shall marry between this and the spring, and still most probably Countess Wilhelmine Walmoden, unless, indeed, there are quite unheard of things to be seen at Ziegenberg—and then I shall immediately take a tour in Switzerland. All this will require a deal of preparation, &c.

Now follows the winding up of a somewhat ordinary love story. In those days of confusion, after the fall of Mainz, when Stein was so busy in deliberation with Count Walmoden, he found leisure to arrange a private as well as so many public matters.

December 29, 1792. I have already told you that in Giessen and Cassel I lived fourteen days with the Walmoden family, where a hundred circumstances, occurrences and utterances convinced me of the pure, benignant character and sound just understanding of Countess Wilhelmine, so that, after my departure, I felt such an insufferable void, such a dark, joyless prospect opened before me, to have to pass my life alone and isolated, that the wish to receive from her hands what for me at least is the only happiness of life, that is domestic happiness, became so strong that I took a decided step and have now the hope to be united with her as I have so long wished and expected. I am convinced that my wishes will be satisfied since an acquaintance of three years has confirmed me in my judgment of the Countess, and since purity of character and soundness of understanding are the sources of all domestic virtues. It is interesting to me too to enter into relations with the people who surround her, for her father is a man of rare knowledge of the world and of mankind. He has much nobleness in his mind and shows much good nature and affection in intercourse with his family, and the Countess is a real angel of kindness, benignity and love.

The marriage took place on the 8th of June, 1793. It was like the marriage in Hermann and Dorothea, which took place in the midst of general confusion and the 'loosening of all the bands of the world.'

Countess Wilhelmine v. Walmoden-Gimborn was granddaughter to George II. of England and the

Countess of Yarmouth. Her father was General and Field Marshal in the service of George III. in Hannover, and was perhaps the most distinguished servant George III. then had in his electoral dominions. Politically this marriage had some effect upon Stein's position. It identified him still more with the high aristocratic circle of Hannover, with which he was already connected by his sister Charlotte's marriage with v. Steinberg, and made him perhaps somewhat more of the nobleman than he had been before. This is most strongly asserted in the Recollections of Stein which were published by Rehberg, whom the reader remembers as his University friend and whom we have just found mentioned by him as one of the three people in the world with whom he felt quite at home. Rehberg was one of the most eminent political writers in Germany and, in particular, was greatly admired by Niebuhr; he himself asserts that Stein had derived from him some of the great principles embodied in the legislation of 1807. Yet it appears that they saw each other for the last time in 1802, five years before Stein achieved his European reputation, and that they also ceased to correspond. Rehberg understood that the friendship was broken off—though I find Stein in one of his letters speaking of it as only suspended accidentally by local separation and the distractions of a busy life —and the account he gives of the breach is this. He was an official in the Hannoverian service and had had occasion to take sides firmly with the government in a matter in which it had been opposed by the clique of aristocratic families. He was himself of plebeian family, and Hannover was a country in which aristocratic ascendancy was complete. He believes that by his opposition he incurred the dislike of Stein's great connexions, the Walmodens and the Steinbergs, whom, however, he acknowledges to have been excellent people in the main, and that Stein gradually yielded to their influence. One may believe this without necessarily assuming that any unkind feeling towards Rehberg ever sprang up in his mind. When there are already a number of hindrances to intercourse between two friends, such as business and distance, it is easy for relatives by quietly mar-ring the few opportunities of meeting that still present themselves to make the separation complete. Rehberg's sketch of Stein is worth inserting here : 'Stein was sharply distinct in his opinions, very lively, in fact vehement in his expressions, alarming to soft complying natures. But he was always busy with the question, and so you found him uniformly disposed to listen and to revise his opinion. But he had a horror of discussing pros and cons, discoursing and embellishing. Steel must have flint, and if the artist's idea wants only a soft clay in order to be embodied, the practical statesman's idea on the contrary only springs out of the collision of hard substances, where sparks fly. Then again every minute for him had its value. Once when I delayed to give an answer to a question I would rather have evaded, he answered it himself, and then added, "If you had been through a campaign or two you would not beat your brains so much."'

At their marriage the Countess Wilhelmine was in her 21st year and Stein near the end of his 36th. We have already learned from his letters to guess at

her character.   He repeats always the same formula
('sharply distinct in his opinions'), viz. that she had
purity of character and soundness of understanding;
on the other hand she had a little family pride, not
very many ideas and not much activity.   So it
proved to be; she was quite unable to enter into her
husband's large ideas about large questions, or to
respond to his passionate energy.   His first feeling,
we are told, was one of keen disappointment, which
he expressed to the Countess Voss in these words,
'Don't you think a man's heart may be quite crushed
when he finds himself deprived of what should be the
true balm of his life?'   But in the end, simple 'purity of
character and soundness of understanding' triumphed.
She had the opportunity of showing the unselfishness
and loyalty of her disposition in the calamities which
fell upon the family in the sequel.   Loyalty was also
part of her husband's character, and gradually he
recovered from his disappointment and came to regard her at least with great confidence and tenderness.   He thinks of her much in absence; after her
death in 1819 he wrote a short sketch of her life, of
which the following paragraph conveys the leading
idea.

'The inclination of her whole nature was towards
domesticity, family life, society, repose; these it was
not decreed by Providence that she should enjoy.
Wife of one whose life had been violently assailed
by the storms of the time, her wishes and anticipations of such enjoyment were dissipated, even though
they had the appearance of a favourable issue, and in
consequence her whole life was a course of self-denial,
effort, sacrifice.'

According to this memoir the newly married pair settled in their new home at Cleve[1], in October, 1793. They enjoyed there but a year of quiet. He says, 'In 1794 I was driven from Cleve by the advance of the French.' The battle of Fleurus had taken place in April, and it had given the whole Austrian Netherlands to the enemy, who were thus brought into the immediate neighbourhood of Stein's district. In October he sent his wife to her parents in Hannover, and himself took up his abode at Wesel. About the same time the negotiations were beginning which ended the next year in the separate peace between Prussia and France. In this very month Möllendorff's army broke up. One part went to Poland, the other was charged with the protection of Westphalia. Stein was charged with the provisioning of this latter division, a task which he remarks had been made the more difficult not only by a bad harvest but by the exhaustion of the country, upon which the Austrian army had been quartered when it retired under Clerfait from the Netherlands, and which had also helped to supply the Duke of York's army on the Weser.

Stein's political education was proceeding rapidly. He had already made himself practically acquainted with the needs of industry; he now studied war. But as he had looked at industry not as a man of business, so he looked at war not as a soldier but as a statesman. His point of view was always that of

---

[1] Pertz prints Köln (v. 428), which is evidently wrong. It is true that Stein's appointment to Cleve was not made out till November, but it was a settled thing in May. Pertz, I. 127, note 36.

the government, his concern always for the welfare of the whole.

For Prussia this disturbed time ended abruptly and ominously in April, 1795, and Stein returned to the task of civil administration and enjoyed a second period of calm—but calm before a storm—of eleven years. Here are a few sentences from his letters to Frau v. Berg, written about this time, which may help the reader to understand what was passing in his mind.

You ask me what will be the result to Germany of all this uproar, this pressure of people, thoughts, opinions. French anarchy and immorality will not prove infectious to the quiet moral German ; in war with that unhappy nation he will perhaps not conquer, but certainly he will not be conquered, and the example of the horrors which his neighbours commit, the misery which two numerous and distinguished classes of the nation suffer will quench many a prejudice and hasten many a good thing. I expect a war of many years, but its influences will be beneficial, it will restore energy and courage, give a new charm to activity, and increase our repugnance to the abominable French nation....

I came back to Mainz to witness the surrender of the town and the departure of the garrison...The expression of licence, stolid insolence, immorality on the faces of the garrison as they marched out was insufferable, and there was not a face among them one could look at with comfort. The town itself showed many outward signs of devastation. The inside of the houses was almost universally ruined, and a disgusting degradation seemed to me stamped on the faces of most of the women....

I think the lot of women in the upper classes of society is less happy than that of men ; the latter are generally educated for definite vocations, and live in the discharge of them. The former are seldom educated for the vocation intended for them by nature, that of mother and educator. We develope in them only the vague wish to please and instruct them in the material means of doing so, and their whole life is devoted to an empty struggle for universal admiration, which is never attained, and an observance of a multitude of aimless duties. Their whole system of ideas consists of incoherent fragments of opinions, usages, and judgments of the great world, and everything concurs to estrange them from their one true vocation.

This last reflection is rather curious, when we consider that the standing argument of conservatives in female education is that women ought to be educated for their natural vocation, that of wife and mother. What strikes Stein as the fault of the established system is precisely that they are *not* educated for this.

In the summer of this year an address of thanks for his services was presented to him by the inhabitants of the district of Wetter in the County. Many such addresses no doubt have been presented to local governors, whose merits were not extraordinary, but this one is written with such enthusiasm that we see plainly that the merits of Stein had made the profoundest impression.

A man began to labour among us, whose exalted uprightness, pure patriotism, rare knowledge, indefatigable activity won universal admiration. He imparted to those he worked with his own heart and intelligence; they strove to emulate him; a noble and pure public spirit was excited among all who wished well to our native land by a single great example, and produced immediately, and yet promises the fairest fruits......The nations of antiquity would have set up public monuments of gratitude to him, the great, the noble, the immortal. We cannot do this; and he needs it not! &c., &c.

CHAPTER IV.

WITHIN THE LINE OF DEMARCATION.

STEIN describes the last stage of his career as a provincial governor in these words : 'In the year 1796 I obtained the post of Superior President of the Westphalian Chambers at Wesel, Hamm, and Minden ; in this province, after a revision undertaken with the College of the Chamber itself, I achieved the laying down of the road from Bielefeld to Minden, the improvement of the navigation and communications of the Weser ; several alterations in the linen factories were attempted ; lastly, the alleviation of villenage was taken into consideration, but not in the revolutionary spirit which cancels all rights. When the secularisations followed through the Resolution of the Imperial Deputation I was charged with that of the Foundations of Münster and Paderborn. It was accomplished with leniency, forbearance, and loyalty ; the native officials were retained, if they were in any way efficient, and the harshness of the thing was as much as possible softened.' These few sentences are all that Stein allots to a period of nine years, nor indeed does this period offer much memorable incident properly belonging to his biography. This last promotion of 1796, which he again owed to the steady patronage of Heinitz, united under his superintendence, as we have remarked, all the Chambers of the then West-phalian possessions of Prussia. The territories united under Stein's control amounted to 182 (German) square miles, with a population of half a million souls. He now took up his residence in Minden, and here, August 2nd, 1796, a daughter was born to him, who was named Henriette, and became in course of time Countess Giech.

He had now an opportunity of continuing, on a greater scale, the engineering enterprises he had begun at Wetter. He did not lose a moment in forming the plan of carrying the great road he had constructed in the County Mark from Bielefeld through the Teutoburger Wald to Minden and Bücke-burg. He proposed also to lay down a road between Minden and Osnabrück, and thus complete the con-nection between the Rhine and the Weser, and to improve the navigation of the Weser itself. All this, as he tells us, he not only planned, but succeeded in accomplishing. But it seems that he found the Chamber at Minden in a very bad condition, and was obliged on first entering upon his office to institute an investigation, which led to some severities. A member of the Board was dismissed and two others induced to retire; a *journalist was put under arrest*. This, I suppose, is the revision of which Stein speaks.

Thus in the routine of vigorous administration several years passed away, varied by little incident. At Minden he was in the immediate neighbourhood

of Hannover, which, as the home of his wife's relations, he was often tempted to visit. He saw a
good deal of Rehberg at this time; he became acquainted with the statesman, who during the next
age represented Hannover in Germany and England
on the Continent, and with whom he always continued on friendly terms, Count Münster; he became
acquainted also with the man who was to share with
himself the glory of regenerating Prussia, Scharnhorst.

About the time when Stein settled at Minden
began a new regime for Prussia. Frederic William
II. died in November 1797, quitting the scene in the
middle of the play, but having lived long enough to
see Napoleon Buonaparte among the most prominent actors. There began a reign which was to last
forty-three years, to begin in uneasy tranquillity, to
pass thence into the depths of misfortune, thence again
to glory and triumph, and to end as it had begun, in
a long period of uncomfortable tranquillity. The
literary movement has advanced much since last we
took note of it, though Stein cares as little about it
as he did then. Klopstock and Wieland have
passed somewhat out of sight, though both are still
living. Just at this moment two poets have united
their influence to take possession of German public
opinion. They succeeded; their names were Goethe
and Schiller. A new philosophy has long been
agitating the minds of the young; it is one which
Stein would approve if he cared for any philosophy, the severe system of Kant. Among those
influenced by it are some who later will aid Stein in
rousing the national spirit of the Germans, in particular Fichte and Schleiermacher.

Prince Louis Ferdinand, a nephew of Frederick the Great, who showed more genius than any Hohenzollern of this period, and afterwards fell early in the campaign of Jena, was in command of a regiment that was stationed in Minden. Stein became his friend, and some letters are preserved which the Prince received from him. Had the Prince been more fortunate he might have learned from the Superior President the secret of adding steadiness and concentration to his energy. Stein lectured the Prince with his usual frankness. He wrote,

It is certain that the philosophical spirit which generalizes relations, and collects isolated objects under a principle or a higher point of view, is the kind of intelligence which makes the great man; but with this kind of intelligence he must combine the force of character which may give him in quiet times industry in work, persistency to pursue whatever influences his development, and in times of action gives him the necessary moral force to bear the exertions of mind and body which the pressure of circumstances requires. It was want of character (we should say, fixed purpose) that in the revolution overthrew the most virtuous and enlightened men, as Mounier, Bergasse, Bailly, even among the Girondists, Condorcet, Roland, &c.

Again in 1799, when the Prince had been removed to Magdeburg out of Stein's influence, he writes—after complimenting him on his progress in the military art :

But while you develope your faculties, while you labour to acquire and extend your information, what makes you, Sir, disregard so many other moral considerations, offend against so many other principles, in regard for which a soul that was sensitive and susceptible of tender inclinations, like yours, would necessarily find its happiness? I confess to you, Sir, I have been much troubled to hear how much you separate yourself from your parents, how much you neglect to meet the desire they show to have intercourse with you....

And you, Sir, who are so sensitive to others' unhappiness, who have never refused help to it, who have shown the most touching care for the simple soldier, the companion of your dangers, you close your heart against the imperious feeling of nature, you separate yourself from her, and hope to be able one day to escape a lacerating regret like that of having harshly repelled the anxious applications of a father on the verge of the tomb !

It is to be observed that the father here spoken of, Prince August Ferdinand, long outlived the son who is here charged with neglecting his deathbed, and died in 1813.

Here are a few sentences from the letters to Frau v. Berg, of this period.

I saw Münster again in passing through ; I confess, he attracts me, he has feeling for what is good and noble, a remarkable passionate love for art, which he has cultivated by his five years' stay in Italy with Prince August (*i.e.* the Duke of Sussex), and he has surrounded himself with works of art.

April 28. What do you say, with your love of great and fine actions, to the vigorous and gallant behaviour of our young hero the Archduke Charles and his brave army, that have cleared Germany of that horde of robbers, the so-called French army—it is melancholy to see us disabled and in a state of palsy while we could restore with energy the peace of Europe on its old basis, the independence of Holland, Switzerland, Italy, Mainz. We amuse ourselves with displays of the art of the military dancing-master and tailor, and the state ceases to be a military state, and changes into a drilling and writing state. When my imagination brings before me the forms of the influential people of the executive, I do assure you I do not expect much.

There was peace on the Continent of Europe from October 1797 (Oct. 17th, Peace of Campo Formio—'the black and complete treachery of

Campo Formio,' as Stein calls it), till the beginning of 1799. Then followed the War of the Second Coalition, which lasted for two years until the Peace of Lunéville was signed, Feb. 9th, 1801. Then again there was peace on the Continent for four years, until the War of the Third Coalition in 1805. These facts, simple as they are, may be forgotten by English readers, since England did not share these alternations of war and peace, but waged war with France without interruption till the Peace of Amiens in 1802, and again from 1803 till 1814.

The choice which Prussia had made under Frederick William II. in 1795, when she elected to stand aloof from the strivings and sufferings of Europe, came up for reconsideration under Frederick William III. in 1799. It was confirmed and repeated though after much hesitation, and though in the end even those of the king's counsellors who were most irresolute by nature, the Duke of Brunswick and Haugwitz, gave their voices for war. An incurable unwillingness to take any important resolution seems on a survey of his whole reign to have been the ruling characteristic of Frederic William III. Neither now nor at the Occupation of Hannover in 1803, nor at the forming of the Third Coalition, nor again, as we shall see, in the crisis of Stein's Ministry, though in each case everything depended on him, could he bring his mind to a clear decision; all the discomfort of his later years arose in like manner from the indecision which, as soon as the excitement of the war had subsided, prevented him from keeping his promise of a con-

8—2

stitution to his people. It is necessary to mark
this early in order that the reader may have a
measure of the commanding ascendancy of the man
who in 1807-8 was able to hurry such a King
through several stages of a political and social
revolution. What this man thought when in 1799
the policy of the Treaty of Basel was ratified,
and a new period of ignominious and ruinous
isolation entered upon, we see in the reflections
just quoted. He was depressed and saddened,
though we may notice now, and even up to the
eve of the catastrophe of Jena, that his disapprobation of the policy of the day is not half
strong enough. He speaks in fact of foreign policy
like a man who does not consider it his province
and has not given much attention to it.

The War of the Second Coalition now runs its
course. The Archduke Charles and Suworoff are
the heroes of the first part of it, Napoleon and
Moreau of the second. For the first time Russia
leads the politics of Europe; for the first and
hitherto the last time Russian armies are seen in
Italy. But in the end the inherent difficulty of
all European Coalitions is again experienced, and
on the other side the reverses of the French
drive them to give their State the form of a
Military Monarchy. The war is decided at Marengo and Hohenlinden. It had two great results
for Europe. It closed the movement properly
called the French Revolution, by establishing in
France, now increased by Belgium and the Left Bank
of the Rhine, a new Monarchy which satisfied the
nation, and it led to a complete revolution in Ger-

many through the territorial changes made by the Treaty of Lunéville.

By the Treaty of Lunéville, the Empire of Germany surrendered all its possessions on the Left Bank of the Rhine. In consequence of this, a number of German States found their territories curtailed, and many German proprietors found themselves forced either to sell their lands, or become French subjects. The determination of the more powerful States thus injured to indemnify themselves in Germany itself at the expense of the less powerful, caused what may fairly be called the German Revolution of that period. Meanwhile Stein was among those who were threatened with what was to him the intolerable calamity of becoming a French subject. His estate of Landskron lay on the left bank of the Rhine. Accordingly, he determined to sell it, and with the price he bought at the end of 1801 a share in an estate called Birnbaum in Prussian territory on the Wartha, a certain v. Troschke being his co-proprietor. By this purchase his connexion with Prussia was naturally strengthened.

In the summer of 1802 he was invited to become a Minister in Hannover, that is, to serve the same sovereign as William Pitt. His connexion with the aristocracy, not to say the royal house, of the country makes the offer appear quite natural. 'It came to him,' says Pertz, 'not through his father-in-law, but perhaps through his brother-in-law, v. Steinberg.' The condition of Hannover, which through its connexion with England was exposed to the hostility of Napoleon, and yet was enclosed within the line of demarcation which had been drawn round the neutral territory of North Germany at the Peace of Basel, must have given matter for painful reflexion to its government. They must have half anticipated what was actually in store for it, viz. a French occupation, and their application to Stein was perhaps caused by a vague hope that his sagacity might find a means of escape. Stein declined, partly on the ground that the age of George III. and his absence made it impossible to carry any considerable reforms in Hannover, but partly also because the interest of Hannover was opposed to that which even then, it appears, he steadily contemplated, the Unity of Germany.

In the path of greatness temptations of this kind perhaps are the most dangerous. To be on the spot when the opportunity for greatness occurs, this is the essential thing. When the Hour and the Man meet we call it fortune, but we should probably call it instinctive foresight if we could know how many alluring offers the Man has refused which would have led him where perhaps every advantage was to be found except the opportunity for greatness. Stein had been proof against the allurements of Austria at the beginning ; but the Prussian service had lost since that time the charm which had belonged to it in the days of Frederick. Humiliation for Prussia could already be foreseen, and on the other hand what comfort, what convenience for a man of Stein's connexions in the Hannoverian service ! But in Hannover the opportunity for greatness could never come, while in Prussia it might be found even in the midst of disaster.

What I have described as the German Revolution occupied the year 1802, the year which followed the Peace of Lunéville. The new order of things was fixed by the Principal Resolution of the Imperial Deputation (Reichsdeputationshauptschluss). This act, together with the establishment of the Confederation of the Rhine in 1806, effected the change of the old Empire into that system of States which at the Congress of Vienna was united into a loose Confederation. The Revolution accomplished three principal things. It swept away, with few exceptions, (1) Ecclesiastical Sovereignties, (2) Municipal Sovereignties, (3) Small Hereditary Sovereignties. It changed a system of States which were of three different kinds, and of every variety of magnitude, into a system of States which were almost all of one kind, and almost all of at least moderate size. The change, as I have said, was made in two Acts. That which was accomplished in 1803 affected only the governments which were not hereditary, that is, the Ecclesiastical and Municipal Sovereignties; the Act of 1806 affected the smaller Hereditary Sovereignties. I have called this a Revolution, and such it was, if that name belongs to every fundamental political change; but it was not caused or accompanied by any popular commotion. The cause of it was simply that, a loss of territory having been suffered in common by a great number of States, some powerful and some weak, those which were powerful indemnified themselves by appropriating that which remained to those which were weak. The Act of 1803 was, it will be seen, a great act of secularisation. Its

chief importance in history lies in its having been
the fall of the temporal power of the Church in
Germany. Among the Powers which profited by
this secularisation was of course Prussia. By the
cession of the Left Bank of the Rhine she had lost
not more than 48 (German) square miles, with a
population of 127,000 souls. The equivalent which
Prussia obtained amounted to 230 (German) square
miles, with more than half a million souls. It was
part of the policy of France to reward Prussia for
her neutrality, and Prussia might almost be satisfied
with the Peace of Basel when she saw the fruits it
brought. For by this accession of territory her
possessions were consolidated as well as increased,
and between the Elbe and the Rhine only small
States, if we put aside Hannover, interrupted henceforth the continuity of her dominion.

To all this confiscation under shameless pretexts,
Stein probably reconciled himself by considering
that it brought Germany nearer what he held its
best goal, unity. Territorial aggrandisement seemed
to him a legitimate object to Prussia or even
Austria, for it would be a step in that direction,
while the aggrandisement of the small States he
judged more severely than others, as a step in the
opposite direction. Accordingly we find him taking
a great part in the secularisations for the benefit of
Prussia, but at the same time protesting emphatically
against annexations projected by an inferior state,
Nassau.

The Prussian indemnity comprised, in Lower
Saxony, Hildesheim and Quedlinburg, ecclesiastical,
and the municipalities of Nordhausen, Mühlhausen,

Goslar; in Westphalia, a great part of Münster and the Bishopric of Paderborn, besides Elten, Essen, and Werden; and in the territory of Mainz, Erfurt and the Eichsfeld. Count v. Schulenburg-Kehnert, one of the most distinguished Prussian officials of this period, was appointed to superintend the whole work of appropriation, and the special task of taking possession of the Westphalian bishoprics was judiciously entrusted to Stein, who had endeared himself to the Westphalians by his long and beneficial administration. The appointment of Stein was made by an Order in Cabinet, dated June 6, 1802. Blücher had already taken military possession of the bishopric of Münster, disbanded the troops, and was establishing the new regime with little tact or forbearance. The inhabitants were falling into a mood like that of Alsace in 1872, when on the 9th of September Schulenburg summoned Stein to his post.

What Stein says about the manner in which he performed his task, namely, that 'it was accomplished with leniency, forbearance and loyalty,' seems perfectly true. No forbearance indeed could disguise the cruelty of the decree of the Diet. The inhabitants of the Bishopric not merely lost their independence and were subjected to the despotism of Prussia; more than this, the territory was actually partitioned, and while the larger half went to Prussia the rest was divided among a number of petty princes. Nevertheless what could be done, Stein did. In the first place he succeeded in obtaining the consent of his superior Schulenburg to the introduction of some representatives of the population of Münster into the Commission which was charged with the reconstruction. Two privy councillors of the old government, Druffel and Forckenbeck, were appointed, and, at the suggestion of Schulenburg, Count v. Meerfeld to represent the old nobility. In the second place he preserved to the people the useful educational institutions which had been founded by Fürstenberg, the admirable minister of the Government now superseded. Stein writes to Frau v. Berg, on November 13th:

H. v. Fürstenberg has diffused a great amount of solid useful knowledge among the people of this part, he has succeeded in providing the educational institutions with considerable sources of income, which may be made still more productive, and must be applied to accomplishing the object for which they are intended. Perhaps he sets too much value on the positive part of his religion, on the form of worship, perhaps he is too anxious for the diffusion of a multiplicity of views about the supersensual, still he has in part attained the object, and you find more outward respect for religion, more people of pious and devout feeling than I have found elsewhere, and he preserves to his fellow-citizens the possession of what is assuredly a jewel the loss of which all our philosophisms cannot replace.

Among the ecclesiastics of the chapter was one who afterwards became Archbishop of Cologne, and continued from this time to be Stein's principal clerical friend. This was the Dean, Spiegel. On the other hand he seems to have conceived a less favourable opinion of another member of the chapter, Droste Vischering, who at a much later time succeeding Spiegel in the Archbishopric of Cologne, became memorable in Prussian history through his persecution by the Government.

Some account of this revolution at Münster has been printed by Freitag from the MS. of a certain

official named Sethe. We learn from it to understand that the hardship of being conquered by
Prussia was much greater then than it would be
now, since it was the *unreformed* Prussian system
that was introduced. For example, in recording the
substitution of Prussian troops for the old episcopal
army, Sethe remarks, 'Among the officers of Münster
reigned much cultivation and scientific knowledge,
and the average of Prussian officers at that time
could not bear comparison with them.' Still worse
than the ignorance of the Prussian officers was the
brutality of the system of conscription, as practised
in Prussia in that age and now for the first time
introduced into Münster; of this Sethe gives us
painful glimpses.

After having for a moment contemplated Stein
labouring at a task which has so often occupied
Prussian officials, that of conciliating a newly-con-
quered population, let us, for the sake of contrast,
pass over a few months, and see what he thought of
similar annexations when they were undertaken by
States of less magnitude than Prussia.

I have observed that the first act of the German
Revolution which was accomplished in 1803, touched
only the ecclesiastical and municipal Sovereignties.
It did not touch any secular Prince, not even the
Imperial Knighthood, though there was no doubt
that the sovereignty of the Knight was a greater
abuse than that of the Bishop or the patricians of a
Free Town, and though it was evident that the
Knights and small secular Princes were as weak and
as easy to spoil as those who were actually plun-
dered. The fact is that as this spoliation was ac-

complished with deliberation, and by the Diet itself, some show of decency had to be observed. It was difficult to find a formula which should justify the indemnification of the great Powers of Germany for their losses in foreign war at the expense of the small Powers. Recourse was had to a distinction which had just so much show of validity as to save appearances, and not an atom more. It was laid down that the *hereditary* rulers who had suffered loss had a right to indemnification. On this pretext the secular princes, as being hereditary, claimed the right of spoiling the elective ecclesiastical princes and the elective Municipalities. But the pretext would not justify them in despoiling the pettiest or the most incompetent Imperial Count or Imperial Knight. The principle however which was veiled under this decent distinction was the simpler one, that the strong had a right to indemnification at the expense of the weak, and the great States were naturally annoyed that their ostensible principle was less comprehensive than their real one. Towards the end of 1803 their impatience began to be too strong to be restrained. The middle States of the West and South West began to threaten the lands of the Knighthood with annexation. The Bavarian Government set the example, and it was soon followed by the Courts of Cassel and Darmstadt. The Prince of Nassau, Stein's powerful neighbour, was roused by this example. On Dec. 31st, 1803, he issued a Patent announcing that he wished to secure the knightly possessions within his territory against other Estates, and assume the sovereignty over them, if the dissolution of the Imperial

Knighthood was to follow. On January 3rd, 1804, appeared an official with soldiers, who took possession of Stein's lordships of Frücht and Schweighausen, and forbade the payment of further dues, with the exception of rent, to the Baron vom Stein. Wieler, an official of Stein's, sent in a protest against this proceeding, and it proved that the spoilers had been somewhat too hasty. The Imperial Government interfered, France was not yet ready, and thus the second great act of spoliation was postponed till 1806. But in the meanwhile Stein wrote the following letter to the Prince of Nassau :—

Your Serenity has by the publication of a Patent, dated the 31st December of the last year, caused the villages of Frücht and Schweighausen, which have belonged to my family for centuries, to be taken in possession with the view

'of protecting them against other Estates (Stände) and 'claiming the sovereignty (Landeshoheit) in case of the 'dissolution of the Imperial Knighthood.'

Your officials added as a commentary on the Patent a prohibition to my subjects to pay me the arrears of their taxes or those falling due, and thus these persons added to an authorized suppression of my independence, a deprivation of my property, which, as it seems, was at least not authorized.

The preamble of the aforesaid Patent refrains, indeed, from deciding upon the continuance of the knightly corporations, but it seems to be doubtful about their utility in relation to the order and defence of the Fatherland.

Germany's independence and stability would gain little from the consolidation of the few knightly possessions with the small territories surrounding them; if those great ends so beneficial to nations are to be attained, these small states must be united with the two great monarchies, on whose existence the continuance of the German name depends; and may Providence grant me to see this happy occurrence!

In the cruel contest from which Germany now momentarily reposes, the blood of the German nobles flowed: Germany's numerous rulers, with the exception of the noble Duke of Brunswick, declined all participation in it, and sought to preserve their tottering existence by emigration, negotiation, or bribing the French generals. What will be gained for the independence of Germany, if its powers are concentrated still further into such hands as these?

The motives alleged in the Patent have no application to the villages taken from me—they lie, with their lands, in the midst of the principalities of Nassau. None of the neighbouring princes could, without travelling for hours through Nassau territory, take possession of them, and there was no reason to expect such an act of violence. Accordingly this protective measure was not called for; moreover, it was decreed by an incompetent court.

I look for protection to the same laws of the Empire on which the personal rights and the sovereignty of the princes depend, and to the Head of the Empire, who has displayed clearly enough his will to those princes who lay themselves open to the charge of arbitrary and violent behaviour towards those weaker than themselves.

Your Serenity promises, in case of the dissolution of the Knighthood, everything to its members which your hereditary love for equity and your respect for honourable families can suggest to you. So instead of a condition resting upon laws and the constitution, we are promised a precarious condition resting upon equity and other unstable foundations. What a prospect! and I cannot reckon even on this.

A nobility, the pride and prop of great monarchies, fares but poorly in a small state: if it is rich, it becomes an object of jealousy, if not to the prince yet to his courtiers; if it is poor, no prospect is opened to it of an improvement of condition; it pines, decays, and dwindles.

If the Knightly Union is dissolved violently, I shall cease to reside in a land which will surround me with objects of bitter remembrance, and where everything will force me to reflect on the loss of my independence and on my new chains.

It is hard to have to leave a family property which can be traced 700 years back, and to have to transplant oneself into remote countries, and to give up the prospect, after a laborious and I may say useful official life, of enjoying repose, and awaiting the passage to a better existence in the ancestral home, amid the recollections of youth. It is harder still to make all these sacrifices not for any great or noble, or universally beneficial object, but merely to escape lawless might, and to—but there is a conscience that judges and there is a God who punishes !

With great respect I remain,

STEIN.

And to his agent Wieler he wrote,

If the Order is dissolved I shall never come back to Nassau, but divide the estate into peasant holdings, farm out the gardens, cut down the timber on the Stein, etc. I will never recognize a robber for my sovereign.

Stein's letter was printed, and excited much admiration. It is not only spirited and impressive, but it expresses so clearly Stein's view of the most important questions of German politics, that it deserves most particular attention. Why, it may be asked, is he so angry at an aggression upon his own sovereignty, which all Germany regarded as an abuse, while he has himself just been engaged in suppressing the sovereignty of the Bishop of Münster, who had recently given to all Germany a model of good government ? One answer of course is that Prussia only carried out a decree of the Diet, while the Prince of Nassau waited for no authority whatever. But this is not the answer Stein would have cared to give. For the decree of the Diet only gave a legal *colour* to the act of Prussia; it was only the great power of Prussia and her great influence with France that enabled her to procure the authority of the Diet for her annexations. Again, he might have defended the Imperial Knighthood from the charges commonly brought against it, and argued that it deserved to be maintained while the Ecclesiastical Sovereignties deserved to be abolished. But it is evident that Stein is not prepared to do any such thing ; his letter contains not one word in defence of the Imperial Knighthood. The position he takes up is far stronger and more statesmanlike than either of these. He argues that whatever may be the demerits of his order, the absorption of its territories into those of the small neighbouring states can only make matters worse, and that all the small states together—Nassau as well as Stein—ought to be absorbed in Prussia and Austria. On this principle he is justified in approving Prussian annexations at the same time that he condemns those of Nassau. He approves neither on such grounds as those alleged by the Diet. He says nothing of any right to compensation. But he declares the annexations of Prussia to be for the well-being of Germany, since the more powerful Prussia becomes, the more probability there is of her creating either a united Germany, or at least a united North Germany ; on the other hand, the annexations of Nassau can do nothing but harm, for Nassau can never become the nucleus of Germany ; and this being so, her interest will always be opposed to the unity of Germany, and the stronger she grows, the greater will be the difficulty of achieving it.

Thus clearly did Stein perceive that the danger of Germany lay not so much in the petty sovereignties, as in the middle States. There was another man who saw it as clearly, the great enemy of Germany, Napoleon. Therefore, while Stein's life was passed in enmity and opposition to all such potentates as the Duke of Nassau, Napoleon rested entirely on them, and by aggrandising as much as possible the strongest of them, Baden, Würtemberg, Bavaria and Saxony, and admitting three of them into the Royal Caste of Europe, he at once procured for himself a faithful following in Germany, and set up in the path of German Unity 'a stone of stumbling and a rock of offence,' which not even the later German revolutions of our own age have yet succeeded in removing.

I must go back a few months to note an occurrence of the summer of 1803, the great importance of which both to Germany and Prussia can in this place only be cursorily remarked.

On the recommencement of the war between England and France in the spring of this year, Napoleon caused a body of troops under Mortier to pass the German frontier from Holland and take possession of Hannover. The proceeding was Napoleonic in its lawlessness, but Prussia took a long step in the downward path which led to Jena, when she witnessed it without interfering. Her neutrality since the Peace of Basel had been inglorious enough, but it had at least left her in the position of the guardian of North Germany. She might boast that her greatness shielded the crowd of small states that were comprehended along with her within the line of demarcation. Now the world saw that the neutrality had not even this value, and that a state conterminous on three sides with herself, and assailed by France for no assignable cause whatever, owed nothing to Prussia's alliance or to having joined Prussia in the Peace of Basel; the

9

world saw Prussia permit the northern frontier of the
Empire to be passed and a French government to
be set up in the heart of Germany. We should be
glad to know what Stein thought of this, but, unfortunately, Pertz gives no letter belonging to this time.
And yet the occurrence must have come home to
him. He was living near the Hannoverian frontier,
and the Hannoverian army, which, in consequence of
the irresoluteness of the government, made no resistance to Mortier, was under the command of his
father-in-law, Marshal Walmoden. The Marshal
was bitterly assailed for his inaction, but published
a justification of himself, which was held conclusive.

In the same summer died Stein's steady friend
and patron, Heinitz. He did not live to see the
full magnitude of the service he had rendered to
Prussia in conferring upon her such a statesman, nor
all the fruits of the influence he had exerted on
Stein's own character by his example. His own
official industry would not preserve his name from
oblivion, but as often as it is repeated that the modern
greatness of Prussia is grounded on the result of
Stein's legislation, so often it ought to be remembered that this again is the result of the discernment
by which Heinitz detected his capacities, and the
pure example by which he helped to develope
them.

The department over which Heinitz had presided was divided at his death, and the superintendence of Mines was given to the companion of
Stein's English tour, Count Reden.

At the end of the year the Commission of Organisation for Münster had completed its task and

was dissolved. On the 1st of December there took its place a War and Domains Chamber for Münster, Paderborn, Lingen and Teklenburg. Stein presided over it, and now resigned the Presidency of the Chamber at Minden. He continued to reside in Münster, sharing the Royal Palace with Blücher, the General in command. Here was born, on May 3rd, 1803, his third and youngest daughter (the second did not live), Therese, afterwards Countess Kielmansegge.

The year 1804 saw the close of Stein's career as a provincial governor. The laborious work of arranging the details of the partition of Münster among so many princes was completed in July. We also find him busy with the organisation of education, appointing Professors, studying the Pestalozzian system. In November came the change which raised him to be a Minister of State.

His last care before leaving Westphalia was to provide himself with a successor to his mind, and he procured the appointment of one of the most eminent men that have adorned the Prussian bureaucracy, his friend v. Vincke. They had worked together in the province since 1798, and the Life of Vincke, by Bodelschwingh, records that they had had occasional differences and that angry letters had occasionally passed between them. But it now appeared that the elder official clearly recognised the merits of the younger. Vincke, for his part, describes Stein as 'an excellent man, perhaps better fitted for Minister than for President,' a judgment which marks both the men. Vincke was himself the model of a local Governor, and saw in Stein some deficiency in the

9—2

minute diligence which characterised himself, but he recognises at the same time that it was a deficiency not caused by weakness but by powers too large for any functions below the highest.

Of Stein's private letters during this period Pertz only gives us one, addressed to Frau v. Berg. It has the following characteristic passage :—

Minden, April 22, 1802. . . . I have travelled through Mecklenburg. The appearance of the country displeased me as much as the cloudy northern climate : great fields, of which a considerable part lies in pasture and fallow, extremely few people, the whole labouring class under the pressure of serfdom, the fields attached to single farms seldom well-built, in one word a uniformity, a deadly stillness, a want of life and activity diffused over the whole which oppressed and soured me much. The abode of the Mecklenburg nobleman who keeps down his peasants instead of improving their condition strikes me as the lair of a wild beast, who desolates everything round him and surrounds himself with the silence of the grave. Assuredly even the advantage is only apparent ; high energy of cultivation, thorough agriculture, is only possible where there is no want of human beings and human power. The selling price, the yield, the security of sale, the possibility of carrying out great public works of general utility is assuredly overwhelmingly greater in lands where there is population and industry than in those where the human being has been degraded into the item in the stock. The short-sighted covetousness of money-making has also entirely taken away the possibility of an increased population by the destruction of the wood which is so necessary in this ungenial northern zone.

The following letter, though official, is highly characteristic and may stand here as a specimen of Stein's unsparing severity in rebuke. The reader should note at the same time that the man who could pen such a fierce reprimand was not commonly unpopular with his underlings; on the contrary evidence remains that he was enthusiastically beloved by many of them.

I think it necessary before leaving this province to communicate to you my opinion, I am sorry to say my very unfavourable opinion of your behaviour.

You have become by your acrid coarseness, which insults all laws of decency and of a liberal education, an object of hatred to those who have the misfortune to be in a position of subordination to you, and of contempt to those who are independent of you. It will be enough to mention your proceedings towards A, B, C; not a day passes on which you do not treat your underlings with harshness and bitterness and drive them into a mood of sullen depression.

To this brutal behaviour is added the complete want of legality which is a consequence in you of your ignorance of law and of a presumptuous disdain of existing prescriptions. . . .

You will do well generally to go to work with more forethought and circumspection in all clerical and educational questions, since there are subjects entirely strange to you, you are entirely destitute of the resources of scientific knowledge, and are restricted to the knowledge of the forms of service.

I recommend to you seriously and in a friendly spirit an alteration in your behaviour; the necessary consequences of it will be that the direction which you conduct with inhuman bitterness and illegality will be taken from you, and in this way a quiet, judicious, and harmonious conduct of business in the College will be secured, since the College needs to be guided and not given up to the discipline of a drill-sergeant, &c.

There is more in the same merciless style. It should be noted, however, that it is not inhumanity which makes his language so rough, but an unbounded indignation against inhumanity. We can understand how useful such energetic control may have been at such a moment when nothing but a studied tenderness on the part of the Prussian

officials could save the unfortunate population, sacrificed to a political exigency, from absolute despair;
we can see in this letter a specimen of the zeal with
which Stein prosecuted his task of alleviating the
bitterness of conquest and partition to the people,
and also how difficult the task was, and what energy
it required.

CHAPTER V.

IT is now time to turn our attention from local to central government, from Münster to Berlin. Some account has already been given of the form of administration in Prussia as it had existed since the reforms of Frederick William I. It will be remembered that there was a Supreme Finance Directory, which had originally been divided into five Departments, under as many Vice-Presidents. This Directory had undergone many modifications of form as the work of Government increased in magnitude and complication. The Vice-Presidents had become Ministers of State, but no rational classification of the provinces of Government had yet been introduced. In fact this development had been retarded by the restless self-will of Frederick the Great. He had created at his pleasure new Departments independent of the Directory, and called Immediate because they were related directly to himself. Frederick William III. had done much to repair this evil, and had incorporated most of the Immediate Administrations with the Directory. Only the Administration of the Province of Silesia still remained completely independent of it. The Directory now included eight Ministers of State, of whom four, Voss, Hardenberg, Schrötter, and Angern administered the country divided into districts, Goltz presided over Military Affairs, Reden had the Mining Department. The remaining two, Schulenburg and Struensee, in a manner divided between them the Department of Finance. Count Schulenburg-Kehnert, who, it may be remarked in illustration of the military character of the Prussian Government, was a general in the army, had the title of Controller-General of Finance and Minister of the Treasury, with the presidency of the Directory. It seems, however, that Struensee, though occupying an inferior position, was regarded as being in a more special sense the Minister of Finance, just as in England the First Lord of the Treasury and the Chancellor of the Exchequer both take their titles from finance, while the inferior Minister is the responsible head of the financial department.

It is to be observed that this Directory, with its various departments, was concerned only with internal government. Foreign Affairs were controlled by the Cabinet Ministry, and the Minister here had for some years been Count Haugwitz. But he was in the habit of asking for leave of absence that he might attend to his estates in Silesia, which suffered, as he complained, from his inattention and required his care all the more as he had long served the State without salary. Since April, 1804, Hardenberg had taken his place as substitute for an indefinite time, and since July it may be said that by a curious arrangement either Hardenberg or Haugwitz indifferently might be regarded as Foreign Minister, not that the duties were divided but that Haugwitz, though absent as a rule, might take Hardenberg's place occasionally, drew part of the salary, and 'particularly in winter when he wished to reside in Berlin took cognisance of all affairs and attended the conferences,' while Hardenberg conducted the ordinary business of the office. I pause to mention this, because it gives us a glimpse of that incurable confusion in the management of Foreign Affairs which brought Prussia to her catastrophe.

Carl August v. Struensee bears a well-known name, and was in fact an elder brother of the unfortunate Minister of Christian VII. of Denmark. He had begun life as a Professor of Mathematics at Liegnitz, and had written treatises on Military Engineering. In 1769 he followed his brother to Copenhagen, where he received an appointment in finance, and was involved in the catastrophe of 1772. In this peril Frederick the Great, who valued his writings, interfered to protect him as a Prussian subject, and he was allowed to return to Germany, where he resumed his literary occupations. In 1782 he was recalled to public life by the offer of a place in the Directory and the Directorship of the Maritime Institute. Still retaining this post, he became in 1791 a Minister of State, with the Department of Excise and Customs. Stein speaks of him merely as an 'intelligent, well-informed statesman,' but to many he appeared a great man. Thus Lord Malmesbury in his Diary of 1793 remarks : 'Among the other Ministers of State none are worth mentioning but Struensee, who is said to be an able financier, although no proof of his ability in this branch is to be found.' Perhaps Mirabeau had

conferred on him this somewhat mysterious reputation by writing in his Letter to Frederick William
II., 'Struensee would subscribe to all my doctrines;
he could point out to Your Majesty a hundred substitutes for the extortions of fiscality.' Schön's description of him furnishes a plausible explanation of
the contrast between Struensee's reputed abilities
and his inconsiderable achievements. 'Struensee
was the only star of the first magnitude in this
assembly. . . . He was indeed the greatest
statesman the Prussian State has ever had, and
would have done immense things had not his high
intellect been in a manner unnerved by his fatal
course at Copenhagen. Such a catastrophe as that
cannot but lead to a habit of thinking of Government as a sort of apparition that comes and goes;
and they say that at the end of Frederick William
II.'s reign, when some one blamed Struensee for
taking no steps against the advancing evil, he said,
"The paste will stick together a few years yet!"
Yet when it was necessary, or when he cared to
make his great intellect felt, he never failed.'

In 1804 Struensee's health failed so completely,
that by the end of September it was necessary
to appoint a successor to him, and he died soon
after. The appointment lay with the King on the
nomination of Schulenburg, but the person who in
this instance decided the appointment held the
office, hereafter to be described, of Cabinet Councillor. His name was Beyme, a name which, in
the sequel, will frequently reappear. He now did
for Stein the service which hitherto had always been
done by Heinitz. The King meditated the appoint-

ment of v. Schuckmann, but Beyme, in a letter to Schulenburg, pronounced him not equal to the post, and named Stein, 'for whom, as a thinker and man of business who had also a rare firmness of cha-racter, he had much respect, and who might be lost to the state if he were often passed over.'

Schulenburg presented Stein's name to the King, who, however, seems to have had an instinctive terror of Stein's originality (as indeed we shall find him later acknowledging): and preferred to take a course of his own.

Struensee had combined two distinct Depart-ments, that of Excise and Customs and the superin-tendence of the Maritime Institute, one of the two great commercial corporations with which the Go-vernment had connected itself. The other, the Bank, was under the directorship of Schulenburg. It was an obvious improvement in classification to put both Bank and Maritime Institute under the same Minister. This might be done in two ways, either by enlarging the functions of Schulenburg, or those of Struensee's successor. The King for a moment tried the former plan. He nominated a certain v. Borgstede to the control of the two institutions in subordination to Count Schulenburg. But it was immediately found that these great Corporations would not submit to the rule of any one below the rank of a Minister of State. It remained, therefore, to adopt the opposite method of narrowing Count Schulenburg's department by placing the Bank under Struensee's successor. And thus Stein, in becoming Minister of State, entered upon larger functions and assumed a more complete control of the national finance than had belonged to the admired financier who had just died.

An Order of Cabinet of October 27th nominated Stein Minister of State, with the charge of Excise, Customs, Manufactures and Trade, and assigned him a salary of 6200 th. with an official residence. A further arrangement with respect to the Institutions of Credit was promised. Stein wrote in answer, on Nov. 3rd, as follows :—

To the King's Majesty.

As your Majesty has been pleased to give me a distinguished proof of your favour and confidence by committing to me the offices of the deceased Minister of State, v. Struensee, I am the more bound to examine myself beforehand conscientiously and rigidly how far I am in a condition to fulfil the expectations of your Majesty, and in this self-examination carefully to put aside personal and selfish considerations.

The department assigned me by the Royal Order in Cabinet of the 27th of last month comprehends the duty of fixing and levying the taxes on consumption, the guidance of the more important parts of the national industry, the administration of the Salt-Tax, and of the manufacture of Salt and some Institutions of Trade and Credit.

My official position hitherto has given me the opportunity of becoming acquainted with the nature of the Taxes on Consumption, with the customary procedure in the levying of them, and with some branches of the national industry, but I want acquaintance with the state of these arrangements in the interior of the Monarchy, since the Westphalian Provinces differ from it so completely in their constitution.

To acquire this knowledge will require time and local investigation, and till then I shall only be in a condition to perform imperfectly what your Majesty may expect from him to whom you confide the conduct of important parts of the public economy.

The direction of the Salt Manufacture and the levying of the

Salt Taxes in Westphalia has been entrusted to me for many years past, but I must acknowledge my very imperfect knowledge of the Institutes of Commerce and Credit.

I am impelled to lay most respectfully these confessions before your Majesty by my reverence for your Majesty's royal virtue and by the fear of counteracting its beneficial working by my imperfection; but having once made these confessions, I may add the declaration that I am prepared to comply unconditionally with your Majesty's further commands.

He wrote a letter at the same time to Beyme, in which he says that personally he prefers a provincial office as at once more independent and more interesting, but that he puts aside such considerations because he is convinced that the civilization and culture of Germany are firmly and inseparably bound up with the welfare of the Prussian monarchy. As Beyme had already informed him that the parts of Struensee's functions which had not yet been transferred to him, superintendence of the Bank, Maritime Institute, &c., were to be placed practically under his control, but with a nominal subordination to Schulenburg, and had expressed a little anxiety lest Stein should rebel against this subordination, Stein now adds that he has no objection to serve under Count Schulenburg whom he knows for a man of clear penetration, indefatigable and powerful activity and extensive official knowledge.

On Nov. 10th the King wrote a letter to Stein to remove the scruples of his diffidence and to confer upon him further, nominally under Count Schulenburg but with practical independence, the Control of the Bank, Maritime Institute, Salt Administration, and Administration of the Sinking Fund, as Struensee had held them. With these new functions there was assigned him an additional salary of 4000 th. out of the funds of the Maritime Institute.

Throughout these proceedings Count Schulenburg plays the part in which the Berlin public had long known him, that of universal nominee to every vacant post. It is said that a worthy citizen who heard of the death of the King's mother, exclaiming innocently, 'Why! who will be Queen Dowager now?' was answered without hesitation, 'Count Schulenburg, of course.'

Stein's financial administration in the two years which brought Prussia to her great shipwreck is not in itself of much importance, but as the Revolution through which he guided the State in 1807 extended to its finance, it will be well to take this opportunity of introducing the reader to the subject of the Prussian Revenue.

The first great period in Prussian financial history is that of the reforms of Frederick William I. I have touched on this subject before, and remarked that the finance of that king was similar to that of the Bursar of some corporation endowed with land. For him the one financial procedure was to increase the production of the royal domains. He rounds off the royal estate by buying up contiguous properties, labours to relieve it of encumbrances, undertakes great works of irrigation, colonisation, &c. The revenues so gained he economises with the utmost care. Where the scale of revenue was so small, parsimony in the personal expense of the king was more than half the battle of finance. It was the masterpiece of Frederick William I. that in an age when the pernicious example of Versailles had demoralised all the courts of Europe, in the age of August the Strong, he set this example of parsimony. It was a great step in other countries when by the institution of a Civil List the personal revenues of the Sovereign were separated from those of which he was only the administrator. But Frederick William refused to have even a Civil List. His predecessor had reserved a Chatulle which for Prussia was extravagant in amount ; this was abolished by Frederick William. Instead of it the Domains Treasury paid him monthly pocket money (Handgelder) to the amount of 52,000 th. a year— the Chatulle had brought in nearly ten times as much. With this yearly sum eked out by Colonel's pay in the service of the Dutch States General, and a small grant which the States General had made in 1688 when they answered for him at the baptismal font, Frederick William voluntarily determined to face the world. If I am not mistaken, it was this example so resolutely set, and in the next generation extensively followed, that retrieved the character of European monarchy at a moment when it was fast settling down into Oriental degradation.

It will be useful to give here for reference a state of the revenue for the last year of Frederick William I.

> Domain Revenue ... 3,300,940
> General War Fund ... 3,616,251
> Total 6,917,191

The General War Fund consisted of a number of imposts, commutation of feudal services, excise, &c., mostly small in amount taken separately.

This revenue was spent as follows :

Army	5,039,663
Reserve Fund	914,416
Civil Service and Court	963,112
Total	6,917,191

Frederick William left to his successor a treasure of 8,700,000 th., and it was with the help of this treasure and in dependence upon the same system of finance that Frederick II. carried through the great struggle of his life. Let us observe the simplicity of Frederick's war finance even when his difficulties were greatest. In the Seven Years War we find no application to banks or other commercial corporations, no establishment of a State Bank, no depreciation of paper money, in fact no emission of paper money, no negociation of loans either at home or abroad, and in the end no national debt. How much more severe was that war to Prussia than to England, and yet the English debt is alarmingly increased by it while Prussia incurs no debt at all! In truth the economy of the Prussian State was still in a primitive phase. Nearly half a century after England and France had been convulsed by bubbles the Prussian King's only notion of providing for the future is to store up great sums of gold in cellars where they lie unproductive, and a still longer time after William III. brought into use against Louis XIV. the formidable weapon of credit Frederick knows nothing of such a weapon. There was not yet any Bank of Prussia ; indeed there was not even any bank *in* Prussia. When cash begins to fail,

Frederick's only expedient is to adulterate the coin, and he is glad if he can reduce to the utmost the evil results of such a measure by scattering the debased coin over the foreign territory occupied by his armies.

A new period of finance opens with the Peace of Hubertsburg. A country now almost ruined and yet obliged by foreign dangers to maintain an army of not less and if possible of more than 200,000 men, looks about for new Ways and Means. Frederick was not on the whole fortunate in his measures. More strange even than his love of French poetry and French philosophy was his admiration for French finance. That which was the infamy and proved soon the ruin of the French Monarchy, became to him a model for imitation. But notwithstanding his Tobacco Monopoly worked by a colony of detested French officials, his Coffee Administration and other mistakes, some steps were taken towards the introduction of a more advanced system of finance. From this period dates that effort to develope the mineral wealth of the Domain Lands, in which Stein took so large a part, and also, what is still more important, the organisation of the principle of credit.

Two years after the Peace, that is in 1765, the Bank was called into existence. Not as in England in order that the wealth of the country might become available to the Government in its necessities, but that the Government might have an opportunity of placing its wealth at the service of the exhausted nation, and by that means of reviving industry. Instead of the Bank advancing money to the

Government, the Government advanced money to the Bank. One establishment began at Berlin in 1765, and in the following year gained permission to issue notes. An independent establishment, also assisted by Government, was started at Breslau. In 1772 was founded the Maritime Institute (See-handlung) in order to revive foreign trade. Here too the Government takes the initiative, holding as many as 2100 shares out of 2300. These corporations once established and the country once accustomed to their paper, it might safely be predicted that the next war would make Prussia acquainted with Government loans and with a national debt.

The Seven Years of Frederick William II. from 1787 to 1795, though less terrible and glorious, were financially almost as trying to Prussia as the famous Seven Years of Frederick the Great. In 1787 there was a campaign in Holland. In 1790 and 1791 the army was mobilised and massed upon the Austrian and Russian frontier, though no hostilities actually took place. From 1792 to 1795 war was waged with France, and to this was added a Polish campaign in 1793, and afterwards a war against the Polish insurrection. At the same time the harvest of 1794 was the worst ever known in Prussia. It was found in this year that the treasure left by Frederick the Great, which had amounted to 55,000,000 th., was exhausted, and now began the Prussian debt. Money was borrowed from all quarters, from Holland, from Frankfurt, from Cassel, from the Maritime Institute. At the death of Frederick William II. in 1797, the Prussian debt amounted to 48,054,903 th.

Great complaints were made in England and Austria upon the sudden retirement of Prussia from the war in 1795. Her financial condition was perhaps not adequately appreciated except by herself. It is a momentous crisis in a nation's history when it begins to have a debt after having always hitherto had a reserve treasure. When a Government is backed by an enthusiastic nation, it can no doubt keep the field even in such a crisis; but the Prussian Government was not in that condition, and in the matter of peace and war had scarcely a choice. So too in judging the policy of inactivity to which Frederick William III. afterwards clung so persistently, we ought not to forget that according to the tradition of his house war could not be undertaken without a reserve treasure.

It was possible in peace at least to reduce if not extinguish the debt, and measures were taken with this object as soon as the Peace of Basel was concluded. A Sinking Fund was established, which was to be fed from the revenues of the Salt Monopoly, which in Prussia belonged to the State. In 1788, the Salt Administration, which till then had belonged to the Mining Department, was separated from it and put into connection with the Maritime Institute. It thus came into the hands of Struensee, and from him it passed to Stein, who, when the control of the Bank was also added to his Department, found himself entrusted with all that part of Prussian Finance which was of modern growth.

Schön, who was already a member of the Directory when Stein entered it, and who becomes from this point one of our authorities, tells us that

Stein disappointed the general expectation that he would prove fully equal to Struensee, and that 'the occasional flashes which his brilliant intellect gave forth, had neither coherence nor consciousness.' He goes on to say that 'as a politician Stein was so full of the foreign relations of the State, of what is called diplomacy, and attached such value to this intrinsically unreal matter, that he had never found it worth his while to develope in himself the idea of the State, or in short to occupy himself at all with the study of the political sciences, political economy or finance. In this he was like Frederick the Second.' Later, I shall introduce Schön himself to the reader, and shall then have something to say on his peculiar character, and shall give, I think, strong reasons for sifting with caution and some suspicion his evidence about Stein. The statements just quoted are surprising enough. So far from attaching excessive importance to diplomacy, the reader already knows on the best authority that Stein had a peculiar distaste for it; up to this time he had had no concern with foreign affairs, and we often have occasion to remark that he did not give them so much attention as we should have expected from a statesman of his rank at such a critical time; later, we shall find that when the department of Foreign Affairs is offered to him, he declines it on the express ground that Foreign Affairs are not in his line. It is in fact the special distinction of Stein in Prussian history, that he does *not* in this respect resemble Frederick II., and that he for the first time vindicated the internal, industrial, economical side of politics from the neglect of a school of statesmen who cared for nothing but foreign relations and diplomacy. In fact, in another passage Schön himself makes this very remark[1]. But he here makes two other statements : (1) that Stein proved himself inferior to Struensee as a Minister of Finance; (2) that he was ignorant of political economy.

It is to be observed that Schön does not actually say that Struensee had accomplished more in that post than Stein now accomplished. On the contrary, he speaks of him as one who might have done wonders, had he not, in Schön's opinion, been unnerved by his brother's catastrophe in Denmark. He impressed Schön as a man of greater ability and acquirement than Stein; that is all, and it will not seem much when we have had an opportunity of observing with how little impartiality Schön judges Stein.

Struensee's abilities may have been great, but he appears to have been timid and wanting in energy. Beyme writes to Stein : 'The deceased Struensee saw how much re-organisation was needed (in the Excise Department), but in his old age he had not energy or vigour to set his hand to the work. He was overpowered by the officials with their routine.' In vigour and decision, if not in acquirements, there can be no doubt that Stein was far superior to him, and it would be hard to show that in thirteen years during which he had held the

---

[1] Speaking of Stein's ascendancy in 1808, he writes, 'The aggrieved diplomatists who were accustomed to give the law had to conceal the spite they felt when they found themselves subordinated to the Department of the Interior' (*Aus den Papieren*, II. p. 48).

post Struensee accomplished so much as Stein accomplished in less than two years.

As to Schön's other statement that Stein had not mastered political economy, it is to be observed that Schön was one of the disciples of a certain Kraus, who from a professorial chair at Königsberg was at this time proclaiming the doctrines of Adam Smith. Stein belonged to an earlier generation; he had commenced his official career only four years after the appearance of the *Wealth of Nations* in its English form. He became in time a reader of it, and his great Edict of October, 1807, is a monument of his acceptance of its principles. In a letter to Vincke dated January, 1806, he expressly says that he had been guided by Adam Smith in his financial policy of the year before. It is possible, however, that he did not make a methodical study of him until he had been appointed Finance Minister; and we might accept Schön's evidence that in 1804 his economical views were not fully formed, if other statements contained in the same passage were not, as we have seen, so manifestly incorrect. Remarks like the following, which occur in a letter of Stein's to Vincke, dated February 26th, 1805, seem to savour of the old-fashioned system. 'Cotton-spinning is for us a business of the greatest importance; we consume 1,500,000 pounds of yarn yearly, and manufacture only 100,000—what an emission of money!' Here, the reader will say, is the well-known confusion of wealth with money that characterised the mercantile system. Cotton yarn is just as much wealth as money is, and the exportation of money in return for it would not make the country poorer. Nevertheless we ought to consider the peculiarity of Prussia, which was obliged to sacrifice every other interest to national defence. It is not clear that Stein is thinking here of the nation and its wealth at all. To the *nation* no doubt money is not synonymous with wealth; but to a *Government* when the question is of paying an army and conducting a campaign, it may be an all-important thing to be able to lay its hand at a moment's notice upon large sums of money. This is the case in all countries; Pitt found it true in England in 1797; but it is especially true in countries like Prussia in which credit is still in its infancy.

Englishmen speak too much as if there had been no political economy, or at least as if there had been no doctrine of Free-trade, before Adam Smith's book was published, forgetting that the world had not yet seen the *Wealth of Nations* when in the last years of Louis XV. the salons of Paris were busy in discussing the Commerce des Grains, nor even when Turgot abolished internal protection in France. Stein, I am inclined to think, before he became a follower of Adam Smith looked up to Turgot as his master. We have remarked already the resemblance of his provincial administration to Turgot's famous administration of the Limousin; in his Ministry of Finance, short as it was, too short to disclose what he may have had in view, he still found time once more to emulate Turgot.

If the great Governments of the Continent were forced by their military necessities to regulate trade with foreign parts in such a way as to prevent a drain of money from the country, there was nothing to hinder them from adopting the principles of free trade at home. The inconveniences that might arise from money leaving the country could not follow from its circulating freely within the country. Internal free trade accordingly triumphed on the Continent, and the principle that industry thrives by the neglect of government was admitted to that extent, before free trade in the sense the English attach to the word was seriously considered. Only a country like ours, shielded comparatively from war and depending upon foreign countries for its wealth, could contemplate free trade between nations ; but free trade within a nation was a favourite notion of continental economists in the latter half of the 18th century. Stein now had the courage to introduce it into Prussia. It would have been well for Schön to have told us what prevented Struensee in thirteen years of office from accomplishing this reform which, since the great days of Turgot, could not escape the notice of any financier, and which it seems the King himself had recommended in 1798. It appears that the internal or provincial Customs of Prussia produced no greater sum than 185,000 th. yearly, but at the same time, being levied upon an ancient system which had become in the course of time extremely intricate and confused, caused the greatest possible hindrance to traffic. They were now removed by the Edict of December 26, 1805.

Another important achievement of Stein's was the reform of the Salt Administration by the Edict of May 14, 1805. A very brief description of it is all that the reader, whom I cannot suppose deeply interested in the business details of old Prussian finance, will expect. The manufacture and sale of salt was an important monopoly of the Government. At the same time the Maritime Institute held a monopoly of the trade in foreign salt. At the crisis of Prussian finance above described, when Prussia first began to feel the weight of a national debt, Struensee had undertaken to save half a million thalers yearly, by uniting the Maritime Institute with the Salt Department, and creating a General Salt Administration. The plan had not been found to work well. Stein sums up the objections to it thus : 'Affairs of quite different kinds are committed to the same Department, viz. Manufacture, Trading Operations, Levying of a Consumption Tax. Each branch demands special skill, special arrangements and a special mode of procedure.' What these are he goes on to state, and then adds : 'The following inconveniences are caused by the combination of such heterogeneous matters in one administration : 1. Onesidedness in the management. Each Head of the Department takes his own peculiar view, which he pursues to the neglect of all others. If you examine recent administrations in this respect, you see under Minister v. Heinitz special attention to manufacture, under Minister v. Struensee, a commercial view, and a combination of the whole to the neglect of manufacture and of details. 2. Expensiveness, if the requirements of such varied affairs are in any degree to be satisfied ; for what a number of officials is necessary to supply the desired skill and the proper oversight for all this business ! 3. Loss to the Revenue, when one or other part of the business is neglected, as has been the case hitherto.' He proposes, therefore, 'to dissolve an aggregate consisting of such heterogeneous parts, and to commit each branch to the department which is furnished with the necessary knowledge and possesses the tools needed for the work;' these departments are, as he explains, for the salt manufacture the Mining Department, for the trade in foreign salt the Maritime Institute, and for the levying of the tax the Excise Department. The elaborate report containing these proposals is dated January 9th, 1805. A Commission was appointed to consider the mode of carrying them out, in spite of the opposition of Count Schulenburg, who disapproved, and when this Commission had reported, the scheme, with some unimportant modifications, became law.

To these two great Reforms, the abolition of internal customs and the re-arrangement of the Salt Administration, Stein himself in his autobiography adds, that he 'succeeded in diminishing the amount of useless writing in the higher boards; that he quite stopped a great quantity of useless paper-blackening, and increased the independence of the provincial posts.'

Stein's experience had lain hitherto exclusively in the western part of the Prussian State; in fact it seems that the officials of the Eastern Provinces had dreaded the appointment to the Ministry of one so Westphalian in his notions, and that the King himself had shared their misgivings. Stein began now diligently to study the Eastern Provinces. The Partitions of Poland were still recent, the administration of the acquired territory still unsettled; perhaps few of us remember how extensive these acquisitions

were, and how much Polish land which now belongs
to Russia was then in Prussian possession. Besides
East Prussia which the Great Elector had vindicated
from Polish overlordship, and West Prussia the
acquisition of Frederick the Great, there was now
South Prussia and New East Prussia. Warsaw
itself was a Prussian town, and the frontier of the
monarchy embraced Bialystock. In March Stein
addressed the Directors of the Provincial Chambers,
requiring from them minute reports of the condition
of their provinces, and suggestions of improvement,
and he devoted the summer to a tour of inspection.
In July he visited Posen, Kalisch, Warsaw, Plock,
Bialystock, Szcenczyn; in August Memel, Königsberg, Danzig, and returned in September by Fordan
and Stettin. One or two letters to Vincke written
during this journey are preserved. He says he is
much interested by what he sees, but evidently he sees
nothing but what concerns trade and administration.
On his return he embodied the results of his observations in a report addressed to the King. He proposed to simplify local government in these provinces
by abolishing cross or overlapping administrative
divisions, and also to make some changes in the
Excise Tariff of East and West Prussia, so as to
adapt it to the interests of the great commercial
towns, i.e. to extend to the Eastern Provinces the
same kind of reform which he had introduced long
before into the County Mark.

It was not till after his return in September that
the two great Credit Establishments, the Bank and
Maritime Institute, passed into his hands from
those of Count Schulenburg. Stein had avowed at

his appointment that his knowledge of those institutions was very imperfect, and Schön would have us believe that he was a mere child in everything that concerned the Money Market. Nevertheless it appears that an immediate revolution in these two corporations was the consequence of his assuming the management of them. The standard of commercial honesty was, it seems, at that time not yet so high as a developed banking system requires, and the business was much in the hands of Jews, of whom Stein says that 'their cunning, perseverance, *esprit de corps*, and want of the sense of honour if only their covetousness was gratified, were pernicious in any State, and had especially a mischievous influence upon the official class.' Three or four great frauds came to light in succession during the autumn of 1805. It was also discovered that the Bank, contrary to the principle on which it had been founded, had lent extensively on mortgage, the security in many cases consisting in Polish lands; this, Stein remarks, led in the sequel to most mischievous negotiations with Napoleon and with Russia when the Polish provinces were so soon after severed from the Prussian monarchy. Altogether he considered the Bank, as he tells us, 'a pernicious institution, drawing to itself as it did considerable sums of money, the application of which was intrusted to officials;' that is, it was pernicious by the strong temptations to which it exposed the official class....He mentions the detection in fraud of the Jew David Ephraim, who 'saved himself by fleeing to Vienna and there becoming a Catholic, while one of his accomplices committed suicide,' according to Pertz, hanged himself before Stein's door. Strong measures were adopted, the Directors subjected to new and stringent regulations, the mortgage business in South Prussia forbidden, speculation threatened with new penalties; finally, the chief Director of the Bank was deprived of his office. To replace him Stein looked to Denmark, as Frederick had done in the case of Struensee, and invited a man who had lately distinguished himself in the direction of the Bank of Copenhagen, and whose name, well known already in England, will frequently reappear in this book, Barthold Georg Niebuhr.

But when Niebuhr arrived in Berlin (it was in October, 1806) he found the scene already much changed, and a few days after it was still further transformed. And here ends our account of the tranquil period of Stein's life. One more financial operation of his remains to be spoken of, but it belongs to war finance, and the enemy is Napoleon.

Prussia did not actually engage in hostilities till October, 1806, but during a whole year before this, or from October, 1805, she was within the penumbra of war. The causes and conditions of this war will be traced in the next Part. It will also be shewn what share Stein took in it, and what effects upon his life it had. But as some slight view has just been given of the history of Prussian finance, and as the great incidents in financial history are always wars, it will be convenient to note at this point what were the financial ways and means by which Prussia, under the guidance of Stein, proposed to maintain the new war which for the first time in Prussian history was to be undertaken with a debt greatly exceeding in amount the reserve treasure of the State.

It was in the latter half of September, 1805, that the King determined to mobilise the army, and was advised by Schulenburg, to whom he applied first, to call upon Stein for a financial plan. For the first time a Prussian King contemplated war without having in his treasury the means of supporting it even for a single year. Stein's report was sent in on October 9th. The document itself does not lie before us, but we are able to make out his views from an additional report sent in by him on October 26th, and from another most elaborate and instructive paper dated December 2nd. He passes in rapid review the possible ways of supporting the war, rejecting at once the notion of throwing the expense upon the enemy's country, and speaking of Frederick the Great's method, which consisted in ' certain operations upon the coinage ' as ' so disturbing and even destructive to trade, and casting such a dark shadow of immorality, that neither the good of the State nor your Majesty's principles will allow you to resort to it if it can possibly be avoided.' Internal loans have, he says, great difficulties, and foreign loans have the same and others of their own. Subsidies are not to be despised, but ' we have in our own history a recent example of their inconveniences in the suspension of the English subsidies late in 1794, just at the moment when a new war was added to that already in progress, and made them specially necessary.' Rejecting these methods, he proposes to resort to paper money.

This was regarded as a great innovation, and

yet paper money in the English sense of the word
had long existed, though not in great quantities, in
Prussia. The Bank of Prussia had almost from the
beginning had the right of issuing notes, and what
is paper money but bank notes? But I must remind
the reader that strictly the two things are distinct.
The truth is that the peculiar connection which exists
in England between the Bank and the Government
fills our minds with preconceptions which make it
difficult for us to follow the financial history of
foreign states, particularly in times long past. The
Bank of England was created to advance money
to Government. Hence when war puts an extreme
pressure upon Government it is to the Bank that
Government applies; and the Bank does not merely
render what help it can and then bid the Government go elsewhere, but shares all the embarrass-
ments of Government, so that what is really the
insolvency of the Government appears here to be
the insolvency of the Bank. This was the case
in 1797, when the immense subsidies of England
to foreign Powers embarrassed Pitt's Government.
The Bank was not allowed to sever itself from the
cause of the Government, but was by Act of Parliament actually forced—not permitted—to suspend
payments in cash. If there had then been no Bank
of England standing in this connection with the
Government, let us ask ourselves what Pitt would
have done in 1797. It is evident that instead of
forcing the Bank to suspend cash-payments he
would have begun to pay in paper himself. He
would have made a certain proportion of his payments in paper, but the paper money thus issued

would not have been bank notes but treasury notes.
Of this kind were the Exchequer Bills issued by
Montague in 1695, while the Bank was yet in its
infancy, for sums as small as £5 ; of this kind also
were the French assignats, which were not notes
of any bank but of the Government itself. Now
the Bank of Prussia did not at all correspond to the
Bank of England. It had been created, as we have
seen, not for the convenience of the Government,
but of the people; the moneys of Government were
not deposited there but kept in the Exchequer;
accordingly Stein, though a close observer of England, did not think of throwing the difficulties of
the Government upon the Bank. The Government
itself issues paper instead of forcing the Bank to
suspend cash payments.

But having determined to issue paper the
Government would have to consider many other
questions, of which the principal would be, Should
the new currency be convertible or inconvertible?
In other words, should the Government suspend
till the return of peace some of its principal payments, or content itself with acquiring the advantage
of a banker who, issuing notes payable at sight,
calculates that only a certain proportion of them
will be presented within a given time ?

If Government contented itself with adopting
the latter course the introduction of paper money
would perhaps amount to no more than Government
undertaking the business of a banker. And it might
be urged that this, so far from being an objection-
able course justified by an emergency, was actually
in itself to some extent expedient. For if the

development of credit in a country be beneficial, if the practice of using a paper currency within limits be convenient, Government may do well in furthering the practice in a country in which it is as yet little known. Thus industry might positively be animated by an issue of Government paper intended in the first instance only to rescue the Government itself from embarrassment. It appears that this was Stein's original proposal ; five millions were to be issued in treasury notes exchangeable for coin at certain fixed centres ; other sums were at the same time to be raised by loans at Leipzig and Cassel.

As the expense of a year's campaign was estimated at 30,000,000 th., it will be seen that Stein proposes only to meet a sixth part of the expense by paper money. To this proposal the King replied in the Order of Cabinet of Oct. 15th, by accepting it in principle, but suggesting that the amount issued should be twenty millions instead of five. In the elaborate Report of Dec. 2nd, Stein gives his opinion upon this suggestion, but in this document is to be remarked that he contemplates no longer a convertible but an inconvertible paper currency. It is to be conjectured that at the moment of drawing it up (it was the month of the battle of Austerlitz), the probability of war seemed greater than in October. As to the quantity of paper money to be issued he finds himself after a close examination able to raise it to nine millions and a-half. Much of the document is occupied with a demonstration that the evils which in other states have sprung from paper money have been caused solely by the excessive issue of it. Denmark,

Sweden and the Revolutionary Government of France are introduced as examples of this, while the history of England is referred to for instances of the safe and moderate use of paper money. It is evidently Stein's idea that the financial perplexities of Prussia, a country industrially, and therefore of necessity financially, little advanced, were best to be met by taking lessons from the rich financial experience of England. He closes by praying that his Report may be examined at a special meeting of the General Directory. Accordingly we have another Report dated January 8th, 1806, in which Stein's Report is criticised, and the conclusion is arrived at that in the case of actual war the inconvertible currency is to be preferred, but if the army was likely soon to return to a peace footing, only convertible paper could be recommended. The King, who knew only too well that Prussia would certainly not proceed to actual war except in an emergency so extreme that it could hardly be contemplated as possible, decided on January 18th for a convertible currency, and decreed that the branches of the Bank and Maritime Institute at Berlin, Breslau, Elbing, Königsberg, Warsaw, Stettin, Münster, and Fürth should be supplied with funds sufficient for cashing all the treasury notes that might be presented.

But we must pause here, for Prussia's turn has come at last. Hitherto England and Prussia have seemed equally to enjoy an exemption from the revolutionary storms of the time. But only England was to continue exempt to the end. The shock was to come upon Prussia more suddenly even than upon France, and it was to be in Prussia as in France a revolutionary shock, for it was to alter all the institutions both of government and of society. It was to inflict scarcely less suffering than in France, suffering continued for seven years. But one calamity, the greatest of all which had befallen France, was to be spared to Prussia. The fury of Civil Discord was not to be let loose there. No guillotine was to be set up ; no emigrant nobles were to infest the frontiers or consume their lives in cursing their country from a foreign shore; the Oder, Spree and Weichsel were to see no noyades. Nay, the years of endurance were to exercise a reconciling, uniting influence upon the different classes of the people; they were to form a period in the national history which could be looked back upon without horror, and if with shame yet also with pride; for in these years the same transition was made in Prussia that had been made in France, but made in the way which in France had after trial been found impossible. It was made under the peaceful guidance of a Minister of the Crown. Prussia too found her Turgot, and, what is more, a Turgot who did not fail.

PART II.

THE CATASTROPHE.

Cependant, Sire, qu'a fait comme roi ce grand homme (Frédéric II.) au prix de tant d'efforts ? Vous a-t-il laissé des états riches, puissants, heureux ? Otez-leur la réputation militaire et les ressources du trésor qui peuvent se dissiper, le reste est bien faible…Une armée ne pourra pas toujours, elle ne pourra pas longtemps faire le fonds de la puissance prussienne.

MIRABEAU, *Lettre remise à Frédéric-Guillaume II.* (1786).

CHAPTER I.

CHARACTER OF THE PRUSSIAN STATE.

At the time it happened the catastrophe of Jena was the most startling and unforeseen occurrence that had been witnessed in modern Europe. No downfall so complete and sudden of a state so great and prosperous had yet been witnessed, and it surprised Europe the more because the State which fell so suddenly fell in war, and at the same time had the reputation of being the peculiarly military State of Europe. Perhaps it has been made to appear even more surprising by the revival of Prussian military greatness that has taken place since. A Jena intervening midway between a Rossbach and a Sedan is a phenomenon to which perhaps European history can produce nothing parallel. In Asiatic history we read of something similar, how the Ottoman Turks, when they had already made themselves the terror of Europe and had the battle of Nicopolis behind them and the capture of Constantinople before them, were suddenly trampled in the dust by the world-conqueror Tamerlane.

However unforeseen at the moment, the disaster when it is studied will be seen to have nothing abnormal about it. But its importance in the history of Prussia is all the greater on that account, and in the life of Stein it is such an occurrence as the

meeting of the States General was in the life of
Mirabeau, or the breaking out of the European war
in the life of Napoleon. It furnished him with the
occasion of those achievements which have made
him memorable.

At this point therefore the biographical narrative
must pause. Hitherto we have looked into the
politics of Prussia just as far as the biography required us to do so, glancing now at Local Administration, now at the Ministerial Departments, now at
Finance. But as we approach the catastrophe
which carried him to the position of a universal
Reformer, we must prepare ourselves to understand
his reforms by contemplating deliberately the Prussian State as a whole. This we shall try to do
without being led further than the occasion demands,
and without losing ourselves in the general history
of Prussia.

The special course of history which a State runs
is often determined by some original peculiarity
in its situation. In the case of England, for example, such a peculiarity is its separation, decided
and yet not wide, from the Continent of Europe; in
the case of the American Union its boundless space
for expansion, and its having no rivals. The controlling peculiarity in the situation of Prussia, on the
contrary, is that it has had neighbours and rivals
overwhelmingly superior, and has been separated
from them by no frontier but what it could make
itself. The immediate consequence of this peculiarity has been that Government there assumes a
much larger province than in England or America.
Self-preservation more than any cause determines the

character of States; it was an easy task in England since invasion was difficult, and easier still in America. England therefore did not want much government, and America wants even less; but Prussia has always wanted as much government as can possibly be had, because the defence of Prussia has always been extremely difficult. For the same reason the government has always taken a military form. Our examination of Prussian finance has shown us the army swallowing up the greater part of the public revenue. We have seen that the machine of administration in Prussia was almost exclusively applied to the creation and maintenance of an army entirely out of proportion to the population and wealth of the country. In this it is evidently involved that the form of government was absolute and that popular liberties were unknown. The huge army would be fatal to the Monarchy if it were entrusted to any other hand but that of the Monarch, and in the hand of the Monarch it was just as necessarily fatal to any thought of liberty. Prussia entered upon a course which, it might have been foreseen, was likely to lead to great vicissitudes of fortune. Everything depended upon the military qualities of the king. A born general on that throne would be the first man of his age, as was Frederick the Great; a genuine soldier there, even without genius, would succeed, as the Emperor William. But even a very clever man would fail painfully, as did Frederick William IV., if his talents were not of the military kind, and ordinary kings wanting in insight and will, such as the two with whom this book is concerned, were likely to steer the State upon the rocks.

Frederick the Great's mean dress, his snuffy coat and uniform never laid aside for any robe of state, and at the same time his indefatigable devotion to business, gave him in his own age the reputation of an original genius and a reviver of antique heroism. When we look closer we discover that his merit lay in discerning clearly the exigencies of an exceptional position, and moreover that in this he was not original but only faithful to the lessons of his father. The Prussian system was devised by Frederick William I. between 1720 and 1730. The army was then greatly increased in numbers and settled upon a firm financial basis ; the nobles were induced to devote their lives to military service ; and it was in order to set them an example of such devotion that the king gradually adopted the practice of appearing always in uniform. Nor in spite of his extravagances was Frederick William one who played at soldiers as so many petty German princes have been accused of doing. As Crown Prince he had witnessed the helplessness of the Monarchy exposed in the great War of the North to the unceremonious invasion of its neighbours. In determining to save it from such humiliation as it endured then, he had created a machinery which proved only too success-ful. Desiring to give Prussia an equivalent for a frontier, he gave her that which raised her in no long time to the rank of one of the great Powers of Europe.

But as this extreme difficulty of defending the country and the consequences of it, namely, the necessity of a government at once all-powerful and oppressive, are the fundamental facts of Prussian history, we should try at the outset to realize them with some exactness and detail. Let the reader look in Macaulay and see what the English standing army was at the time when it was first established. He will read that in 1698 the House of Commons was divided upon the question whether it should consist of 7000 or 10,000 men. And that was a time when Louis XIV. was threatening Europe and when our country was at the head of the party of resistance to him, a time when Europe was on the point of being convulsed by the momentous controversy of the Spanish succession, and England was a rich and great country. If we pass over thirty years to the administration of Walpole we find that after the period of the victories of Marlborough, and when England was flushed with glory and prosperity, her standing army on the peace establishment still amounted, and indeed continued much later to amount to little more than 17,000 men. Let us now turn to Prussia under Frederick William I., whose reign was contemporary with the administration of Walpole. Prussia was then an exceedingly poor country; it had no great or ancient reputation to maintain. The age was for the most part peaceful, and in such wars as there were Prussia had little share. And what was the population of Prussia? At the death of Frederick William in 1740 it was about 2,240,000, less perhaps than a fourth of the population of the United Kingdom at the same time.

And now what was the Peace Establishment of Frederick William I., which he left to his successor? It amounted to about 80,000 men.

England however, it will be said, had a fleet, and

had never professed to be a military state. Let us
then compare the army of Frederick William with
other continental armies. It was nearly equal to
that of Austria, which had a population perhaps
about six times as great. It was half as large as
that of France, whose population was about nine
times as great. But if we wish correctly to estimate
the effect which this incredible military force must
have had upon the state which maintained it, we
must take several other facts into consideration.
We shall find that both as increasing the absolute
power of the Government and as a burden upon
the people, the army of Frederick William was
much more formidable than could be inferred from
its greater proportionate numbers. For about one-
third of it consisted of foreign mercenaries, and of
the rest the rank and file consisted not in any
degree of the educated classes, who might be capable of some regard for liberty and some jealousy
of arbitrary power, but of agricultural serfs, who
even in their own homes lived under a subjection as
complete as in the camp. Moreover, overwhelming
as is the force which a vast unintelligent standing
army gives to a Government even at the present
day, there are now in every State counteracting
influences, some shadow of a Parliament, some pre-
tence of a free Press. In Prussia the local Parliaments had almost everywhere passed into insignificance—there was no Mutiny Bill—and in the time
of Frederick William the Press had no freedom;
nothing counteracted the brute force of this mass of
armed slaves, ruled with iron severity and officered
by their hereditary masters, the noblesse, who had

made themselves in turn, as it were, serfs to their King and Commander-in-chief, for the Articles of War bound the officer to obedience 'even against his own honour.' If we reflect on all this, we shall recognize that Frederick William when he organized this army, achieved a work not less important politically than it was in a military sense. He created not only a new Great Power in Europe, but also a new form of Government. For in resting so mainly on his army, and drawing from it such unlimited power, he contrived a new variety of monarchy, so that the Prussian State from this time does not resemble the model of the France of Louis XIV., but anticipates modern military bureaucracies, and furnishes a model to Napoleon.

But what a burden upon the people must this army have been! The Prussian State of our own time may be called rich. It has acquired new territories, some of which are very productive, it has developed new industries, such as that mining industry of Westphalia which we have been contemplating; it has reaped the benefit of that agrarian and industrial revolution which we are about to follow the course of.

Moreover its military system has been made just and equal, so that the modern German army is regarded by many with pride as a sort of school of virtue. The old system could not be thought of in this way; it was terribly oppressive and demoralising and caused vast misery to the Prussian peasantry.

The rulers who figure in history as conquerors are commonly those who have inherited an exceptional army. Alexander used the army Philip had made; Napoleon reaped the benefit of the *levée en masse* of 1793; Cromwell, as Protector, awed Europe with the army which had been formed in the Civil War, an army such as no English king had ever commanded. Nor did Frederick the Great withstand the temptation of using the potent instrument his father had put into his hands. But the ambitious aggressions of this king ought not to lead us to think of the Hohenzollern as an essentially ambitious dynasty, or of Frederick William as having had ambitious views in creating his military system. It is well known that he never showed the least ambition himself, and in more than one of his successors a certain backwardness to war may be observed which, when their great military means are considered, is remarkable. The king, with whom we shall here be principally concerned, was throughout his long reign peaceful to a fault. But it is impossible to create a great army for purposes of defence which shall not be capable of being used for offence also, and used for offence and for unjust offence such an army is certain at times to be. The true view of Prussia in the 18th century seems to be, that it was a state which found itself unable to be safe without being dangerous at the same time, which created for legitimate purposes a weapon it was always suspected of wishing to use and sometimes did use for illegitimate.

Frederick the Great had a more cultivated mind than his father, and talents which his father never had any opportunity of showing; but the idea on which Prussian greatness was founded was conceived and realised by the father, not by the son. Sybel even goes so far as to say that Frederick, though a great general and diplomatist, was not a great organiser[1], and Mirabeau remarks that he was an example rather of a great character in a great position than of a great genius raised by nature high above the ordinary level. It must be admitted that he sometimes made mistakes that a man of much original insight would hardly have been in any danger of making. But he maintained with invincible tenacity his father's idea of defending Prussia by the sustained energy of its people, called out and stimulated by the unsparing rigour of the Government. Accordingly, we find that after the great trial of the Seven Years' War, when Frederick William's foresight had been justified by the event and the country saved, 'so as by fire,' from its enemies, the King is far from abating his exactions. From the beginning of the Peace he is busy in devising new burdens. No allowance is made for the terrible losses the country had suffered. The army is greatly increased in numbers, though not quite in proportion to the increase of population. At Frederick's death in 1786 it amounted to 200,000 men in time of peace, and the revenue annually levied had risen from nearly 7,000,000 th. to nearly 20,000,000. It is true that the population had now risen to 6,000,000, but it seems to have felt the burdens laid upon it ever more and more, partly, I suppose, owing to the losses caused by the war, partly to the abject poverty of

---

[1] 'So genial er sich im Angesichte des feindlichen Feldherrn oder Gesandten zeigte, so wenig schöpferisch war er auf dem Gebiete der Verwaltung und der Organisation.' *Ueber die Entwickelung der absoluten Monarchie in Preussen.*

the province of West Prussia, which was added to the kingdom in 1772.

In 1786 occurred in Prussia that grave crisis which cannot always be avoided in countries where the stress of government is laid upon the hereditary monarch. Frederick William II. succeeding his uncle was like Rehoboam succeeding Solomon, like the first Stuart succeeding Elizabeth. A system had been formed in which almost everything depended on the personal qualifications of the king, and now the ablest of the Hohenzollerns was succeeded by the most inefficient. Frederick William II. did not want activity but he wanted clearness and fixed purpose. Accordingly he is to the fall of Prussia what Frederick William I. was to its rise. As the latter paved the way to the glories of Rossbach and Leuthen and deserves half the credit of them, so did the former guide Prussia on the way to the catastrophe of Jena, and the responsibility of it belongs to him almost more than to the unlucky sovereign under whose auspices it occurred. As the process of decline initiated by Frederick William II. was witnessed in its whole course by Stein, it will be necessary that we should give here a clear account of it.

CHAPTER II.

FREDERICK WILLIAM II. AND FREDERICK WILLIAM III.

IT has often been remarked that the countries which prove richest are those which are poorly endowed with natural wealth. Where nature has been lavish, there man is commonly found a pauper, as though demoralised by a natural poor-law. But the Dutch, to whom nature gave not even house-room, became the richest nation in the world; and the richest nation now is the English, to whom nature has given not wealth, but only the tools by which wealth is made, i. e. coal and iron. In the same way we have remarked that great military power has been forced upon Prussia by the very fact that her position is one of extreme military weakness. It is impossible for her to take the precautions necessary for her safety at home, without becoming formidable to her neighbours. Hence her history falls into periods in which her influence has extended into wider regions, in consequence of the new measures of self-defence she has been forced to adopt. To protect Prussia the peaceable Frederick William I. created an army, and it had the immediate effect of raising Prussia into a great German Power formidable to Austria, and of adding to her Silesia and West Prussia. But it is to be observed that Frederick the Great in his turn is peaceable with respect to Europe. He does not seem to have thought of making Prussia into a great European Power. While within Germany he is always prepared to take part and even to intervene with arms in controversies which only concern him as an Estate of the Empire, as for instance in the case of the Bavarian Succession, outside Germany on the other hand he only intervenes where his own interests seem directly to require it. In the politics of Poland and Russia he takes part, because they are his neighbours, but in the dispute between England and her colonies he does not feel called upon, as not only France but even Austria does, to take any part. Nevertheless at his death it appeared that in spite of Frederick Prussia had entered upon a third stage in her course, and had insensibly become one of the great European Powers. An army of 200,000 men could not but be a most serious weight in any scale in which it might be laid. The reign of Frederick William II. exhibits a series of Prussian interferences in the general controversies of Europe, to which there is nothing similar in the reign of Frederick the Great. He interferes in Holland, and restores the government of the hereditary Stadtholder; he is on the point of interfering in the great Eastern controversy raised by Joseph and Catharine, and is actually at the head of his troops when Leopold's dexterity entraps him into the Convention of Reichenbach; he interferes in Poland to quell the insurrection of Koszciusko; finally he interferes in France after the French Revolution. Prussia's *début* as one of the Great Powers of Europe is not fortunate. In all these interferences except the first she failed, and in 1795 a period of reaction commences in which she tries to combine the formidable resources of a Great Power with the unpretending modesty of a small State, and in this unhappy attempt finds her ruin.

The times were altering fast when Frederick died. They had in fact already become revolutionary, for we ought not to date the transition in Europe from the movement in France, which country was indeed somewhat late in taking the prevalent infection. An ominous rift or schism already showed itself in almost every European State. Where Frederick had seen simple Powers, which it was the problem of statesmanship to balance against each other, his successor saw in almost every country two Powers in conflict, the government and some opposition party, popular or other. It had been so earlier with England which had been at war with her colonies, it had long been so with Poland, but in 1786 the war of people and government raged in the United Netherlands and over the whole vast extent of the Austrian Monarchy, including Flanders and Hungary. In 1789 the rift showed itself at length in France. Meanwhile Prussia was and remained through the whole period quite free from this evil, and accordingly was just in the position in which she could assume a commanding influence in Europe. Each of these domestic discords invited foreign intervention ; it was by means of such discords, by assuming them to exist everywhere and by creating them where they did not, that revolutionary France afterwards gained her ascendancy in Europe. The same chance had presented itself earlier to Prussia. United at home and controlling an army of 200,000 men, she could avail herself of the divisions of all her neighbours.

But though Prussia escaped the evil of intestine discord, she underwent in the end under pressure of a different kind a revolution similar to those which were caused by intestine struggles in other countries. She revised her institutions after Tilsit, and under the guidance of Stein. And as this Prussian Revolution is the subject of this book, it is not irrelevant to take note of the other great revolutions of the age and to mark their character, so that when the time comes we may understand whether the development of Prussian institutions was parallel or not to that of other states. Frederick William II. then was engaged during most of his reign in watching three great constitutional struggles, not to mention other smaller ones, in the nations round him. These were in Poland, in Austria and in France. In Poland and France revolution actually took place, and Prussia interfered in both countries, assisting in the partition of the first and sharing the discomfiture of the intervening Powers in the second. The Austrian movement, which for a long time threatened completely to overturn the system of Europe, was checked at the last moment. In 1790 the Austrian States passed into more judicious management than that of Joseph II., and, instead of becoming the source of disturbance to Europe, proved once more as usual the ballast of the ship ; and the same skilful hand that had stayed revolution at home—that of the Emperor Leopold—at the same time warded off Prussian intervention.

These revolutions, two realised and one abortive, were in appearance different, yet not altogether so different as they appeared. That of Poland was one of a class now much overlooked, yet not uncommon in the 18th century. It proposed to cure the intolerable evils of the aristocratic form of republicanism by the establishment of hereditary monarchy. The example had been set within a few years by the Dutch, and analogous movements had taken place at other times in Denmark, Sweden, and Russia. In May, 1791, almost at the same time that the first French Constitution was promulgated, the Poles converted their State from the helpless elective monarchy, which had already suffered partition, into a solid hereditary monarchy under the House of Saxony. And if this revolution did not save the State, if on the contrary it hastened its destruction, this was not because the change itself was ill-judged, but for the opposite reason, that it threatened to revive Poland in such strength as to thwart the ambition of Russia and actually to endanger Prussia.

The Austrian movement has the strongest superficial resemblance to the rising of England against the Stuarts. Joseph's innovations are of the same kind as those of our Charles I., and are resisted in a similar way. In Flanders and Hungary he sets aside the old half-federal provincial organisation and the Assemblies of Estates : he substitutes uniform administrative districts and purely bureaucratic boards of government. The encroachments of Charles I. were trivial compared to these. By such acts Joseph gradually in the course of ten years roused a spirit of rebellion over his whole empire, and before his death was compelled to cancel most of his innovations.   In the Resolution of Jan. 28th, 1790, just before he died heart-broken, he wrote with a kind of pathetic frankness, ' I undertook alterations in the administration simply with the view of further- ing the public weal by them, and in the hope that after closer examination the people would become favourable to them.   But now I have acquired the conviction that the people prefer the old arrange- ment and seek and find their whole happiness in it, I yield therefore to their wishes and declare the forms of administration, as I found them at my accession, again legally existing.'   At first sight, I say, we seem to have before us the war between Charles I. and his Parliament.   There is indeed one very obvious difference.   The Stuarts lean to Catholicism, and when they take away religious liberties it is not in their own interest but in that of an imperious Church, the Anglican in the case of Charles I., the Roman in that of James II. Joseph, on the other hand, violates religious liberty in the interest of the State, and his special object of jealousy is the power of the Catholic Church, because it is independent of the State and alien to it.   But in secular policy how does Joseph differ from the Stuarts ?   Is not his object the same as theirs, viz. absolutism ?   Has he not the same enemies, viz. Assemblies, local liberties ?   And yet modern Liberalism, which condemns the Stuarts so unreservedly, counts Joseph among its founders, and at most censures him only for over-haste and for that recklessness about means to which enthu- siasm and conscious good intentions are peculiarly liable. When we look more closely we see the reason of this, but at the same time we see the apparent resemblance between the Austrian and English movements disappear. Those Austrian Assemblies were not like the English Parliament, and the absolutism Joseph would have introduced, though not a good sort of government, would have had a very real advantage over the system he would have swept away. For he desired to sweep away Assemblies which either represented the separate interests of a part of the Empire without the least regard to the whole, or else represented separate social classes, and served only to strengthen class prejudices and perpetuate discord. They were rather like our Convocation, in which professional prejudices are strengthened by discussion among members of the same profession, than like our Parliament, in which prejudices are moderated and interests reconciled by the fusion of different classes. The despotism Joseph would have introduced was in his mind only a means of giving unity to Government. It was intended to establish the supremacy of the State over all class feelings and interests.

The same remark is to be made about the third and greatest of the movements of that age, the French Revolution. It has the same superficial resemblance and the same substantial unlikeness to our English revolutions. The French Revolution waged more implacable war against local and provincial liberties than any despot could do. The substitution of Departments for Provinces was plainly borrowed from Joseph, and was moreover in exact accordance with all the tendencies of

the old Bourbon absolutism.   In fact it may be said
in general that the Revolution carried further and
completed the work commenced by the great cen-
tralising kings.   But here too, as in the case of
Joseph, despotism was only a means, not an end;
the end aimed at was to establish the unity and
supremacy of the State.   That intense particularism,
that war between province and province, town and
town, town and neighbouring country district, that
universal indifference and insensibility to all public
interests which Turgot has described, was to be
brought to an end, and the State was to be set up
as the object of universal devotion.   The State
therefore, whether in the republican or monarchical
form, was to have a commanding authority and a
very wide province, and however much speculative
republicanism might be professed, the Liberalism of
that generation favoured in practice a very absolute
form of monarchy, as conversely absolute monarchs
had been the first favourers of Liberalism.

If then we look at all these movements together,
the Polish, the Austrian and the French, and observe
what is common to them all, we may see that the
idea peculiar to that age and which made it revolutionary was the idea not of liberty but of government,
the idea of an omnipotent state.   We may see too
that such an idea could not easily excite any
ferment in Prussia, for the State there was omni
potent already.   What Joseph wanted, what Napoleon
afterwards realised, Frederick William the First and
Frederick the Great had possessed in full measure
long before.

United within herself and armed to the teeth, it

might be thought that Prussia, in the midst of States convulsed by revolution, would have accomplished great things. And, indeed, Frederick William II. in his reign of 11 years (1786—1797) did make acquisitions of territory. Yet few reigns have been more inglorious. The principal incidents are the Treaty of Reichenbach, the interference in France ending in the separate Peace of Basel, the second Partition of Poland in 1793, the third Partition of Poland in 1795. To Prussia her participation in these two partitions of Poland was perhaps not the most disgraceful part of her policy during this period. It had, indeed, most disgraceful circumstances ; for instance, a few months before the Partition Treaty signed at St Petersburg, Jan. 23rd, 1793, Prussia had in another treaty solemnly guaranteed the integrity of the Polish territory!   Nor is it possible to overstate the demoralising effect of these partitions upon European politics.   The enormous series of political immoralities which make up the foreign policy of revolutionary France and of Napoleon seem directly traceable to them, and I confess I think the true mischief-maker, the true revolutionist in the system of Europe, was Frederick himself. But when once the anarchy of Poland had been allowed—very much by Frederick's vigilance in preventing reform— to become intolerable, still more when the policy of partition had once been adopted, there is something surely to be said in excuse for the Government which did but inherit it. After the first partition had opened the flood-gates of lawless aggression, Prussia might argue with some plausibility that she herself and Austria were compelled, if they would not see Russia swallow up all and push her frontier into the very heart of Germany, to share the spoils with her. The misfortune was, that this lower international morality could not be localised and treated as belonging to a special and exceptional case, but was caught up by France, enraged to see other Powers enriched while she went empty away, and became for a whole age the international morality of Europe.

But whatever judgment we pass upon these partitions it was not in his Polish policy that the King showed himself degenerate. Frederick the Great would have treated Poland, I imagine, much as his nephew did, only that he would have shown himself more anxious to justify his usurpation by giving the blessing of good government to the annexed territory. It was by his submission to Austria at Reichenbach, and the series of mistakes to which that led, the unsuccessful intervention in France, the violation of the Treaty of The Hague, and finally the abandonment of the Empire by the Treaty of Basel, that Frederick William II. discredited Prussia in the eyes of Europe, forfeited a commanding position and prepared disaster for his successor.

Between his accession and 1790 this king had an opportunity, had he been an efficient statesman and soldier, of raising Prussia much higher than the point at which Frederick had left it. Frederick had depended almost entirely on his military force. This was undiminished, and in addition his successor had in almost every surrounding country the support of one of those revolutionary parties which had now sprung up. To all this was added in his first years the alliance of England. He had in Herzberg a minister trained under Frederick, and fully capable of understanding the situation. With a little energy and a free use of the Prussian army it is evident that he might have dictated terms to both Austria and Russia, for he could rouse both Flanders and Hungary against Austria, and Poland against Russia. It was by taking advantage of only some of these favourable circumstances that France, a few years later, annexed Belgium, brought Holland to complete subservience, and afterwards humbled Austria and broke up the Empire. Frederick William did enter upon this career. His intervention in Holland made that Power almost as dependent on him as it was afterwards on France; but here he stopped. After rousing the hopes of the disaffected in Poland, in Flanders, and also in Liège, which had risen against its Bishop, after entering upon a great plan, framed by Herzberg, which would have rescued Turkey from the assault which had been made upon her by Russia and Austria, and secured as an equivalent for Prussia the most desirable acquisition of Danzig and Thorn, then Polish enclaves in Prussia, after putting his formidable army in motion, he suddenly yielded everything to Leopold at Reichenbach. It is true he met with difficulties—Poland was refractory—England and Holland opposed the plan; but such difficulties would scarcely have arrested his uncle or even an inferior general at the head of such an army. The year 1790 and the Treaty of Reichenbach mark the abandonment of the strong and clear policy of Frederick. Then began the period when the State, its operations being now on a larger scale than before, is first guided with an irresolute and capricious energy, and then allowed to sink into a dangerous inaction.

No doubt Frederick William's position was advantageous only on condition that he had not only a strong will, but also either practical talent in himself or the power of finding it in others. The Treaty of Reichenbach was unsatisfactory, but had he taken the bolder course and commenced a campaign, he might have failed still more disastrously through military mismanagement. This was what happened to him in the next crisis of his reign. He interfered in France, and had he found there, which was probably what he expected from the divided state of the country, as little resistance as he had found in Holland, had he succeeded in restoring Louis XVI. as he had restored the Stadtholder, he would no doubt have raised Prussia to a commanding eminence in Europe. But here the power of action failed him as resolution had failed him before. He found in Brunswick a general who had the same indistinctness of conception as himself, the Polish troubles began, and he gradually found himself involved in undertakings to which the resources of Prussia were utterly unequal. Then the Diet treated him shabbily, and in his dealings with the Sea Powers the influence of Haugwitz, a statesman whose fate, or rather whose unfortunate character it was to introduce confusion into every affair with which he was concerned, is perceived for the first time. Financially embarrassed, damaged in reputation, and without a friend among the Great Powers, unless it were France, Prussia resigns herself in 1795 to a policy of neutrality which brought her in the end no better fortune than her previous policy of intervention.

How much mischief had been done to Prussia by the unsteady government of Frederick William II. was, I think, very little suspected at the time. When he died the reputation of Prussia was indeed much sunk from its old level, but no ruinous calamity had happened, and the State had made great acquisitions of territory. Some time passed before it could be understood that Prussia had entered upon a new age under the guidance of incompetent statesmen. A new system of foreign relations, a new military system, new principles of finance, were wanted, and this king's reign had consumed eleven irrevocable years in which, while the fund both of reputation and of money was exhausted, none of these wants was supplied, and the high departments of State were filled with officials entirely incompetent to supply them. The system of hereditary personal government had broken down, as sooner or later it must, and Prussia paid dearly for having entrusted her destinies at such a critical moment to a man without character or clearness of understanding.

Meanwhile in domestic affairs as well as foreign the soul was departed from Prussian policy. Through two long reigns, that is for seventy-three years, and indeed with only a short break for a hundred and forty-six years, the government of Prussia had been conducted with an intense earnestness, and with the clearest insight into the wants of the country. Except in the history of the House of Orange, no parallel can be found to the series of monarchs who ruled in Prussia between 1640 and 1786. So much the more fatal was the sudden interruption of this apostolical succession, occurring at a most critical moment. 'The Round Table was dissolved,' when a common man without vocation, without principles of action, sat in the seat of the great Elector, of Frederick William, and of Frederick the Great. Frederick had almost atoned for his ambition by the zeal with which he had laboured in Silesia and West Prussia for the welfare of his new subjects. But after the second and third partitions of Poland all the scandals were witnessed that ordinarily accompany lawless spoliation. The confiscated land was prodigally squandered among unworthy favourites of the king, and the population, though accustomed to the horrors of Polish anarchy, complained loudly of the treatment they met with at the hands of their Prussian governors. Corruption was infecting the military system, though indeed little noticed as yet—for Gentz, in the letter to Frederick William III., published on his accession in 1797, finds nothing to criticize in the army. Frederick the Great himself before his death had been aware of the danger, and the campaign of Jena in the end revealed it to every one. At the same time the example of the court was peculiarly dangerous to public morals. Frederick himself had helped to infect his people with French manners, and had unsettled their religious belief, but the vigour of his character and sternness of his discipline ensured a kind of survival at least of public virtue. His successor set an example of unbridled profligacy in which all discipline was lost, and he coupled with this a rigid persecuting orthodoxy. The people who had learnt already to associate

energy and heroism with irreligion, were now taught
to associate religion with vice, misgovernment and
disgrace. The king's religious views partook of the
bewilderment which marked his somewhat gross
character. He was a gaping spiritualist, and surrounded himself with the superstitious, and particularly with those who were superstitious and
vicious at the same time. Wild stories are told
of his Court, and the reign seems to answer in
Prussian history to that of Charles II. in English
or Louis XV. in French. Yet the corruption is of
a different type. The king is no cynic, but a senti-
mentalist; his vices arise from ungovernable passion
and not from a cold pursuit of pleasure, and they
seem rather connected with his religiousness than at
war with it. Such antinomian orgies must have
been peculiarly repugnant to Stein, and I notice that
when he writes of the encouragement of religious
principles among the people, he loves to use the
compound adjective 'religious-moral' (religiös-sitt-
lich), as though to guard himself against being supposed to recommend the religion of Frederick
William II.

In Prussia, of all countries, it might be said,
'Regis ad exemplum totus componitur orbis.' Religious hypocrisy was soon understood to be the best
means of winning the king's favour, and it appeared
on a grand scale. Honest men began to conceive
a disgust for the public service. Thus, for example,
writes in 1793 one who was afterwards among the
most distinguished of Prussian officials, and has
been already mentioned as Stein's successor in his
provincial government, Ludwig v. Vincke: 'It must

be my most earnest endeavour to acquire information of every kind to make me thoroughly competent
for a public post.   It will be my greatest concern for
four years more to study political economy and
jurisprudence in their fullest extent; if then I feel
myself thoroughly competent to serve my country in
a public post, and yet cannot reach this object of all
my exertions without first becoming a Rosicrucian,
Spiritualist, or Adept, without first becoming a hypo-
crite, a sneak, an intriguer, and a flatterer, in a word,
without deviating from the plain path of honesty,
which I have marked out for myself ... then indeed
it would be impossible for me to remain a moment
longer in such a service.'

No sign of the decline of Prussia was more distinctly visible than the degeneracy of public men.
Frederick had left behind him an energetic foreign
Minister in Herzberg, a model of unselfish devotion
in Heinitz, and lower down in the civil service
Stein and in the military service Gneisenau.   But
under Frederick William II. Herzberg had to give
place to Haugwitz, a man who may be called the
Ruin of Prussia, in whom the confused ineffective-
ness and corrupt religiousness of his master were
reflected.   A Brunswick by the same sort of elective
affinity came to command the army: a Wöllner
brought in Government to the support of orthodoxy,
and caused a royal rescript to be sent to Kant on the
publication of his *Religion within the Limits of Pure
Reason*, threatening him with 'Our highest displeasure'
if he should repeat the offence ; Bischoffswerder and
Lombard were politicians of the same order, and
the elder Stein was at this time more prominent than

the younger. Hardenberg, though not to the taste of the higher class of politicians who came to the front with Stein in 1807, and by no means a model of private virtue, yet deserves to be excepted as superior to the other politicians of the age of Frederick William II.

And yet in spite of this general decay the King in his public character need not be charged with anything more inexcusable than being totally inadequate to a task for which very few men would have been qualified. Stein who was fond of drawing characters, and draws them generally with the most unsparing severity, has been very lenient in his description of this king. He says that he 'combined a lively feeling of his dignity with a strong memory enriched by the study of history, a just understanding and a noble benevolent character; but these good qualities were clouded by sensuality, which gave his mistresses ascendancy over him, by a love of the marvellous and of spiritualism, which caused commonplace designing men to gain influence over his mind, and by want of perseverance. Yet a great part of the errors of his reign ought to be ascribed to the nation, which cringed at once without reserve or decency before his favourites Bischoffswerder and Wöllner, and before his mistresses, who in the sequel frustrated his better political designs and abused his generosity in a dishonourable manner in the matter of the granting away of the Polish lands.' Not a word here of his fatal foreign policy. But to all foreign questions, it seems to me, Stein, wrapped up in the business of his office, was for a long time inattentive. That a retired thinker like Kant should pronounce the King 'a brave, honest, humane and—putting aside certain peculiarities of temperament—a thoroughly excellent prince,' is perhaps less surprising. Yet that he was full of good impulses seems to be true, and also that he did not fail in diligence; what he wanted was clearness and consistency.

Frederick William III, though he too committed great errors for which he was mercilessly punished, assuredly deserves our esteem and, if ever sovereign did, our pity. He inherited a declining government, he was surrounded from the outset with pernicious advisers, he had been ill-educated and had grown up with a bad example before him; it was hardly to be expected in these circumstances that he should see that anything required reform. But he had remained uncorrupted; whatever in the former government had been repugnant to good sense and good feeling he discerned as clearly as if he had not grown up in the midst of it. Everything scandalous disappeared at once; the reign of the Countess Lichtenau of course was over; and by the side of an honest, though homely and taciturn, young king, appeared a young queen, fascinating and virtuous, the idol of the nation. The ecclesiastical policy of Wöllner was soon abandoned; his Edict of Religion, which had aimed at disciplining the clergy by methods better suited to the army, but had declared at the same time that 'out of the king's genuine regard for freedom of conscience' even those of the clergy who were notoriously infected with the errors condemned, i.e. Socinianism, Deism, &c., should be allowed to retain their preferments

provided their public teaching were rigidly ortho-
dox; this Edict in which the Government seemed
to advertise for hypocrisy was now referred to
with cold disapproval in an Order of Cabinet, in
which the times when there was no Edict of Religion were spoken of as 'times when there was certainly more religion and less hypocrisy than now.'
In about a year Wöllner himself had to retire. So
far the new King's plain good sense carried him.
But though so much was improved, no one could
for a moment imagine that Prussia had got back her
great race of kings. He had even less that was
great about him than his predecessor. Frederick
William II. had had a high heart, an ardent imagination, much knowledge, and extraordinary physical
vigour. In his chivalrous championship of Germany, he is thought to have aspired to revive the
legendary fame of Arminius. Frederick William III.
is at the same time the most respectable and the
most ordinary man that has reigned over Prussia.
He betrays throughout his reign a lowly estimate
of himself, an unassuming modesty, which if it be
a virtue is of all virtues the least kingly, and which
at the same time decided his whole policy. We
have seen how necessity and financial exhaustion
had forced Prussia in 1795 to retire from the
European quarrel. The neutrality which his father
had submitted to because he could not avoid it was
congenial to the new King's character. It suited
at once his benevolence and his distrust of his
own abilities. He raised it into a principle, and
may be said to have based his foreign policy on the
maxim that Prussia was not a great Power. In

shunning the mistake of attempting to play too great a part in Europe he ran into the other extreme, and seemed to wish to be a simple Elector of Brandenburg again, as in the days before the mighty Prussian army was created. What came of this rare political meekness, for which not the advice of any Minister but the King's own personal disposition is responsible, we shall see.

The same diffidence is traceable in that reluctance to take any important decision which we have already noted to be a characteristic of his reign. And indeed a less modest man might have felt oppressed by the burden of responsibility which a King of Prussia had to bear since the interests of the State had grown so large and the times so dangerous. But was his diffidence in itself reasonable or morbid? Were his abilities as humble as he himself supposed? The sequel will help us to decide. It may be enough here to remark that at least he showed little discernment in the choice of his advisers. He did not find out the demerits of Haugwitz. He entrusted Brunswick with the management of another campaign. Stein, as we shall see, was forced upon him. He had indeed been trained in a bad school to read character; he had grown accustomed to his father's officials; perhaps their mediocrity consoled him for his own; at least we seem to see him affected with real terror at the approach of Stein. When in the latter part of his reign and of Stein's life we find him gathering round him a new group of narrow-minded intriguers and repelling those to whom he had owed most, such as Stein himself and W. v. Humboldt, we ought to remember in his excuse to the society of what counsellors the circumstances of his youth had accustomed him.

The following account of this king's education deserves to be inserted here, as he will accompany us through the whole of this book, and as it is written by Stein.

The beginning of his education was entrusted to one named Behnisch, a hypochondriacal dreamer tortured with misgivings about the sin against the Holy Ghost and with apparitions. Not till his sixteenth year did the Prince get rational teachers; meanwhile he was left to emptiness, shyness, want of the habit of work. Count Karl v. Brühl and Major v. Schack had the charge of his adolescence. The first was honourable, honest, benevolent, and amiable; the outside, the social talents and accomplishments of a man of the world, he possessed in the most favourable degree; the last was a sensible officer of infantry, who had been trained in the Establishment for Cadets, and through garrison life had grown punctilious, petty, careful. Stronger men with higher views would have developed, exalted, strengthened and inspired the young Prince's sound understanding and moderate disposition. When he reached manhood, Major-General v. Köckeritz was assigned to him as Aide-de-Camp. He became his inseparable associate, and soon his friend and confidant. He had passed his whole life in the petty service of the Potsdam garrison, where the suppression of individuality, devotion and monkish obedience were inculcated with the utmost rigour. Here his narrow understanding had been formed into a representative of commonness and subordination; capable only of the shallowest views, he desired nothing but repose and peace without and harmony within, that he might be able to enjoy his cards and his pipe without disturbance. How could such an automaton have any sense of national honour and independence, or conceive that in the crisis of our age these blessings could only be preserved by struggle and effort, and that circumstances presented themselves in which it was a duty to exhort to such a struggle at the sacrifice of comfort and interruption of the ordinary course of one's vegetation? In the sequel the king learned to know the man, and withdrew his confidence from him, but was too goodnatured to dismiss him; he allowed him to be present at the ordinary Conferences; here he heard a great deal which he imparted to those who were ready to make use of his communicativeness, and made himself the instrument in tittle-tattle which did public mischief.

And now the catastrophe approaches. Under this well-intentioned and respectable king, Prussia looks on quietly while the Empire with which she is connected is transformed, invaded, and finally brought to an end by a foreign conqueror, and almost immediately afterwards being forced into war without an effective ally, sees that army, to maintain which so many kings had wielded despotic power, and so many generations of Prussians had submitted to intolerable burdens, that army which had been 80,000 when the population was less than two millions and a half, and 200,000 when the population was 6,000,000, and now that the population, greatly augmented by acquisitions of territory, had grown to 9,000,000, was 250,000, collapse with greater suddenness, and bring the country after it with more instantaneous downfall, than the old-fashioned armies of old-fashioned States for whom no House of Hohenzollern had ever laboured.

Before we go back to Stein's life, let us endeavour to understand these two great events, the fall of the Empire and that of Prussia.

CHAPTER III.

NAPOLEON AND THE EMPIRE.

THE destruction of the Empire, and the temporary prostration of Prussia, were accomplished by the same military power wielded by the same hand.

Along with the causes above assigned for the unfortunate policy of neutrality now adopted by Prussia, the fact ought to be mentioned that her importance as a military Power in Europe had changed in the last years of Frederick William II. Frederick the Great had left behind him an army which even in numbers was perhaps the first, and in everything else was incomparably the first in Europe. His successor therefore inherited resources, which had they been used with ability would have made him the arbiter of Europe. But this pre-eminence was exceedingly precarious. It resembled that which Holland at one time, and Sweden at another, had enjoyed, but which neither had been able long to retain. It depended not on great means, but on making the very utmost of small ones.

Frederick William II. could make an imposing appearance in France and Poland at once, but his resources dried up so fast that before long he was under the necessity of retiring from the contest. Prussia, it was evident, would have to descend to the second place as soon as one of the richer States of Europe should be led by circumstances to make military exertions at all similar to her own. This was what happened now. Room had been left for the greatness of Frederick by the degenerate indolence of France; France now began to enter upon the same course as Prussia with means incomparably greater.

The army of France, which under Louis XIV. had amounted at one time to 446,000 men, had sunk under Louis XV. and Louis XVI. to a level of numbers, not to mention discipline, actually below that of Prussia. In 1784, for example, it was officially declared to amount to 163,000 men; but critics reduce this total, some to 155,000, some even as low as 140,000. Thus inferior in numbers, and since the disasters of the Seven Years War incomparably inferior in military reputation, France had at this time fairly resigned to Prussia the military leadership in Europe, while politically she sank into a kind of vassalage to Austria. But from 1795, roused by her Revolution, she again takes the lead among the Continental States. She may be said to have done so by adopting the system of Prussia, that is, a purely military government controlling a monstrous army. Only in Prussia the despot came first and created the army, whereas in France the army was first called into existence by the pressure of invasion; and afterwards, as could not fail to be the case, created the despotism. In three years after the accession of Frederick

William III. the transformation was complete. After Brumaire France was precisely what Prussia had been under Frederick, a purely military State ruled despotically by a great soldier, only with the advantage of a population three times as great. In the autumn of 1793, the French army numbered more than a million; in 1794, about 871,000. It fluctuated considerably; at the end of 1795 it did not amount to 450,000. At length, on Sept. 5th, 1798, General Jourdan's law was promulgated which fixed the method of recruitment on the basis of voluntary enlistment supplemented by conscription. For the next two years this method produced an army of nearly 350,000. The new system was now completed by the establishment of the Consulate and the placing of the whole military force in a single skilled hand. The enormous armies afterwards levied by Napoleon are known to every one.

Here then was a military Power far greater than had been witnessed in Europe before. Materially, it was much greater on the whole than had been at the command of Louis XIV.; and it was wielded with as much effectiveness, and in some respects with more skill than that of Frederick. It threatened all weak States with conquest, and all tottering institutions with destruction. Could the effete Empire which had been shaken to its foundations by France in 1740, hope to escape its old enemy thus transformed and reinvigorated ?

The career of Napoleon is the triumph not of mere genius, but of genius controlling infinite resources. France, owing to a number of causes, the jealousy with which she had witnessed the

partition of Poland and the English conquests of
India and Canada, the passion of shame which had
been inspired in her by the disasters and disgraces
of Louis XV.'s reign, threw herself into war as
she had done once before under Louis XIV., but
waged it this time at once with the advantage of
being directed by a military specialist instead of an
Oriental despot, and with the joyous energy of a
nation newly relieved from the old regime, and a
peasantry prosperous for the first time. The power
thus set free shook the globe, and the control of it
gives an unparalleled greatness to the position of
Napoleon.

> 'Condensed blackness and abysmal storm
>   Compacted to one sceptre,
>   Arm the grasp enorm.'

When we see him fighting singly against a coalition of States, we are not to think of him as overmatched. He had for the most part as much force
at his disposal, putting aside the force which resided
in himself, as all his enemies together. So much
force was not needed for the destruction of an
institution so feeble as the Empire, and yet other
means helped him to bring it about.

Besides her immense army and vigorous military
organization, France had two principal means of
conquest. The first has been already mentioned;
it was to take advantage of that schism between
peoples and governments which had already broken
out in so many countries of Europe. The discontent which Joseph's innovations had excited in
Flanders, helped France to get possession of that
country, and what was practically the conquest of

Holland was in appearance simply the rendering of assistance to the Patriots against the Stadtholder. The Revolutionists counted upon this schism existing in all countries alike. They thought they saw it in England, and were encouraged by it to provoke her to war. They even created an opposition in the United States to the government of Washington. But their views were exaggerated. There were many countries of Europe where even in spite of much misgovernment there existed,—could be called into existence,—no revolutionary spirit. Germany belonged to this class of countries. Only in one or two States, such as Mainz, was it possible to create the shadow of a revolution. Over the rest of the country an individual here and there was roused to enthusiasm, and literary men admired and appreciated the Revolution in a speculative way, but the prevalent temper was that of political Philistinism, to use the German word; in other words, a decided unwillingness to interrupt 'the ordinary course of one's vegetation,' on account of any political views whatever. In the destruction of the Empire then, this first great political weapon was little used by the French. In Germany the French rulers for the most part had to make tools of the governments themselves, and use them against each other, for there existed no people which could be used as a tool against the governments. In rare cases, however, when the object was actually to set up a French government in Germany itself, as was done when the kingdom of Westphalia was created, it was found that the Germans could be made, as I may say, mechanical tools though not active dupes. If they had no animosity against their own governments they had a complete indifference to them, and had besides a talent for mechanical official drudgery quite peculiar to themselves. Trouble and expense were saved to France just as much when German officials consented to serve King Jerome simply from soullessness, and did his work for him like so many automata, even when that work consisted in plundering Germans for the benefit of France, just as much as if they had taken the French side from revolutionary enthusiasm.

But on the whole it was another weapon which the French principally used in the destruction of the Empire.

Napoleon in his flying visit to the Congress of Rastatt said to the publicist Martens, 'You are a teacher of public law; that will have to be modernised. Does not public law consist now-a-days simply in the right of the stronger?' This candid utterance seems to show that Napoleon did not regard himself as introducing a new lawlessness into Europe, but as reaping the full benefit of a principle already acknowledged. The partition of Poland had in fact been secretly generalised by all leading politicians on the Continent. It was understood that the old system of Europe was at an end, and the vast consequences of this fact were beginning to be understood. Only under the shadow of that ancient system could the multitude of small and powerless States that were then to be found in Europe subsist. Napoleon had already no doubt settled it in his mind that small republics like Venice and Genoa, the numerous Italian duchies, the States of the Church,

and all but a very few of the three hundred and odd
States, republican, ecclesiastical and hereditary, which
made up the Empire, were henceforth to be regarded
as so much plunder, in the proper distribution of
which statesmanship was now to consist. 'Public
law was to be modernised;' in other words, all the
small States in Europe were to be annexed by the
larger. And in his view the whole mass of booty was
to be thrown into two heaps, of which one, as large
as possible, was to be France's own share, and the
other was to be employed in bribing the other Powers
for French ends. It was not always possible to
overcome the enemy by force, and there were States
which could not be assailed by the revolutionary
method of inflaming the people; but there were few
States which were not surrounded by feeble neighbours, whose territories they were eager to annex,
and prepared to wink at French spoliation if they
might be allowed to share it. And if there is one
principle in which Napoleon's diplomacy may be said
to be summed up it is this principle of so-called
'indemnities.' The student of that age is at first
perplexed by the perpetual recurrence of this word,
and may have some difficulty in understanding it.
Such a student may be assisted by a remark of
Charles Fox, who says somewhere of these indemnities that they are 'in plain terms robbery.' From
the beginning to the end of his career Napoleon's
bargains are regularly made at the expense of third
parties. At Campo Formio he appeases Austria by
handing over to her Venice. At Tilsit he offers
Russia a large share of Turkey. In his negotiations with Fox, England is to have in exchange for

Sicily the Balearic Isles which belonged to Spain, and at another time the Hanse Towns.

Now this principle was specially applicable to Germany, for it was in Germany that the small help- less States most abounded, which was fortunate for France, since it was just in Germany that the revo- lutionary propaganda had no success. Accordingly in the destruction of the Empire it plays fully as great a part as the military successes. When we see at Campo Formio and afterwards at Lunéville, great acquisitions made by France, after great victories won over Germans, we are apt to suppose that the great German Powers lost as much as France gained. But this would be a mistake. In the first place, Prussia was outside of the conflict, and gained by every settlement almost as much as France. Probably the King may have consoled himself for the igno- miny of his policy by reflecting that Prussia in pro- found peace was steadily adding to her territory, and, as it were, making France fight for her. But, what is more startling, neither did Austria, though in both cases clearly the defeated party, lose anything either at Campo Formio or at Lunéville. What France took was not taken from her. At Campo Formio, for the land she ceded in Italy, the population of which was reckoned at 1,200,000, she received new lands with a population of 2,000,000; and if she yielded her possessions in the Netherlands, she obtained in a secret article the promise of French assistance in obtaining the Bishopric of Salzburg, and a piece of Bavaria between the Inn, the Salza, and Tirol. At Lunéville, too, her 'indemnities,' though not equal to those of some other German parties to the treaty, were reckoned a full compensation for her losses. Upon whom, then, did the loss fall, since it was not upon the defeated party? The answer is that it fell upon the helpless small States. The German Church was disendowed to pay for Austrian defeats, as the French Church had been robbed to save France from bankruptcy. And the German Republics, the Free Towns, were robbed with the consent of the great French Republic, which now made no difficulty of sacrificing in Germany the principle of republicanism to that of hereditary despotism.

But what then was precisely the policy of France, since it could not be her interest either to aggrandize Prussia or to save Austria from the consequences of her defeats? She evidently considered it wise to secure, even by an enormous bribe, the inaction of the redoubtable Prussian army; and her own acquisitions, both at Campo Formio and at Lunéville, were such that the power, both of Austria and Prussia, if not absolutely, was yet relatively much diminished. The time came when the growth of France had been such that it was no longer necessary for her to bribe either Austria or Prussia, and that was the time for both those Powers to suffer defeats which were also crushing disasters. After sacrificing their helpless fellow-States of the Empire, they found themselves attacked in their turn. Prussia after Jena, Austria after Austerlitz, and again after Wagram, were made to disgorge all and more than all their ill-gotten plunder, and the calculation of France succeeded in the end, for to her in the end almost all the booty fell. But it was not only by her more rapid growth in territory and resources that France was thus able

to overwhelm the very Powers she had herself helped
to pamper. Two other circumstances greatly favoured
her plans. The first was the growth in Germany
of a third Power dependent on her and therefore
devoted to her. For indeed her bribes were calculated to have different effects upon different German
Powers according to their magnitude. Great Powers
like Prussia and Austria had at times to be bribed
for the pressing purpose of securing their acquies-
cence in some settlement favourable to France, but
to enrich them only made them more dangerous and
more haughty. On the other hand, small Powers
like Baden and Würtemberg were turned into devoted adherents by the 'indemnities' France procured for them. They could never become dangerous
to France, and France alone could guarantee their
acquisitions and maintain them in the new position of
importance she had given to them.

Thus between the great Powers of Germany,
who were enriched only until it should be convenient
to overthrow them, and the small States who formed
the fund of bribery, there were a number of middle
States who were attached to France in a condition
of clientship. At the head of these were the States
which were in course of time raised by Napoleon
into kingdoms, Bavaria and Würtemberg, and after
these Baden, to which at a later time Saxony was
added, and many smaller States, among which Nassau,
Stein's aggressive neighbour, was conspicuous. They
were a wedge driven into Germany on the south-
west, while Saxony brought France into connexion
with Slavonic Europe and with the vulnerable point
of the three great Eastern Powers, Poland.

The other circumstance which made the destruction of the Empire easier was that the settlements of Campo Formio and Lunéville and the transformation of Germany effected in the Principal Resolution of the Imperial Deputation (1803) deprived the Austrian State, though they did not diminish but rather consolidated its power, of the peculiar influence it had hitherto exerted over the rest of Germany. Its local position with respect to Germany was now changed. We are accustomed to think of Austria as the State of the south-east of Germany, and in 1866 we saw her severed by a single stroke from the Germanic body and sent into a kind of eastern exile. But before the transformation above mentioned, the connexion of Austria with Germany was far more intricate and far less easily dissoluble. She had possessions in the extreme west as well as in the extreme east; instead of leaning on one side of Germany she laid her arms round it. She was the shield of Germany against France through her possessions in the Netherlands and through her Suabian territories (Hither Austria). The Government was itself dissatisfied with the want of connexion in the different parts of the State, and seems to have been well content to part with the Netherlands. Austria did no doubt bring out of the struggle with France a much more compact territory, but at the same time she lost the position which gave her a natural authority and preeminence in the affairs of the Empire.

By the same change her majority of votes in the Diet was lost. This will be seen if we pass in review the changes made in its three Chambers. The highest Chamber or Council of Electors had con-

sisted of eight members. To the original and well-
known seven had been added Bavaria at the time
of the Thirty Years War, and Hannover late in the
17th century. This gives nine votes, but in 1777
by the merging of the Houses of the Palatinate and
Bavaria one had been lost again. Of these eight
votes, three were ecclesiastical, and the presidency
belonged to an ecclesiastical elector, Kurmainz.

The change made in 1803 in this Chamber was
as follows. Of the ecclesiastical Electors, only Kurmainz remained. In place of the others came Baden,
Würtemberg, Hessen-Cassel and Salzburg. Thus
the whole number of votes was now ten.

The Second Chamber or Council of Princes had
consisted of 100 votes, partly single, partly collective.
Of the single votes 34 had been spiritual and 60
temporal, of the collective two spiritual and four
temporal.

By the loss of the left bank of the Rhine the
number of votes was now reduced to 82, of which 26
were spiritual and 56 temporal.

The Chamber of Imperial Towns now disappeared, only six Imperial Towns being preserved.

Upon this transformed Diet the following observations are to be made. (1) The spiritual element
has practically disappeared; the Empire has been
secularised. This does not appear from the above
brief statement, in which the respectable number of
26 votes in the College of Princes is called spiritual,
until we add that the possessors of these votes were
not really spiritual princes but, for the most part, the
temporal princes who had entered into possession
of the secularised bishoprics. Only three spiritual

votes, properly so called, were left. (2) The majority
has passed from the Catholic side to the Protestant.
It is calculated that in the old Diet the Catholic
votes had been 55 and 57 (according to the alternation
of the Foundation of Osnabrück and of the collective
vote of the Westphalian Imperial Counts), and the
Protestant 45 and 43, but, in the new, 52 or 53
Protestant votes to 30 or 29 Catholic.

Thus was the Empire both secularised and
protestantised in 1803. And this change undermined the preeminence of Austria, which had depended on the steady Catholic majority in the Diet
and on the fidelity of the spiritual vote.

The institution called the Empire had long lost
the power of political action. All its organs, the
legislative at Regensburg, the judiciary at Wetzlar,
the executive at Vienna, were alike paralysed. But
it still subsisted as a kind of mould in which all the
political thinking of German politicians took shape,
and in this character had still a considerable influence
of the restraining or prohibitive kind. It had formed
a certain political morality which bound the different
German States to each other. Powerless as it
seemed, the Empire had mainly prevented Prussia
and Austria from swallowing up the multitude of
helpless principalities and bishoprics with which
they were surrounded. But now that 'public law
was modernised' and that under the influence of
France the universal scramble had actually begun,
it might be fairly said that the Empire without any
act of abolition had ceased to exist. When Napoleon's envoy on August 1st, 1806, announced to the
Diet that his master did not any longer recognize

14—2

the Empire, its best friend—contemplating the transformation it had undergone—might have silently
acknowledged to himself, ' Neither do I.' But with
the imperturbable conservatism which then characterised Germans they might long have gone on making
believe that it still existed, had it suited Napoleon's
purpose to permit them. It was he who brought to
an end an institution which may be said in some
sense, as Mr Bryce asserts, to have lasted for 1858
years, and to have been brought into existence by
Cæsar's victory of Pharsalia.

Napoleon accomplished several vast changes in
the world, but they were commonly changes which
he did not intend. It was so in this instance. To
destroy the Empire was the very last thing he wished.
He hoped to live in history as the new Charlemagne
who had restored it and given it a new lease of life.
If he proved to have been its destroyer, this was
because he suppressed the old form of it, and the
new form under which he revived it proved short-
lived.

The mere disappearance from the world of an
institution which, however venerable, had long outlived itself, would not be very important. But it
is most memorable in German history, if the Fall of
the Empire be understood to mean not merely the
dissolution of the Diet at Regensburg but the dis-
endowment of the German Church, the secularisation
of Government, and the consolidation of the country
from an intricate medley of small and heterogeneous
states into a comparatively simple group of states
moderately large and resembling each other. It is
made more memorable still by the fact that the idea

of German unity outlived the change. Symbolised now by nothing but the infamous and contemptible Confederation of the Rhine, German unity was nevertheless not forgotten. Particularism had always been too strong for it, and seemed now to have extinguished it completely. Germany seemed partitioned as effectually as Poland; there remained indeed German governments, but that all those who spoke the German language, or the bulk of them, should be united under one government, seemed now to have become impossible. Since this apparently impossible problem has actually been solved, and so great a political Power created in the act, the fall of the old abortive Union has become far more interesting than it seemed at the time, as part of the process by which the new Union was evolved.

Mr Bryce has put before us the Fall of the Empire in its relation to the past by describing at length what the Institution was that fell. It should be considered also in reference to its consequences, to that which has taken the place of the fallen Empire. And as I have said, the student of history should understand by it not the mere dissolution of the Diet and abdication of the Emperor, but a complex event extending over several years. Considered in this way the Revolution of Germany consists of four distinct occurrences—

(1) The Principal Resolution of the Imperial Deputation of 1803. The whole German Revolution was implicitly contained in this. It secularised the Empire and withdrew it from the influence of Austria, and it inaugurated the absorption of the small States by the large.

(2) The War of the Third Coalition, Battle of Austerlitz, and Peace of Pressburg. These occurrences advanced the German Revolution by a step, because Bavaria, Würtemberg, and Baden fought in this war on the side of Napoleon against Austria, and thus gave the clearest evidence of the practical non-existence of German unity.

(3) Creation of the Confederation of the Rhine, July 12, 1806. By this act the French Empire took the place of the German Empire, and France assumed the same position with respect to the middle States of Germany that Austria had hitherto held. To induce the middle States to consent to this final treason it was necessary once more to have recourse to the fund of bribery. The ecclesiastical and republican States had been spent in 1803. There remained the small Principalities. These had been passed over in 1803 for want of a pretext for spoiling them, but 'public law was now modernised' so far that pretexts could be dispensed with. They were now handed over to the Princes who formed the Confederation of the Rhine by a great act of mediatisation. The original members of the Confederation were, from the Electoral Chamber, Bavaria, Würtemberg, Baden, Mainz, *i.e.* four votes out of ten ; from the Chamber of Princes, Hessen-Darmstadt, Cleve and Berg, Nassau-Usingen and Nassau-Weilburg, Hohenzollern-Sigmaringen and Hohenzollern-Hechingen, Salm-Salm and Salm-Kyrburg, Isenburg-Birstein, Aremberg, Lichtenstein, v. der Leyen. But this was only a nucleus ; in the end almost all the German States except the two great ones entered the Confederation.

This act constitutes the conquest of Germany by Napoleon, but so far it was only temporary and was rescinded in 1813. What was permanent in it and makes it a stage in the German Revolution was the completion of the process by which the small states were absorbed, and the elevation of the middle states of the south-west into independent states of such magnitude as to form a counterweight in Germany to Prussia and Austria, and a most formidable barrier against all future schemes of German unity.

(4) On August 6th, 1806, the German Revolution receives its formal completion by the abdication of the Emperor Francis II.

The modern history of Germany starts from these four occurrences in the same way as the modern history of France starts from the meeting of the States General in 1789, the Constitution of 1791 and the fall of that Constitution and of the Monarchy in 1792. Before this German Revolution was fully completed there had begun a new period in the aggressions of France. Her army and military government had enabled her, as has been shown, to bring to an end the old system of Europe and particularly of Germany. But hitherto, though constantly at war with the other great Powers, she had yet, as we have seen, effected this great change in concert with them, and in such a way that both Prussia and Austria had gained by it as well as herself. The campaign of Austerlitz marks the moment at which she threw aside this temporizing policy. The area from which her armies were drawn now included, besides France proper, the whole left bank of the Rhine with Belgium and Holland, Switzerland, Piedmont, much of

Lombardy, and the south-western States of Germany itself. It was indeed absurd to suppose that such a force could be successfully resisted by a coalition from which Prussia stood wholly aloof, and in which England only furnished subsidies. Henceforth the French Empire stands in Germany face to face with the two great Powers, Prussia and Austria, and with no desire or interest but the subjugation of both. Napoleon's contemptuous violation of Prussia's neutrality during the campaign of Austerlitz showed that he clearly comprehended his new situation.

The Empire fell on August 6th; and on Oct. 14th, or a little more than two months after, was fought the battle of Jena. If Napoleon could succeed in isolating Prussia, and in engaging her alone, it was evident from a mere comparison of force that he must crush her, and he did succeed. The defeat of Prussia was not in itself surprising; it was in fact inevitable. What at the time seemed amazing was that this meeting of two giants, the army of Napoleon and the army of Frederick, instead of leading to a more obstinate contest than had yet been witnessed, resulted in the most sudden and complete collapse on the side of Prussia. The army which had been the wonder of the world succumbed ignominiously and may be said to have carried the State with it in its fall. We ought to find, when we examine the legislation of Stein and of his colleague Scharnhorst, the explanation of the disaster that made such legislation necessary. In the history of an age which witnessed the downfall of so many states in succession, this particular catastrophe has a peculiar interest. That systems so manifestly rotten as that of Spain, so manifestly superannuated as that of the Empire, so manifestly unwieldy and insufficient as that of Austria, should fall or suffer disaster was not surprising, but it might be thought that Prussia of all states had the least reason to expect to share their fate. She at least had been careful to set her house in order. During two long reigns her Government had set to all Europe an example of intelligent activity. It had been so alive to the peculiar needs of the country that it had devised new and strange institutions to supply them. If it seemed that Napoleon had received an unlimited commission to clear the world of the ruins of an obsolete system, Prussia might have boasted, even more than England, that he could have nothing to say to her. In her organisation almost everything was new and modern, and similar to the system of Napoleon himself. And she might well have thought that if on any side she was safe it was on the military, for to the perfection of her military system everything else had been postponed, and in the Seven Years War it had borne the rudest tests. Could it be that barely twenty years of slackness on the part of Government had deprived her of all these advantages? Thus it proved, and Napoleon was allowed, before he reached his zenith, to destroy something else beside feudalism, the newest product of the political genius of the eighteenth century, the system of Frederick the Great.

CHAPTER IV.

NEUTRALITY OF PRUSSIA.

As Stein is more nearly interested in the fall of Prussia than even in the fall of Germany, it will be necessary before we return to his personal history to mark in the summary way adopted in these chapters the series of mistakes and misfortunes by which Prussia was forced in 1806 to engage Napoleon at such disadvantage and with such calamitous results.

I have marked the Treaty of Reichenbach, concluded in 1790, as the first stage of Prussia's decline. It was then that her foreign policy lost its independent character, for by that treaty the power of Prussia was placed, in a manner, at the service of Austria. The Treaty of Basel, concluded with France in 1795, marks as clearly the commencement of the second stage. It closed abruptly, no doubt, the period of subservience to Austria, but not in such a way as to restore to Prussia her independent influence on the politics of Europe, rather so as to deprive her of all influence upon them, and to convert her from a tool of Austria into a cipher. Prussia now retired behind her line of demarcation, preserving her territories on the right bank of the Rhine, but abandoning the whole left bank, nominally indeed only to the provisional occupation of the French, but really to their definitive possession. Henceforth up to 1806, though the course of affairs in Europe becomes more and more unprecedented and portentous, Prussia declines to interfere. The policy of the Treaty of Basel was that which Frederick William III. inherited when he came to the throne two years after it had been concluded, and he adhered to it with unwavering tenacity and apparently with stronger conviction than any of his ministers. But it is to be observed that a policy of non-intervention after 1801, and even after 1797, had a very different meaning and effect from the same policy at the time when the Treaty of Basel was concluded. For at that time the aggrandisement of France could hardly yet be considered very formidable. She had indeed annexed the Austrian Netherlands, reduced Holland to subserviency, and was in military occupation of the Left Bank. This was an expansion that would have appalled Marlborough, but then what the French constantly urged was really worthy of consideration, namely, that all the other great Powers were in a similar course of enlargement—Russia, Austria, and Prussia by the absorption of Poland, while England had become a world-empire. Frederick William II. when he signed the Treaty of Basel was not obliged to consider himself as signing the abolition of the balance of power and of the old system of Europe. But in the next two years the aspect of affairs altered. The Peace of Campo Formio, achieved through the victories of Bonaparte, contained the germs of a European revolution, and particularly of a revolution in the system of Germany. The destruction of the so-called Holy Roman Empire was involved in the principle then first adopted, of giving indemnities at the expense of the spiritual and republican Estates to the sovereigns who lost territory by the cession of the Left Bank to France. From the very beginning therefore it may be said that Frederick William III. in adopting the policy of the Treaty of Basel surrendered the system of the Empire and the system of Europe, and consented to a territorial revolution in Europe.

This he did at a time when his intervention might have averted such a revolution, at any rate for a considerable time. For in 1797 the cause of old Europe was by no means lost. And in the oscillations of human affairs there came a moment when everything lost seemed on the point of being retrieved. In 1799 Bonaparte with the best army and best generals of France was in Egypt, and had been cut off from France by the destruction of his fleet. At the same moment a new and redoubtable force was added to the other side by the adhesion of Russia. Catharine had regarded the disturbances of Western Europe with the eyes of an Eastern conqueror. She cared nothing for their result and considered only that the longer they lasted the better was the prospect for her designs on Poland and Turkey. But her successor Paul changed the face of affairs by one of those whims of the Czar to which Europe has had to submit many times from before the accession of his father Peter III. He entered into the conflict not only with a great army, but with a great general. If now the old coalition could be revived with the addition of Russia, with Bonaparte absent and Suworow present, all might be recovered that had been lost at Campo Formio, and ancient Europe saved at the last moment. The opportunity was lost. Bonaparte returned, usurped the government of France, and retrieved the loss of Italy by the campaign of Marengo. In the autumn of 1800 the decisive victory of Hohenlinden was won by Moreau, and at the opening of the new century, on the 9th of February, 1801, the Treaty of Lunéville was signed.

At Lunéville old Europe passed away and the French ascendancy, against which so many generations of statesmen had contended, was re-established, an ascendancy which might perhaps have been made permanent had it been watched over by more rational statesmanship than Bonaparte's. But how was the opportunity lost, and how was France allowed to recover herself ? Solely by the obstinacy with which Prussia clung to her policy of non-intervention. It is scarcely possible that the Directory should have maintained the contest if in the early part of 1799 Prussia had joined the Coalition. Accordingly we find that at this crisis even the most irresolute and the most blind of the counsellors, upon whose advice the King was accustomed to depend, the Duke of Brunswick and Count Haugwitz, were in favour of demanding from France with threats of war the restoration of the independence of Holland and the evacuation of the territory between the Rhine, the Meuse and the Moselle. But the King fell back upon himself, and outdoing even Haugwitz in resolute irresolution and in the energy of his inaction, overruled the advice of his Cabinet, and witnessed from a secure distance the downfall of Europe and the establishment of the

military monarchy which was to humble his own
pride. Stein felt the importance of the crisis. He
writes, April 28, 1799, ' It is disquieting to see us
halting and in a state of paralysis when we could
restore the tranquillity of Europe upon the old
foundations—the independence of Holland, Switzerland, Italy, *and Mainz*.'

Nevertheless we ought not to suppose that the
King had no case, and that the strong arguments
in favour of intervention were not opposed by any
other arguments of at least apparent weight. It was
true that never had a fairer opportunity presented
itself for checking the advance of France. But this
did not at that moment appear so urgently necessary
as from our knowledge of the sequel we are apt to
suppose. Jealousy of Austria was still, as it had
long been, a much stronger passion of Prussian
politicians than jealousy of France. We have seen
how this animosity had smouldered secretly all
through the first revolutionary war, and how it had
been heated further by the partitions of Poland.
The treaty of Campo Formio and the Congress of
Rastatt had kept it alive up to the moment when
Frederick William took this decision. It was not
between selfish inaction and his duty to Europe that
he hesitated, for the danger to Europe which was
really at hand was not yet generally perceived. To
him the policy of curbing France seemed doubtful
because it would either deprive him of a friend upon
whom he counted to protect him against Austria or
drive France and Austria to renew that formidable
alliance of the past age which had not long been
dissolved. These misgivings concurred in Frede-

rick William's mind with another which lay deeper still, with the prejudice which the experience of the last reign had created against all ambitious foreign policy. The policy of Pillnitz was just then in particularly bad repute. It had been attended with infinite vexations, humiliations, and failures. It had dragged Prussia in the wake of Austria; it had embroiled her both with Austria and with the Sea Powers; it had cost her an effort which had embarrassed her finances, and it had in no respect advanced her interests. Prussia had blessed her good fortune in being rid at Basel, even at some expense of reputation, of all the complications to which intervention had led; and this feeling of relief was still too fresh in 1799 to allow her statesmen keenly to appreciate the advantages which in the changed circumstances intervention might now bring.

But if the King decided at this time against intervention, the question arises what he meant his relations to be on the one side with France and on the other with the Powers of the Coalition. Since he did not mean to oppose France, did he meditate siding with her? The contest going on round him was so gigantic, and he seemed so inextricably involved in it by the situation of his States, that during the six years that followed the breaking out of the second European war in 1799 he could not win any confidence for his professions of neutrality, and was always suspected by both belligerent parties of being secretly in the opposite interest. Was he really on the side of France, and if so, what is to be thought of such a policy?

As a matter of fact, of those who disapproved
the King's policy many did so on the ground that it
did not favour France decidedly enough.   The sur-
viving representative of the age of Frederick, Prince
Henry, took this view.   He urged that the existing
Constitution of Germany must be broken up, and
that this must be done by an alliance between
France, Prussia and the German princes against
Austria.   He made light of the danger to legitimacy
of an alliance with revolution; this danger he said
was only serious to small States, not to great Powers.
We can indeed imagine that if the two great military
nations, if the armies of Napoleon and Frederick had
been heartily united in changing the system and
re-arranging the map of Europe, certainly great
things might have been accomplished.   Prussia must
have guaranteed a Confederation of the Rhine,
that is, must have surrendered a third, and a very
large third, of Germany to France.   But as a compensation France would have had to guarantee to
Prussia a similar leadership in North Germany.
A North-German Confederation must have been
established in which Prussia would have held such
a position that she could in a short time have
created a solid and extensive North-German State,
in which the system of Frederick would have been
introduced and which might have furnished the
means of raising the Prussian army, say, to 350,000
men.   It might be argued that this at least would
be a solid gain for Germany, and that to aim at
more would be chimerical, that the Unity of Germany could not be maintained, and that it was
necessary to give up a large part of it to the

foreigner in order to strengthen and secure the rest. Meanwhile by this course a great danger, or rather *the* great danger that hung over Europe, might be averted.

What was this? If Prussia held aloof from France, or indeed if she did not heartily join her, France would surely gravitate towards the only alliance which the nature of the case suggested to her—an alliance which every statesman of those days must have thought of with anxiety[1], as both likely to prove unavoidable, and at the same time fatal to the civilization of the world. Everything at that moment concurred to bring France and Russia together. Both were launched in the career of unbounded conquest; yet they were so distant from each other, and the direction of their conquests was so different, that their interests could not easily clash. Germany with its feeble organisation, with its States divided by jealousies, lay between the dominions of Napoleon and Paul, or Alexander, just as Poland had lain in her anarchic helplessness between Frederick and Catharine. The partition of Central Europe was the problem put before the two autocrats, and it was one which it was the more easy to solve because if Napoleon was bent upon having almost all Germany he could always compensate the Czar in Poland and in Turkey. Accordingly, from the moment of Napoleon's accession to supreme power in France, that is, from the moment when system was introduced into her

[1] See for instance Gentz 'On the State of Europe before and after the French Revolution,' p. 288 of the English Translation by Herries, 4th Edition, 1803.

foreign policy, a steady gravitation of France and
Russia towards each other sets in. Long before
the Peace of Tilsit was realised, it had been indi-
cated by significant symptoms. The friendship so
suddenly conceived by Paul for Napoleon, the revival of the Armed Neutrality at Napoleon's suggestion, after Paul's murder the way in which
Napoleon and Alexander in concert presided over
the German Revolution of 1803, almost as if they
had been directing a Polish election, Napoleon's
remark made to Haugwitz at Vienna in December,
1805, 'The Russian alliance is perhaps the one which
suits me best'—these were symptoms of what was
to come, and when once the Peace of Tilsit was
concluded, a condition of stable equilibrium seemed
to be reached, and the slavery of Europe to be as
settled and irretrievable as if it had already lasted a
hundred years.

It might have been different if Prussia with her
mighty army, instead of effacing herself, had entered
decidedly, with conviction and energy, into the task
of re-arranging Europe in concert with France. Her
alliance would have served the turn of France
almost as well as Russia's; it was long before
Napoleon would allow himself to despair of obtaining it, and we have evidence on the other hand,
particularly in a memoir drawn up by Lucchesini,
that the politicians of Prussia had not overlooked
either the great prospects such an alliance opened
or the serious danger of exasperating Napoleon by
refusing it.

Frederick William III. was still more incapable
of this revolutionary course than he was of resolving

in favour of the Coalition. It required an audacious disregard of existing and traditionary relations, which was quite foreign to his character, while it was a course which could only prove advantageous to Prussia if pursued in the most unreserved manner. Even within Germany he desired no aggrandisement, and his close personal friendship with the young Czar, which is believed to date from their meeting in June, 1802, made him unwilling to take a course which would probably have embroiled him with Russia. But as he thus ended by joining neither side, are we to suppose that he had no settled scheme of policy? The policy of absolute and immoveable neutrality, though it seemed to the belligerent Powers so strange that they never could believe Prussia to be sincere in professing it, was yet capable of being defended by some plausible arguments, and may perhaps have seriously appeared to Frederick William not only the right course, but a course which it was his special merit to have discerned to be right.

He may have argued that Prussia was a very poor State, and scarcely equal to the burden of its own defence; that it was a mistake for such a State to pretend to a leading part in the politics of Europe; that the bad consequences of such a pretension had appeared plainly in the recent intervention, when she had been obliged by want of resources to withdraw ignominiously from the war she had entered on with so much confidence. He may have remarked that the Prussian army, though so enormously large in proportion to the population, had not been originally created and did not exist for aggressive purposes, but was merely a substitute for the frontier which Prussia had not received from nature; and that this was remarkably shown by the fact that the creator of this army, Frederick William I., though the most military, was at the same time the most pacific of sovereigns. It was even shown in the career of Frederick the Great, who though an ambitious disturber within the German system itself had yet never seemed to aspire to the position of a leading European potentate. He may have supposed that in withdrawing into a purely defensive position he was reviving the genuine policy of Prussia and returning to the original idea of Frederick William I., who after his early experience of the great Northern War seems to have vowed that he would create such an army as should for the future secure the safety of Prussia, even though war might be raging all around her. Such a case had now arisen. War was all around; the giants of Russia, France, England, Austria were hurling rocks at each other. Now was the time for Prussia to use her army, and to use it, not by interfering in the European conflict in which she must be overmatched, but by preventing the neighbouring Powers from fighting over her body and trampling her to death in the melée.

Such perhaps was the King's reasoning. But the policy of combining the modesty of a secondary State with the military resources of a great Power was peculiarly liable to be misunderstood. What the King called a humane desire to save his people from war was construed as pusillanimity, and at the same time neither side seemed able to think of his

neutrality as serious. Thus it was not so much
Prussia's neutrality as what the world was allowed
to suspect behind the neutrality which led to such
disastrous consequences. Neutrality by itself need
not have brought about the isolation in which Prussia
found herself when in 1806 she was driven to war
with Napoleon, and at the same time did not get
the help of England and Austria. Why did those
Powers then hold back? Not because her policy
had been neutral, but because it had been incomprehensible, suspicious. They did not help her because
they had ceased to believe that she had the spirit to
help herself. She had carried her complaisance
towards Napoleon to such a length that she had lost
all credit for self-respect. Her show of resistance
came now too late; it was not believed that she
would really fight.

In the diary of Sir G. Jackson, under date Oct.
25, 1805, we read in an account of a conversation
with Lord Mulgrave: 'Lord Mulgrave then put
many questions to me respecting the character of
the King of Prussia himself....I should observe that
he seemed to have mistaken the hitherto wavering
and timid policy of that monarch for cowardice and
spoke of him as a man deficient in personal bravery.'
An unjust charge, no doubt! but still it may be true
in a certain sense that his policy was dictated in
good part by simple fear. Thus at least writes no
less an authority than Hardenberg, speaking of
Napoleon's outrage on Sir George Rumbold in
1804: 'The King *would* not see how nearly it
concerned him and the Prussian State....I say "*would
not*," for there is no doubt that he fully understood

it all, but he could be inexhaustible in colourable reasons when the question was of maintaining a false position once taken up, and in such cases his better judgment was overpowered by his repugnance to any decided measure. Distrust of his own ability to cope with the formidable Napoleon, a presentiment of the misfortune that fell in the sequel so heavily upon him, were at the bottom of this repugnance.' In other words, not want of personal courage, but a very natural feeling of incapacity to conduct with credit a campaign against Napoleon, was the secret motive of the policy of neutrality.

What first gave the world reason to suspect this was the King's conduct in the matter of the French occupation of Hannover in 1803. There could not be a better opportunity for Prussia. It was just such an act as she might have entreated France to commit in order to give her an occasion of showing the difference between a policy of non-intervention and a policy of mere passiveness. Had she then stepped forward and forbidden Napoleon to set foot within the line of demarcation, her position would have been immediately made intelligible to all Europe. She would have appeared as the potent and resolute defender of North Germany, neutral indeed as between France and Austria or France and England, but respecting herself and ready also to sacrifice something to the interest of her fellow States in North Germany. And there is every reason to believe that she would have given a rough check to the insolence of French diplomacy. It is not likely that Napoleon at that moment would have ventured to defy Prussia. Russia was already grow-

ing decidedly hostile; Austria was insulted even
more than Prussia by the contempt shown to the
Empire in the occupation of Hannover, and war had
just begun with England.   In these circumstances to
provoke Prussia was to call into existence that universal Coalition of Europe against him which he was
able to prevent till 1813, but which crushed him
when it was formed.

   This grand opportunity was lost. Prussia allowed
Napoleon to introduce a French army into the heart
of the Empire, and Haugwitz wrote to the Hannoverian Ompteda, throwing the responsibility this time
also upon the King: ' The King is determined once
for all to show to all Europe in the most open manner
that he will positively have no war *unless he is himself
directly attacked.*'   This does indeed assert in words,
that Prussia had still spirit enough left for a war of
self-defence; but when self-defence is so rigidly interpreted as to exclude the defence of one's nearest
neighbours and of those whose safety is intimately
involved with one's own, it becomes almost a word
without meaning.   Public opinion in Germany itself
was then so demoralised that we are told that the
King's declaration was received with approbation by
such political writers as Archenholz, and nowhere with
marked disapprobation.   But its effect upon foreign
statesmen must have been very different.   It must
have confirmed the suspicion which since 1799, if
not since 1795, they had entertained, that the self-
defence of Prussia was no defence at all, and the
policy of non-intervention was in fact only the want
of a policy.

   In so difficult a path as that which Prussia had

elected to tread, a false step such as this could not be retrieved. From this time till the fatal year 1806 Hannover remains an insurmountable difficulty to the Prussian Government, and the only rational course now left to her was to make quiet preparations for war with France, and to give an eager adhesion to the new Coalition which was formed in the next year. Not only was this necessary to the recovery of her reputation, but it ought, I think, to have seemed absolutely necessary as a measure of self-defence. Up to this time the ascendancy of France had not fixed the attention of Prussia as the peculiar danger of the time. She had feared sometimes Austria, sometimes Russia, sometimes a league of France with Austria. And in calculating the chances of the future she had thought of France as probably a friend, as possibly a powerful protector. There was indeed a short period after the Peace of Lunéville when it seemed possible that France would cease to be an aggressive Power. The accession of Napoleon marked in many respects the termination of the revolutionary age. France had seemed to read a sort of recantation when she became Christian again and established an orderly government, out of which, it might be guessed, a new monarchical dynasty would soon arise. For a moment it was reasonable to hope that she would also sheathe her restless sword. All that could be expected from war she had realised, and Frenchmen may now feel on looking back that the secure ascendancy gained at Lunéville has been lost and lost irretrievably to France through the suicidal attempt to raise it higher still. So long as Napoleon stood at the parting of the roads, and had not yet made the bad choice, the Powers of Europe might leave him alone and Prussia cling to her neutrality. But the period of uncertainty was but a moment. William Pitt soon became convinced that 'Bonaparte would never be anything but a rapacious plunderer;' Russia was gradually alienated; Austria felt herself threatened by the changes she saw making in Italy; and during the year 1804, under the auspices of Pitt, now again at the head of the English Government, the Third Coalition was formed in the hope of averting before it was too late the Universal Monarchy from Europe.

The illustrious historian, v. Ranke, who has lately traced with infinite care and subtlety the course of Prussian policy during this period, is inclined to regard it as controlled by a fatality which no political skill could have withstood. He writes, 'I know not whether we have a right to speak so much as we do of mistakes made, opportunities lost, oversights committed. Over the heads of the parties concerned the result was evolved with a necessity which had something inevitable in it like a fate.' And as he tells the story the King seems no longer blind or glaringly mistaken, and even Haugwitz is brought decently through the campaign of Austerlitz, the Treaty of Schönbrunn and the Treaty of Paris. Undoubtedly we are apt to make individuals too much responsible for the great disasters of history, as if an enormous calamity could not happen without an enormous blunder. Neither the King nor Haugwitz was below the average of mankind in intelligence, and both acted merely as most men would have acted in their circumstances, that is to say, they followed routine and had not insight or energy enough for a new resolution. But we need not surely go further than this in fatalism. The necessity of which v. Ranke speaks is merely that which masters all those who will not use their own eyes or their own wills. When he says that 'it was after all not to be expected that the King, whose policy had its root in the idea of neutrality, should abandon it and give himself up without reserve to the Coalition,' *i. e.* in 1805, I am inclined to answer that during the years 1803 and 1804, when the rest of the world were becoming gradually alive to the danger which threatened Europe, the King ought to have opened his eyes too, and to have abandoned his idea of neutrality. In the occupation of Hannover he had had a warning which had not been given to Russia and Austria. The power of France was now brought close to him in the most alarming manner. His force had been, as it were, cut in two, for a French army and a French government were now planted between his possessions in Brandenburg and those in Westphalia. They had taken the place not of an Austrian or Russian power, which he might have feared almost equally, but of the power of George III., whose predecessor had fought in this very territory as an ally of Frederick the Great against France. After this change had happened we may admit that if the policy of neutrality were still maintained, all the rest up to the catastrophe of 1806 followed by a sort of necessity. But for this very reason we may urge that this policy, always questionable, became from that moment untenable.

In fact, from this time till the campaign of Austerlitz, Prussia is found constantly humbling herself before France. Only once, in the matter of Sir George Rumbold, she finds courage to resist, and wins a small diplomatic victory.

We have now reached the date of Stein's appointment to the Ministry of Trade. The Third Coalition was beginning to be formed while he was taking possession of his new office. We may perhaps obtain some measure of the discredit into which the Prussian Government had now fallen by noting the treatment it receives from both belligerents when the war breaks out in October, 1805. Prussia's position at that moment might have made her the arbitress of Europe. Her army would turn the balance into whichever scale it might be thrown. We might therefore expect to find Napoleon on the one side and Russia and Austria on the other competing for her favour, or at least most anxious not to provoke her hostility. We find just the contrary. We see both sides treating her with a reckless contempt, which shows that nothing was hoped and at the same time nothing was feared from her wooden immobility. Both sides begin by openly violating her neutrality.

On September 19th Russia announced that she intended to march 100,000 men through South Prussia and Silesia. She seems to have believed that Prussia could be roused from her torpor by this kind of friendly violence, and hurried along in the tide of war. No sooner had Russia ventured upon this step, than Napoleon himself—apparently as a mere military measure, the Prussian Government

being disregarded as completely as if it did not exist
—marched a *corps d'armée* on October 3rd across
the Prussian territory of Ansbach. But Frederick
William was not quite a lamb. The one *casus belli*
which he admitted was now realised; Prussia was
now directly insulted. She was roused at last. In
the last days of September she was on the point
of joining France to punish the Russian insult; on
October 14th a violent revulsion has taken place,
and she is already taking steps for joining the
Coalition to punish the insult of Napoleon. The
Russians are allowed a passage, and armies are
assembled on the southern frontier, in Westphalia
and in Franconia. Seldom has Europe witnessed
a more tremendous month than the October of
1805. Three days after the Order of Cabinet was
issued in which the resolve of Prussia was made
known,—a resolve which, had there been energy
either in Prussian statesmen or Prussian generals,
would have been fatal to Napoleon's fortunes,—
occurred the great capitulation of Ulm, striking an
almost mortal blow at the Coalition in the hour
when it seemed triumphant. And this catastrophe
again was only four days old when the battle of
Trafalgar destroyed the fleets of France and Spain,
and with them the whole offensive power of Napoleon's empire against England.

On November 3rd the Treaty of Potsdam was
signed, by which Prussia undertook to mediate, offering Napoleon terms which he could not accept
without descending at once from the imperial position he had hitherto held, and in case the terms were
not accepted within four weeks to join the Coalition

with 180,000 men. The scene in which the Czar and the King of Prussia swore eternal friendship at the tomb of Frederick the Great gave proper solemnity to the great event which seemed to decide the fate of Europe by setting the greatest military Power after France on the side of the enemies of France, and creating at last that fourfold Coalition which hitherto it had been impossible to realise.

Stein, as we have seen, was called upon, as soon as war seemed imminent, to report upon the means of raising the necessary supplies. His report was sent in on October 9th, and has been examined above, but as it recommended measures likely to excite disturbance in the public mind—for example, the introduction of paper money—he sent in another memoir recommending that these measures, the necessity of them and the good intentions of the government in adopting them, should be explained to the public in a pamphlet published by authority. Pertz prints this memoir as containing no doubt the substance of Stein's views, but remarks very justly, in my opinion, that it can hardly have been written by Stein, as it altogether wants the curtness and definiteness which characterise his style. It is indeed an empty and wordy production.

Was then Prussia now really entered upon a new and less inglorious career? Was her neutrality over? Was she won at last to the cause of Europe? It is well known how differently all turned out. The humiliations which followed have been usually attributed to the weakness of Haugwitz, but, as we have seen, v. Ranke believes that the circumstances were beyond his control. If, in his interview with Napoleon at Brünn on November 28th, he said nothing of the bold demands he was commissioned to make, the reason, we are told, was that Prussia's military preparations were not sufficiently advanced. He had been told by the Duke of Brunswick that the breach must be postponed till the middle of December. 'No one is to be blamed; in the circumstances it could not be otherwise; but the whole position had from the outset something ambiguous about it.' But on December 2nd the Russians and Austrians, instead of waiting for the Prussian adhesion, removed all Napoleon's difficulties at once by rushing into the battle of Austerlitz, just as two years later the Russians risked the battle of Friedland without waiting for Austria. On December 6th a truce was signed, the Russians retired from the contest, and on the 7th Haugwitz presented his congratulations to the victor. The Coalition being now dissolved and Napoleon's power so enormously increased, he could not avoid signing the Treaty of Schönbrunn, by which Prussia fell back into her former condition of neutrality, or rather adopted a neutrality which was nearer by several degrees to a position of dependence on France. At a Council of State, held under the presidency of the King, it was decided to ratify this treaty only conditionally, and Haugwitz was once more sent to obtain from Napoleon at Paris the required modifications. Napoleon had required from Prussia some cessions of territory to Bavaria, and as an 'indemnity' he had offered Hannover, or, in other words, a war with England. It had been decided to accept only a provisional occupa-

tion of Hannover until a general Peace. But
Napoleon's consciousness of power had been growing ever since the battle of Austerlitz. Pitt died
just at this juncture; and, in an unhappy moment, it
was resolved at Berlin, for financial reasons, to put
the army on a peace footing. On February 15th
Haugwitz, under the threat of immediate war,
signed a new treaty of unqualified hostility to
England, and in other respects more unfavourable
to Prussia than the Treaty of Schönbrunn, and this
treaty was ratified on March 3rd. The lowest point
of humiliation was now reached. The neutrality of
Prussia was destroyed, and it might seem that
nothing remained to her but to become a servile
accomplice of France. Such then was the end of
Prussia's neutrality. She had always intended to
defend her own honour, but now it appeared that
she could not do this without being prepared to
defend much more. At one crisis she found her
army not ready, and at another she found it reduced
again to a peace footing. On looking back she
might have confessed that she could not afford to
wait to be insulted by such a Power as France now
was, but must be ready when the insult came both
with soldiers and with alliances; in other words, she
might have confessed that her policy of neutrality
had long been inadequate, and that she ought to
have joined the Coalition.

CHAPTER V.

THE CATASTROPHE OF PRUSSIA.

AFTER the treaty of February 15th, as we have said, Prussia appeared condemned to a servile dependence upon France like that of Bavaria and Würtemberg. But she preserved herself from this degradation, though in a strange way. In the months which intervened between the treaty and the outbreak of war with France, the position of Prussia may be described by saying that while hitherto she had refused to take sides either with France or Russia, henceforth she takes sides with both at once. At the time when it had been determined to ratify the Treaty of Schönbrunn with modifications, which it was too hastily assumed that Napoleon would accept, the Duke of Brunswick had been sent to St Petersburg. He had carried assurances that the King held union with Russia to be indispensable both to his own State and to

Europe, and had proposed a method by which the effect of those provisions in the Treaty of Schön-brunn which seemed, or rather which were, inconsistent with such a union might be nullified. Prussia was to make a secret Declaration that her engagements to France would never stand in opposition to Russian interests. The Czar was to reply with an analogous Declaration. While the matter was under deliberation came the news first of Napoleon's rejection of the modifications and then of the treaty of February 15th. The Duke left St Petersburg, but his visit had cleared away much ill-feeling and paved the way to that friendly relation between the two courts which lived on through all vicissitudes to the end of the European war, and was a principal cause of the overthrow of Napoleon. Yet this happened at the very moment when Prussia carried her compliance with France to its extreme point.

We have noticed already the curious condition of the Foreign Department in Prussia. Haugwitz and Hardenberg, though differing greatly in their views, were both at the same time Foreign Minister. This arrangement, which in ordinary times might seem inconvenient, began to be in place when the Government had two conflicting systems of foreign policy at once. Haugwitz now represents the State considered as subservient to France, and therefore opposing Russian interests for example in Turkey, while Hardenberg represents it considered as friendly to Russia and hostile to France. For the purpose of concealment Hardenberg retired to his estate of Tempelberg, while the Russian ambassador

Alopæus received at the same time leave of absence from Berlin and took up his residence in the same neighbourhood. The secret of this negotiation was kept not only from Napoleon, but even to a certain extent from Haugwitz. Hardenberg communicated with the King chiefly through the Queen, and his colleague had no official knowledge, and perhaps no definite knowledge of any kind, of his proceedings. This, as we shall see later, was not the only curious feature in the system of the Prussian Foreign Department at that time.

In this way Prussia still retained her middle position. She was still the arbitress whose ultimate decision would go far to decide the fate of Europe. But it seems that her feelings were no longer, as they had so long been, impartial, for she could not now disguise from herself that the danger from France far outweighed every other danger. Nevertheless it still remained Napoleon's evident interest not to alienate Prussia, and he had much to give which she would have found it difficult to refuse. In the middle of 1806 it was still not improbable that the close of the year would see Prussia united more closely than ever with Napoleon, and perhaps even admitted into his Confederation of the Rhine, or, what was more likely, heading a North German Confederation only one degree less dependent on him.

It turned out otherwise for two reasons; first because Napoleon did not, just at this crisis, bribe Prussia, but inflicted upon her new injuries and slights, and next because when she began to resent his conduct he thought he saw signs that a new coalition was forming against him, which he might crush in the birth. It would be a mistake to attribute his conduct to mere arrogance or to a desire to punish Prussia for her ambiguous bearing in the last campaign. In order to understand it we must bring before our minds the crisis through which Europe was passing.

Another stage seemed to have been accomplished in the transformation of Europe, and a certain if not a long period of repose seemed likely to begin. England and Russia still remained at war with Napoleon, but they could no longer hope to be able, for the present at least, to put any restraint upon his power, their recent attempt to do so having simply ended in the fall of the old Germanic Empire and in the creation of a new one under his Protectorate. The abdication of the German Emperor and the creation of the Confederation of the Rhine could be foreseen at the beginning of this year and actually took place in August. It was therefore to be expected that England and Russia would now make peace with France, and this was the more likely because the Opposition in Europe had lost its great statesman Pitt, and because his place had been taken by the leader of the French party in English politics. Napoleon himself was probably not disinclined to make peace, for his new position in Germany as head of the transformed Germanic Body required to be strengthened and settled; but then the terms of peace must be such as to express the superiority he had acquired, that is, they must be ignominious to England and Russia. His mind then was occupied in the spring

16—2

and summer of 1806 with these two great subjects, negotiation with England and Russia, and organisation of the Confederation of the Rhine. In comparison with these two great affairs it was not unnatural that his relations with Prussia should seem of secondary importance, particularly as he had long understood that in those relations he was 'yoked with a lamb that carried anger as a flint bears fire.'

He may therefore have been but half aware how insupportably affronting and damaging to Prussia were some of the measures which he now took in settling Germany and in negotiating the general peace. First let us observe what a change and what a loss to Prussia was involved in the organisation of the new Confederation. Her position in the Germanic Body and the Diet had for ages been to Prussia the substantial question of external politics. Even Frederick had thought comparatively little of non-German Powers. He lived in the Germanic world, and all his ambition was bound up in maintaining there his position among his co-Estates, and in conducting the warm and sometimes warlike, but still on the whole constitutional, opposition to Austria. This Germanic World had now passed away like a dream. Golden Bull, Imperial Chamber, Aulic Council, the Roman Emperor himself—all was gone. And in the new organisation which had taken its place Prussia played no part at all. She was not, she did not wish to be, a member of the Confederation of the Rhine, and yet this was the only symbol now left of German unity, and Prussia asked herself whether she had ceased altogether to belong to Germany.

Napoleon was not so busy as wholly to overlook the discomfort which these new arrangements caused to his ally.   He even went out of his way to suggest that Prussia should make herself the head of a North German Confederation.   This plan had already been suggested and discussed at Berlin, and was now seriously taken up.   Prussia was to be in this Confederation what Austria had been in the Empire; Saxony and Hessen were to stand next in dignity, and the Hanseatic Cities were to enjoy special privileges; Hildesheim was thought of for the Federal City.   Negotiations were set on foot, and it was determined, independently of all such schemes, to form a close alliance with Saxony and Hessen.

But now it was perceived how much influence Napoleon's arrangements with England and Russia might have both upon the success of such a scheme and upon Prussian interests in general.   In spite of the resolution often expressed by English statesmen to keep English altogether separate from Hannoverian interests, it was impossible to prevent George III.'s right to Hannover from becoming one of the most important questions of the negotiation. Now the possession of Hannover was the one equivalent which Prussia had received for so many sacrifices and compliances ; from its geographical position Hannover was a possession of almost indispensable importance to Prussia, particularly at a moment when she meditated making herself the centre of a North German Confederation.   Yet when Lord Yarmouth, the English negotiator, insisted upon the restoration of George III. to his

Electoral dominions, Talleyrand after a few days delay announced that 'Le Hanovre ne fera pas de difficulté.' It was not exactly intended to rob Prussia, but in the fashion of that age it was proposed to find an 'indemnity' for her to the amount of 400,000 souls somewhere in the neighbourhood of the Prussian States.

In the first days of August there fell upon the Prussian Government in quick succession the news of the establishment of the Confederation of the Rhine, of the abdication of the Emperor, and of Napoleon's intention, which Lord Yarmouth had revealed in conversation at Paris, to give back Hannover to George III. Meanwhile Haugwitz himself, so identified with the French Alliance, had already taken alarm; he had come upon indications that Napoleon was working underhand in Dresden and Cassel against the North German Confederation. He now read his recantation in the most explicit way by advising the King to mobilise his army; thus it was by him and not by Hardenberg that the decisive step was taken. For it proved decisive, though there is no reason to think that it was meant to lead to war. Napoleon, it was felt, must at last be taught that there were limits to Prussia's patience; a display of spirit would bring him to reason, and he would not be so rash as to bring upon himself the army of Frederick at a moment when he had not concluded peace with England and Russia.

But almost simultaneously with this demonstration on the part of Prussia came another occurrence which appears to have determined Napoleon to

accept at once the challenge thus offered. A treaty
with Russia which Oubril had been induced to sign
at Paris on July 20th was awaiting ratification. It
was a treaty which would have had the effect of
breaking the understanding between Russia and
England, and thus of leaving England isolated and
the Continent pacified under the ascendancy of
Napoleon, as it afterwards was through the Treaty
of Tilsit. But now came the news that the Czar
had refused his ratification. Napoleon writes to
Berthier on September 3rd, 'I was going to send
you orders for the return of the army when I received news that the Emperor of Russia had refused
to ratify the treaty;' and again two days afterwards,
'The new circumstances of Europe lead me to think
seriously of the situation of my armies;' and on the
same day, 'Send officers of the Engineers to make
good reconnaissances at all risk on the outlets of
the roads that lead from Bamberg to Berlin.' It
appears that Napoleon connected in his mind the
Russian refusal of ratification with the Prussian
mobilization, that he divined the secret negotiations
which had actually been going on between the two
courts, and that he thought he saw a new coalition
between England, Russia and Prussia ready to
assail him, a coalition which it was desirable, since
Germany was already full of his armies, to crush
before its forces could be brought together.

And thus we are brought to the catastrophe of
Prussia. At the end of the First Part we reached
this point by one route, and now we have reached
it again by another. Naturally the Life of Stein
and the Times of Stein cannot be completely brought

together into a single narrative until he arrives at
the head of affairs.   So long as he was confined to
internal affairs while the fate of Prussia was decided
by the course of foreign politics, the connexion of
his life with his times is positively slight.   Even at
this point it does not immediately become close, for
as a civilian he could not exert any decisive influence over the course of the war.   It is advisable
therefore, now that the time has come for breaking
new ground, to continue a little further that outline
of general Prussian history which has occupied us
hitherto in this Second Part, and to give a general
view of the catastrophe which now overtook the
State before we inquire how the personal life of
Stein was affected by it.

Frederick William might take up arms, to all
appearance, with considerable confidence.   Not only
were his relations with Russia now cordial and his
chance good of obtaining before long the help of
England and Austria, but he had reason to think
highly of his own resources.   Those of Frederick
the Great, when he withstood so gloriously the
united arms of Austria, Russia and France, had been
by no means so considerable.   Since the territory
had been enlarged by three partitions of Poland;
Hannover, which then to be sure was allied to
Prussia, now belonged to her, and Saxony, which
then was hostile, was now an ally.   The army was
to all appearance what it had been so long, and
indeed was more self-confident than ever.   General
Rüchel said on parade at Potsdam, 'His Majesty's
army can produce *several* generals equal to M. de
Bonaparte.'   The country had enjoyed eleven years

of peace while other states had exhausted themselves in war. All this time, whatever mistakes
had been made by ministers and diplomatists, the
soldier's drill at any rate had not been intermitted.
What could reasonably be conjectured but that
Prussia would fight at least on equal terms with
France, and if not actually victorious would at least
prove absolutely unconquerable?

Not but what prophetic voices made themselves
heard. Thus wrote in this very summer Heinrich
v. Bülow:

The love of hoarding may be shown in armies as well as in
money. He who from horror of war lets his army, that is, his
capital, lie idle in garrison service, where it rusts and bastardises
and sinks into a spiritless militia of the sort that German students
call Philistine, and that you could hunt into flight at the first
opportunity with tailors, or apothecaries, or perriwig-makers, he
must look on while more adventurous speculators earn wealth
and power and honour, and must grow impoverished and paralysed while he pines in inaction. Napoleon is an adventurous
monarch who keeps his capital out; the rest who have either
invested in bad speculations or abandoned themselves to the sloth
of timidity are astonished when they awake from the dream of
stolid materialism, at the new condition of vassalage in which
they find themselves so suddenly. The fact is certain, Prussia
has lost her independence since she forgot how to make use of
200,000 men. The most enormous blunder was the removal
of the Demarcation—as if Prussia felt herself unworthy to rule in
North Germany. Frederick William II. was not quite without
a policy, for the Demarcation was his work and he would never
have submitted to the occupation of Hannover. Minister Haugwitz deserves to be praised after so many blunders, *first for avoiding war, for it would have been conducted without skill*, next for
bringing Hannover to Prussia. The possession, to be sure, is
precarious, because our independence altogether is precarious,
and it is the lowest of all degradations to steal at another man's

order; in fact, it is altogether a new part to play, and without example in history.

And speaking of the last war he says:

Twenty-three thousand men and sixty cannon were surrendered without a blow; on the French side perhaps two or three hundred men suffered contusions. The occurrence is unique in history, and characterises the present generation, which belongs to those spoken of by Rousseau, when he says that Europe will see races spring up and die out on her bosom that are not worthy to live. A campaign without a battle, decided purely by strategy, the whole war conducted through the legs without even the use of the forefinger! It is an easier thing now-a-days to conquer all Europe than to subdue a horde of Calmucks.

In those ominous days of August, 1806, this prophet was suffering the fate of Jeremiah. He was arrested, and his trial commenced with a medical examination to ascertain that he was not out of his mind.

But in a single week between October 10th and October 17th all the divisions of the Prussian army were defeated at Saalfeld, Jena, Auerstädt, and near Halle, Prince Louis Ferdinand being killed and the Duke of Brunswick receiving wounds from the effects of which he died soon after. Then began the surrender of the fortresses; Spandau, Prenzlau, and Stettin fell before the end of the month, and on the 27th Napoleon entered Berlin. During most of the month of November the taking of fortresses continued. The example of weakness which had been set at Prenzlau by Prince Hohenlohe was followed almost everywhere, until at Magdeburg a garrison of 24,000 men surrendered without striking a blow.

Such was the sudden military collapse, which, when a political disaster in the following year was added, left Prussia a ruined and conquered, nay a more than conquered state. Napoleon himself had confidently expected success in the field in spite of all the apparent military strength of his enemy, for he bore in mind the fundamental superiority of France. On October 12th he had written to the King, 'Your Majesty will be defeated....Europe knows that France has thrice the population of your Majesty's states and is as completely organised for war as they are.' But the immediate downfall of the whole system which followed his first successes must have astonished him no less than the Prussian Government. It is particularly to be noted here as the first revelation that was made to all the world of the necessity of that radical reform of the Prussian State which is the main subject of this book. The following words were written as early as March, 1807, and not by Stein but by Hardenberg: 'A radical treatment of the defects of our administration is absolutely and urgently necessary. Necessary both with respect to the system and to the persons. The question at this moment is of discovering additional resources to save ourselves; later it will be of a thorough regeneration.'

In the war, that is between October 1806 and July 1807, we may distinguish four periods.

The first of these ends at November 21st, and may be called the period of military collapse. Politically the earliest result of the disasters was the downfall of the nascent North German Confederation, of which the union of Saxony and Hessen with Prussia formed the nucleus. Saxony is now won over to Napoleon and enters the Confederation of the Rhine, while he proclaims the deposition of the Elector of Hessen. The other cause of the war had been Napoleon's intention of pacifying England at Prussia's expense by restoring Hannover. The King now saw that Hannover must be ceded, and hoped at this cost to be quit of the war. But it was seldom easy to shake off Napoleon, and now followed the surrender of the fortresses. His demands after this become unlimited; the territory as far as the Elbe is to be made his by formal cession, and other conditions are announced which would reduce the king to complete vassalage in the provinces still left to him. By the Convention of Charlottenburg it was engaged that the Prussian troops should be withdrawn into the north-eastern corner of the monarchy; that Thorn, Graudenz, Danzig, Colberg, Lenczyk, Glogau, Breslau, Hameln, Nienburg should be surrendered, and that the Russians who were supposed to be marching to the King's assistance should be sent back to their own country as soon as they arrived. The demand was also made that Prussia should join France in war against Russia if the Russians should enter Moldavia.

This last demand shows what Napoleon was meditating. He meant not merely to humble or rob Prussia, but to make her an active vassal. The Prussian army was not merely to cease to fight against him; it was to become a part of his own army and to be directed against Russia. The Convention was signed and laid before the King for ratification. He was called upon to decide the momentous question whether he would break with Europe and place himself on the side of France, while at the same time he parted with the power to exact terms from France by handing over his principal fortresses to French garrisons. We shall see that Prussia did in the end sink as low as this Convention would have brought her; in 1812 her army actually did march with Napoleon against Russia. But in 1812 she only submitted to the most overpowering compulsion, and therefore did not forfeit the sympathy of Europe; it would have been otherwise had she accepted the same terms in 1806. The King's decision was taken after a deliberation held at Osterode on November 21st, and it is the first step taken by the government of Frederick William III. in a better course of policy. The ratification was refused on the advice of Stein, Voss, and Beyme, and against the advice of Haugwitz, Prince Henry, Schrötter, Generals Kalkreuth and Geusau, and Colonel Kleist. This turning-point is also marked by the retirement of Haugwitz, which now took place. His last appearance in the councils of Prussia is thus simultaneous with Stein's first expression of an opinion on national policy. Hardenberg was not present at this deliberation, but his opinion agreed with that of Stein. He wrote: 'Russia will take from us all that Napoleon leaves. This abominable armistice is worse than war.'

The second period is that of the Battle of Eylau, and ends with Napoleon's offer of a separate peace to Prussia, and the King's refusal after a second deliberation held on February 29th, 1807. In this period we see Prussia for the first time fighting as she was to fight in her War of Liberation, that is in alliance with Russia. Her affairs have decidedly revived. She is indeed only able now to assist Bennigsen with a modest force under Lestocq ; but this force distinguishes itself, and a gleam of hope lights up the general gloom when this new Coalition instead of dissolving at the first touch of Napoleon faces him at Eylau, and there in one of the bloodiest battles of history administers the first check he has yet received in his victorious career. It was a hopeful moment for Prussia when on February 16th General Bertrand, sent by Napoleon, had an audience of the King at Memel, and announced that his master was anxious to have the undivided honour of restoring his Majesty to his dominions, and would concede everything that was necessary in order that he might resume his old position among European sovereigns.

This was an attempt to accomplish by flattery and guile what had been attempted at Charlottenburg by force. A second time the King remained firm. He refused to desert his ally. And in this case it was the advice of Hardenberg that decided him. Haugwitz had been succeeded as Foreign Minister by Zastrow, a military man not much less French in his inclinations than his predecessor. His reign was now brought to an end, and for the first time the Minister who had all along been faithful to the cause of Europe, the Minister who was destined to guide the State afterwards through its darkest years, and also through its years of victory, came—gradually and with many marks of reluctance on the part of the King—to the head of affairs. Stein has now left the scene. In the first week of the new year he quitted for a time the Prussian service.

The third period ends with the Battle of Friedland, June 14th. Under the direction of Hardenberg the alliance of Prussia and Russia takes the dimensions of a great European coalition. The Treaty of Bartenstein is signed; Sweden promises help and England engages to furnish subsidies; there began to be hopes of the adhesion of Austria. The combination is almost identical with that which we shall meet with again at the beginning of the War of Liberation, and Hardenberg's language begins to show some of the elevation that characterised that period. He proposes to banish from politics mistrust and arts of deception, to establish an entire reciprocal confidence, hasten a complete concert among the Powers that have good intentions, and to substitute for delays, hesitations and incoherence in the choice of means, rapidity, energy, perseverance, and wise combinations.

But for the present all such bright prospects vanished with the disaster of Friedland and the unexpected consequences that followed it. A second blow fell on Prussia even more crushing than the first, and this time a blow which she had not drawn down by any fault of her own. We have remarked before Napoleon's peculiar art of concluding bargains at the expense of third parties. What glorious treaties for France had been those of Campo Formio and Lunéville! No doubt, and the reason was that

Austria had been induced to cede what did not belong to her. A better opportunity for practising this trick than had ever occurred before now presented itself. Russia had been beaten at Friedland, and might perhaps have been induced to submit to a disadvantageous peace. But the Peace of Tilsit which was now concluded was not disadvantageous for Russia; on the contrary, it was a peace by which Russia gained much; it was such a peace as she might have concluded after a successful campaign. How was this? It was because Napoleon was satisfied with one concession. He only asked that Russia should abandon her ally. After Eylau he had offered a separate peace to Prussia, but she had refused to desert Russia. After Friedland he made a similar offer to Russia, knowing well that it was in his power to offer her an almost irresistible bribe, and his offer was accepted. I have spoken before of 'whims of the Czar.' A violent whim of Peter III. had saved Frederick the Great, and his son Paul had changed the face of Europe during the war of the Second Coalition by suddenly passing from friendship with England and Austria to a violent animosity against both. The case before us is not so similar as it appears. It is understood that Alexander's change of policy was not voluntary, but was forced upon him by an importunate peace party among his generals and advisers. It was not unnatural that such a peace party should form itself. Russian feeling had indeed all along been in opposition to France and had sympathised with Prussia at the beginning of the war. But Prussia was then a great Power, and there was a fair prospect then of liberating Europe by assisting her. Now the aspect of affairs was changed, and it might fairly be asked what Russian, almost what European, interest could be promoted by continuing the war. The only object left was to secure better terms for Prussia, and voices were sure to be raised against shedding Russian blood and drawing down the inexorable anger of Napoleon upon the country in the sole interest of a foreign state. Such a party now arose, headed by the Grand Duke Constantine, and Bennigsen was supposed to have become a convert to its views. It is said that the Czar was invited to remember what had been his father's fate.

But if Russia was to abandon an ally who could do nothing for her, why should she lose the opportunity of making at the same time an alliance which might prove most profitable? Thus was brought about the Treaty of Tilsit, by which every vestige of old Europe was erased and the Napoleonic system fully established, a system more fatal to civilisation than any which had ever been dreaded by the statesmen who for a century and a half had watched over the balance of power. The Military State coalesced with barbarism, and Europe was left at the mercy of military Commissions, such as shot Enghien and Palm, or of the autocratic will which wielded the terrors of the knout and of Siberia. An observer might indeed have consoled himself by reflecting that Europe had not been fairly beaten, but had partly been taken by surprise, and partly had thrown up the game. Russia abandoned the Coalition just as Austria was on the point of joining it. If the day should come when there should be only one mind in Prussia, Russia, Austria, and England, and when all should be alike in earnest, nothing that happened in this campaign gave evidence that Napoleon would have any chance of success against such a coalition.

Besides establishing the ascendancy of the French and Russian Czars, the Treaty of Tilsit effected the partition of Prussia. The three partitioning Powers were nominally Russia—for by a new refinement in the science of partition this Power received from her late enemy part of the territory of her late ally—Saxony and the newly established kingdom of Westphalia. But the share of Russia was in itself insignificant and brought the Czar little but infamy; the other two Powers, being members of the Rheinbund and creatures of Napoleon, merely disguised the gains of France. The territory left to Prussia contained a population of only 4,938,000 souls, whereas it had been 6,000,000 at the death of Frederick the Great and had increased in the twenty years which had passed since that event to not less than 9,744,000. But it would be a great mistake to infer from these figures that Prussia was simply reduced to the position she had occupied in the early part of the reign of Frederick the Great. Her downfall was much deeper and more complete. Under Frederick or Frederick William I. the State, though not rich or large, was perfectly independent, and was capable, though with great exertion, of keeping on foot a wonderful army. But the land was now so impoverished that whereas in Frederick William I.'s time an army of 80,000 was levied on a population of less than two millions and a half, Scharnhorst did not now think it possible to raise more than 70,000 from a population of nearly 5,000,000. And lest by recurring to her old policy of unheard-of military exertions Prussia should even with her reduced territory recover something of her importance, Napoleon by a new treaty signed on September 8th, 1808, exacted an express engagement that the Prussian army for ten years to come should not exceed 42,000 men, that is, should scarcely exceed the half of what it had been nearly a century earlier, and before Prussia had made any claim to rank among the great Powers of Europe. Thus if her population was reduced by about one-half, about four-fifths were taken from her military force. But her *relative* military importance was diminished far more than even this calculation would show. For an age of gigantic armies had now set in, and whereas a century earlier even a force of 42,000 men was important, it was a drop in the bucket in the midst of the hosts which Napoleon and Alexander were accustomed to bring into the field.

But when all this has been considered the reader must not suppose that the depth of Prussia's fall has been in any degree measured. With so small a population and army and without a frontier, it is true that no state in that lawless age could be independent. Between France and Russia in alliance, such a Prussia had no course but submission or complete destruction. Yet in this respect she would only be on a level with the other German States. If she had descended from her position of rivalry with Austria, she had not in respect of population or army sunk below the level of those middle

17—2

States which formed the principal members of the Confederation of the Rhine. Indeed in one respect she never did sink to their level, for though practically her subservience to Napoleon was much the same as theirs, though she accepted the Continental System in obedience to him and furnished him with assistance in his Russian war, yet she never in the utmost extremity consented formally to join the Confederation, and she never, like Bavaria and Würtemberg, accepted honours and rewards from the foreigner for treason against Germany. But Prussia had not the happiness of being left alone in her humiliation. The conqueror did not relax his hold upon the territory after he had imposed these terrible conditions. In addition to them all there was a war-indemnity to be paid. It was fixed, as will be explained fully in the sequel, at a sum greater than Prussia, now an insignificant state, poor by nature, heavily burdened and totally without credit in the money market, could pay, and till it was paid Napoleon maintained his hold upon the country. For the five years that followed, Prussia is to be conceived, in addition to all her other humiliations, as in the hands of a remorseless creditor whose claims are decided by himself without appeal, and who wants more than all he can get. She is to be thought of as supporting for more than a year after the conclusion of the Treaty a French army of more than 150,000 men, then as supporting a French garrison in three principal fortresses, and finally, just before the period ends, as having to support the huge Russian expedition in its passage through the country.

I shall explain in another place the course pursued by Napoleon, and shall point out that the terms actually enforced upon Prussia were almost as much more unfavourable than those agreed upon in the Treaty of Tilsit as these again were more unfavourable than any terms which Prussia had submitted to in any earlier treaty. It was not in fact from the Treaty of Tilsit, but from the systematic breach of it, that the sufferings of Prussia between 1807 and 1813 arose. It is indeed hardly too much to say that the advantage of the Treaty was received only by France, and that the only object Napoleon can have had in signing it was to inflict more harm on Prussia than he could inflict by simply continuing the war.

Such was the downfall of Prussia. The tremendousness of the catastrophe strikes us less because we know that it was soon retrieved, and that Prussia rose again and became greater than ever. But could this recovery be anticipated? A great nation, we say, cannot be dissolved by a few disasters; patriotism and energy will retrieve everything. But precisely these seemed wanting. The State seemed to have fallen in pieces because it had no principle of cohesion, and was only held together by an artificial bureaucracy. It had been created by the energy of its government and the efficiency of its soldiers, and now it appeared to come to an end because its government had ceased to be energetic and its soldiers to be efficient. The catastrophe could not but seem as irremediable as it was sudden and complete.

The summary account which has now been given of the fall of Prussia will have led the reader to discern three distinct causes for it. First, the undecided and pusillanimous policy pursued by the Prussian government since 1803 had an evident influence upon the result by making the great Powers, particularly England and Austria, slow to render it assistance, and also by making the commanders, especially Brunswick, irresolute in action because they could not, even at the last moment, believe the war to be serious. This indecision we have observed to have been connected with a mal-organisation of the Foreign Department. Secondly, the corruption of the military system, which led to the surrender of the fortresses. Thirdly, a misfortune for which Prussia was not responsible, its desertion by Russia at a critical moment, and the formation of a close alliance between Russia and France. In order to acquire a thorough comprehension of the event, it would be necessary to trace in detail the operation of the first two of these causes, and also to inquire what in turn were the causes of these causes, how the government came to be irresolute and the military system to be corrupt. These questions will be fully considered in the course of this biography; on the second or purely military question I insert for the present a few sentences from an instructive memoir by the distinguished Prussian general, Gneisenau.

The inability of the Duke of Brunswick to form a sound plan of a campaign, the irresolution so natural at his age, his bad fortune in the field, the army's distrust of him, the dissensions of the chiefs of the staff, the neutralising of some of its ablest members, our army's want of practice in war, the want of preparation for it visible in almost all departments, the habit formed in the years of peace of occupying it with useless minutiæ of elementary tactics, invented to gratify the people's love of shows, our system of recruiting with all its exemptions which obliged only a part of the nation to bear arms, and prolonged the term of service of this part unreasonably, so that in consequence it served with reluctance, and was only kept together by discipline; our system of encouraging population, which allowed the soldier to burden himself with a family, the support of which when war called him from his hearth was mostly left to public charity, and whose lot often made the anxious father long for the end of the war; the system of furloughs, which tempted the chief of a company by his pecuniary interest to send the recruit home half-drilled; the bad condition of our regimentary artillery, which could never vie with the numerous horse artillery of the French; the bad quality of our weapons; the incapacity of most of our generals; and, to sum up all, our conceit, which did not allow us to advance with the time,—forced from the patriot a secret sigh, and nothing remained to depend on but the intelligence of most of our officers.

The following remarks taken from the same memoir, which appears to have been sent to the King soon after the first disasters, should also be read.

Thus are we brought to the humiliation of having to look for help and rescue to our neighbours or to an ignominious peace. And even this will not help us, for it is after all but a palliative. The tone of the army is deteriorated, the incapacity of several generals exposed. Below no confidence, and no force of will or ability above. Those who might have helped are no longer in a condition to do so. Pusillanimity rules almost everywhere, and the age is so emasculate that the idea of falling with decency passes for a poetical flight. Whether a new dynasty is to reign over the Baltic lands is a matter of indifference not only to the common people, no, even to men in high offices. Each man wants only to save himself and his own comfort, so that to the man of honour nothing is left but to envy those who fall in the field of battle. On certain suppositions no doubt the monarchy may still be saved, but the disgrace of the army which melted away to nothing in consequence of deserved misfortune is not to be effaced. Many have voluntarily allowed themselves to be taken, and multitudes offered their capitulation to the enemy when they might have saved themselves......Two battles lost in one day in such disastrous circumstances was a trial too hard even for Prussia. Whatever Europe might think of it, this monarchy was nevertheless no military state, although its system of taking its place among the great Powers of Europe placed it under the necessity of maintaining a great army by heavy impositions. But this was its only military side. Otherwise nothing was organised for unity. The separation of all branches of Government, the enormous formality and the distinct constitution of each province made a remodelling of the fabric of the State almost impracticable. Thus when the army was destroyed the very hope of independent recovery vanished, as the formation of a reserve had been neglected, and afterwards was made impossible by the fact that the chief part of the munitions of war, which were unjustifiably collected in a metropolis disadvantageously situated, fell into the enemy's hands along with it, and even what was brought away from it was lost afterwards in the fortresses that were surrendered.

It is now time to return to the narrative of Stein's life.

CHAPTER VI.

STEIN DURING THE WAR.

FROM a letter written to Vincke on January 3rd we learn Stein's view of the state of affairs just after the Treaty of Schönbrunn.

I trust your Excellency's disquiet about the present condition of public affairs may be somewhat alleviated by the following considerations.

Had a great force, moral and intellectual, guided our state, it would have led the Coalition, before it suffered the blow which overtook it at Austerlitz, to the great goal of the emancipation of Europe from French ascendancy, and after that blow it would have restored it. This force was wanting; I can as little blame him to whom Nature had denied it as you can reproach me with not being Newton. I acknowledge the will of Providence, and nothing is left but faith and resignation.

Hannover is to be occupied and administered. You imagine the case of our taking advantage of circumstances and uniting Hannover with our state. But it is otherwise. Bonaparte has occupied Hannover, and will assuredly not give it back to England at the Peace. Austria demanded it for the Elector of Salzburg, but Bonaparte refused it to him and offered it to us. We occupy and administer till the Peace, when it will be assured to us.

Is Prussia to reject this aggrandisement, which rounds her territory and strengthens her in population and revenue?

Is she to leave in the same condition this point of attack for England, which endangers her own security? What is to happen? Is the war to go on in North Germany, and the forces of the Allies to be scattered or driven into the sea?

Assuming—not admitting—your discontent to be reasonable, is your discouragement and despondency justified by this? has the Prussian monarchy no interest for you but your personal relation to the sovereigns? in what relation does this state stand to Germany, to European civilisation—is its existence a matter of indifference, is it unfavourable to the elevation of humanity? What a contrast makes our perpetual grumbling at the government with the devotion of the Austrian to his monarch, who began a war in thoughtlessness and ended it in cowardice!

The letter to which this is the answer and unfortunately also the other letters of Vincke to Stein just at that critical period are lost. Of Stein's to Vincke two or three others remain breathing the same spirit as this, that is, a spirit rather of resignation and faith than of satisfaction. But we may suppose that Haugwitz' crowning achievement of Feb. 15th changed this mood for one of active alarm. At any rate, in the month of April, when next we hear of him, he is one of the most energetic members of an opposition party which has sprung up among the officials. With him are joined the Minister Schrötter, and the two Generals Rüchel and Phull. The combination supports Hardenberg against Haugwitz and the secret influence of the Cabinet Secretaries; Hardenberg, however, as he himself tells us, was in no sense a member of it, and took no part in its consultations, preferring to press his views upon the King independently from his place in the Foreign Department. What the objects of the new party were and what measures they meditated, can best be seen from a Memoir written by Stein near the end of April. It is entitled 'A Representation of the Faulty Organisation of the Cabinet, and the Necessity of forming a Conference of Ministers.' As it is the earliest exposition of Stein's views on general politics, and at the same time throws more light on that crisis of Prussian history than perhaps any other contemporary document of equal length, the reader will, I believe, thank me for inserting it entire.

Every considerable public functionary is called on to investigate the condition of the affairs of this monarchy by the danger which threatens it of losing its independence and the richest sources of its national wealth, and by the discontent of the nation at the condition of degradation in which it finds itself, and at the loss of its ancient, well-earned renown.

The Prussian State has no constitution; the supreme power is not divided between the Sovereign and the representatives of the nation. It is a very new aggregate of many single provinces brought together by inheritance, purchase and conquest. The Estates of these provinces are local corporations, to which is entrusted a co-operation with the provincial administration, but which are entitled to judge of and guide only local and not general affairs, if the course of imperial business is not to be impeded and misdirected.

As the Prussian State has no political constitution, it is all the more important that its governmental constitution should be formed on correct principles; and as it has this, which has only been undermined by the course of time, it requires to be restored in a form adapted to the present condition of things.

According to the governmental constitution legally existing, the whole extent of the administration is divided between these principal departments—the Military Board, the Cabinet Ministry, the General Directory, and the Ministry of Justice; the Administration of Finance and Police for Silesia stands by itself.

The point of union of all the principal departments and of the Silesian Ministry is the Council of State, which now consists of fifteen members.

It is confined however at present to a few unimportant affairs, only assembles on special occasions, and may be regarded as non-existent in respect of character and efficacy.

Frederick William I. governed independently, deliberated, resolved and executed through and with his assembled Ministers. He formed the still existing Administrative system, and ruled with wisdom, vigour and success.

Frederick the Great ruled independently, did business and deliberated with his Ministers *in writing* and by *conversation* and executed through them; his Cabinet Councillors wrote his will and were without influence. He possessed the love of the nation, the respect of his neighbours, the confidence of his allies.

Frederick William II. ruled under the influence of a favourite, of his courtiers, male and female. They came between the throne and its regular advisers.

Had these asserted their position with energy, unity and dignity, and withstood the Cabal in its commencement, its influence would certainly have been much restricted. But they fell down before the idol, each individual sought to advance him and himself through him, and so the State fell into a condition not far from dissolution.

At present the Sovereign does business, deliberates and resolves under the influence of his Cabinet, and of the Cabinet Minister Count Haugwitz, who is affiliated to it and dependent on it, and of his friend General Köckeritz; with these the Sovereign works, deliberates and resolves, while his Ministers make proposals and execute the resolutions arrived at in this assembly.

Thus under Frederick William III. a new State Council has grown up, and the question arises, Is the Institution useful, and does the excellence of its personal composition compensate the imperfection of the arrangement itself?

This new State Council has no legal or publicly recognized existence; it works, resolves, executes in the King's presence and in the King's name.

It has all power, the final decision of all affairs, the nomination to all posts, but no responsibility, as the King's person sanctions their proceedings.

To the higher officials remains the responsibility for proposals, and for the execution of them and exposure to public opinion, while the Members of the Cabinet are removed from all danger.

All unity among the Ministers themselves is dissolved, as it is useless, as the results of all their common deliberations and common resolutions depend upon the consent of the Cabinet, and all turns upon obtaining this.

This dependence on subalterns, whom the feeling of their independence misleads into an insolent behaviour, hurts the self-respect of the higher officials; one grows ashamed of a post of which one has only the shadow, since the power itself has become the spoil of a subordinate influence. If the pang of injured honour is suppressed, the sense of duty is blunted along with it, and both these powerful motives to activity are paralysed in the officials.

The spirit of obedience is lost in the underlings of the heads of departments, since their feebleness is well known, and every one that can gets near the idols of the day, tries his fortune with them and neglects his superiors.

The Monarch himself lives in a complete separation from his Ministers; he stands neither in a direct business connection with them, nor in a connection of intercourse, nor in that of special correspondence; a consequence of this situation is onesidedness in the impressions he receives, the resolutions he forms, and complete dependence on his courtiers.

This onesidedness in views and resolutions is a necessary consequence of the present constitution of the Cabinet, where all internal affairs are brought forward only through one and the same Member, who stands in no permanent connection with the administering Boards, and before whom the affairs come only on single occasions, very often only through single reports of a single Minister on the most important internal affairs of the Provinces.

Thus we miss in the new Board of Cabinet a legal constitution, responsibility, close connection with the Boards of Administration, and participation in the execution.

As then from these considerations the faultiness of the arrangement of the new State Council of the Cabinet appears, the question rises :—

Does its personal composition mitigate the faultiness of its
arrangement?

The Cabinet, so far as it does not concern the military administration, consists of the two Members of Cabinet, Beyme
and Lombard, and united with them, and dependent on them,
the Minister, Count v. Haugwitz, and the King's friend General
Köckeritz.

The Member of Privy Cabinet, Beyme, had a reputation as
Member of the Judicial Chamber for his straightforward, open
bearing, his thorough and healthy judgment, and his industry, and
his knowledge of law.   But he wants the knowledge of the principles of political economy, which is necessary for the conduct of
internal affairs.

The new situation he entered into as Member of Cabinet
made him arrogant and dogmatic; the vulgar presumption of his
wife was prejudicial to him, his intimate connection with the
Lombard family undermined the purity of his morals and his love
of what is good and diminished his industry.

The Member of Privy Cabinet Lombard is debilitated and
enfeebled physically and morally, his attainments are only those
of a French bel esprit, the solid sciences which draw the attention
of the Statesman and the savant have never occupied this frivolous
person.   His early participation in the orgies of the Rietz family,
his early acquaintance with the intrigues of those people, have
stifled his moral sense and put in its place a complete indifference
about good and evil.

In the impure feeble hands of a French poetaster of mean
extraction, a roué, who combines with moral corruption an entire
physical prostration and decay, who idles away his time in the
society of empty people with play and debauchery, is the conduct
of the diplomatic relations of this State at a time which has not
its parallel in the modern history of States.

As to the Minister v. Haugwitz, who is affiliated to the
Cabinet, his life is an unbroken series of disorders or evidences of
corruption.

In his academic years he handled the sciences in a shallow,
impotent way; his manners were sleek and supple.

Next he followed the fools who thirty years ago formed the
genius-clique in Germany, strove after the nimbus of sanctity

which surrounded Lavater, became a Theosopher, a spiritualist, and ended by sharing in the revels of the Rietz and in that woman's intrigues, became her obsequious attendant, and wasted the time that belonged to the State at the ombre table and his powers in every sort of brutal sensuality. He is branded with the name of a treacherous betrayer of his daily associate, of a shameless liar and an enfeebled debauchee.

General Köckeritz is a narrow-minded, uneducated person, of a common character and way of thinking, which leads him inevitably to insipidity in his views and opinions and in the choice of his acquaintances; to this he adds a very mischievous turn for thoughtless gossip.

Thus the composition of the Cabinet does not compensate by its qualities the faultiness of the institution itself, and a necessary consequence of the incompleteness of the arrangement and of the choice of persons is

> the dissatisfaction of the inhabitants of this country with the government,
> the decline of the Sovereign's reputation in public opinion, and
> the necessity of an alteration.

It is consequently necessary that an immediate connection between the King and the highest officials should be restored, that the persons who have the presenting of State affairs to the King for his final decision should be called to it legally and publicly, and their assemblies properly organised and clothed with responsibility.

The public business may be arranged in the following divisions: (1) War, (2) Foreign Affairs, (3) General Police in the widest sense of the word, (4) Public Revenue, (5) Justice.

Each of these departments would be entrusted to a Minister who, in the assembled deputation of the Council of State, would lay the affairs belonging to his sphere before the King, and the King would decide after the voting of all the members of such a Privy Council of State for internal affairs.

The Ministers are to lay affairs personally before the King, and give in their opinions; each is then to see the proposals developed by the Cabinet Secretaries, who are to be excluded from the audience, and laid before the King for ratification after the draft of the Order of Cabinet has been signed by all the Ministers.

The High Chancellor needs only to be present at these meetings on special occasions that concern legal matters.

The Cabinet Secretaries are to work in a common office in the Palace. Here the Ministers are to assemble daily to deliberate on the affairs to be laid before the King, and to sign the drafts.

The regular and frequent assemblage of the Ministers is necessary, that affairs may be conducted in common and not in a onesided way, on consistent principles, and not according to accidental views and fancies.

The sphere of the Privy Internal Council of State would comprehend all affairs that have hitherto been brought to the immediate decision of the King; experience would afford materials for a more exact and proper definition of the sphere.

A complete melting down of the forms of business and an alteration of principles demands an alteration in the persons to whom the public administration is confided.

The present Members of the Cabinet will either not put up with the subordinate position which is intended for them, or will undermine it and avail themselves for that purpose of the influence which habit, knowledge of character and experience of business gives.

The recent occurrences when we saw solemnly sanctioned treaties evaded in the moment of fulfilment, and soon afterwards reversed, are a fearfully instructive example *how necessary it is to alter the persons when measures are altered.*

The new administration can besides only inspire confidence by the dismissal of the members of the old, since these are deeply fallen in public opinion and in part branded with contempt.

I can suggest no other way of bringing about this alteration but

> a combination of a number of officials of mark, who shall lay before the King the necessity of an alteration, and shall declare that they will resign their posts in case the proposal is not accepted.

If his Majesty does not resolve to adopt the proposed alterations, if he perseveres in acting under the influence of the Cabinet, it is to be expected that the Prussian State will either dissolve or lose its independence, and that the respect and love of the people will entirely depart from it.

The causes and the persons which have brought us to the brink of the abyss will fairly push us in; they will bring about situations and relations, in which nothing will remain to the honest Statesman but to abandon his post, covered with unmerited shame, without being able to help or to take part in the wickednesses that will then be committed.

He who reads with attention the history of the dissolution of Venice, of the fall of the French and Sardinian monarchy, will find in these occurrences ground to justify the most dismal anticipations.

STEIN.

The above is translated not from the version of Pertz, but from the more complete copy recently printed in Ranke's Life of Hardenberg. A comparison of the two versions shows that Pertz, apparently not knowing how incomplete his copy was, has done Stein some injustice. He represents the Memoir as originally intended to be laid before the King, for he writes, 'Stein resolved, whatever might be the consequence to himself, to keep the oath he had taken as Minister, and reveal the truth to the King. Accordingly he drew up his statement.' Now the reader will see from the last paragraphs, that the Memoir is not addressed to the King, and cannot have been intended, in the first instance, to be laid before him. It must have been intended to be circulated among the rising party, as containing a clear expression of their views, and a suggestion of the best course for them to take. This observation is really of some importance. As addressed to the King, the Memoir would seem written in a very unusual tone. We might, up to a certain point, admire

its unsparing frankness, and think highly both of the
Minister who could write the painful truth in such
plain language, and of the King who could permit
it thus to be written.   But we should have, at the
same time, to acknowledge that Stein pushes frankness to rudeness, for the attack upon Köckeritz,
who at the same time is expressly described as 'the
King's friend,' could scarcely be considered as less
than an intentional insult to the King.   It is true
that according to Pertz this attack was ultimately
suppressed in deference to the advice of Stein's
friends.   'He showed the paper,' writes Pertz, 'to
Minister v. Schrötter, and at his suggestion softened
several passages, and particularly refrained from
demanding the dismissal of General v. Köckeritz.'
And Hardenberg writes in a letter sent at the time
and intended to be read by the Queen, 'Minister
Stein has presented to the Queen, through the
Countess v. Voss, a Memoir which he showed to
me, and which he intended, after altering some passages aimed at General Köckeritz, to lay formally
before the King.   The purport, unfortunately, is as
true as it can be, but the style so strong and harsh,
that so far from gaining its object it would be likely
even to increase the evil, since the King presumably
would think he heard the voice, not of truth, but
only of passion and of some violent private pique.'
Most readers will gather from this passage, what
after all it does not say, that the alteration of the
passages referring to Köckeritz was suggested by
Hardenberg.   But could not Stein, we ask in
astonishment, see for himself the glaring impro-
priety of those passages ?   The explanation is found

as soon as we discover that the Memoir was originally intended to be read only by his fellow officials.
When by an after thought he resolved that the
King too should see it, it would be a matter of
course that the offensive passages should be omitted,
along with the paragraph in which it is proposed
to put pressure upon the King.

Whether, even after these alterations and some
softening of the invectives upon Haugwitz and
Lombard, the paper did not remain too 'strong and
harsh' to produce a good effect on the King's mind,
we may well doubt with Hardenberg. The reader
will have other opportunities of observing Stein's
incurable frankness. It is however to be noted in
mitigation, that in a letter written at this time to
Rüchel, he declares his belief that the King hated his
Ministers, and only wanted an excuse to get rid of
them. Under this impression then he resolved to
take measures for laying the Memoir in its softened
shape before him. He introduced it with a preface
addressed 'to the King's Majesty,' in which he cited
the oath he had taken to speak the truth frankly,
declared that he was actuated by no personal considerations, that the step he took might expose him
to the King's displeasure, and if it was also possible
that it might bring him personal advantages, he renounced all such advantages beforehand. Accompanied with this apologetic preface, the Memoir was
then laid, not before the King, but before the
Queen.

I have not given so much importance to this
Memoir on account of any effect it produced. Stein
himself seems to have been uncertain whether the

King ever saw it, for he speaks of it as a paper which 'had probably not remained unknown to the King.' I rather imagine that the Queen suppressed it; the letter from Hardenberg which I have just quoted, and which was intended to be read by the Queen, was likely, and was apparently intended, to determine her to do so.

But the document is of the utmost importance to us, as laying bare those defects in the Prussian system which had been the secret cause of all the vacillation and feebleness of her foreign policy. The defect upon which Stein lays most stress is different from that which we have noticed above; he says nothing of two rival Ministers holding the Foreign Department at the same time, because the abuse had quite recently disappeared. Early in April Hardenberg had retired, and the Department was now held by Haugwitz alone. How abusive that system had been, and at the same time how service-able the King had found it for cloking the nullity of his foreign policy, may be shown by a single example. Prussia had on a single occasion behaved with spirit towards Napoleon. She had demanded of him in 1804 the extradition of Sir George Rumbold, an English *chargé d'affaires* carried off from Hamburg by French troops. At this time Haugwitz was absent, and Hardenberg advised the King in the strongest manner to remain firm. In this extremity the King sent an express to Haug-witz in Silesia with a letter, in which he proposed the question in the following terms:

I have demanded satisfaction from Bonaparte for his breach of neutrality and because Rumbold was actually accredited to my person in relation to the Circle of Lower Saxony. His extradition is demanded. If Bonaparte evades the demand by having recourse to subterfuges, what should Prussia do to maintain her dignity and to fulfil her engagements both to Russia in conformity with the existing arrangement and to her co-Estates in North Germany? Several persons vote in favour of war, *but I do not* (underlined by the King). I think there are means of settling the matter without proceeding to such extremities......Think of it, and assist me with your views. You know that I have reserved to myself the right of having recourse to you in critical circumstances, and these are as critical as possible.

Is it possible to imagine a more undisguised entreaty for pusillanimous advice, or a more deplorable ministerial position than this of Hardenberg?

But it now appears that there was another abuse behind. The complaint which was most loudly made at this time by all who were dissatisfied with the management of affairs in Prussia was of the influence of the Cabinet Councillors or Cabinet Secretaries.

In order to understand this we must dismiss all the English associations that have gathered round the word Cabinet. The Cabinet which Stein considers to be faultily organised is not a Committee formed of the Heads of the Principal Departments, but a totally different institution. I have traced above the gradual differentiation of the Ministerial Departments out of the General Directory established by Frederick William I. There was indeed a recognised Council or Board in which all the Heads of Departments deliberated together, but this was not called the Cabinet; it was called the Privy Council of State, otherwise the Privy Ministry of State, and is referred to, it will be seen, by Stein as practically obsolete. The same great organiser, Frederick William I., who had created the General Directory, had also created in 1728 the Cabinet Ministry (Cabinets-Ministerium), which consisted of personal confidants of the King, and which was occupied chiefly with Foreign Affairs. In giving the name of Cabinet to a Committee of Foreign Affairs Frederick William was in accordance with the original usage of England, though that usage has altered since, for it is known that in the reign of Charles II., when the Cabinet or Cabal was struggling for existence, it was in like manner a Committee of Foreign Affairs. But though not the Ministers generally, yet naturally the Minister for Foreign Affairs sits in the Cabinet. Accordingly he is called the Cabinet Minister.

From the beginning the King's personal authority had been felt in the Cabinet much more than in the General Directory, as in every Monarchy Foreign Affairs are supposed to concern the King more directly than domestic. Thus the restless personal government of Frederick the Great had had its head-quarters in the Cabinet, and the Cabinet Secretaries had been the clerks whose business it was to draught and carry his orders.

In his time they had been 'without influence,' as Stein says; but suppose—as Stein does not venture to say—that in the place of Frederick the Great a king of ordinary abilities should arise, it might be expected that the influence of these clerks would increase. They had this advantage over the Ministers, that they were about the person of the Sovereign, and would be at hand if ever he should feel the inclination to ask advice or to lean on some one. After the abnormal and demoralised reign of Frederick William II., in which mere favourites had supplanted Ministers and Members of Cabinet alike, this perversion had actually taken place. Under the present reign the Members of Cabinet had gained power, and had been formed into a kind of Council, which had superseded the older Cabinet of Ministers.

Thus in Prussia the Ministers were not formed into any Council, and there was a Cabinet not consisting of Ministers. This is the point, and here, according to Stein, lay the mischief. A despotic government is generally thought to be effective in war and foreign policy; why had the despotic government of Prussia proved so exceptionally feeble without any exceptional feebleness in the sovereign? The answer is, that the energy of a despotism arises from the union of the executing and the resolving powers in one person or council, so that all resolves are at the same time founded on detailed practical knowledge, and executed with conviction and intelligent comprehension. But in the despotism of Prussia no such union existed. The Ministers executed, and had the practical knowledge of affairs; but they had little share in resolving, and were excluded from deliberation. Meanwhile deliberation was in the hands of the Members of Cabinet, who could not have any practical knowledge of affairs. To this was added, that they deliberated without responsibility, both because they advised what they would not be called on to execute, and because, being a secret and unrecognised camarilla, they were screened by the responsibility of the King. It is to be observed that these Members of Cabinet not only had an inordinate influence over affairs in general, but in particular that the Foreign Minister was a tool in their hands, so that at the time when it might be doubted whether Haugwitz or Hardenberg was properly Foreign Minister, it was certain that the real control of Foreign Affairs lay with neither.

We have now before us an account of this abusive system written by Hardenberg, whose acquaintance with it was much closer than that of Stein. He fully confirms Stein's statements, but enters more into detail.

The King was still supposed, like Frederick the Great, to govern personally without a Council of State, but the irresponsible closet Council of State still existed, more powerful than a public, constitutional and responsible one would have been, accessible and susceptible to every intrigue, domestic or foreign.

General v. Köckeritz, fully informed on all matters and present at all deliberations, Colonel v. Kleist in respect of military affairs, Privy Cabinet Councillor Beyme for the Interior, Privy Cabinet Councillor Lombard for Foreign Affairs. The deliberations in Military and Internal Affairs were combined. Those relating to Foreign Affairs were held separately ; if Count Haugwitz came to the King, which in the end happened but seldom and only on very important occasions, Lombard might not be always present, but the Count did nothing without him. His (*i.e.* Lombard's) younger brother, an ignorant, effeminate young Sybarite, the Count had selected for his confidential friend, and given him a place in the Department though he had neither merit nor any of the requisite readiness. Lombard was the real directing Minister, who saw the King as often as he wished, who could influence the King's resolutions before or after the Count's formal advice had been given, and could besides avail himself of the influence of General v. Köckeritz and the other two members of the

Cabinet, who were fully informed of all political relations. If Lombard was absent or ill, Beyme took his place. None of these men do I accuse of bad intentions; I believe none of them to have been corrupted; yet their influence and their conduct of business were among the principal causes of the downfall of the Prussian Monarchy.......It was most difficult for the Ministers to obtain access to the King. Except those of Foreign Affairs and for certain purposes Count Schulenburg, the rest scarcely ever saw him in business, some never. Nothing remained but written reports which were laid before the King by the Cabinet Secretaries. Between the Ministers and them there was either war with very unequal weapons, or the Ministers had to give way to their opinion. Many times the most beneficial plans could not be carried through till a negotiation with the Cabinet Secretary had taken place; often hindrances were put in the way of them without any sufficient knowledge, if they were opposed to the personal interests of the Cabinet Secretary. Lombard ventured to hear Foreign Ambassadors, who applied to him, and to negotiate with them......I myself experienced that an addition of salary and a money grant, which the King had sanctioned at my instance and had issued the orders in due form, was later declared to have been unduly obtained because it had not passed through their hands, and that they actually annulled the grant after I had retired from affairs.

If there was imbecility in Prussian foreign policy under such a system we need not surely be surprised. The characters given by Stein of Lombard and Haugwitz also agree with those given by Hardenberg, but they have the less interest for us because these two politicians now retire from public life. The character of Beyme, which it may be observed is much less severe, should be noted by the reader for several reasons. Beyme had been the adviser of Stein's appointment to the Ministry of Trade, and this attack upon him might have been, indeed was, regarded as a mark of ingratitude on Stein's part; to

us it must rather seem a proof of the strong sense of
duty and public exigency by which he was actuated,
knowing as we do from the instance of Heinitz how
far removed he was from the disposition to ingratitude. But it is also important because Beyme's career
was by no means over, because a struggle against his
influence forms the next passage of Stein's life, and
led to Stein's dismissal in the middle of the war.

During the summer of this year the reconsti-
tution of Europe, under French ascendancy, was
rapidly proceeding. Louis Bonaparte became King
of Holland in June, and Cardinal Fesch became
Coadjutor to the Electoral Arch-chancellor Dalberg.
In July and August took place those events which
have been described above as completing the German Revolution, viz. the creation of the Confederation of the Rhine and the abdication of the
Emperor.

The consequence of this Revolution to Stein was
that he was mediatised. What had so long hung
over him befell at last on the 8th and 9th of September, when the Prince of Nassau announced the
annexation of the Stein territories, the cessation of
all rights of sovereignty in the house of Stein, and
its subjection to the law courts and to the government of Nassau.

Meanwhile, what progress were the opposition
party among the Prussian officials making? A few
slight traces remain that Stein at least did not cease
to plan and to hope. It is interesting to come upon
the following words, written Aug. 11, in the letters of
Gentz to Johannes Müller. 'The Minister v. Stein,
who was here a few days, is the first statesman in

Germany. Certainly if I lived in Berlin he should not be long without work; with his deep views and great character the only question would be of assuring him support, for he is fully resolved to act. But quite alone he positively can't, and what am I to expect from Berlin?' When we consider that these words were written to Berlin, where Stein was better known than at Dresden, and that they were written after a conversation with Stein, in which he had announced his intention of acting, we may perhaps conclude that they are a kind of testimonial given by the distinguished publicist to Stein, and intended to be shown in the most influential circles. That Stein just at that time was collecting such testimonials, appears from a passage in a letter written by General Rüchel to Hardenberg on August 15th. The letter accompanies a copy of a Memoir which had been presented on that day to the King, and Rüchel says, 'Have the goodness to take a copy, but with your own hand, of this rough exemplar, and show it to Stein when he comes, that he may see that I have kept my word[1].' And in the Memoir itself we read, 'Your Majesty must take into your counsels a man of rank, reputation, honour, firmness, and trustworthiness. Schulenburg has the misfortune of being frequently absent when the storms of the time threaten. Minister v. Stein is such a man. He has great resources and manly energy.' A little earlier than this (July 23rd) Blücher is found writing to Kleist about 'my friend Rüchel and Stein,' and says,

[1] Ranke, v. 377.

'I wish the latter were our Foreign Minister, and the present one (Haugwitz) were in hell[1]!' But no result had come of all these wishes and efforts when the catastrophe arrived.

It was on August 9th, or three days after the abdication of the last Roman Emperor, that the King issued his orders for setting the army on a war-footing, and a little more than two months afterwards the catastrophe of Jena and Auerstädt occurred. Once more, and for the last time, the old fault was committed, which Stein had so recently pointed out. The men were not changed with the measures; Haugwitz remained at his post; and, while he was Foreign Minister, no Austrian or English statesman could be justified in stirring hand or foot to assist Prussia. Up to the moment of the catastrophe no one knew whether there was really to be war or not.

At this last instance of the King's perverseness the alarm became general. A new remonstrance was drawn up at the instance of Prince Louis Ferdinand by the distinguished historian Johannes Müller. It was signed by the Prince, by the King's two brothers, Heinrich and Wilhelm, by the two distinguished generals, Rüchel and Phull, and by Stein, and was presented to the King on September 2. The purport of it is identical with that of Stein's earlier memoir; but as it is drawn with far less force and distinctness, it need not be given here. The following sentences will be sufficient as specimens.

---

[1] From a letter printed lately in the *Kölnische Zeitung*.

The whole army, the whole public, and even the best-disposed foreign Courts, regard Your Majesty's Cabinet, as it is organised at present, with the greatest distrust. This Cabinet, which by degrees has so forced its way between Your Majesty and the Ministers that every one knows that everything is done through three or four persons, has long forfeited all confidence, especially in political affairs. The insolent way in which Bonaparte has abused Your Majesty's love of peace is ascribed to them. The public voice speaks of corruption. We leave that undiscussed, because prejudices and other personal inclinations and relations may tempt to as bad actions as money. Enough that the universal conviction, grounded on notorious facts, is that the Cabinet plays in every way Bonaparte's game, and will either purchase peace by the most shameful compliance, or in war adopt the feeblest measures, or if Your Majesty prescribes strong measures and honourable generals are prepared heartily to carry them out, will hinder if not betray them, and so bring the utmost disaster on Your Majesty and your noble House and faithful subjects.

Again, Your Majesty has in your dominions a multitude of the ablest men, by whom these few, whose dismissal is necessary, may most easily be replaced. It is even easily possible to simplify and facilitate the whole system of affairs. *But the principal thing is, that only by the dismissal of the Cabinet Minister, Count v. Haugwitz, and of the two Members of Cabinet, Beyme and Lombard, is it possible to bring confidence, steadfastness and tranquillity into men's minds and well-grounded hope of the good result of affairs.*

The unfortunate King was deeply hurt by this remonstrance, which was such as Kings of Prussia were little in the habit of receiving from their subjects, and gave Stein in particular to know of his disapprobation through General Phull. It was now proposed to send in a second paper with the additional signatures of Blücher, Hohenlohe, and Schmettau, and at the same time that all those who signed should resign their appointments. But as it appeared that the King would prove quite immove-

able, such a plan seemed on second thoughts unpatriotic, and was given up.   On the day when Johannes Müller's paper was presented, Stein wrote a few
lines to Vincke, expressing his fears, but adding,
'We must all stand fast, and do what we can at our
posts; think of the Emigrés.'

The soldiers now naturally advance to the front
of the scene, and while the heat of the first campaign
lasts, there is little to tell of Stein.   He was suffering from an attack of gout when the news of the first
great disasters reached him at Berlin.   He left that
town for Danzig on October 20th, that is, a week
before Napoleon entered it.   Thus he was not among
the seven Ministers who, without waiting even for
their own Sovereign's consent, took the oath to Napoleon's government, retaining their offices ; and while
Prince Hatzfeld, who had become commandant of
Berlin, feeling himself by anticipation an official of
Napoleon, opposed the sending away of the military
stores, lest they should *not* fall into the conqueror's
hands, Stein sent off to Stettin and Königsberg the
funds of the Treasury, Bank and Maritime Institute,
and thus furnished the Government with the means
of carrying on the second war.

One of our minor personages disappears at this
point from the stage.   It was Count Schulenburg
who, as commandant of the troops in Berlin, put up
the celebrated announcement: 'The King has lost
a battle.   The first duty of the citizen is now to
be quiet.   This duty I charge the inhabitants of
Berlin to perform.   The King and his brothers live.'
Henriette Herz comments upon it as follows.
'How laconic !   And yet part of it is superfluous.

For who in Berlin thought of disturbing his quiet? The announcement was read, but few countenances showed any expression of fear, most no expression at all; at the utmost one or two people went away shaking their heads with an air that seemed to say, Really, it has come a little too quick! The people thus charged to be quiet were so childishly disposed to quiet, that when the General, the preacher of quietism, rode out of the town a few days after at the head of a few troops that had remained behind, they crowded round him entreating that they might not be forsaken. "Surely I leave my children with you," was the warrior's reply. The people looked at each other with a bewildered air. Scarcely any one knew who these children were. Some saw in the words a symbol or mystery, some palladium hitherto unknown. But the children had a literal existence; they were simply Princess Hatzfeld and her husband, the Princess a very good friend of mine, but I am sure she must have been very much astonished to hear that she had been left behind by her father as a pledge for the safety of Berlin. And this was the General's last appearance!'

By the middle of November the first burst of the storm was over. The Prussian army was dissolved, and the question was to be decided whether the King should submit at once unconditionally, or determine to resist in reliance on the help of Russia. If he should decide for resistance, it was evident that reforms must be undertaken, and doubtless it was now at last clear even to the King that he must part with Haugwitz, and seek for a minister of quite another kind. At this point Stein begins to draw

attention on himself as the hope of the State.
Hardenberg was out of the way, and though people
apparently had the habit of thinking of Stein rather
as a financier than as a statesman, they could not
help remarking the large make of the man, something lion-like in his bearing, qualities sharply con-
trasted with those of Haugwitz, a style of speech
curt, distinct and imperious, a powerful mastery
of every task he undertook, the 'deep views and
great character' which Gentz had so lately recognised in him. Such a man might be fit for other
occupations besides finance. But to procure his services you must offer him his own terms, and this the
King was not at once prepared to do. The State
must sink lower yet before he could interfere to save
it. Not till after Tilsit did his hour come. But
in the middle of the war, just when Prussia's first
defeats are over and she is beginning her second
struggle with the help of Russia, occurs an abortive
negotiation between the King and Stein, which,
though it ended in anger and alienation, brought out
strongly the characters of both, and particularly
afforded grounds to hope that the statesman who
showed so little eagerness to rule, and who knew his
own mind so clearly, would, when his time came,
bring the same clearness and unselfishness into the
conduct of affairs.

It has been mentioned above that Stein was one
of those who counselled the King not to ratify the
Treaty of Charlottenburg, or, in other words, not to
break with Russia and attach himself irredeemably
to France. The Council at which he gave this
advice was held at Osterode on November 21st;

the Protocol shows that he took a certain lead in the deliberation, for Köckeritz, the King's friend, is reported as saying no more than that he fully concurred with Stein, and Beyme, who, it is to be observed, does not speak, but only adds his own opinion in writing at the end of the Protocol, in like manner grounds his opinion on 'the reasons alleged by his Excellency v. Stein'. On the same day the Ministry of Foreign Affairs was offered informally to Stein through Beyme and Köckeritz; and though, in a letter to the latter written on the 21st, he declared himself disqualified by want of special knowledge, and recommended that some one should be chosen who was well acquainted with Russia and Russian politics, mentioning particularly General Goltz and Count von Goltz, yet he received, on Nov. 29th, the following formal offer from the King.

MY DEAR MINISTER BARON VON [1] STEIN,

The Minister of State and Cabinet, Count v. Haugwitz, has at present such a severe attack of gout that it has become clear to him that he is absolutely compelled to retire altogether from business for a long time. I must therefore entrust the Portfolio of Foreign Affairs *ad interim* to other hands, and have reposed my confidence in you, since I can promise myself from your talents and acquirements that you will conduct the affairs of the Foreign Department altogether in the spirit required by the present condition of the State, and I am also convinced that you will secure the confidence of the Courts with which I must maintain the closest connexion. For the conduct of your department in the meanwhile you are to make proposals to me. But I must impose it on you as a duty to hasten your arrangements for entering upon the Foreign Department, as Count Haugwitz wishes to depart as early

[1] So the King writes.

as to-morrow, and until your arrival I must entrust affairs to
the Member of Privy Council, Beyme.   I am, your affectionate
king,

FRIEDRICH WILHELM.

The letter came from Ortelsburg, where the
King was, to Stein at Konigsberg, and was accompanied by a letter from Beyme, in which he tried to
make out the provisional form of the appointment
not only to be the most convenient for the King and
Haugwitz but also for Stein himself, as making it
easier for him to retire from the post if he found his
repugnance to it insurmountable, and as being in
fact an express concession to Stein's scruples.

Of the three persons against whom Stein had
declared war two were now gone, Haugwitz and
Lombard; only Beyme remained. The King probably thought that this would satisfy Stein, and that
he would not require a more complete submission to
his wishes.   But the system was not altered; if particular Members of Cabinet were gone, the Cabinet
itself remained, and probably Stein was not propitiated by His Majesty's anxiety to make it clear that
the retirement of Haugwitz was not caused by any
sense at last awakened of his misconduct or incom-
petence, but purely by an attack of gout. He answered by a long letter of refusal, which seems in
part, at least to an English judgment, strangely pedantic and unreasonable, but which was probably
well-judged on the whole. After stating generally
that he finds it impossible to accept the appointment
'even in circumstances in which any statesman truly
devoted to the monarchy and His Majesty's person

and house would be eager to make every sacrifice of personal inclination and interest,' he proceeds thus :

It was a principle of an earlier time proved to have been wise by the shameful experience of the present, that in the manifold affairs of internal and external administration every one should from early youth be destined by special guidance and personal preparation directed to one end, and acquisition of qualifications for a single department of affairs, in which subsequently, ripened by manifold experience, he strove to attain the degree of excellence which Nature and circumstances permitted him. So long as a legal condition of public international relations subsisted in Europe, before the question of right in these relations was first disregarded and then despised as a folly, the vocation of the diplomatist, of the Minister of Foreign Affairs, was a vocation requiring comprehensive acquirements slowly and with difficulty attained, never mastered by one not completely devoted to it from his earliest youth in the same degree as by one who had chosen it early and exclusively.

No doubt in the confusions and desolations in which everything perished which assured to our fathers progress in prosperity and indomitable fortitude in adversity, this principle too not only in relation to this matter but in everything has been exploded, while every one thinks himself capable of everything of which he can form to himself a distinct conception; as if early cultivation and continued experience did not produce the real and true capability in every department of affairs. But the consequences of this self-confidence or of confidence reposed on similar grounds (i.e. the King's confidence in Haugwitz) are only too plainly to be seen in the course of public affairs, since all old relations have been disturbed, all formerly observed principles of the relations of States neglected or despised; and if I acted against these principles, which are expressed not as the feeling of the moment but as a vital and deep-rooted conviction; if in my 50th year, after serving for 27 years in quite other departments of Your Majesty's and your royal predecessor's service which have occupied me exclusively, I should consent to pass into a department of ministerial business which is foreign to me, I should become guilty of an inconsistency which would not answer to the confidence by which Your Majesty was determined to make me this flattering offer.

This seems not very promising. Surely it was no time for such nice scruples. There would be no room in the world for great or heroic actions, and history would sink into a mere mechanical routine, if it were established as an absolute principle that no one is to travel out of the vocation in which he has been trained; if a Cromwell must decline to command troops because he had been trained in farming, or Clive because he had been a civilian. Indeed there would be no room for that very self-government which Stein was himself to introduce in Prussia, for the very principle of self-government is to depart from that general rule of the division of labour which is here represented as not less absolutely binding in politics than in other affairs. At the same time Stein's pedantry is interesting both as illustrating the strongly conservative bent of his mind, and also for the strangeness to English ears of this recognition of government as a matter requiring so much special training. Stein's contemporary, William Pitt, was put at the head of affairs with little experience in any department, indeed with scarcely any experience of any kind; and if it be thought that he was an exception to all rules, what shall we say to his successor Addington, who, with abilities rather below than above the average, passed from being Speaker of the House of Commons to the head of the executive administration, or of Percival, who, with the training and qualities of an advocate, was made first Chancellor of the Exchequer, and then Prime Minister? Nor, again, can we read this passage without feeling what strangers we English have become to the affairs of Europe, and how little we can be thought to belong to the European system. To Stein it appears that a Minister of Foreign Affairs ought to have a special training, because the international affairs of Europe had till lately belonged to a *legal* system of things, and therefore required a knowledge of precedents and cases like that possessed by a lawyer. It is surely long indeed since English statesmen ceased to think in this serious manner of Europe as constituting a kind of federal state.

But to these somewhat general considerations Stein adds two definite reasons for refusal which deserve more attention. The first is that the man evidently marked out for the place, by the wishes both of foreign Courts and of the people, is Hardenberg, for whom, at this time, he professes the greatest esteem.

Stein at this time, as an opponent of the Haugwitz system, was in foreign policy a kind of follower of Hardenberg. On the matter which had just been debated at Osterode, we find them in correspondence and in entire harmony of opinion. On November 18th Stein had sent on to Hardenberg letters relating to the Convention of Charlottenburg, with the remark: 'It is impossible to accept the propositions; we can only consider ourselves now as the auxiliaries of the Russians and our country as theirs; all the advantages we concede to Napoleon must turn against the Russians and consequently against ourselves.'

To this Hardenberg replies on the same day: 'I am entirely of Your Excellency's opinion, that this abominable armistice, which surrenders almost the whole Monarchy to the enemy, is pointed against our only remaining ally, and is worse than the war. While that affords still some lucky chances, Napoleon's conditions lead to complete and certain ruin.'

But Hardenberg and not Stein had all along been the representative of the policy of resistance to France, and now that the King had come over to the same side had evidently a right to the vacant portfolio. Yet he had not even been summoned to the Conference at Osterode. Hardenberg has himself clearly explained his own grievance: ' It had been quite overlooked that I still actually held the post of first Cabinet Minister by the King's own will (*i.e.* he had not been dismissed, but had only received an indefinite leave of absence). Even if there were supposed to be reasons for not just then entrusting the conduct of affairs to me, still I was neglected and slighted in a very singular way.... The Minister v. Stein felt this far more strongly than I did myself.'

No doubt the excuse for passing Hardenberg was Napoleon's declared hostility to him.

But, in the next place, Stein proceeds: ' The Ministers of Your Majesty feel that they have a right, in consideration of their unreserved devotion to Your Person and readiness to devote their powers entirely to Your interest and the good of the nation, to receive, along with the responsibility for the measures executed through their department, the free and unconstrained introduction of them, and the unimpeded and immediate discussion of everything relating to them with Your Majesty.'

And then he recapitulates what he had vainly

urged before upon the King, how the Council of State had fallen into practical desuetude, how the Cabinet had taken its place, and what mischiefs had followed. And we feel that the real reason for his refusal is his conviction of the radical unsoundness of this system, rather than the bureaucratic punctilio which he himself alleges, and that it is a reason fully sufficient to justify the act. Haugwitz, as we have seen, when he was nominally Foreign Minister had been in reality the mere vassal of Lombard, and now since the retirement of Haugwitz Beyme had been acting provisionally as his successor, and so was just in the position to reduce any new Foreign Minister that might be appointed to a similar condition of dependence.

He concludes as follows : ' My resolution to encounter every fate with the Monarchy and Your Majesty's House is known to Your Majesty. I may hope that Your Majesty will neither misinterpret nor receive unfavourably my candid confession; but if my views or the expression of them should draw upon me Your Majesty's displeasure, I am compelled, in circumstances in which the alteration of a system from which much misfortune has arisen appears to me the first condition of deliverance, most humbly to beg that Your Majesty may be pleased to grant me my dismission.'

A contest now begins between the King and what we may call the Hardenberg party among his Ministers. It is a contest which marks that a change is taking place in the Prussian political system, and yet it is not like the constitutional contests of England, because publicity is wanting, not merely the large publicity of an age of free journalism, but even the minor publicity inseparable from a Parliament, even where its debates are not reported. Only a few officials were privy to what was going on, but in this narrow world a resistance was now offered to the King which would have been inconceivable in the time of Frederick the Great. An official refuses to accept an appointment because he considers that another official has a better right to it, and at the same time because a certain reform is not made which he regards as essential. And very soon there follows combination among the discontented officials to put constraint upon the King. It does not appear that he had any personal objection to Hardenberg, or any reason for passing him over, beyond a vague impression that some one less unacceptable to Napoleon ought to be chosen, and he seems to have been ready to allow that some alteration must take place in the constitution of the Cabinet. But it was really a serious matter for a King of Prussia to submit to dictation, and we need not be surprised if he felt that he was asked to surrender once for all the absolute authority he had inherited. On the other hand, we cannot condemn the Opposition for insisting on a formal and definite capitulation, for the deplorable condition of the Foreign Department had been caused precisely by the want of definiteness in the attribution of functions. Policy lost all character where no one knew whether Haugwitz, or Hardenberg, or Lombard, or Beyme, or Köckeritz, or some combination of these, or on the other hand none of these but only the King himself, was to be considered as directing Foreign Affairs.

The King for his part now proposes a compromise. He causes Beyme to draw up (Dec. 10th) a paper, in which was recommended the formation of a Council consisting of three Ministers: (1) a directing Minister, whose own department can open the most productive sources of revenue for the expenses of the war; (2) a General of ability, sagacity, and power, who, as a virtual War Minister, may unite under his control all the separate branches having relation to the conduct of the war in the position of President of the Supreme Board of War; (3) the Minister of Foreign Affairs. This Council is to discuss with the King all great matters that concern the conduct of the war or the foreign relations of the State, and all considerable legislative proposals in either civil or military affairs. A Cabinet Secretary is to be present in order to draw the Protocol, and to execute more promptly any royal orders that may not endure delay. This new Council is to have a practical, but, like the English Cabinet, no legal existence ; and all existing institutions, including the old Cabinets, are to subsist unaltered. Stein's proposal that all the Ministers shall form a Council, which shall take the place of the Cabinet, is disapproved on the ground, first that the Ministers could not undertake so much work, additional to the work of their departments ; secondly, that each Minister would simply maintain the independence of his own department, and oppose the union of branches of authority that have been unnaturally divided. Beyme supports this view by a curious picture of the complete want of unity among the different administrative depart-

ments, to which, rather than to Cabinet government, he attributes the public disasters, declaring
that 'if the government by Cabinet had not been
maintained, the government would have fallen to
pieces, even in the fullest internal peace, by an
internal war of all the Executive Boards among
themselves.' He challenges any Minister to produce a single example of the mischievous working
of the Cabinet upon his own department. A studied
vindication of the King pervades the document;
his predecessor is, as delicately as possible, made
responsible for all that has happened; he himself
is acquitted of everything but excessive amiability
—'the age required a Sulla on the throne; how
could a Titus prosper there?' an over-ambitious
conceit, which makes Hardenberg exclaim, 'Good
God! did the age require that Prussia should be
ruled by a monster?' This document was answered
by Stein with a curt refutation, in which he pronounced the proposed Council existing side by side
with the old Cabinet a system either 'useless or
abusive.'

On the other side, the Opposition also took a
decided course. On December 14th, a memorial
signed by Rüchel, Stein, and Hardenberg, was laid
before the King, in which the formal abolition of the
old Cabinet, and the institution in its place of a
Ministerial Cabinet (*Cabinetsministerium*) was advised as an indispensable measure, and Hardenberg
accompanied this paper with a declaration in his
own name, the opening sentences of which make
it clear in what a strong light the point at issue
presented itself to his mind. He writes:

The existence of the former Cabinet by the side of the Council which is to be organised, for which we have considered the title Cabinetsministerium (already in use) the most suitable, and which is to take the place of the other, only as a public Board with responsibility and a share in the executive power, we have all regarded as exceedingly prejudicial, and particularly on account of present circumstances we have considered the dismissal of both the present Cabinet Secretaries from the King's person indispensably necessary, since almost everything depends on increasing the confidence of the foreign Courts from which alone we can expect rescue ; and everything depends on uniting king and people in the bonds of mutual confidence, whereas, with respect to Beyme and Lombard [the younger Lombard is here spoken of] an unfavourable opinion is so deeply rooted in all these Courts that nothing can have strength enough to root it out, or at any rate there is no time for such an experiment, and we should never be trusted so long as it was thought possible that they might have influence : and within the country, there is just the same opinion of them which hurts the mutual confidence I spoke of, the more because these men are thought to rule the King. ...... With respect to the conduct of foreign affairs, which I am to undertake again, the matter is so important that I must remain firmly resolved not to undertake it, if these men remain at their posts and about the King, and a Cabinet beside the Ministerial Cabinet is allowed to continue.

The course now taken by the King may have been intended only to save his dignity, and it is possible that he fully purposed in his mind to adopt the system his Ministers recommended. The misfortune was that he could not save his dignity and reassure his Ministers at the same time. He did not resent the memorial of Dec. 14th, which, though respectful in form, was certainly peremptory in substance; Hardenberg alone, who had declared himself determined not to accept office except on the conditions stated in it, was passed over in the

King's answer. That answer was conveyed in a letter addressed to Rüchel, Stein, and Zastrow, enclosing a decree regulating the future conduct of the government. Three Ministers were to form a Council, much as in the scheme suggested by Beyme. The first was to be a War Minister, and Rüchel was appointed to this office; the second a Minister of Internal and principally Financial Affairs; 'for this office', adds the King, 'I have selected the Baron v. Stein, Minister of State, who is so honourably known to me as an active mind, capable of great conceptions'; the third a Minister of Foreign Affairs, and to this post Zastrow is appointed. The decree concludes with these words: 'It is my will that the Privy Cabinet Councillor Beyme be called to the deliberations of the Council as Secretary; partly in order to keep the minutes, partly also, in case it were necessary, to be able to draft the instructions immediately, in order that they may be laid before me without loss of time at the audience of the members of the Council.'

This document is dated December 19th. It may have been intended to cover a concession of all that was required; under such a system the old Cabinet might have gradually fallen into disuse, and Beyme might have become insignificant. On the other hand, the wording of the decree was equally consistent with the supposition that the King granted nothing, for when Beyme was called Privy Cabinet Councillor, it was implied that the old Cabinet was not abolished. Another feature of it was unsatisfactory, viz. the appointment of Zastrow. He had been one of the negotiators at Charlottenburg, and had just returned full of conversations he had had with Napoleon, and notions he had formed as to Napoleon's intentions. Hardenberg, in rejecting a proposal that had been made to him on Zastrow's suggestion, that he should return to office simply changing places with Stein, had, it seems, remarked that it would be better to give the Foreign Department to Zastrow himself, and the King had immediately determined to do so. Zastrow belonged to the party which, among the military men, answered to the party of Haugwitz and Lombard among civilians; and no one who held Stein's opinions could allow himself to make one in a Council consisting of four members, two of whom favoured a policy which he regarded as pernicious. On the 17th he writes to Hardenberg: 'Zastrow has communicated to me the King's letter. I have refused decidedly; I stand by the paper we have signed, which General Rüchel has laid before the King. I shall be firm, dear Excellency; no Cabinet, no secret influence, and no Council without *you;* we must hold together to destroy the intrigues of Beyme and the others.'

And again in a letter to Schulenburg, dated the 18th, he sums up his objections as follows: (1) 'Unless Hardenberg enters the Council I can have nothing to do with it, for I cannot do without his assistance and support in a career completely strange to me; (2) there must be security that the King has formally dismissed Haugwitz and Lombard; (3) Beyme is an object of suspicion and dislike at the Court of St Petersburg, and extremely odious to a great part of the public, so that the King would in great part recover the confidence of his subjects by dismissing him; (4) it would be indispensable, unless the plan is to be stifled in the birth, to put in practice the principles stated in the paper signed by Rüchel, Hardenberg, and myself, that the coexistence of a Cabinet and a Council is an arrangement inadmissible, contradictory, and absurd, which no man of sense can have anything to do with.'

Accordingly, while Zastrow accepted the appointment offered to him, Stein wrote on Dec. 20th a respectful refusal, addressed however not to the King but to Rüchel, alleging that the persons who inspired the public with mistrust were not removed, and that he was discouraged by the little forbearance and kindness with which Hardenberg was treated.

Rüchel was now commissioned by the others to make a report to the King to the effect that the proposed arrangement seemed impracticable; but that Stein had no intention of abandoning the King's service, and would continue to perform his former functions, and obey the King's commands, only declining to yield to the delusion, that a real Council in direct co-operation with the King existed, or to assume a responsibility to which in such circumstances he was not equal. It is difficult to understand that Stein can have been technically justifiable in taking this course. He might decline the appointment offered him in the King's Order of Dec. 19th, but that Order introduced by royal authority a new state of things; and one does not see what right Stein or Rüchel could have to declare the new arrangement impracticable, and that they remained in their old offices under the old arrangements which the King had now abolished. This seems to have been the view taken by the King himself. He took no notice of Rüchel's report, but assumed that Stein's declaration that he remained in the King's service was equivalent to an acceptance of the appointment offered to him, reasoning probably that Stein could not remain in his service except on the terms offered by himself, and at the same time, as we shall see, resenting Stein's conduct in sending his refusal to Rüchel rather than to himself. This misunderstanding soon brought on a catastrophe. Papers were sent from the King to Stein, on which he was required to report, as holding the office conferred on him by the Order of Dec. 19th. He sent them back, declaring that the matter did not belong to his department. They were returned to him by Köckeritz after it had been ascertained that he could not from illness attend the King personally, with a message pointing out that by the new arrangements the matter came within his province. Stein replied simply by referring to his letter to Rüchel, and declaring that he regarded the new Council as nonexistent.

The royal family were at this moment leaving Königsberg for Memel, and Stein was preparing to follow them. It was Jan. 3rd, 1807, and Stein was to leave that night, though he was ill himself, and one of his children in a dangerous state, when, at seven o'clock in the evening, came the following autograph letter from the King:

I had formerly prejudices against you. I always indeed looked on you as an active-minded, talented man, capable of great conceptions; but I thought you at the same time to have the eccentricities of genius, in one word, to be a man who, considering his own always as the only true opinion, was not suited for a practical post where there are continually points of contact which would soon disturb your temper. These prejudices I overcame, as I have always striven not to choose the public servants from personal liking, but on serious grounds. And here it is a most unaccountable thing that the very persons whom you now attack and want to overthrow are those who were then your most powerful advocates—(The King speaks evidently of Beyme) —and I yielded. You succeeded the deceased Struensee. I soon convinced myself that the conduct of your department was exemplary. I began to think of bringing you nearer to myself in order in due time to give you a greater sphere of action. An ironical sally about the proceedings of the last summer, improper in a ministerial report, drew upon you a deserved reproof from me. You made no reply—Was it from a conviction that you were wrong? I waive that question. Not long after, I saw your name at the bottom of a paper signed by several, which on account of its singular form I choose to pass over in complete silence. In spite of all this, I continued to treat you with confidence and receive your advice on all principal affairs. Your judgment was always that of an acute understanding. Accordingly I thought of ways to bring you nearer to the most important points of the machine of State, and for this reason committed to you the Portfolio of Foreign Affairs to hold at least *ad interim*. You refused to accept this honourable post in a bombastic essay; chiefly on the pretext of your want of information in this department. Although this refusal at that time could not but embarrass me much, still I admitted your reasons, and in order to meet your views still more in respect of an improved method in the conduct of public business I issued the Order of Dec. 17th (19th?) of last year, which *I presume* to be known to you. I say, ' I presume,' since your persistent silence, which at first I laid to the account of the state of your health, must otherwise remain completely inexplicable. (The King seems to mean, inexplicable except on the supposition that the Order was *not* known to you.)

I cannot possibly attribute your silence to mere defiance or disobedience to my commands, for in that case I should have to provide you with a suitable lodging.   I am indeed well aware in what an insolent manner you have expressed yourself orally and in writing in the presence of Generals Rüchel, v. Zastrow, and v. Köckeritz, and that just now you have twice refused to report on an affair which was sent to me by yourself, and accordingly was plainly to be regarded as belonging to your department.

From all this I have been forced, to my great regret, to admit that unfortunately I was not mistaken in you at the beginning, but that you are to be regarded as a refractory, insolent, obstinate and disobedient official, who, proud of his genius and talents, far from regarding the good of the State, guided purely by caprice, acts from passion and from personal hatred and rancour.   Such officials however are just those whose conduct works most prejudicially and dangerously upon the coherence of the whole.   I am *really sorry* that you have reduced me to the necessity of speaking to you so clearly and plainly.   However, as you give yourself out for a lover of truth, I have told you my opinion in good German, and I must add that if you are not disposed to alter your disrespectful and indecorous behaviour the State will not be able to reckon much on your future services.

FRIEDRICH WILHELM.

Königsberg, Jan. 3, 1807.

The harsh words printed in italics had been crossed out by the King.

Stein replied on the spot as follows:

I have received Your Majesty's Order in Cabinet of Jan. 3rd, in a moment when I had prepared myself for a journey to Memel, which was in many respects burdensome and serious, and was about to start this night.

As Your Majesty regards me as a 'refractory, insolent, obstinate and disobedient official, who, proud of his genius and talents, far from regarding the good of the State, guided purely by caprice, acts from passion and from personal hatred,' and as I am equally convinced that 'such officials work most prejudicially and dangerously upon the coherence of the whole,' I am forced to beg Your Majesty for my dismissal, which I look to receive here, as in these circumstances I am compelled to abandon my purpose of going to Memel.

Jan. 3rd, 1807.   STEIN.

The King answered on the following day:

As the Baron v. Stein under yesterday's date passes sentence on himself, I have nothing to add.

                                   FRIEDRICH WILHELM.

Königsberg, Jan. 4th, 1807.

No notice was taken of an application which Stein made in answer to this for a formal letter of dismissal. It would surely be difficult to find a parallel to the violence and suddenness of this explosion, considering how well-intentioned and estimable were both the parties concerned. The King, it must be confessed, writes, as he says, in good German, and Stein answers with cold defiance. The necessity which, a few months later, the King was under of humbling himself before Stein, recalling him and loading him with honours, has led history to give its verdict entirely against the King. The same verdict was given at the time by the best politicians who were in a position to judge. We have letters from Niebuhr, in which he sides passionately with his chief, asks Stein whether Beyme's plan of a Council did not remind him of Ariel's speech in the *Tempest* :

> You shall be viceroys here, 'tis true,
> But I'll be viceroy over you :

and stigmatises the King's letter as the 'monstrous inconceivable letter.' From the same letter of Niebuhr, it appears that not only Hardenberg, who was himself labouring under a sense of injury, but also Altenstein and Lord Hutchinson, the English Ambassador, took the same view; so did Vincke, to whom a few months after at Nassau Stein showed the papers. Indeed, the mere fact that, in the extremity of the fortunes of Prussia, the King chased from him both Hardenberg and Stein, the former with slight, the latter with fierce anger, and so left himself in the hands of a Köckeritz and a Beyme, speaks for itself. What may be alleged in his excuse is partly that, as we have said, it was an unprecedented thing for a King of Prussia to surrender his own will to that of his Ministers so absolutely as was now required of him (no one can read his letter, I think, without seeing that his respect for Stein's character and abilities amounted almost to terror), and that he may well have felt that, if he yielded then, he was likely never to recover his liberty; but partly also, I cannot but suspect, that Stein's neglect of usual forms had made him reasonably angry. He clearly charges Stein with leaving him entirely in the dark as to whether he accepted or declined the appointment of Dec. 19th; from which it appears that he regarded the letter to Rüchel, in which Stein declined the appointment, as entirely informal, and as disrespectful to himself. He also charges him with first acting as if he still held his office, when he laid before the King the paper which was the occasion of the dispute, and then acting as if he had ceased to hold it, when on the paper being sent back to him, he refused to report on it; evidently implying that Stein's plan of refusing the appointment of Dec.

19th, and at the same time continuing to hold his former office, just as if the Order of Dec. 19th had never been issued, was a mere impertinence, of which he could take no notice. I have seen no defence of Stein's conduct on these points; it is difficult to imagine that it can have been formally regular. Possibly, in the confusion of the hour, Stein may have supposed such irregularities unavoidable and venial, while the King may have been more punctilious, or may have unjustly attributed them to intentional disrespect; but it is possible also that the less favourable view of Stein's conduct was not unjust, for there is no mistaking his despotic and irritable temper. He may have become exasperated in the course of the dispute with the party of Beyme, and he may in consequence have forgotten the tact and forbearance which were especially necessary when the King was, however much for his own good and for the good of the State, to be humiliated. That nothing of this sort is hinted in Niebuhr's letters does not prove much; for Arndt, speaking of Stein and Niebuhr together, calls them two of the most irritable men in the world, and adds, 'Niebuhr was the more irritable of the two.' Hardenberg passes the following sentence : 'Both parties were wrong : the King in refusing to listen to the voice of truth raised so often and from all sides, and in writing in such harsh language to a meritorious man ; the Minister in not using gentler and more respectful forms towards his master.'

Moreover the account which Stein himself gives of these occurrences conveys to me the impression that he was not altogether satisfied with his own conduct. He says indeed of his dismissal, what he was perfectly justified in saying, that it made an unfavourable impression on the public; but when he describes his own conduct which led to his dismissal it is with a comment which is much more like an apology than a vindication. He says:

> I was afraid he (*i.e.* Beyme) would abuse his inordinate secret influence, and I insisted on his dismissal as the condition of my acceptance of the position offered me. Illness and deep resentment against the authors of the disastrous political system which was pursued had in truth greatly embittered and exasperated me.

So far from justifying his conduct in detail he does not even say that he thought it right in the main.

The King's letter suggests two other remarks. First, the retrospective recital with which it opens does not mention Stein's Memoir on the Faulty Organisation of the Cabinet. We may surely gather from this that the King had not seen it. Secondly, it draws a very curious picture of Stein's character. Strongly marked as that character was, he could hardly mistake it altogether, and yet he does to all appearance seriously mistake it. His notion that Stein was a man 'who considered always his own opinion as the only true one,' was perhaps a natural conjecture to be made by a king, for the angularity and combativeness of Stein's manner might be taken as marking dogmatism by one who, as he could not descend to a regular wit-combat with his subject, could not be expected to find out that in this instance they only marked earnestness and a deter-

mination to arrive at definite and solid conclusions.
Those who knew him more intimately are careful to
assure us of this. Rehberg says expressly, ' He was
always busy with the subject,' and Schön's studied
depreciation of him unconsciously bears the same
testimony. Stein, according to Schön, was not a man
of ideas, and if his statesmanship appears particularly
rich in ideas, the reason is that when he was brought
into the society of men of ideas he very readily took
the infection and raised himself for the time quite to
their level. It is startling to find the same man—
and that too a man of remarkably open character—
described in such contradictory terms by those who
had themselves known him. A man full of ideas
but incapable of entering into those of others, says
the King. A man *without* ideas but with a remarkable readiness in appropriating the ideas of others,
says Schön. The King's mistake is easily explained,
and Schön's misrepresentation only too easily; but
he would hardly have ventured on it if Stein had
really been the self-absorbed egotist he seemed to
his prince.

CHAPTER VII.

STEIN IN RETIREMENT.

THE dismissal of Stein took place on January 4th 1807. While the court removed to Memel he remained in Königsberg till the end of the month. He was meditating the publication of the documents relating to the affair, and proposed to commit the editing of them to Niebuhr. In the end he decided to postpone the vindication of himself to more peaceful times, and complaining of the annoyances to which he was exposed at Königsberg, 'constantly hearing a number of things contemptible in their vulgarity and yet disturbing through the consequences they had,' and of his unendurable situation, 'ever excited without being able to act, without occupation, and in the disagreeable condition of the labourer waiting at the corner of the street to be hired,' he decided to retire to his home in Nassau. This however was not easy to effect, until the battle of Eylau, on February 8th, reopened the communication between Königsberg and Danzig. On February 16th he is at Danzig with his family, writing thus to

Niebuhr: 'I expect nothing from the ingredients of the Court of Memel—it is a soulless, meaningless combination, capable of nothing but corrupt fermentation. If they ever want me again I shall demand a guarantee against unworthy treatment, and assume that the supreme direction of affairs is to be placed in the hands of intelligent, reasonable, and estimable persons.   H. v. Hardenberg seems still to look for a favourable turn: I admire his patience and hope that it may be well grounded, but for myself I look for nothing from empty, slow, flat people.' This reminds us of his description given above of Köckeritz. From Danzig he made his way, just before the siege of that fortress was formed by the French, in spite of the disturbed state of the country to Berlin, and from thence to Nassau, where he arrived at the end of March. Here a respite of three months was allowed him, and then came the summons which called him to the great struggle of his life. In August he was once more to leave his patrimonial mansion. He was to enjoy for thirteen months the painful eminence of first minister in a ruined State, then to hurry into banishment, and to hear that his house and lands were seized by the enemy, then to drift upon the great wave of war eastwards as far as St Petersburg, and again west as far as Paris, and after seven years to see his home again in a world tranquillised at last, and to outward seeming much the same as he remembered it in his youth before the French troubles began, yet in reality, as he learned in an old age but half contented, different and growing ever more strange to him.

The period of the war had been as unhappy to
Stein personally as it was to the State.   In September, 1806, he had been attacked with gout, and it
had never left him since.   He reports himself 'very
ill' when he left Berlin in October, 'very ill' at
Königsberg in November, 'ill' at the time of his
quarrel with the King, and now that he had repose
and was able to devote himself to the recovery of
his health, he did not shake off the gout till May,
and was laid up again in August with fever.   His
mind was all this time disquieted, not only by the
misfortune of his country, but, as he tells us, 'by deep
discontent on account of the mediatisation that had
befallen him.'   How he occupied himself during this
interval we are able to judge from an essay On the
proper form of the Central and Provincial Councils
of Finance and Police in the Prussian Monarchy,
which he wrote at Nassau, in the month of June.
It is a document of great importance both in the
constitutional history of Prussia, and as the earliest
exposition we have of Stein's general views.   At
the beginning he refers to his paper of April, which
has been given above, and undertakes to determine
in detail the character of that responsible ministry
working under the immediate oversight of the King,
which he had before declared should be substituted
for the existing irresponsible Cabinet.   He enters
at great length into the distribution of the different
functions.   On this subject, we shall find an occasion
later of considering his views ; what deserves to be
noted at present is, that the question of administrative reform occupies him principally.   This agrees
with a remark made by his friend Schön, who says

of him, 'When he came to Memel his first thought was to reform the administrative system,' and it agrees also with what we should expect, since the public calamity had been traceable much more directly to administrative abuses than to any other cause. But though he begins here, Stein does not end here. When he comes to the question of Provincial Administration, we find the following important passage. After remarking that there had hitherto been a great want of uniformity in the government of the different Provinces, and particularly that in some of them Estates or Corporations of certain classes of Proprietors had had more or less share in the government, while in others it had been exclusively in the hands of bureaucratic Boards, he proceeds as follows :

In this multiplicity of Provincial Administrations the question arises which of them deserves the preference. The Provincial Colleges, consisting of paid officials, are easily and generally infected with a hireling spirit, a devotion to forms and official mechanism, an ignorance of the district governed, an indifference, often an absurd antipathy to it, a dread of alterations and innovations which impose more work upon the Members, of whom the better are already overburdened and the less able are indisposed to work.

If the proprietor is excluded from all share in the Provincial Administration, the link which unites him to his country remains unused, the information which he has gained from his relation to his estates and his neighbours unproductive; his wishes and the improvements he knows of to remove abuses which affect him are lost or suppressed, and his leisure and the powers he would gladly on certain conditions devote to the State are spent in every kind of luxury or wasted in indolence. It is really monstrous to see that the possessor of an estate or other property of great value is deprived of an influence over the affairs of his province, which a strange official, ignorant of the country and having no connection with it, possesses to no purpose.

In this way by removing the proprietor from all participation in the administration public spirit and monarchical spirit is killed, disaffection towards the government is nourished, official posts are multiplied, the cost of administration is heightened, since the salaries must be fixed in proportion to the wants and position of the officials who are to live solely on their pay. Experience shows the correctness of this remark; if for example the important functions of the Landräthe were committed to paid officials out of the class of non-proprietors, undoubtedly the branch of administration entrusted to the Landräthe would become more expensive.

He goes on to quote D'Ivernois on the cheapness of administration in England as compared to France, and adds :

My own official experience too has given me a deep and lively conviction of the great advantage of properly constituted Estates, and I regard them as a powerful instrument for strengthening the Government through the information and the estimation of all cultivated classes, for binding them all to the State by conviction, sympathy and co-operation in national affairs, for giving the forces of the nation a free activity and directing them to the public good, for diverting them from idle sensual enjoyment, or insubstantial metaphysical cobwebs, or pursuit of purely selfish ends, and for keeping up a well-constituted organ of public opinion, which at present we make vain attempts to guess from expressions of individual men or individual associations.

He then descends into details, where the reader is not yet prepared to follow him. He then raises the question how far the Polish provinces may be allowed to share in these improvements, a subject which he discusses in a very interesting manner, and with a great display of knowledge of Polish affairs.

That the reader may understand the observation I have to make on this essay, it is necessary that he should learn at this point what the reforms made by Stein in the period we are now approaching, definitely were.   They consisted then of

(1) A Land Reform, by which a process was commenced, which ended in the abolition of serfdom in Prussia, the removal of shackles which prevented all free-trade in land, and the creation of a class of peasant proprietors.

(2) A Municipal Reform (Städteordnung), by which the military bureaucracy which up to that time had ruled in the towns made way for the self-government of the citizens.

(3) A Reform of the Administration.   This was sketched by Stein during his term of office, but was not actually completed or put into practice till later.

I have enumerated these Reforms in what is generally considered the order of their importance, and I have placed first that with which Stein's name and fame is especially connected.   Now, when we refer to the essay of which an abstract has just been given in order to find what were the ideas with which Stein set out, we observe that the Reform I have placed last is foremost in his thoughts, and the great Land or Social Reform, which I have placed first, is nowhere mentioned.   It is true that the subject of the Essay is government, not industry, that it deals with the political, not with the social question, and that for this reason it was not to be expected that serfdom and peasant proprietorship should be discussed in it.   But in the autobiography of Schön, in which the ministry of Stein is chronicled by one of his coadjutors, the Emancipating Act is declared to have been discussed and matured at Königsberg before Stein's arrival, and to have owed to him little more than his signature. This view is at least negatively confirmed by the essay before us. We find indeed proofs of Stein's sympathy with the labouring classes, but there is nothing to show that he had busied himself with any great schemes for their relief. Evidently, what he values himself upon is his plan of administrative reform.

He had quitted the scene in the middle of what I have marked as the second of the four periods into which the war may be divided. The third and most hopeful period began about the time that he reached Nassau. It might just then be supposed for a moment that Prussia had found her destined saviour in Hardenberg. The general confidence he inspired was such that England and Austria might be expected soon to render effectual help to Prussia, and as to reforms he had views not less clear than those of Stein concerning the most urgent reform of all, that of the Foreign Department. But, as we have remarked, the sudden change of Russian policy which followed the Battle of Friedland introduced a fourth period of the war and brought a new and overwhelming calamity on Prussia. It brought to an end at the same time the Ministry of Hardenberg.

Napoleon's art of diplomacy was very similar to his fashion of making war. It was a singular mixture of cunning and audacity made more effective by extreme rapidity. But it was expressly adapted to confound courtier diplomatists of the old type, just as in war Napoleon seemed sent to confound the spirit of military system and pedantry. It could be foiled by intelligence and firmness, and accordingly Napoleon makes it a principal object to avoid having to deal with intelligence and firmness. In the negotiations which now began this is unusually visible. The Czar had a vigorous minister in Budberg, and therefore Napoleon, though anxious to treat the Czar with the utmost forbearance, seeks excuses for excluding him, declares that he is not a Russian, and asks what had led Alexander to choose him, till Budberg finds it necessary to fall ill and refrain from appearing at Tilsit. But it was still more essential that Prussia should not be represented by a man of ability. For a long time Napoleon's dealings with Prussia had been calculated on the assumption of imbecility in her councils. Haugwitz and Lombard were now gone, and the question with him was how to replace them with tools equally serviceable to himself. Half the advantages he had gained might be endangered if just at this last moment he should find himself encountered by an intelligent diplomatist.

Hardenberg was at this moment not only Foreign Minister but occupied a sort of dictatorial position which was soon to pass to Stein. Even after the complete change of front on the part of Russia he by no means looked forward to such a fate for his country as actually overtook her at Tilsit. If an alliance is now to be formed between France and Russia he still believes that the support of Prussia

is important to both Powers. He imagines a great
alliance of the three States, necessarily under the
leadership of Napoleon and directed against England. To accommodate all the parties interested,
he thinks the best means will be to make a partition
of Turkey in Europe in such a way as to give France
the command of the Mediterranean. Russia is to
have the Principalities, Bessarabia and Bulgaria;
Dalmatia, Servia, Bosnia and part of Wallachia are
to go to Austria; all Greece with Thessaly and the
islands to France. Meanwhile the kingdom of
Poland is to be restored in the House of Saxony,
but Prussia while she cedes her Westphalian possessions is to acquire Saxony, Lübeck and Hamburg,
and to be placed at the head of a North German
Confederation. It is startling to find that Hardenberg regards such a solution as still possible on
June 22nd, that is, not three weeks before the
Treaty of Tilsit, and when the change of Russian
policy had already taken place. Partly this is
because he does not count upon such a complete
desertion of his ally as the Czar was guilty of, but
partly also he is far from considering that Prussia
was yet at the end of her resources. His sketch of
what the King might still have done is as follows :—

There were still troops left on the Memel, in Swedish
Pomerania, in the three fortresses of Pillau, Colberg and Graudenz, in Cosel and Glatz, though both these last places were on
the point of falling, and Colberg too could not have held out
much longer. But much would have been possible with spirit
and effort, when once his resolution was known. The harbour at
Memel lay full of ships; we had money left too. If the King
took ship, as he might have done, passed to the Isle of Rügen,
on the way took help to Colberg, asked England for money arms

and ammunition, which in that case might have been had at once, since the English Ministers had full powers, and ships with artillery and munitions of war were already under way in the Baltic, which the English afterwards sent back again; if in an appeal to his subjects and to Germany he described his situation and ordered a *levée en masse*, which would certainly have had an indescribable effect, since everything had actually been prepared in Westphalia, Hessen and Lower Saxony by the Prince of Wittgenstein, by the President v. Vincke at Münster, and Colonel D'Ivernois of our light infantry (brother of the author) and only waited for the landing which had been resolved on of 17,000 English and Hannoverians with arms and munitions; if the King himself had appeared at the head of his troops and pressed boldly forward in the rear of the French army into the heart of his States; if the attempt had been made to seize some strongholds that were slightly garrisoned, such as Stettin, Magdeburg, Spandau, Hameln;—he might perhaps have fallen covered with fame and honour, but he might also, before Napoleon could bring back his army from the Weichsel, have assembled a formidable and dangerous Power between him and France, have set all Germany in motion, and by this example have induced Austria to strike in, and so have become the Liberator of his State and of the world.

Frederick William was indeed not the man from whom such a resolution was to be expected, but despair sometimes gives courage, and a resolute diplomatist who can support himself by pointing to such a possibility occupies a position of some strength. It was accordingly all-important to Napoleon that he should not encounter any such resolute diplomatist. He declared war at once upon Hardenberg. 'So long as a foreigner, educated about the person of the Prince of Wales and entirely English in his sympathies held office, he could not,' he said, 'negotiate with any feeling of confidence.' It was in vain that Hardenberg protested that 'it

was absolutely false that he had any ties whatever
with England or any partiality for that Power, and
equally so that he had been educated with the Prince
of Wales; that he had quitted the Hannoverian
service twenty-five years before on account of a very
marked difference with that Prince, not at all dishonourable to himself, in an affair which had destroyed his domestic happiness; that he had been in
the Prussian service seventeen years, that he had
transferred to Prussia all his possessions and had
sold all his lands in the Hannoverian country.' On
July 3rd Napoleon insisted that all negotiation must
be broken off if either Hardenberg or General
Rüchel remained in the King's service, and that
he must receive an answer on the next day. On
July 6th Hardenberg left the King and Queen, who
were then residing at the village of Piktupöhnen
near Tilsit, and went to Memel. He was not to
return to power till 1810.

In Stein's biography these occurrences are of
interest, partly because we shall see that he himself,
as soon as he began to make himself formidable to
Napoleon, was treated by him in just the same way,
the fall of Stein in 1808 being almost precisely
similar in its circumstances to that of Hardenberg
in 1807, but principally because Stein was destined
to succeed to the place now vacated by Hardenberg.
The latter relates that at the first meeting of the
sovereigns on June 26th, on the raft in the midst of
the river Memel, Napoleon expressed his hostile
feelings towards himself, and that on the King remarking that he had no one to whom he could
entrust his affairs with the same confidence, Napo-

leon named to him Schulenburg, Zastrow, and Stein.
Another version makes him say, ' Prenez le baron
de Stein; c'est un homme d'esprit.' What did
Napoleon know about Stein at this time ? Clearly
not much; otherwise he would have seen that it
could hardly be worth while to insist on the dismissal of Hardenberg if Stein was to be appointed
in his room. But it appears that Stein on his
journey home to Nassau had passed through Berlin
and had made there the acquaintance of the French
Governor, General Clarke. Clarke had been at first
alarmed at hearing of his arrival, thinking, I suppose,
that he had been sent to rouse an insurrection,—
particularly as the Battle of Eylau had just happened
and Prussian affairs seemed reviving,—but on learning from Stein that he was retiring from public
business treated him in a very friendly manner, and,
as Stein learnt afterwards, mentioned him in favourable terms in his letters to Napoleon. It was much
to learn that if Stein were appointed Napoleon
would not interpose his veto. Hardenberg was of
course most anxious for his appointment, for it may
almost be said that he had fallen a sacrifice in
January to his zeal for Hardenberg's honour and
interest. In the last private interview which the
retiring Minister had with the King, on July 6th, he
tells us that he ' begged him to take the Minister
v. Stein again into his service, to forget what had
passed between them, and to assign him with confidence the same position which he himself had hitherto occupied near his person (*i.e.* a sort of dictatorial
position), and that he represented to him earnestly
and in heartfelt language that Stein was the only

man from whom help could be expected.' 'To this proposal,' he adds, 'the King after some objections gave his assent, and commissioned him to carry it into effect ; provisionally '—this looks like a little flash of obstinacy—' until Stein's arrival he would resort again to the advice of the Privy Cabinet Councillor Beyme.' The next day Hardenberg informed Beyme of this arrangement, who 'made no objection, though he did not seem quite to like the recall of Stein.'

Meanwhile the expulsion of Hardenberg had fully served its immediate purpose. Haugwitz himself, or almost more than Haugwitz, reappeared in Field-Marshal Count Kalkreuth, upon whom now the negotiations devolved. He had pledged himself upon his honour, if the King would employ him, to conclude an honourable peace. The King should only cede a few Catholic Churches, perhaps Münster and Paderborn. He would know how to speak to Napoleon as General to General, though indeed his most conspicuous military achievement had been the surrender of Danzig, which gave rise to suspicions of treachery. Kalkreuth seems to have had an amusing vein of caustic humour, but it struck most Prussian politicians with absolute horror to see him entrusted with important negotiations. ' His whole art,' says Hardenberg, 'consisted in vain gasconades and flatteries of the French Generals.' 'The vainest puppy perhaps that ever lived, and now quite in his dotage!' says Altenstein. 'The very children laugh at him.' The worst apprehensions were more than fulfilled. As to the Treaty itself, little choice was left to Prussia in the end but to accept it ; but what completed the ruin of the country was the Convention signed on July 12th, and to have signed this without question was the masterpiece of Kalkreuth.   Two days later Roux writes as follows to Hardenberg :—

Your Excellency has predicted the disastrous issue of our negotiations.   But what is the loss of so many provinces in comparison with the incalculable evils which the Convention signed since by Count Kalkreuth will bring upon us?   Either complete insanity or flagrant wickedness has actuated the Marshal ; no other explanation is admissible, and he has only to choose between the gibbet and the lunatic asylum.   But I do not despair of seeing him awarded the civic crown !

In August the summons reached Nassau in the form of a letter from Hardenberg written by command of the King.   In the following passage of it I think it is not difficult to read the writer's disapproval of Stein's violence in his collision with the King, and his anxiety lest the same fault of manner should now prevent him from acquiring his proper influence :

Let not a word be said of bygones between you and the King. The King has profited much by adversity, and his constancy does him honour.   If you hit the right way of doing business with him you will get his consent to all good and useful measures, as I was always able to do.   Be careful to avoid the appearance of wishing to rule him.   He has the good quality of enduring contradiction and of esteeming those who tell him the truth, if it is done with the respect due to a prince, without harshness, and from real love to him and his service.

The letter also reassures Stein about Beyme, of whom it testifies that his behaviour has been excellent and that he has sought no undue influence since Hardenberg's return to office in April.

Along with this letter was enclosed another from Blücher, and a passionate appeal from the Princess Louise Radziwill, a sister of that Prince Louis Ferdinand who perished at Saalfeld.

No greater honour could be paid to Stein, than such a unanimous appeal to him as the only man capable of saving the State; but could he hope to accomplish anything? Want of principle, purpose, and intelligence had ruined Prussia, but it was by no means clear that she could now be restored by principle, purpose and intelligence. The task recommended to him was the care of a ruined State, overshadowed by what might almost be called a Universal Monarchy, by which it was likely at the next change of affairs to be absorbed. When at the end of the following year he laid his office down again, having done his best, it was by no means clear that any progress had been made, nay, four years later the public ruin seemed in no wise averted, but rather more inevitable than ever. Nothing, he might fairly say to himself at the outset, could help Prussia except a disaster befalling France so entirely beyond precedent that it might be called impossible.

In such hopeless circumstances it does, no doubt, behove a good citizen at least to fall at his post. He is to sacrifice his repose and his private happiness for his country. But here lay the misfortune of the German States at that time. Prussia was not Stein's country; nor was it Scharnhorst's, nor Gneisenau's, nor Blücher's, nor Hardenberg's, nor Niebuhr's. These were so many officials who had been attracted into the Prussian service from various quarters. It had afforded them a livelihood, and they did their duty to Prussia faithfully while they received their salaries. Were they under any obligation to do more? At any rate, if one of these officials had been harshly treated by his employer and driven away with ignominy, could he be called upon, could he with any justice be expected, not merely to forget such an injury, but actually to expose himself and his fortunes to new risk in behalf of such an employer, particularly when it was scarcely possible that he could do any good? We have seen that, as an Imperial Knight, Stein had from the beginning thrown more of the spirit of chivalry into his work than was usual with German officials, yet with him too statesmanship was a *profession* in a sense in which it is not so to English statesmen. Administration was the business to which he had been trained, in which he had acquired skill, and which perhaps had become almost necessary to him. An English politician, when he is thrown out of office, or has lost the popular favour, does not think of applying for office to some foreign sovereign; but during these months of Stein's retirement we find Niebuhr instructed to make inquiries whether the Czar could find a place in his service for Stein, and for a short time it seems not unlikely that he may take the place of Romanzow, a Russian official, whom he has encountered before and is to encounter again, as Minister of Trade. Surely there were now brighter prospects at St Petersburg than there were likely to be in future at Berlin, if the King should ever return to Berlin!

Before Stein's answer was sent, Niebuhr wrote words which, as usual with Niebuhr's words, were not encouraging :

You will not be daunted by the summons to rescue from destruction and to restore internally a country so completely ruined, however mournful the spectacle and gigantic the undertaking, however dark the future and external destiny. But your Excellency *will* be daunted, because you will be filled with the presentiment of the opposition that awaits you, by the permanent marring of all comprehensive enterprises through the mediocrity and baseness that will scarcely be forced even from their present dominion, by the folly of the hope that a better day must follow the night of incapacity and vulgarity. The giants piled up mountains and rejoiced in their strength, but the stone of Sisyphus was a torment of hell.

Stein had been seized with a tertian fever on hearing the news of the Treaty of Tilsit, and was so weak as to be unable to write. He dictated to his wife the following answer :

To the King's Majesty.

Your Majesty's commands concerning my re-entrance into Your Majesty's Ministry of Home Affairs reached me on the 9th August, through a letter of Cabinet Minister Hardenberg, dated Memel, July 10th. I obey them without conditions and leave to Your Majesty the making of every arrangement, whether concerning business or the persons with whom Your Majesty may see fit that I should work. In this moment of universal misfortune it would be very unjustifiable (unmoralisch) to take account of personal considerations, the more so as Your Majesty gives so high an example of constancy.

I would commence my journey at once were I not afflicted with a violent tertian fever. I will however set out as soon as my health is restored, which I hope will be the case in 10 or 14 days. I am uncertain which way I shall take. That by Berlin seems to me unsafe, as I am without passports, since I should have to pass through the French cantonments and be examined by each commandant. I shall therefore take the way of Copenhagen, and only in extreme need, if circumstances should arise which I am not in a condition to foresee, that of Galicia. I humbly submit to Your Majesty a single observation. At this moment the most urgent question seems to be the satisfying of the demands of the French officials. General Schulenburg has declined the commission given him by Your Majesty: in case Your Majesty has not already made another choice, I humbly suggest to Your Majesty that Your Majesty will be pleased to entrust this commission to Count v. Reden. He has continued to conduct his business, in this period of misfortune, with complete self-devotion. With him might be conjoined Privy Councillor Niebuhr, who is familiar with the Currency Question and the French language.

STEIN.

Thus arrives the decisive moment in Stein's life. What was generally thought of the man to whom the Prussian Monarchy thus turned in its extreme need? We shall find that he was universally regarded, even before he had any great achievements to show, as a man of massive power. He was not considered amiable or soft in his manners; but at that moment people thought with some pleasure of his roughness, for the manners of Haugwitz had been so soft! The second volume of Schön's Remains, lately published, contains some letters written to Schön during Stein's absence at Nassau, about the time when the King's summons went out to him, and when it was still uncertain whether he would accept it. They are written by two Prussian politicians of considerable mark, the one Altenstein, who was the leading man in the ministry that succeeded Stein's, the other Niebuhr, and they show us clearly in what light Stein was regarded by official men at that time. These letters come to us from Schön and were written to him; when one of them institutes a comparison between Schön and Stein which is in favour of the former, the reader will of course bear this in mind; but they are at least not written *by* him. I extract from them all the references to Stein that they contain.

The first shows us Hardenberg in the very act of writing the letter to Stein above quoted. It is from Altenstein, who had been a devoted follower of Hardenberg. He writes (July 10):

> The Minister begs to be remembered. He would have written to you himself...but had to finish the letter to Stein which is to go with this. It is a faithful description of the newest phase with Hardenberg's views, that he may do his whole duty to the State and Stein. I trust he will come. A powerful man like that is often attracted by difficulties, and no doubt in the mean time he has acquired new views for our wretched notions. A letter from the Princess Louise too will do something to win him. I should advise him to risk it—to risk it just as you would on the chance of its not lasting long. He may set good things in motion even if he does not accomplish great things.

On July 12th the same Altenstein describes a conversation, at which he was present, between Hardenberg, Rüchel, and Beyme:

> Beyme declared with great vehemence that he staked all his hopes on Stein; that that was the only resource, and that it must be the whole study of the King to make no arrangement that can cramp Stein, and to leave it entirely to him to organise everything round and under himself. I need not tell you that Rüchel quite agreed, and Hardenberg spoke very decisively.

Again on July 19th:

> I am convinced that my view about the pitiful state of things is right—that the misery is all the greater because dirt is a thing

one cannot take hold of ; but in the end one manages to drive a
strong pile into the dirt-sea, and so make the first beginning of
building a firm fabric which now resting on it comes into existence.   Stein will be this pile, and if he does not come *you* (*i.e.*
Schön) must be it.   The King must begin to think of you now.
What is said against you he will not much notice, because his
hopes are centred in Stein, and if Stein fails him you will remain.

To the same effect in another letter :

Everything depends on our Don Juan coming, and I hope he
will.   If not, I hold to my opinion—Niebuhr quite agrees with
me—that you must try your hand.   You are the only one, and
no doubt you would be better than Don Juan himself, who indeed
has many prejudices, did not, *as you very justly remark*, the
system of keeping down and keeping back that lies in our whole
constitution make it harder for you to come forward.

And in the same letter :

Schlaberndorf thought he was in for many annoyances ; Stein
had treated him rudely and he could not put up with it.   He
was afraid he would take the Prussian State, which was like a
mortally feeble infant, in his Cyclop hands and squeeze it to
death.

Niebuhr writes near the end of July :

Get me at any rate a furlough for two months that I may go
to Denmark—I must go, to watch the course of things a little,
and see whether Stein (Tu es Petrus et supra hanc petram ædi-
ficabo ecclesiam meam) accepts or not.   If not, everything will
follow its tendency to dissolution and rottenness, and if he does,
—well ! we shall see.

And lower down, with reference to the Imme-diate Commission :

Instead of such a many-voiced concert I with less taste for
music would have heartily begged for a single grand organ with
the whole congregation singing to it and led by it.   I have sent

a letter to Stein frankly describing my condition, and laying my future fate in his hands. Yes! but only in *his*. And only to fulfil former promises and because I have more regard for him in his rough strength than for anyone else. You understand that I do not care so much for amiability, and at times positively dislike it.

It is not uninteresting to notice in these extracts the commencement of the habit of playing upon Stein's name. When he was fairly installed as Minister and exciting admiration by his energy, this habit grew among his admirers. As may be seen from Niebuhr's letter quoted above they were not struck merely by the correspondence between the Minister's name and his character, or the destiny which made him the Ararat upon which the ark of Prussia's greatness rested. The play upon words was *borrowed*, and the main interest of it consisted in its being borrowed. It was borrowed from the most memorable play upon words ever made in the world, from the saying which is inscribed in mosaic on the base of St Peter's dome. In the later improvements of the conceit its Biblical character is plainly to be observed. Other allusions to the name of St Peter were collected from the New Testament and applied to Stein. The description of him which it became the custom to inscribe under his portraits and which pains were taken to circulate widely among the people, is said to have been invented by Professor Süvern, and ran thus: Des Guten Grundstein, des Bösen Eckstein, der Deutschen Edelstein. It is evidently composed by adding the sentence from the Gospel to a verse from the 1st Epistle of St Peter—A Rock whereon all

good is built, to evil a stone of stumbling, but
to all true Germans precious. I take it that no
greater mistake could be made than to judge of this
play upon words by its wit or ingenuity. It is not
wit but popular poetry. What gave it vogue was
its startling and almost providential appositeness
at a moment of extreme peril and anxiety. At
such moments the most philosophic temperament
is affected by omens. Leaders are then carefully
watched to find out whether they are lucky or not,
and often it is observed of some conspicuous man
that without excelling others precisely in ability he
seems to 'have a star.' This was so in that age
particularly, when the lurid comet of Napoleon's
fortune seemed likely to become a fixed star in the
heavens. The search for omens fixes easily on
proper names; we know how the ancients changed
the names of Maleventum and Epidamnus because
of the omen. We know too how the feeling was
not confined to the vulgar; we remember how the
most elevated of all ancient poets, when his imagination is brooding over the siege of Troy and all the
misery that had come from the beauty of Helen, is
struck by something in the first syllable of that name
that his Greek ear associates with disaster and destruction, and how accordingly the chorus in the
Agamemnon breaks out, 'Who can it have been that
named her so all-appropriately?' The reader of
Æschylus may find this a little quaint, but he finds
it also, I think, impressive and perfectly natural.
And yet in Æschylus the play upon words rests
upon a mere illusion. Assuredly it was a much
more striking coincidence that when Prussia had

been brought to the brink of ruin by irresolution and sentimentalism, in short by a want of manly angularity, in its rulers, a deliverer should come from one of the castles of the Rhine country, and this deliverer should bear the name—significant once before in the annals of Christianity—of Rock. In such a case it seems to me a trait of high and simple poetry that first Niebuhr, and then Süvern, and then the whole nation, should welcome him with the cry of, Who can it have been that named him so all-appropriately?

PART III.

MINISTRY OF STEIN.—FIRST PERIOD.

Mit ihrem heil'gen Wetterschlage,
Mit Unerbittlichkeit vollbringt
Die Noth an einem grossen Tage,
Was kaum Jahrhunderten gelingt;
Und wenn in ihren Ungewittern
Selbst ein Elysium vergeht
Und Welten ihrem Donner zittern—
Was gross und göttlich ist, besteht.

HÖLDERLIN.

CHAPTER I.

CONSTITUTION AND TASK OF THE MINISTRY.

STEIN now becomes once more a Minister of the Prussian State. But we remember that when he received his dismissal in January, the King had already begun to alter, in some degree, the old relations between the Ministers and himself, and also the old distribution of functions among the Ministers. Further alterations had been made since that time, so that Stein was now called upon to occupy a post which was newly created and had only as yet been held for about two months by Hardenberg. To understand what this newly created Ministerial Office was, we must trace slightly the history of the Prussian Administration from the beginning of the year.

We marked the King's refusal to conclude a separate peace with Napoleon as the beginning of the third period of the war. The King had been led to that decision by the advice of Hardenberg, and this is the moment of the revival of that states-

man's influence, and of the decline of the influence
of Zastrow, who had, as we remember, succeeded
Haugwitz in the Foreign Department on Stein's
refusal to accept the portfolio.   But the revival of
Hardenberg's influence was only gradual.   The
King had persevered in the middle course which
Stein and Hardenberg had rejected.   His Council
of Ministers now met regularly, and Beyme drew the
protocols, and passed and repassed between them and
the King.   The Ministers were Zastrow, Schrötter
and Voss, who had taken Stein's place.   Hardenberg had no department, but the first mark of the
King's favour for him was that he was now required
to attend this Council, which he only consented to
do under protest.   The new system led to nothing
but confusion, if we may judge from the contempt
with which it inspired Niebuhr.   Thus he writes at
the end of March :

> Hardenberg and Zastrow are at daggers drawn.   Voss takes
> a high tone and bears himself as Prime Minister.   Schrötter
> curses the Russians....Beyme is a patriot and speaks of the great
> interests of humanity.   If new languages do not spring up at last,
> as at the Tower of Babel, the old story must be a fiction.

So notorious was their discord, that a French
newspaper had the remark :

> The most extreme misfortune has not yet brought union to
> the fugitive Court of Prussia.   In spite of the most terrible
> lessons, it is more divided now than in the time of its prosperity.

But April brought a great and beneficial change.
The Czar Alexander arrived at Memel on the 2nd.
He treated Zastrow with much coldness, but on the
other hand he honoured Hardenberg with a visit

which lasted two hours. The two monarchs determined to go to a place called Kydullen on the Russian frontier, in order to see some Russian reinforcements which were to arrive there. Hardenberg and Zastrow were to accompany them, but the latter, piqued at the Czar's coldness, feigned illness and did not go. The other Ministers and Beyme also remained behind, and thus for the first time the King fell into the hands of Hardenberg, and that at a moment when his powerful friend, the Czar, was at hand to push his interests. On the 10th the King, who had been surprised and displeased at the con duct of Zastrow, gave the Foreign Department or, as it was technically called, the post of First Cabinet Minister, to Hardenberg. He shall tell us himself how in a few weeks he was advanced to a higher position still.

On leaving Memel the King had taken no man of affairs with him but Colonel Kleist and me. Except purely military matters, I alone laid all public affairs without exception before him. Cabinet Councillor Beyme had remained in Memel. This was the first time that Cabinet business was conducted by a Minister. At the same time I was present at the transaction of all military business and took a share in the discussion of this too. The King came to like this; I had the happiness to win his confidence more and more; I could go to him at all hours in the day and as often as I chose; he was not displeased at my freedom, which was often very great, yet always accompanied with the decorum and respect due to a Sovereign—[this seems pointed at Stein]—and marking devotion and honest purpose. As early as April 28th he committed to me internal as well as external affairs.

An Order was now draughted in which the King declared that he had grown convinced, while he had been with the army, of the urgent need of such rapidity and energy in the conduct of affairs connected with the war as was only possible through unity and avoidance of prolix communications and discussions between several Boards; that accordingly he ordered the Minister of State and Cabinet, the Baron v. Hardenberg, to assume again the sole management of the Foreign Department, and at the same time the conduct of all other affairs having relation to the war, with the exception of affairs purely military. These other affairs committed to him are then defined to be the provisioning of the army with the purchase of corn in foreign countries, war finance, a general control of the Post, the Censorship, and Secret Police, also of the Treasury, Bank, and Maritime Institute. Permission is given him to select for himself such officials as he may consider most efficient for the conduct of such important affairs.

Thus was created for the first time in Prussia a sort of Premier. It may be said that the plan originally proposed by the party of Stein and Hardenberg had been, in a manner, tried and had failed. Beyme had said that there was danger of a war of all the Departments against each other, a danger which he considered to have been averted by the power of the Cabinet. This was a very inadequate defence of the Cabinet, but the danger itself now appeared to be far from imaginary; much such a war had actually broken out when the Council of Ministers was introduced. Some controlling authority was actually needed, and we may perhaps consider the influence of the Cabinet Secretaries, pernicious as it was, to have been forced into existence by a real want, which was evidently the failure of energy in the King himself. The same need was now met by another method, a method infinitely preferable, the appointment of a Premier. It naturally gave offence to some of Hardenberg's colleagues; Voss, for instance, writes to him, 'If that one of us who has the good fortune in our present situation to be near the King's person chooses to seize the opportunity of appropriating the offices of his colleagues, very serious scenes will take place, which would not occur under the rule of a Cabinet,' and he thinks 'that this dictatorial power will hardly take deep root in our Constitution; it does not suit the Prussian character nor that of the Prussian king, and can show only unhappy precedents in the history of Brandenburg.' Nevertheless, as an occasional form of government suited to difficult times, it was certainly found successful. It gave to Prussia the Stein-Hardenberg legislation; after being superseded at the end of 1808 it was restored in 1810, and it carried Prussia through her dark time and through her War of Liberation. At the outset however it does not appear that Hardenberg deliberately intended to introduce so great an innovation, for in his letter to Stein of July 10th he says, 'I hoped that I should soon share the burden with you,' and that this was not a mere courteous profession appears from the following, which was written by Niebuhr to Stein on July 28th:

Hardenberg sent me word, and confirmed the announcement himself when we met, that he had undertaken the premiership as far as internal affairs are concerned only until the King should send Your Excellency such an invitation to resume the Ministry of the Interior as would give you full satisfaction, and you should

make the sacrifice to the country of returning in spite of all that
has occurred. I believe that he said the same thing to the Czar,
and that the latter then firmly hoped for your speedy return as a
benefit to Prussia, in which country he then took so much interest,
and would have considered it his duty to do all in his power to
bring it to pass. At that period however Hardenberg, who I
think wished to excite in the King's mind a desire to have Your
Excellency once more in his service before making any proposi-
tion to him, seems not to have made any sufficient progress in
this design.

Thus the country had two full months to grow
accustomed to a sort of dictatorial government.
Let us now inquire what powers were given to Stein
on his return. He had his first audience of the
King at Memel on October 1st. He describes
him as 'deeply depressed, believing himself pursued by an inexorable fate, and thinking of abdication'; the Queen as 'gentle and melancholy, full of
anxiety but also of hope.'

It was arranged that he should have the control
of all civil affairs, that the King should adopt his
plan of reconstruction, and further that Beyme
should not have access to the King. Accordingly
Beyme was named President of the Kammergericht
at Berlin, Stein's plan was sent in and adopted, the
Order of the Red Eagle conferred on him as an
acknowledgment of his merit, and lastly he was
desired to make proposals concerning the way in
which he would conduct the administration. In the
end it was decided, as indeed in the general dissolution of all government and the necessity of
a complete revision of all institutions was indispensable, that Stein should have not only the full control
of Civil Affairs and Finance, but also the presidency

and a voice in the Foreign Department (though he did not take the Foreign Portfolio), a share in the control of Military Affairs, a control over the department of Justice and over the various Commissions which were sitting to conduct the reconstruction of the State and to settle and satisfy the claims of the conqueror. This was his dictatorial position in the Executive, but besides this he received a kind of indefinite commission as legislator. The Order of Cabinet which gave Stein his powers runs as follows :—

MY DEAR MINISTER BARON V. STEIN,

The present condition of the State and its future reconstruction make a complete unity in the administration desirable. According to the intention already orally expressed I entrust to you hereby the conduct of all the Civil Affairs of my State. You find according to its present condition by way of administrative principal organs, the Prussian Provincial Ministry, the provisional Ministry of Justice, the Combined Immediate Commission and the Commission for the carrying out of the Peace at Berlin. It is my will that you lay before me the reports of these Boards, assume Presidency and a vote in the Conferences of the Foreign Department; conduct the affairs of the Combined Immediate Commission, the administration of the General Coffers and of the General Control or State Book-keeping, also of the Bank and Maritime Institute ; and you are authorised to require from all these as well as from all and every the Departments of my State any information that may be necessary or may seem useful within the sphere of your operations. And as the future arrangement of the military system as well as the transitional arrangement of the army is so intimately concerned with the financial state, with policy and with the future constitution of the State, it is my will that you take part also in the deliberations of the Military Commission.

The necessary instructions to the different Departments you are yourself to have draughted and to lay before me for ratification.

After the recovery of the Provinces which are now still in the occupation of the French the restoration of a free and independent administration will require other machinery: and on this subject and on your relation to this I expect from yourself the project as your affectionate king,

FRIEDRICH WILHELM.

Memel, 4th October, 1807.

If we compare Stein's dictatorship with Hardenberg's, we may see that it has the difference which might be expected from the fact that in the interval between them the war had come to an end. Hardenberg is a Foreign Minister to whom, in order to increase the military efficiency of the Government, a control over the other Departments is given in addition. Stein is a Home Minister in a State ruined by war and misfortune, to whom a similar control over the other Departments is given that he may accomplish a work of extensive but peaceful reconstruction.

The Immediate Commission mentioned in the above document consisted of officials brought together by Hardenberg on his first assumption of dictatorial powers. These were at first Schön, Niebuhr, Stägemann, Altenstein; after Hardenberg's retirement it was proposed to constitute them into a Provisional Government pending the arrival of Stein, but Altenstein and Niebuhr declined the task, and Klewitz was afterwards added to the Commission. We shall see that the deliberations of this Commission before Stein's arrival had done much to ripen some of the most important projects, and so to make his short ministry so fruitful of legislation.

The Military Commission mentioned is of equal importance. As the summons to Stein went forth on the day following the conclusion of the Treaty of Tilsit, scarcely more than a week was allowed to pass before Scharnhorst was promoted to the rank of Major General (it is interesting to observe that he was at this moment tempted by handsome offers to enter the English service and become director of an Artillery School, to be established after the model of that of Hannover), and on July 25th the Military Reorganisation Commission was created, with Scharnhorst for President; the other members being Massenbach, Count Lottum, Bronikowski, Gneisenau and Grolmann, who was to be Secretary. Bronikowski afterwards retired and Boyen and Count Götzen were added to the Board. Such is the Military Commission in which the king now gives Stein a seat.

Stein and these two Commissions : these were the agencies by which the reconstruction of Prussia was now commenced.

It is to be observed that the Order of Cabinet given above does not represent the King's personal view of what he thinks is required by the State, but Stein's own view which the King passively adopts. This will be seen by comparing the document with Stein's report to the King, dated the day before, on the powers which he desires to receive. The King for the most part adopts and sends back to the Minister his own expressions. By referring, however, to the words of the report, we ascertain somewhat more precisely how Stein conceived his own position.

First, we remark that he regarded it as exceptional and dictatorial, for he says :

At present when the State is still occupied by a foreign Power the province of the internal administration is very confined, and foreign relations also are very simple, and the arrangements under which the general conduct of civil affairs can be carried on are different from those under which it will be proper to carry it on after the reoccupation of the land.

Secondly, we may discover from his closing paragraph, of which the King's closing paragraph is a somewhat abridged repetition, precisely what he considered to be the task set him.

When the Monarchy is recovered and a free independent Administration is restored, other Administrative Institutions will be formed, and the relation of the Minister towards these will become somewhat different, with a view to which a special plan may be elaborated by way of preparation.

In other words, Stein considered that his first business was to pay the French and get rid of them. When this was done he thought that it would fall to him to establish a new administrative system, which should be free from the faults which had proved so fatal in the old.

Observe that there is not a single word here about the *revanche* or about recovering the lost provinces beyond the Elbe. The King is not told that henceforth it must be the business of Prussia to put herself in a condition as soon as possible to take the field again and recover her position in Europe. Since this was accomplished we are tempted to take for granted that it was contemplated, but it does not seem likely that Stein had such a design even in his imagination. He does indeed speak, as a matter of course, of a reorganisation of the army ; but then and for a long time after the utmost that was hoped from such a reorganised army—and even this was scarcely hoped—was that it might serve to defend the remaining territory of Prussia. But now let us note further what Stein does not say. He does not say that the recent catastrophe shows the necessity of extensive and thorough-going reforms; that the serfs must be emancipated, that a yeomanry must be created, that a parliamentary constitution must be granted. What he says is precisely in accordance with his reflexions written down at Nassau. He says simply that the administration will need to be reformed. In other words, a bad system of administration has led to a great military disaster; as to the distress that has fallen upon us in consequence, we must bear it as we may; all that we can do is to correct the mistake that led to it, and so take care that it does not befal us again.

The weakness of such a scheme was that it passed far too lightly over the problem of setting the territory free and satisfying the French. 'When this is done, so-and-so will be necessary.' But how was it to be done? This inquiry, as it proceeded, gave Stein quite a new view of the magnitude of his task, and he came to see that the financial and military ruin of the country, which his simple scheme of administrative reform assumed as already repaired, could not be repaired without other legislative changes quite as great and much more startling than the administrative reform itself. It is now time to look more closely at the financial condition of the country as it was left by the Treaty of Tilsit.

We are told of the stupefaction with which the Treaty itself and the Convention as to the evacuation of the territory, which was signed at Königsberg on July 12th, were read in Berlin. But probably few

of those who were thus stupefied had any conception
of the wretchedness of the situation into which this
settlement had brought the country.   For the Convention contemplated the absolute evacuation of all
the territory which was to be left to the Prussian
Monarchy by November 1st, and of all except the
duchy of Magdeburg by October 1st, and had this
been carried out, the state of things anticipated by
Stein, when the country should be free to receive his
reformed administration, would have taken place a
month or so after his arrival.   But the Convention
went on to say (Art. 4), that the evacuation should
take place within the period mentioned on condition
that the contributions imposed on the country should
have been paid, and that they should be regarded as
paid if security sufficient and recognised as valid
should be given for them.   But since no exact sum
was stated and no authority named which might declare what was the sum due, it was evident that this
article deprived the Prussians of all security that
their country would ever be evacuated, and that
Kalkreuth in signing such a Convention had delivered his country bound hand and foot to a conqueror.

That is, so far as in him lay, he had done so;
not that it is at all certain that the fate of Prussia
would have been in any respect different if he had
insisted on the most reasonable terms.   For the
truth is that the Treaty of Tilsit (I am speaking of
that concluded between France and Prussia, not of
that between France and Russia), whatever might
be its value to Napoleon, was to Prussia not worth
the paper it was written on.   Prussia derived from

the circumstances of Europe just so much protection as saved her from destruction, but she scarcely owed any protection to the Treaty. Treaties at best are contracts which it is difficult to enforce, but a treaty with Napoleon in 1807 could scarcely be anything but a snare. Of moral obligation we need say nothing; but that public opinion of Europe, that dread of retribution from other States, that feeling of the importance of commanding the respect and confidence of foreign Governments—all these considerations, which do so much in the ordinary circumstances of Europe to give validity to treaties, had little weight with Napoleon. International law ceases just where a Universal Monarchy begins, and Napoleon, who from the beginning of his career had broken treaties systematically, had now seldom any reason for observing them. It is declared in the Treaty with Russia (Art. 4) that the king of Prussia is restored to part of his States as 'a mark of the Emperor Napoleon's regard for the Emperor of all the Russias,' and there seems reason to think that in some sense this is literally true; namely, that Napoleon refrained from actually annexing Prussia out of fear of endangering the Russian alliance. But when enough had been done to satisfy the Czar, Napoleon did not mean to be bound any further in his dealings with Prussia by the text of the Treaty of Tilsit.

The result was that the cessions made by Prussia proved to be real, but the equivalent for which they were made was not received. Instead of evacuating the territory in October or November, the army of occupation, more than 150,000 men, remained throughout the whole term of Stein's ministry, living at the expense of the country. It was not till the end of 1808, just the time of Stein's fall, that they marched out, and then apparently for no other reason than that they were wanted in Spain, and not without imposing quite new and paralysing conditions as the price of their departure. In fact, a new treaty now took the place of that of Tilsit, precisely as if Prussia had been worsted in a new campaign. At the Convention of Paris of September 8th, 1808, more territory was ceded, and the stipulation restricting the Prussian army to 42,000 men, unknown to the Treaty of Tilsit and apparently rendering the dependence of Prussia irremediable, was introduced.

But that we may see clearly the relation in which Prussia stood to France during this period, let us go on to note that this second arrangement thus arbitrarily substituted for the Treaty of Tilsit was observed only by Prussia, not at all by France. It provided that Glogau, Stettin and Cüstrin should be held by the French with a total force not exceeding 10,000 men, until the contribution, now fixed at 140,000,000 francs (reduced afterwards on the intercession of the Czar to 120,000,000), should be paid, but that when half the contribution should be paid Glogau should be evacuated.

In May, 1811, the King submitted to Napoleon that this condition had been fulfilled, and therefore that he had a right to claim Glogau, but so well did he understand Napoleon's view of the treaties that he did not venture to prefer the claim without offering a new and most humiliating concession, that of an auxiliary force to serve under Napoleon in the

Russian war then expected. Napoleon excused himself from giving any answer to these proposals. In August came a despairing appeal from Hardenberg, asserting that the force garrisoning the three fortresses on the Oder amounted to 23,000 men instead of 10,000, costing the exhausted country 250,000 crowns a month. What was the result of these expostulations? Just as before, the result was simply that the breach of the old treaty was made the foundation of a new one. On February 24th, 1812, a new treaty of alliance was signed at Paris, with a secret article making the alliance offensive, and three conventions were signed the same day, the first of which stipulated that Glogau, Stettin and Cüstrin should continue to be occupied by French troops, while the third exacted enormous supplies for the French army about to invade Russia. And even this new treaty, as Schöll observes, was only executed so far as its obligations fell on Prussia. The French occupied two additional fortresses, those of Spandau and Pillau, and appropriated supplies enormously in excess of the amount stipulated.

From this general view we may estimate the difference between the condition and prospects of Prussia as they were in reality and as they seemed to be at the time of the Treaty of Tilsit. When Stein arrived at Memel at the end of September he had reason to think that the French troops were on the point of marching out, that in another month all of them would have departed, and that when this should have happened France would have no further claims, or at least no considerable claims, upon the Prussian Government. He knew indeed that Napoleon claimed pecuniary payments, and a Commission was already named to arrange them with the French Intendant-General, Daru. But what he supposed the debt to amount to we may judge from the estimate which that Commission formed of it. They stated it at 19,000,000 francs, and as the income of Prussia in the year 1805-6 had been about 27,000,000 thalers, this, though a serious, could not seem a quite overwhelming burden. By the simple course of instructing Daru to demand about 150,000,000 francs, Napoleon completely altered the face of affairs, and converted Prussia from a humbled but independent state into a conquered and enslaved country. Henceforth it seemed evident that the French did not mean to be shaken off, and that that happier condition of the country which Stein had looked forward to was a chimera.

Perhaps the reader ought here to be guarded against misconceptions to which these figures may give rise. Napoleon's claim, as we have seen, was finally fixed at 120,000,000 fr. This is equal to £4,800,000. Now when we consider that the Prussians the other day exacted from France a sum more than forty times as large, and that France paid it apparently with little effort, we may be inclined to think that the Prussians made an unreasonable outcry about Napoleon's treatment of them, and that in fact it was rather mild than otherwise. But we are to consider two things.

First, it is one of the most violent figures of speech to say that France paid her debt easily, or indeed paid it at all. Of course we know that she only changed her creditor and accepted a permanent

charge upon her revenue in place of a pressing overwhelming debt. All that this proves is that her
credit was still good in spite of her misfortunes; in
other words, that Europe did not believe the ruin of
France as a State to be at hand. Had France been
unable to borrow, the burden of the debt would have
been felt most painfully. Now this was the case of
Prussia; she was entirely unable to borrow. In
the first Revolutionary War Frederick William II.
told Lord Malmesbury, as an excuse for not ful-
filling his engagements to England (December, 1793),
'that I have not in my treasure enough to pay the
expenses of a third campaign, that I cannot raise a
new tax on my subjects, that to attempt it would
drive them to the worst consequences without its
producing anything, and that the nature of the Prussian Monarchy is such that it cannot bear a loan.'
It is true that that King did afterwards borrow, but
those were the prosperous times of Prussia. What
credit could a State command which had concluded
the Peace of Tilsit, which lay helpless in the hands
of Napoleon, and which he showed the clearest intention of reducing still lower as soon as the opportunity should arrive?

Secondly, we are to consider that the wealth of
Europe has increased since the beginning of this
century in an incalculable degree, while the value of
money has fallen. And besides this general consideration, we are to remember that Prussia after the
Peace of Tilsit was quite a different State from the
Prussia of the year before. Its population was now
less than 5,000,000, it was completely exhausted by
the war and by having to support the army of

occupation; it was originally a poor country, and its industry had long been cramped by the mercantile system, while its trade was now destroyed by the war with England which Napoleon had imposed upon it. What the distress of Prussia actually was during this period may be estimated by one simple fact, more convincing than much highly coloured description, that in 1810 Altenstein, the Minister who succeeded Stein, in reporting upon Ways and Means, came to the conclusion that the only way left to appease Napoleon was to offer the cession of Silesia. It is evident that, all the left bank of the Elbe and almost all the Polish provinces having gone at Tilsit, such a new dismemberment would have been nearly equivalent to the destruction of the State.

When then we inquire how it was that Stein, who began apparently with nothing more in view than a reform of the administration, found himself involved before long in innovations which completely transformed the State, the explanation which presents itself is that he found the evil far greater than he had supposed. Instead of the Peace of Tilsit which he had looked for, he found no Peace of Tilsit, but complete subjection to France. He found that he was called upon not merely to rectify a faulty system which had caused disasters, but also to repair the ruin which those disasters had produced, and which proved to be far more overwhelming than he had pictured it. Thus he was to a certain extent taken by surprise when the reins of government were put into his hands, and when he returned after an absence of more than half a year to a country which may be said to have been conquered and ruined since he left it. Meanwhile those who were to be his colleagues had this advantage over him, that they had never been compelled to quit their posts. From July to October the Immediate Commission had had the problem constantly before them. Reports had been arriving from which they could form an estimate of the impoverisnment of the country, and they had deliberated incessantly on the means of relief. There has been much controversy in Germany upon the question whether that Land Reform, which is so peculiarly associated with Stein's name, was really his work or that of his colleagues. It must be freely admitted that he was not in any way the originator of the scheme, that it had occurred to others while he was still at Nassau, and that it had been elaborately discussed by the Immediate Commission perhaps before it had even occurred to his mind. Whether in these circumstances he can still deserve to be spoken of as its author will be considered below. But it is evident that the fact does not by itself show that there were men on the Commission superior to Stein in statesmanship or enlightenment, but only that they had had several months start of him in the investigation of the subject.

It was not probably till he had been several months in office, perhaps not till he was on the point of leaving it, not till that summer of 1808 which Schön describes as 'a splendid glorious time,' that Stein or his associates fully realised the greatness of the work in which they were engaged. Then indeed they were in a condition to philosophise upon it, and to expound it in the elevated style of 'Stein's Political Testament'.   But I take it that a mistake would be made if we were to conceive Stein as working on the *à priori* method, as beginning with a comprehensive idea of the way to regenerate a country and then translating this idea into concrete institutions.   It is true that neither he nor his colleagues had any of that aversion to general principles to which we are accustomed in English politics ; still those officials who were practically most influential, and notably Stein, began with partial views.   By slow degrees through common discussion and common study of the tremendous exigency, their ideas gathered comprehensiveness as their feelings gained solemnity, until in the end they found themselves elevated to a kind of prophetic mood. When this had once taken place, they became perhaps subject to a certain illusion, and half believed that the great principles had been more clear to them from the beginning than they actually were.   There is perhaps a touch of this illusion in the sentence with which Stein opens his account of his Ministry :—

We started from the fundamental idea of rousing a moral, religious, patriotic spirit in the nation, of inspiring it anew with courage, self-confidence, readiness for every sacrifice in the cause of independence of the foreigner and of national honour, and of seizing the first favourable opportunity of beginning the bloody and hazardous struggle for both.

This is certainly no exaggerated description of the spirit of the Stein Ministry in the summer of 1808, but we should perhaps be misled if we accepted too literally the expression, 'We started from the fundamental idea.'

CHAPTER II.

THE period of thirteen months upon which we now enter is memorable both in the history of Prussia and of Europe.

In Prussian history it makes the first and busiest part of a period of constitutional developement which is the second of three such periods which Prussia has had. The first period of the kind was the reign of Frederick William I., which saw the creation of that peculiar military and administrative system which has been described above. The third is the period which followed the disturbances of 1848, when the government of Prussia became constitutional and parliamentary. These three points mark a course of progress essentially different from that of England, the main reason being that our constitution developed itself mainly before the period of great standing armies had begun, and

that of Prussia afterwards.   But on the Continent
other States may be seen to have pursued a similar
course.   The Stein-Hardenberg legislation answers
in many ways to the French Revolution, which like-
wise looked back to the military absolutism of Louis
XIV., and on the other hand stopped short of
successful parliamentary institutions.   Much more
closely parallel has been the case of Russia.   Peter
is so similar to Frederick William I. that he may
be thought to have been his model, while the reforms
of the present Czar resemble those of Stein in the
same striking manner.   Russia's third stage of developement is still to come.

In general history this period is memorable for
the first hopeful rally of Europe against Napoleon.
The first object of the reforms undertaken in Prussia
was to repair the ruin caused by the war, but a
further purpose soon began to be entertained.   It
was gradually perceived that the country had not
merely been humbled and impoverished, but that it
had been practically conquered.   Little more than
the name of independence was left, and in point of
harsh treatment the country was not better but
much worse off than if it had actually made a part
of Napoleon's empire.   It also appeared probable
that annexation was in reality only delayed.

Let us pause here for a moment to ask why
Napoleon subjected Prussia to such unspeakable
oppression from 1807 to 1812, and yet refrained
from annexing the country.   His forbearance can
hardly have been, as he said, an effect of magnanimity, for it was a cruel rather than a merciful forbearance.   The truth seems to be that until the year

1812 he was prevented by a series of difficulties arising not out of anything done by Prussia or her Ministers, but out of the foreign relations of his Empire. In the first months after the conclusion of the Treaty of Tilsit, Napoleon was obliged to respect the wishes of the Czar. He did not think his new alliance would be safe if he should alarm Russia by extending his direct influence beyond the Elbe. This scruple made him hold his hand till the Spanish rebellion and Junot's failure in Portugal materially weakened his position and forced him to withdraw his army of occupation from Prussia. In 1809, Russia allowed him to crush Austria, but when this was done he was aware that he must not touch Prussia until he was quite prepared for a Russian war. This involved vast preparations and a solid Austrian alliance cemented by marriage. Prussia had respite while these arrangements were making. Her subjugation was involved in the defeat of Russia, and the occupation of the country by the French troops in 1812 was so complete that no shadow of independence could have remained to Frederick William had the fortune of the campaign gone against Alexander. Had Napoleon's foreign relations been but slightly different; had he been a little more independent of Russia in 1807, a little less engaged in the Peninsula in 1808, above all had he been moderately prudent and successful in 1812, Prussia would not have been saved by the efforts of many Steins or many Scharnhorsts. Nor did they deceive themselves. They trusted in Providence, and in the midst of a course of events so unprecedented hoped to see in time an unprecedented disaster befal their enemy. In the meantime they prepared to be ready when such an opportunity should come. They elaborated instruments which were altogether contemptible when compared with the force they had to encounter, yet such as would prove useful when once the miracle should have happened.

Gradually Stein and his colleagues become aware of the extremity and imminence of the danger, and accordingly about the middle of his short time of office the Ministry becomes warlike. It derives courage from despair, it realises that Prussia has almost nothing to lose, and Stein's name is now published to Europe as representing a great conspiracy to resist Napoleon by raising the masses. In the meantime the popular rising in Spain takes place, Scharnhorst is pushing his military reforms, and the first clear indications are given that in the European struggle the moral forces are passing over from the side of France to the side of Europe. The Anti-Napoleonic Revolution commences, in the bosom of which was nursed that nationality doctrine, that doctrine of the unity of Germany, and that new military system, which together were to give the nineteenth century so much of its character. In this great German and European movement Stein and his colleagues have almost as great a share as in the internal reconstruction of Prussia. But they are not able to carry it so far. Stein has retired somewhat into the background, and Scharnhorst is dead, when the overthrow of Napoleon actually takes place, and Germany does not reach its goal of unity till that whole generation has been laid in

the grave.   Later events have cast a glory upon the
Ministry of Stein which was by no means observed
to shine upon it while it existed.

It is not fair, nor is it the intention of this book,
to credit Stein personally with all that was then
accomplished for Prussia and Europe.   If on the
whole he deserves to rank first both for the importance of his achievements and for the force and
height of his character, yet he can only be considered *primus inter pares*.   He ought not to be
allowed to eclipse Scharnhorst or Hardenberg, and
others of less note worked under him whose names
ought by no means to be lost in his.   As to Hardenberg, it is impossible to trace the history of
Prussia in this age without at the same time tracing
his biography ; the others demand a digression, and
this is the point at which such a digression may
most conveniently be made.

For at this point we become aware that the
scene is occupied by new actors.   The mischievous
school of politicians which we have had to do with
hitherto disappears from it.   Lombard vanished
early in the war, then Haugwitz ; of that clique
Beyme only remains to give us trouble.   The equally
mischievous military clique, of whom it was remarked with surprise that their counsels were more
pusillanimous than those of the civilians, the clique
of Zastrow, Köckeritz and Kalkreuth, now also lose
their influence.   They become an Opposition which
has its headquarters at Berlin, and of which we shall
hear much in the sequel.   At times they recover
part of their credit, and when the trials of the
State are over and the Restoration Period opens,

they return, as it were, with the Bourbons and become once more the ruling party. But for the present another party is in the ascendant, a party which Hardenberg may be considered to have founded, and of which Stein, after having been until his dismissal in January the most distinguished member, and then the martyr, now appears as the head. It is a party full of ability and patriotism. I give here some account of four members of it, selecting two from the military section and two from the civilians.

Gerhard Johann David v. Scharnhorst was a Hannoverian by birth, and about two years older than Stein. He was born in 1755, at Bordenau, on the Leine, not far from the town of Hannover. His father had been a soldier, and had risen to the post of Quarter-Master, but seeing no prospect of further promotion on account of his humble birth, had retired from the army. The story of his marriage illustrates the curiously intricate gradations of rank which are found in Germany even among the peasantry. He himself, we are told, was a Brinksitzer, and he ventured to raise his eyes to the daughter of the Freisasse of Bordenau. She encouraged his suit, but her parents were indignant at his presumption, for in the hierarchy of the village, which ran thus, (1) Freisasse, (2) Vollmeier, (3) Halbmeier, (4) Höfling, (5) Köther, (6) Brinksitzer, (7) Kirchhöfner, (8) Häusling, there were not less than four ranks between him and the object of his wishes. The marriage took place at last, but not till after a child had been born. Gerhard was the second child, and passed much of his boyhood in field-work for his father, first at a farm Hämelsee on the Weser, then at another farm at Bothmer. On the death of his father-in-law the elder Scharnhorst laid claim to the property at Bordenau, and obtained it at last, but not till after a lawsuit which lasted ten years, and involved him in expenses, we are told, amounting to the surprising sum of 280 thalers. The career of the younger Scharnhorst was decided by an acquaintance which his father made with one of the most distinguished soldiers and military writers then living in Germany, the Count Lippe-Bückeburg. Of him Gneisenau says in a letter to Varnhagen v. Ense, who had written his life:

> You have praised Count Lippe highly, but much below his deserts; he was far greater even than you have represented him. Some time ago I spent some time at Bückeburg, and there I read his MSS. in the archives. The man had worked out in detail our whole *levée en masse* of 1813, Landwehr and Landsturm, the whole modern military system from the largest outlines down to the smallest minutiæ : everything was known, taught, worked out by him beforehand. Think what a man it must have been in whose mind ripened so far back the greatest military conceptions, the realising of which later in the end actually crushed the whole power of Napoleon.

This was the patron of the young Scharnhorst, who, in 1773, entered the military school founded by him at Wilhelmstein, and continued in his service till his death in 1777; it is indeed startling to find those ideas of a popular army which Scharnhorst was to realise familiar to the patron of his youth, who died nine years before Frederick the Great. On the death of the Count, Scharnhorst exchanged the Bückeburg service for that of his own State, Hannover. He entered a regiment to which a

promising regimental school had lately been attached, and began to distinguish himself as a lecturer
on military subjects.   In 1782, he removed to Hannover itself, with the rank of an ensign of artillery,
and began now to appear as an author.   He wrote
an Officers' Handbook, a History of the Siege of
Gibraltar, and other similar books.   It was his
deliberate opinion—and his biographer has found
among his papers the outline of an essay which was
intended to establish it—that there cannot be an
intelligent army or any great development of military
skill without a good military literature.   In 1785,
he marries Clara Schmalz, sister of Dr Theodor
Schmalz, a man afterwards of considerable note,
whose acquaintance he had made while Dr Schmalz
was engaged in writing a Life of Count Lippe-
Bückeburg.   In 1788, he appears as editor of a
periodical called the New Military Journal.   And
now comes for him as for others the French Revolution.

Politically, Scharnhorst viewed it in much the
same way as most intelligent Germans of the middle
class, that is, with warm goodwill and sympathy in
its first brilliant year, but with a strong revulsion of
feeling when its dark period commenced.   But it
was the military aspect of the revolution which
naturally seized his attention most forcibly.   In
March 1793, his sovereign George III. summoned
the Hannoverian army to join the English expedition which his son, the Duke of York, was commanding in the Netherlands; and here begins Scharnhorst's practical experience of war.

In the following years Stein and Scharnhorst

begin, though unconsciously, to approach each other. They watch the same conflict though from different points of view, Scharnhorst from the middle of the fray, Stein as a civilian and spectator. Both retire from the field of European warfare at the same moment, for when the line of demarcation was drawn after the Peace of Basel, Hannover as well as Prussia was sheltered by it. Scharnhorst, as well as Stein, saw nothing of war between the Peace of Basel and the campaign of Jena, for when the French occupied Hannover in 1803, he had already exchanged the Hannoverian for the Prussian service. We remember that Stein's marriage in 1793 connected him with the Hannoverian family of Count Walmoden. Scharnhorst about the same time enters also into close relations with the Count, who in the campaign of the Netherlands held at first the position of general of the cavalry and at the end of 1794, when the Duke of York left the army, which by that time had retired into Holland, took the supreme command of the united English and Hannoverian troops. Accordingly, when in 1795 Scharnhorst returned to Hannover, having greatly distinguished himself in the two campaigns and risen to the rank of Major and Assistant Quarter-Master-General, it was natural that Stein and Scharnhorst should become well known to one another, as it has been already related that they did. Scharnhorst continued in the Hannoverian service till the year 1801, and rose to the rank of Quarter-Master-General. The Duke of Brunswick, while in command of the Army of Observation, by which the line of demarcation was protected and to which Hannover fur-

nished a contingent, having become acquainted with
his merits, tried to tempt him to abandon the service
of his native state for that of Prussia. Scharnhorst
refused; but the Prussian offer was repeated, and at
last in 1801 he yielded. It appears that he considered himself entitled to rise in time to the command of a regiment of cavalry, and that he came to
learn that, in consequence of his want of nobility,
he could not expect such promotion in an aristocratic country like Hannover, and in particular that
the Privy Councillor v. Lenthe, who governed
Hannover from London, was firmly resolved not to
allow it.

In the Prussian service Scharnhorst received the
commission of Lieutenant-Colonel in the 3rd Regiment of Cavalry, which was quartered in Berlin,
and, as before, his talent for teaching was put to
profit by giving him a place in the Academy for
young Officers. A Military Academy for Nobles
had been founded by Frederick immediately after
the Seven Years War, but the teachers in this
institution were chiefly French, and the instruction
somewhat too general. In 1791 an Academy for
the Artillery had been founded. Some teaching
was also provided for young Infantry and Cavalry
Officers. Over this last department, with a nominal subordination to Lieutenant-General v. Geusau,
Scharnhorst was now placed. He continued principally occupied with these professional duties from
1801 to 1805. He drew up a scheme for organi-
zing more completely the instruction in his department; a scheme which in 1804 received the
King's approval, and was carried into effect.

Scharnhorst's influence was devoted during these years to creating an intelligent opinion in military circles on military subjects. The doctrine which he preached was the inadequacy of the military system of Frederick, and the necessity of adopting the new warfare which the Revolution had called into existence. Not only by his lectures, but in other ways, and particularly by a Military Society which he founded in 1802, and which, commencing with 9 members, numbered in 1805 not less than 188 (among whom was included Stein), he strove to excite the leaders of the Prussian army to earnest thought on the principles of their art. It may be supposed that he had some opposition to encounter. He held in fact a prophetic function, and his teaching in the midst of the aged and inveterately blinded representatives of the Frederician tradition was in fact, like that of Heinrich v. Bülow, the announcement of a wrath to come, of a destruction to happen after forty days. No wonder that the 'pedant' and 'theorist' was slighted by such heroes as Yorck. He was indeed exposed to so much petty persecution that he became anxious to leave the Artillery. But he had a supporter in the King, who in 1802 raised him to the rank of noble, and afterwards placed him in the staff with the position of third Lieutenant-Quartermaster-General.

His two colleagues were Phull and Massenbach, both well known in the military history of the time. The first afterwards entered the Russian service, and held an important position in the counsels of the Czar in 1812. The second was the trusted adviser of Prince Hohenlohe in the campaign of Jena. Both were, like Scharnhorst, men of ideas and theories. But when Scharnhorst by becoming their colleague was brought into comparison with them, he was seen by the more intelligent observers to differ from them as the true philosopher differs from the mere sophist or dilettante. While they had plausible views which they recommended either by declamation or by oracular airs, he had definite judgments which were unaffectedly explained, and which challenged the strictest examination. The young military theorists delighted to call Scharnhorst their master; Clausewitz names him the father of his mind, and Müffling, who belonged to his brigade, says, ' We of the third brigade thought that in the other two brigades much conceit but little practical mastery was developed.'

This was the career of Scharnhorst till the war came upon him. What he, in his prophetic soul, anticipated of the war escapes him in a letter to his son, dated Dec. 19th, 1805. He dissuaded him from becoming a soldier, for, he says,

You will not serve the French, and the other armies are for the most part in such a condition that little honour for the future is to be gained in them. As to the Prussian army, (he says) it is animated by the best spirit; courage and ability, nothing is wanting. But it will not, it must not, it cannot in the condition in which it is, or into which it will come, do anything great or decisive. This is my confession, which I should not make to a lad like you if in writing I had not my dearly loved son before me, whom I would gladly guide on his course of life.

Scharnhorst was present at Jena, and says: ' On the left wing, where I was, we won, and I may say only through courage and ability. All the arrangements were left to me.'

In the general rout which followed he attached himself to Blücher, and entered Lübeck with him, was driven out with him, and at last surrendered with him at Ratkau, when the old hero wrote, ' Ich kapithullire, weil ich kein Brot und keine Muhnitsion nicht mehr habe.' Scharnhorst was immediately exchanged for Colonel Gérard, and made his way to the King at Königsberg. He writes from Rostock to his daughter Julia, on Nov. 22nd :

When Schmidt is sleeping by me in the carriage I have the miserable liberty of giving myself up entirely to the outbreak of grief. Now are the bravest most sad and afflicted, and the most spiritless most cheerful and contented. Never have I seen a man more unhappy than the finest fellow I ever knew, General Blücher. It comes home to me doubly, as I know all the blunders, the stupidity, the cowardice, that have brought us to our present pass. The real, the only consolation is, that I made proposals, from the beginning, to avert our calamity, the institution of a national militia, the universal arming of the land in the last summer, the strengthening of the regiments and a closer political alliance.

Again, on the 28th from Danzig :

If I can manage it, I will serve in the Russian armies but as a Prussian officer; for I will not take a post in the Prussian army; General Kalkreuth is no man for me. But at present I will not on any terms leave the Prussian service; that I think would be dishonourable. Besides, the Prussian State will never be quite ruined, and, in any case, will maintain an army in time of peace. Possibly, however, it will be smaller than hitherto.

Scharnhorst, it is evident, did not yet quite foresee the Peace of Tilsit. On Dec. 4th, after arriving at Königsberg, he remarks that 'The medley of people half unhappy and quite unhappy, of people that feel nothing and people that feel extravagantly, is so *bizarre* and so universal, that we have a really romantic life.'

The King received him well, and even allowed his resolution not to serve under General Kalkreuth. He appointed him Chief of the Staff to General Lestocq, who commanded the Prussian contingent which joined the Russian army of Bennigsen. The following sketch is given by an eye-witness of Lestocq's head-quarters :

A multitude of people of the military and diplomatic class, with those belonging to both, were crowded together in the Russian and Prussian head-quarters, of all of whom alike it was a question whether they could have been invited thither or had come in order to act as partisans.

All seemed to take the line of saying much and doing nothing. One only said nothing and did much, the noble Scharnhorst, who had associated with himself one as silent and thoughtful as himself, Captain v. Ziehen. If the deep military views and the genuinely humane qualities with the Solonian wisdom which formed a trinity in the character of this unique person, had been united by that energy which in the confidence of moral power gives courage to step forward manfully and make one's will prevail, he would, as Charles V. once did at Speyer, have easily put to silence the squeaking of the mice, and sent the crew of spoiled children either into the battle-field to meet the enemy, or back into the drawing-rooms of Königsberg and Petersburg, which would certainly have given another turn to the campaign.

At the battle of Eylau, the Prussian contingent greatly distinguished itself, the General following the counsels of Scharnhorst, who received from the King by way of acknowledgment the 'Ordre pour le Mérite.' But like almost all the Prussian generals in this war, Lestocq was too old, and during the remainder of the campaign Scharnhorst had to struggle against his prejudices, his incapacity, and his preference for bad and blind advisers. The difference rose at last to an open quarrel, and Scharnhorst went so far as to write to the King representing the absolute necessity of superseding Lestocq. But the battle of Friedland, in which the Prussians had no share, followed by the Peace of Tilsit, suddenly changed the scene.

This was almost the end of Scharnhorst's experience of actual warfare. The next battle at which he was present was that of Gross-Görschen, fought at the beginning of the War of Liberation, and here he received wounds of which he died. He was not permitted to see the successes for which he more than any other man had prepared the way.

The Peace of Tilsit brought Scharnhorst to the head of the military administration as well as Stein to the head of the civil, and these two names are inseparably associated in the regeneration of Prussia. Scharnhorst, as he meddled less with politics, and as his reforms had a more direct and visible effect in restoring Prussia, is more universally praised by contemporary writers than Stein. Even Arndt, Stein's principal eulogist, in a poem in which he assigns to each of the heroes of the struggle of Liberation a peculiar epithet, pronouncing Blücher, for instance, the bravest, and Stein the strongest, seems disposed to keep the epithet 'greatest' for Scharnhorst. Everything we know of him gives us an exalted idea of his character, but it was not his lot to achieve splendid successes on the battle-field, and as to his views and sentiments,

nothing is preserved which in any striking manner confirms the opinion which his contemporaries
formed of him. We have little from his pen which
travels beyond the details of military organisation.

We may notice particularly in Scharnhorst the
academic character which official life tends to assume
in Prussia. The person who did most to save
Prussia from Napoleon has the stamp and led the
life rather of a Professor than of a Commander. His
principal occupation, until he took the lead in the
War Administration at the age of fifty-two, had
always been lecturing. The topics of his biographers and eulogists are much the same as those of
the biographers of Kant or F. A. Wolf. His style
of exposition is discussed; his tendency to repetition and prolixity, which arose from his earnest
anxiety to make his views clear; his want of ease
and fluency, which however, as he warmed with
his subject, he gradually overcame; the profound
influence he acquired over intelligent young students; the gradual prevalence of his ideas and the
influential school he founded; his love of thoroughness and dislike of dilettantism—and so on, until
it requires an effort to realise that Scharnhorst followed the profession of Blücher, and not rather
that of Kant.

Between him and Stein, the two greatest men of
action whom Germany produced in that age, there
was a contrast almost as interesting as that which
has been so often remarked between her two great
poets Goethe and Schiller. It was the more singular
because it reversed the contrast of their professions.
Stein had the temperament of the soldier, and

Scharnhorst that of the civilian. While Stein impressed every one by his vividness and fire, Scharnhorst, on the contrary, impressed no one. 'He seemed,' says Clausewitz, 'to the people of the great world, and even to the intelligent part of it, a dull *savant* and pedant, while military men took him for an irresolute, unpractical, unsoldier-like book-writer.' Yet in another way he accomplished as much, and overcame as many difficulties as Stein. He reached his end as certainly by perceiving it clearly, and travelling towards it persistently, by reticence which perplexed opposition, compliance in secondary matters which propitiated it, and a certain stillness and apparent insignificance which disarmed it, as Stein reached his end by force and rapidity. He could not, like Stein, inspire others with enthusiasm, but, on the other hand, he was peculiarly free from Stein's great fault, the want of secrecy. Perhaps Stein is pointed at by Scharnhorst's disciple Boyen, when he writes of his master as follows:

This modest bearing in a soldier, this submission to the opinion of others when he thought the question immaterial or merely formal, misled the judgment of hasty observers who fancy the great man always reveals himself in thunder and lightning; fiery passionate natures have always, I think, misunderstood him. It was my experience that in business he never said a word more than the matter in hand immediately required; there was never a trace of that *abandon*, that unbosoming, that revelling in the future which has more than once been a snare to celebrated men...... Such caution was so much a part of Scharnhorst's character, that perhaps at times he pushed it to an extreme; still he was always actuated by the noble resolve never to prejudice the interest of his sovereign by any unseasonable confidence.

Stein and Scharnhorst stand together at the head

of the work of political reconstruction in Prussia, with as conspicuous an eminence as the two Dioscuri of German literature had recently held at Weimar. No third politician raised himself to their height until, just after Stein's retirement, and during the Ministry of Altenstein, Wilhelm v. Humboldt appeared with his great educational reform. But both Stein in the civil department and Scharnhorst in the military had most distinguished coadjutors, of whom it is proper in this place to give some account. With Stein worked in particular Schön and Niebuhr; with Scharnhorst, Gneisenau.

Theodor v. Schön was born in 1773. His father had been a friend of Kant's, and had even had the honour of a Privatissimum from him at Königsberg. He held an office in the province of East Prussia, and when Theodor in turn came to Königsberg for his education, procured from Kant a scheme of studies for him. The son was quite as much under the philosopher's influence as the father had been. The first volume of Schön's Remains exhibits Kant's portrait as a frontispiece, and the last sentence in the volume contains Schön's confession of faith. 'Without Kant's philosophy and Sauerkraut I should long have been in my grave.' He explains, however, that by Sauerkraut he means the broth only, and perhaps something may depend also on the way in which the philosophy is taken. But another Königsberg Professor influenced him almost as much as Kant. He says himself, 'Kraus was my great teacher, and I followed him without reserve.' It was from Kraus, the apostle of Free

Trade in Germany, that he gained that idea of the connexion of national wealth with industrial liberty, which was to be embodied partly by his exertions in the Emancipating Edict of Stein's Ministry. In 1793 he began his administrative career, obtaining the post of Referendarius under v. Schrötter, Superior President of East Prussia. In 1796 and 1797 he travelled in Germany. The following observations, which he made upon Silesia, deserve to be quoted.

> The interesting men in Breslau were very much isolated. The nobility lived only with each other, and the citizens only with their equals. Only in Breslau was to be found a cultivated citizen-class; in the country there were only noblemen and serfs. In Prussia free blood remained free for all after generations; but in Silesia the air carried serfdom, and the child born on a knightly estate of non-noble parents was a serf. Where these are the ground-tones in a country, there can be little question of culture, and the well-informed cultivated man feels himself isolated.

Again:

> My journey through Silesia for six months was, through the recommendation of Minister v. Hoym, a real pleasure-trip. I was received and treated in an extremely friendly way, people were obliging, and all this was made more agreeable by the Silesian good humour which showed itself everywhere. I made the acquaintance of a number of people, but it is remarkable that I only met or found two country noblemen that had a touch of scientific culture. These were a H. v. Haugwitz at Leobschütz, and a H. v. Reibnitz at Glatz: but even here you had to avoid hurting the two prejudices of the Province: you must not question that Silesia was the most beautiful of countries, or say that the condition of the common man, that is, the serf, was horrible. On the last head I often could not restrain some expressions of opinion that in Silesia were heretical, and this led to ill-feeling and coldness. A bill of fare for servants in serfdom, drawn up by the Country Police Board, laid it down that every man- or

maid-servant was to have four pounds of meat in the year, and
the bread too was so sparingly apportioned that the diet con-
trasted harshly with that of the Magdeburg or Halberstadt districts.
The consequences were palpable ; the labourers were so weak,
that on a Silesian estate it was necessary to have some 33 per
cent. more hands than an equal estate in the Magdeburg district
had.   Thank God ! it is otherwise since the Edict of Oct. 9th,
1807, and as when the common man is elevated the higher class
rise with him, the Silesian nobility stands there now clearer, freer
from prejudice and more cultivated.

In 1798 he was in England, which he viewed
with much enthusiasm.

It was through England that I became a statesman.   Where
the labourer, busy among the cabbages, called out to me in exul-
tation that he had read that my King was about to join the
Coalition against France along with England—there you have,
in the truest sense of the word, public life.

So that the intelligence of our agricultural population is what strikes him most ! He also remarks
that the popular character of the legal administration
diffuses a knowledge and an acquaintance with legal
formulas which is to be found in no other country of
Europe.

If *we* see England remarkable for the degradation of its agricultural class, and for the general
want of acquaintance with the law, we are not probably to find fault with Schön, but to remember
that he compared our peasantry with serfs, and our
acquaintance with law with that common on the
Continent before the Code Civil.

In 1800, as it appears, Schön was attached to
the General Directory at Berlin, obtaining a place
in the Department of v. Schrötter who was Minister
for the Province of Prussia.   At this time Stein

was still Superior President in Westphalia. He declares

That it was one of the strangest Collegia that can ever have existed. The very numerous Collegium was composed of individual—to be sure very few—eminent capacities and men with an accurate scientific training, and of a great number of persons whose education had not raised them above common clerks' work and the most ordinary unintelligent business routine.

He goes on to make an exception in favour of Struensee, upon whom he passes the enthusiastic judgment that has been given above. The next ablest man he finds to have been Hardenberg.

The marked peculiarity of Schön, as it appears in his Remains, is what he calls his belief in the power of ideas and in the all-importance of scientific culture. It is on such a principle that he classifies all the public men whom he has occasion to characterise. They are divided first into two classes, those who are capable and those who are not capable of ideas, and of these two classes the former is again subdivided into those who have only an undeveloped capacity for ideas and those who have in addition received a philosophic training, or, better still, a 'philosophical and poetical training.' It is to be noted that he does not merely require of the statesman that he should be intellectual and well-informed and should generalise; he must apply to politics a special philosophical system. For those who only study politics inductively and historically Schön has a standing contemptuous epithet; he calls them Dealers in Notices, and applies this phrase at one time to the Historical School and at another to Stein himself.

Schön has left more criticisms upon Stein than any other man who knew him well. These we shall deal with as they come before us. In general he regards his chief as belonging to the second of his classes, that is, as capable of receiving ideas and even of originating them, but as entirely without philosophical and poetical culture. Hardenberg, we may observe, he regards in much the same way. He testifies, but always with much contempt, to Stein's great historical knowledge, and one is led to inquire how such a rigorous critic will regard Niebuhr, who also is indifferent to philosophy and depends, even more than Stein, on history. Curiously enough Schön's observations on Niebuhr are eulogistic in the extreme, although Niebuhr is as decidedly the Conservative as Schön is the Radical of the set, and though Niebuhr for his part seems to shrink from Schön's opinions and plans with a kind of terror.

Some of Schön's criticisms upon Stein have been quoted already. Here are other specimens.

He did not venture with the intelligence with which Heaven had gifted him originally to oppose the positions of political science; nay, when he was pressed he even gave them his sanction, not to seem unintellectual, but he himself never came to a scientific construction in public affairs.

Stein would have been much embarrassed if he had been required to give an answer to the question, What is a State? and, To what end do we live and ought we to live in a State?

Perhaps most of the great statesmen of history would have made an equally poor figure if they had been subjected to an examination of this kind. It is thus that we commonly find by the side of the practical statesman some absolute theorist who condemns him for his compromises and despises him almost in proportion to his success. A criticism of this kind is of little importance even when it is true, for the statesman must at least humour the prejudices of his contemporaries, and will scarcely perhaps be powerfully influential unless he shares them. But such criticisms are seldom even true, for they assume the philosophy of politics to be far more settled than it is. What Schön calls science would not now be acknowledged to have a right to that name, and Stein's historical eclecticism may well have come nearer the mark. At any rate it was not from ignorance, but deliberately that he disregarded his friend's systems. So Schön tells us:

It was by my intercourse with Fichte at Königsberg that the view upwards was first opened to me, and his society laid in me such a firm foundation in this respect that the tendency in everything to seek and hold the higher point of view runs, I am sure, through my whole life. Stein chid me as an idealist, for he was too good-natured to apply to me the hard name of metaphysician, and my *esprit à système*, as he expressed it, was often so disagreeable to him that he complained about it to Hardenberg.

In 1805 Schön opposed the plan of paper money, proposed by Stein with a view of meeting the expenses of the war which seemed then in prospect. In giving an account of his opposition, he adds, 'And yet Stein belonged, beyond question, to the very small part of the members of the General Directory who were of conspicuous merit, and rose above the ordinary routine.' He goes on to describe how the first disasters of the war in 1806 gave the death-blow to the reign of empty

formalism; and how even before the war there had
grown up, between a policy of drifting in foreign
affairs and the idea of national independence, two
parties, the Haugwitz and the Hardenberg-Stein
party; how the quarrel between the King and Stein
at Königsberg made for internal affairs the beginning of the struggle of the 'good old time' with
the feeling that the old mixture could not last;
how Stein 'vomited fire and flame in a case where
fire and flame were wasted,' and then retired to
Nassau. Under Hardenberg, Schön became a member of that Committee which, after his departure,
was erected into a Provisional Government. Here
he made for the first time the acquaintance of
Niebuhr, and says that 'almost every day the compass of the gifts with which God had endowed him
became more evident, and his truly noble character
attached him more and more.'

Schön's share in the achievements of the reforming ministry was certainly greater than that of
Niebuhr, who, indeed, had very little direct share in
them. But Niebuhr was more of a personal friend
to Stein than Schön was, for he continued to meet
and correspond with him in later life, whereas Schön
never saw Stein after the year 1813. Moreover,
he is so interesting in his personal character, so
illustrious by his achievements in the field of learning, and so peculiarly related to England as the
only German political thinker who has ever attracted
our attention, that some account of him seems called
for in this place.

In the year 1760 an expedition of discovery to
the East was sent out by the Danish government,

All the members of it, except one, died in Arabia in the first year; but the survivor, Carsten Niebuhr, pursued the journey alone, and did not return to Denmark till 1767. He was a Hannoverian by birth. On his return he settled down in Copenhagen, and married a Danish lady in 1773. His son Barthold George was born there in 1776. As, a year or two later, the father received a small government office at Meldorf in South Dithmarsch, a province of Holstein, the son grew up as a Holsteiner. He seems to have derived from his mother a melancholic irritable temperament, and from his father strong German feelings. When the Revolutionary war broke out, he tells us that 'his father was delighted, because he hoped that the conquered German and Burgundian provinces might be regained, provinces which he always included in Germany when teaching his children geography.' The great event of Niebuhr's boyhood was the French Revolution, which found him thirteen years old. He is surely the only instance of a clever boy in that age, who from the beginning regarded the Revolution with unmixed horror. But, indeed, horror of revolution was always the ruling passion of Niebuhr. The Revolution of 1789 made his boyhood despairing; and that of 1830 broke his heart before he had reached old age.

Though Meldorf was a very dull country town, Niebuhr did not grow up without the society of intellectual men. He found himself, indeed, in the midst of a literary circle which we have had occasion before to mention. The school which had formed itself at Göttingen among the students, while Stein was a student there, seemed to have scattered itself over Holstein and the neighbouring parts of North Germany. Boie, the editor of their organ the *Deutsches Museum*, was now actually living at Meldorf, and in the most intimate inter-course with the Niebuhr family. Voss, the great translator and the author of *Luise*, was Rector of a school at Eutin, and, as he had married Boie's sister, often visited Meldorf. The two Counts Stol-berg were to be found in the same neighbourhood; and the celebrated poet, in admiration of whom they had first united, Klopstock, was still living at Hamburg. Thus both at home in Meldorf and when for a few months he was at school at Ham-burg, and afterwards at the Holstein University of Kiel, Niebuhr found himself surrounded by the same literary clique.

It is not necessary to say much here about the surprising gifts he displayed from early boy-hood. A wonderful power of acquiring and retaining knowledge was united in him with independence and elevation of thought, and in some departments with a rare power of original combination.. The persons we have hitherto had to deal with have been in the main men of action ; but Niebuhr is one who in practical politics had only the use of his left hand. If Schön brings to practical statesman-ship ideas derived from books, Niebuhr carries back to books strong impressions and images derived from an experience of life unusual in literary men. In his Roman History, and in his professorial lectures, he handled history with an intensity and realism which were quite new in

Germany, and which he evidently owed to having himself lived among kings and statesmen, himself fled before an invader, himself followed a war of liberation.

The following remarks on Phocion, for instance, bring the Berlin Opposition vividly before us, and for Demosthenes we might almost read Stein :

He was personally hostile to Demosthenes ; an aversion which is intelligible to those who have observed the conduct of men at the time of the Confederation of the Rhine. I have known people whom I am very far from believing to have been dishonest, but who were incapable of any enthusiasm, sacrifice, and confidence, and who imagined that misery did not really consist in being enslaved by a foreign ruler, but in the evils which follow in the train of war and in personal sufferings, and that nothing was more foolish than sacrifices of any kind, for that there was extremely little prospect of success and that many thousands were indifferent who ruled over them. When they were told that with such principles all nationality was sacrificed as well as that existence by which human life is raised above mere animal comfort, or when they were asked what great misfortune it could be under such circumstances to die, or what is death, or what is any misfortune compared with servitude—how often have I wished to die together with all those that were dear to me ! and I would have thanked God for it and for the fact that I had as yet no children—they would answer, You are an enthusiast ! adding with indignation, You are the cause of all our misfortunes ! Those who dissented from them were even in danger of being denounced by them as fanatics and as the authors of all mischief.

Passages like this, and in general his enthusiasm for the ancient world, might lead us to picture Niebuhr as a man of antique grandeur of character. But he had to struggle with a somewhat feeble inherited temperament as well as with the morbid sentimentalism of the atmosphere around him. Assuredly he did not strike those who knew him as an eminently masculine character. Rather it would seem that his worship of the Roman virtues was like a woman's admiration of manly strength and arose from a conscious want of them. Thus when Stein describes Niebuhr he calls him 'gentle and loving,' and Niebuhr for his part clings to Stein with a sort of womanly devotion, describing him as 'a man in the highest sense of the word and as one in whose presence he feels ennobled and strengthened.' Schön hints that he clung to *him* in the same way :

> Each of us wanted the other. His eminent intellectual gifts often through his childlike simplicity ended in mere theory when he was called upon to act. He was the noblest of vines, but needed a tree-trunk to twine round before he could come to blossom and grape ; and where he found a capacity for ideals there he eagerly clung and climbed. But where he did not find this, such coarse natures revolted him so that in his childlike way he could not conceal his repugnance, nay his detestation, and so made a multitude of enemies.

Putting aside Schön's assumption of the part of elm to the vine, which seems to me little supported by facts, this description tallies with the conception of Niebuhr, which we should gather from his letters. There too, along with singular elevation and purity of feeling, we discover an abiding sense of feebleness and a feminine disposition to cling. He speaks of the difficulty he has in 'subjecting his poor heart, which will go on sentimentalising and blundering, to his head.' And in the classics we see him worshipping the image of a manhood

and a self-reliance which he does not find either
around him or within him. Thus in a letter to
Stein after deploring the want of public spirit in
Prussia he says, 'It is only to be remedied by an
intense study of antiquity.'

Niebuhr entered political life in 1796, that is,
in his twentieth year. But he was not yet a Prussian. Holstein, we remember, was at that time,
though included in the Empire, under the government of the King of Denmark. Niebuhr became
private Secretary to the Danish Minister of Finance,
Count Schimmelmann. His home was now Copenhagen, and it continued to be so for ten years until,
on the eve of the campaign of Jena, he was induced
to enter the service of Prussia. Here is a glimpse
of the state of German literature as it looked to
Niebuhr watching it from Copenhagen, and with his
Klopstockian predilections.

Do you in Holstein read as little as we do here? It seems as
if the literature of Germany were visibly on the decline. Schiller
and Goethe are worse than dead. Wieland's *Agathodæmon* is
insufferable. The new generation is dwarfish. *Is Voss to stand
alone? Even Klopstock* has by no means distinguished himself in
his last production. O confess it, the bloom of our literature is
over, and besides the usual course of nature which has proved
itself the same in all nations, it is the French Revolution, our
infamous policy, and shameful undervaluing of our own people,
the want of cultivation among them resulting from this general
indifference, and the desecration and shocking abuse of philosophy,
that have brought us to this wretched pass.

He soon left Count Schimmelmann for a post
in the Royal Library; in 1798 he visited England,
and thence proceeded to Edinburgh, where he re-

mained for about a year attending lectures at the University; and on his return to Copenhagen in 1800 received an appointment in the Colonial Department of the Danish administration. At this time he married Amelia Behrens, daughter of the Prefect of North Dithmarsch, and sister of his life-long friend and biographer, Madame Hensler. When Nelson bombarded Copenhagen in April, 1801, Niebuhr was running about the streets within to pick up information, and devising expedients to conceal the worst from his young wife. He writes:

> Such a resistance was never seen. Nelson himself has confessed that never in all the battles in which he has taken part has he witnessed anything that could be compared to it. His loss is greater than at Aboukir. It is a battle that can only be compared to Thermopylæ; but Thermopylæ too laid Greece open to devastation.

In 1804 Niebuhr rose to the chief direction of the Copenhagen Bank, retaining at the same time his position in the Colonial Office. He begins, however, gradually to feel dissatisfied with his position, and much for the same reasons as had made Scharnhorst discontented with the Hannoverian service only a few years before; he was offended by a proposal to promote a young nobleman over his head. In September, 1805, the direction of the Berlin Bank and of the Maritime Institute passed, as above related, out of the hands of Count Schulenburg into those of Stein, and the change was followed by the detection of frauds in the administration of those institutions and by the dismissal of many officials. It was then that Stein resolved to offer Niebuhr a leading position in the Bank, and the fact is a proof that his direction of the Copenhagen Bank was considered successful. The proposal—it was not the first he had received from Prussia—reached him in March, 1806, and it was accepted on April 1, Niebuhr stipulating that he should not be employed in any service hostile to Denmark. That was the last dismal moment of the old régime of Prussia. After he had accepted the offer, but before he had left Copenhagen, war between Prussia and Napoleon was determined on. He left Copenhagen in September and, after a short visit to his parents in Holstein, reached Berlin on the 5th of October, nine days before the battles of Jena and Auerstädt. In a few days he was hastening to Stettin with the treasures which Stein committed to his charge. From Stettin he went to Danzig, thence to Königsberg, and thence followed the royal family to Memel, which he reached early in January, 1807. From Königsberg in December he writes—it shows us his first impression of Prussian society—

There is an everlasting talk—mostly without the slightest comprehension of the matter—about abuses, about the aristocracy, the Russians, the misunderstood French, the great Emperor, and about ruinous measures, and so forth. Of course there are many, very many, who think otherwise; but indignation makes one's blood boil when one is forced to listen to such things.

Now follows the dismissal of Stein; how passionately loyal Niebuhr was to his chief on this occasion has already been shown. In Hardenberg's short Ministry of 1807, Niebuhr found himself a member of the Immediate Commission, where he made the friendship of Schön. During this whole period he, naturally enough, was anxiously endeavouring to escape from the service which he had entered at such an unfortunate moment. He repeatedly sent in his resignation, meditated a return to Copenhagen, considered schemes of entering commercial life. When the Commission is reconstituted after Hardenberg's retirement he declines to return to it. His reasons may be partly gathered from the following letter written to Stein in July.

Before long it will be decided whether your Excellency accept office or not. In the latter case I shall insist on my dismissal, being quite decided neither to take part in an ill-organised, many-headed administration like the present Provisional Commission, nor yet to act under the worse than mediocre men of the late administration, whom I learnt to know thoroughly at Memel last winter. I have further declined a seat in the Provisional Commission because it is impossible to transact business under such a form, and also because it is impossible to remain any longer a member of it without falling out with friends, since their principles are really too monstrous and the consistency with which they apply them more appalling still, and without exposing numberless weak points to the enemy, for innovations are in contemplation, some of which I do not feel able to judge of completely, and others I cannot judge at all. Besides I am a pure Mahometan, a strict Unitarian in administrative affairs, and abhor all Commissions and the like with my whole heart.... Your Excellency might misunderstand it, or at least I might displease you if I should say much to you of the extent of my affection and unreserved devotion. You know the genuineness of those feelings which possess a young man not dead at heart for one of the few great men of his age, if he is so happy as to have been near to him.

He continues characteristically :

I should have liked to have added some facts which would be interesting to your Excellency, respecting the Russian and Slavonic languages : the affinity which I have discovered between them and the Persian, and how they are by no means so difficult as people believe them or make them, &c.

Thus Niebuhr voluntarily dropped out of the number of those whom Prussia now thanks for her memorable reform, and his share in it is limited to the suggestions he made before Hardenberg's retirement, some of which are taken up by Hardenberg in his plan of reform soon to be considered. The reasons for retiring, which he gives in this letter, should be considered together with the remarks quoted at p. 330. His objection to Commissions would be obviated by Stein's acceptance. Are we then to suppose that his true motive was simply a dread of the greatness of the proposals likely to be made and of the warmth of the controversies likely to arise ? Such dread of responsibility seems altogether morbid when we consider that in the legislation now undertaken the Commission had only a consultative function. But I think he was influenced at the same time by the suspicion that Beyme's power was intended to continue.

To these rapid sketches, intended to introduce the reader to the remarkable group of men at the head of whom it was Stein's glory to be placed, one more must be added, that of Gneisenau.

Gneisenau's great time was the War of Liberation itself. The success with which the Prussians in that war held their ground against their old conquerors, and defeated them in so many engagements, at Dennewitz, at the Katzbach, at La Rothière, and in the battles round Paris, was due, in the first instance, to the reformation of the army and the State which had taken place in the years of humiliation. But after this it was due to good leadership, and if in the eyes of the world Blücher stood out as the leader, Gneisenau in the background was the real strategist and tactician, while the old hero contributed little more than a fiery valour and a power of exciting enthusiasm among the soldiers. In this instance, as in several others, the triumph of Prussia at the end of this period wears too much the appearance of good luck, because the ability which really achieved it was masked, and not visible to the spectators.

But though Gneisenau acted the part of head to Blücher, he has less of the school about him than any of the characters we have yet introduced. It is true that he too was in some sense a University man; but, on the whole, his character is simply that of a noble, simple-minded, but most intelligent soldier. He attends no lectures of Kant or Kraus, he does not learn manliness by 'an intense study of antiquity,' he founds no school of military science. He wins his reputation in strictly soldier-like fashion, namely, by a splendid exploit, the defence of Colberg, and the King and his counsellors were induced to select him for this task very much by his strikingly soldier-like appearance, which was such that his biographer reports the opinion of a distinguished general, who had seen all the great Prussian, Russian, Austrian, and French commanders of the age, that not one of them equalled Gneisenau in this respect. But for this

very reason, since this book avoids military matters
as much as possible, only a few sentences can be
given in this place to that part of his biography
which ends with his entrance into the group which
surrounded Stein after the Peace of Tilsit.

August Wilhelm Antonius Neithardt v. Gneisenau was born towards the close of the Seven
Years War, and in the thick of it. His father was
a Saxon lieutenant of artillery, who was serving
against Frederick in the army of the Empire. He
was born on October 27th, 1760, at Schilda in
Saxony, and a week afterwards mother and infant
were involved in the flight caused by Frederick's
last victory of Torgau. The mother died in a few
weeks of the fatigue she had suffered and of the
fright caused by dropping her infant at night out
of the cart in which she was travelling. Thus deprived of his mother, and handed over to the care
of strangers by his father, he was for some years
much neglected, and, it is said, was set to mind
geese on a common. A stranger, observing his
condition, wrote an account of it to the father of
his dead mother, a certain Captain Müller, living
at Wurzburg, and in good circumstances. Müller
took him into his house, and at the age of seventeen he was sent to the University of Erfurt. His
father, in the course of a wandering life, had settled at Erfurt some five years before, and had
been appointed to a post there by the Electoral
Government of Mainz, to which Erfurt belonged.
The young Gneisenau's studies were intended to
prepare him for the army. He entered the service
of the Emperor, and appears to have served in

Bohemia against Frederick in the War of the Bavarian Succession (1778). He then took service with
the Margrave of Ansbach and Bayreuth, where he
is found in 1781; and as the English Government
was then hiring mercenaries from the Margrave,
among other German princes, for the American
War, this led to his crossing the Atlantic. After
the surrender of Cornwallis at Yorktown, the regiment of Chasseurs, in which he had the commission of Unter-lieutenant, sailed to Halifax,
where it remained for some months, and then
proceeded to Quebec. This gave Gneisenau opportunities of studying popular war, and so far
was probably of much use to him; but it gave him
no actual military experience, for the war was
already practically at an end when he reached
America. He returned late in 1783. Growing
weary of the petty service of the Margrave, he
now, as Stein had done five years earlier, applies
for employment to Frederick the Great (Nov. 4,
1785), and receives from him the Commission of
Premier Lieutenant with a post in the guard at
Potsdam. In July, 1786, finding his pay not sufficient to support the expense of life at Potsdam,
he entered the regiment Chaumontet, and was stationed until the year 1793 at Löwenberg in Silesia.
When the Three Years War of Prussia began, he
found himself, not as Stein and Scharnhorst, concerned in the Campaigns of Flanders and the Rhine,
but engaged in that other enterprise which, to her
great misfortune, Prussia undertook at the same time,
the partition of Poland. He spent nearly three years
in Poland, where he learnt Polish, and was advanced

to the rank of Captain.   After this he was stationed
at Jauer in Silesia, where, on October 19th, 1796,
he married Caroline v. Kottwitz.   In the ten years
that followed, for Gneisenau, as for other Prussian
officers, there was little to do.   He watched with
admiration the opening career of Bonaparte, whom
he declared later to have been his master in war
and politics; but he had no opportunity of practising the lessons he learnt in a period when
Prussia had forgotten the maxim which Gneisenau
himself lays down, 'If you want to be a military
State you must engage in war.'

When at last Prussia entered the European
conflict once more, Gneisenau's anticipations were
as gloomy as those of Scharnhorst:

As a patriot I sigh. In the time of peace we have neglected
much, occupied ourselves with trivialities, flattered the people's
love of shows, and neglected war, which is a very serious matter.

The exclamation which follows is significant:

O-my country, my *self-chosen* country!

He was present at Saalfeld, where Prince Louis
Ferdinand fell, and received a bullet in the leg;
present also at Jena, where it is thought that
he learnt the lesson which he afterwards practised
with so much success at the Katzbach and at
Waterloo, viz. the great importance of an unsparing
and unceasing pursuit.   After his defeat, Prince
Hohenlohe meditated a retreat to Stettin and sent
Gneisenau with Knesebeck forward to see that
provisions might not be wanting along the road.
From Stettin Gneisenau went by Danzig to the

King's head-quarters at Graudenz, and afterwards arrived early in December at Königsberg.

It seems to have been here, and at this time, that he began to attract attention. He made the acquaintance of the Princess Louise Radziwill, to whom he was able to relate, as an eye-witness, the circumstances of her brother's death at Saalfeld, and at her house he was introduced to the distinguished circle to which he was henceforth to belong, the circle of Stein, Hardenberg, Niebuhr, &c.

This was the time of the King's first abortive attempt to place Stein at the head of affairs. The better party had for the moment the upper hand, and Gneisenau now sent in a plan for carrying on the war by a united operation of the Prussians, Swedes, English, and Russians, with the sea for their base, upon the French communications. Some attention was given to the plan, and Lord Hutchinson, the English ambassador, promised the active assistance of England in equipping the troops; but at this moment the King's quarrel with Stein put an end to all such schemes, and threw the control of affairs into the hands of Zastrow and the unpatriotic party. He was now sent off as Brigadier, with four newly-formed battalions, to the province of New East Prussia. The biographer remarks, that these new levies, who, when Gneisenau took the command of them, had nothing soldierly in their appearance,—a troop of ragamuffins, some in long coats, some in short, and exhibiting every variety of head-dress, round hats, three-cornered hats, fur caps, and even nightcaps,—were the same who, a few months later, immortalised themselves at the siege of Colberg, and, being received, as a reward, into the new guard formed by the King, marched seven years later into Paris with the King at their head. For the present, however, Gneisenau, as an officer distinguished for enterprise, was placed at the greatest possible distance from the enemy, and entrusted only with the duty of keeping open the retreat across the Niemen, and saving what stores it might be possible to rescue in case of a general wreck. But he made an opportunity even here of showing a remarkable power of winning the obedience and affection of soldiers. In his correspondence of these months, we see the ideas of the new age, of the Anti-Napoleonic Revolution, beginning to take shape. Valentini writes to him of a German La Vendée, a rising against the French under the leadership of a Prussian Prince, to be followed by a universal German constitution.

On March 17th Gneisenau received orders to march at the head of two battalions to reinforce the garrison of Danzig. He was compelled to proceed to Danzig by sea, taking ship at Memel, where the King then was. He found the King in the act of giving audience to one who brought a letter from the besieged garrison of Colberg, begging, as a matter of life and death, for a new commandant. The appearance of such a striking figure as that of Gneisenau at this moment might well seem almost an omen, and the estimable mischief-maker Beyme, passing him on the stairs, received a powerful impression. For the present, however, his destination remained unchanged. He sailed to Danzig, where he arrived on April 4th, and remained till April 24th,

assisting Kalkreuth in his defence of the place.   He
writes from the ship :

> But, but, our generals and governors ! It will give us a
> curious passage in history ! The renowned Prussian army, un-
> practised and unsoldiered through long peace ! If you want to be
> a military state, then you must engage in war. War is an art,
> and every art wants practice.

Receiving the order to proceed to Colberg at Danzig, April 23rd, he started at once, and arrived on
the 29th.

We must not be led further in speaking of the
defence of Colberg, than just to note in what its
importance consisted and what share Gneisenau had
in it.   Stettin had fallen, and Colberg, a place of
much less importance in itself, was now the only
fortress on the Baltic by which a communication
was preserved for Prussia with England and Sweden.   The siege began near the end of February,
under the conduct of General Teulié, who arrived
from Stettin with about 5000 men.   In the month
of April Marshal Mortier arrived with reinforcements, and at the end of that month the invading
force amounted to about 9000 men.   Within the
town were, at the beginning of the siege, about
4000, at the time of the arrival of Gneisenau about
6000 men; provisions came by sea, but ammunition
was somewhat short.   In these circumstances the
place was held triumphantly until the end of the
war, that is, till the beginning of July, and Gneisenau may be said to have carried his bat out, although in the latter half of June the besieging force
was raised to 16,000 men.   This defence is not only
to the Prussians the most creditable exploit of the

war, but it marked in the most striking manner the
change that was coming over the age, the new forces
that were mustering, and the new period that was
about to open under the auspices of Stein and
Scharnhorst. In the first place, it was here that
Schill began his career, and won the reputation of a
popular hero. This may be considered the beginning of the popular war in Europe, for Schill was
in the field even before the great Spanish Rebellion
took place. The times were so completely changed
since France had proclaimed the rights of man, that
opposition to the French was now the most popular
cause, and a man of the people was blessed by the
people for his heroic resistance to French tyranny
as freely as any other champions of liberty had ever
been blessed. It was a sign of hope for Prussia
that, in the general want of public spirit, she should
still be able to produce this Ferdinand Schill, this
lieutenant of dragoons who had escaped with a
wound from Auerstädt, and that he should be able
to find companions and to found a reputation. Not
only was the character of the Prussian soldiery re-
deemed by the exploits of Schill and his followers,
but civilians here exhibited all the spirit which they
had so conspicuously failed to exhibit elsewhere in
Prussia. No one distinguished himself more than
the mayor Joachim Nettelbeck, an old man at
the head of a brewery, who had passed much
of his life at sea, and who, as we may learn
from the narrative of the siege which he has left
us, by no means adopted the maxim proclaimed
by Count Schulenburg to the population of Berlin,
that 'the first duty of the citizen, when an enemy

398 LIFE AND TIMES OF STEIN. [PART III.

appears, is to be quiet.' On the other hand, it is remarkable that the patriots, whether among the citizens or soldiers, have an instinctive distrust of the military commandant. After the shameful surrender of Stettin, Magdeburg, and the other principal fortresses, the impression had gained ground that all the old officers were traitors. Colonel Loucadou, the Commandant of Colberg, did all in his power to confirm such an impression. As a matter of course he was sixty-five years old; he had the greatest jealousy of Schill and systematically opposed all his proceedings; and his conduct provoked on one occasion two of the younger officers to show their pistols and speak mysteriously of shooting any man who should mention surrender.

Thus when Gneisenau took the place of Loucadou a change happened corresponding to the dismissal of Haugwitz and Zastrow and the appointment of Stein and Scharnhorst at the centre of affairs. And it is this which gives the defence of Colberg its peculiar importance. It was not simply a brilliant military exploit, but the abandonment of a bad system and the first successful trial of the new principle which was to save Prussia in the end. Gneisenau availed himself of the patriotism of the people; under him soldiers and civilians worked together in a common cause, and he had the happy talent at once of inspiring and directing them. Thus it was due to him that the war did not end without one happy presage for Prussia. A false system had ruined the country, but Gneisenau at Colberg had had the skill and the good fortune to show what could be done under a more natural system and thus to point out how Prussia could be saved, namely, by substituting for a military caste estranged from the people and led by old men, an army working in sympathy with the people, and vigorously conducted. No one, therefore, had a better right to be called to the councils of the statesmen who were to regenerate Prussia, as Gneisenau was called by the King's letter of July 25th, appointing him a member of the Reorganisation Commission, over which Scharnhorst was to preside.

That friendship of Blücher, which was to be so important to Gneisenau in the later war, was gained by this exploit at Colberg. On hearing of the King's appointment, Blücher wrote to Gneisenau:

Go, and my best wishes accompany you! I see what you are reserved for, and rejoice in it: remember me to my friend Scharnhorst, and tell him that I lay it on his conscience to provide for a national army. It is not so difficult as is supposed: you must begin with a measure of height, there must be no exemptions whatever, and it must be a disgrace not to have served unless bodily infirmities prevent it. The soldiers once well drilled must live at home two years and only be called out the third; that will give the country relief, and we shall not want population. Besides, it is a mere fancy that a good soldier will forget everything in two years in such a way as not to be serviceable again in eight days. The French have taught us all this differently, and the soldier had better forget our empty pedantries. The army must be formed into divisions, the division be composed of all arms and manœuvre together in the autumn. The yearly reviews must be abolished. *Here you have my Confession of Faith*, give it to Scharnhorst and write both of you your opinion. Remember me to General v. Yorck when you see him, and remain the friend of—your friend

BLÜCHER.

This name, which alone of all the Prussian names

mentioned in this biography is a household word in
England, compels us to pause a single moment.
Blücher has little to do with Stein, little to do
with any reform either civil or military.   I have no
excuse for giving even such a rapid sketch of him as
I have given of Gneisenau.   But as that knowledge
of his biography which is universal in England is
strictly limited to a few hours of his life, as well as
for other reasons, it will be advisable to insert here
two or three of the leading points in his career.
Gebhard Leberecht v. Blücher then was already
sixty-five years old, for he was born in 1742.   He
was not a Prussian but a Mecklenburger born at
Rostock, nor did he begin his military career in the
Prussian service but in the Swedish, and his first
enemy was Frederick the Great.   Being taken prisoner by the Prussians in the Seven Years War, he
after some delay was induced to enter the Prussian
service, and he was present at the battle of Kuners-
dorff.   He continued in the service till 1771, when,
being offended at a promotion made over his head,
and getting no redress from his general, he wrote to
Frederick himself thus :

Von Jägersfeld, who has no other merit besides being the son
of the Margrave of Schwedt, is preferred to me.   I pray Your
Majesty for my dismissal.

Frederick answered this letter by placing the
young captain of horse under arrest, that he might
think better of it.   But as he did not change his
views in three-quarters of a year of imprisonment,
he at last extorted from Frederick the following :

Captain v. Blücher is relieved from his service, and may go
to the devil !

Blücher's military career seemed terminated. He soon after married a young Pole, and devoted himself to farming an estate belonging to her father, in which occupation he was so successful that after a time he was able to purchase for himself an estate in Pomerania, and here in his new character of agriculturist, came again into friendly relations with King Frederick ; but he did not return to the army for fifteen years, that is, till after the death of Frederick. Thus it was not till the Revolutionary War, when he was fifty years old, that he gained any considerable military distinction. In the Rhine Campaigns of '93 and '94 Blücher, at the head of the Red and Brown Hussars, became renowned as the great cavalry officer of the day, and the year after the Peace of Basel, with the help of some friends, he published at Münster a narrative of his adventures. After this late but splendid commencement it was his misfortune, in an age of unceasing wars, to pass in inactivity eleven years, during which he declined from middle life into old age. But two wars were still reserved for him. In the campaign of Jena, the campaign of old men, Prussia was saved from absolutely unrelieved disgrace only by Blücher's spirited resistance. But he was overwhelmed by superior force at Lübeck, and having capitulated at Ratkau, remained a prisoner till after the battle of Eylau. In the Convention of February 26th he was exchanged for General Victor, who had been carried off at Stettin by Schill. Unfortunately, however, no opportunity was given him in the second period of the war, when the Prussian honour was partly retrieved, of rivalling the achieve-

ments of Scharnhorst at Eylau, or Gneisenau at
Colberg.   He was to have been placed at the head
of a force which the King of Sweden was to support
both with men and money, but delays were inter-
posed, and the Peace of Tilsit came upon Prussia
before anything was done.   Blücher must have considered his career closed by this treaty.   He can
hardly have anticipated that he should live through
the whole period of Prussia's humiliation, and that
in the seventh year after Jena and the seventy-first
year of his life he should stand at the head of
great armies, and, counselled by his friend Gneisenau, should beat the Marshals of France, defeat
Napoleon in a pitched battle at La Rothière, and
see the tyrant's last armies dwindle away before
him round Paris, and finally, having been more
than any other man the hero of German liberation
in 1813 and 1814, should divide with Wellington
the honours of the crowning day which gave peace
to Europe.

In order to give the reader a complete idea of
the various abilities which co-operated in the period
after Stein's recall for the restoration of Prussia, it
would be necessary to add here several more biographical sketches.   In particular it would be necessary to describe the men who undertook to reform
public opinion, and who took the lead in the moral
regeneration ; Fichte, since Kant's death the most
conspicuous philosopher ; Schleiermacher, the most
eminent theologian and preacher of the age ; E. M.
Arndt, the popular poet and song writer, and, more
permanently influential perhaps than all, Wilhelm
v. Humboldt.

But for the present the reader has had enough of such sketches. It remains, before proceeding with the narrative of Stein's ministry, to suggest a single reflexion which arises out of them.

That such a number of remarkable men should arise together in Prussia must not lead us to hasty conclusions as to the wonderful genius of the Prussian nation, or the wonderful effects of the encouragement of education and free thought by Frederick the Great; and this for the simple reason that scarcely any of these remarkable men were Prussians. Thus Hannover sent Scharnhorst, and, we may add, Hardenberg, while Niebuhr was of descent partly Hannoverian, partly Danish, and by education a Holsteiner; Blücher and Queen Louise were Mecklenburgers. Arndt came from the island of Rügen. Gneisenau and Fichte were Saxons. Stein himself was a Franconian educated in Hannover. Not one of these had any connexion with Prussia until they were grown up. Of the whole number, only W. v. Humboldt, Schön and Schleiermacher were born Prussian subjects.

It is interesting to consider this practice of drawing statesmen from abroad, which has prevailed in some countries but not in others. It gives absolute governments a greater range in the choice of ministers than popular governments enjoy, for no popular government will endure foreigners in prominent office, as the reigns of William III. and George I. may teach us. And indeed the practice, where it is usual, is commonly a mark of a very low political condition; thus Spain since her decline has frequently been ruled by foreigners, and Russia almost habitually. The case of Prussia is in a medium, for though she chose foreigners freely in the time of Frederick the Great, and even later had the Italian Lucchesini, nay even since the Peace took the Dane Bernstorff straight from Denmark and gave him the portfolio of Foreign Affairs, yet as a general rule she has been served by Germans of some kind. Her Ministers even when not Prussians have not been *foreigners.*

Thus Prussia has been in the condition of a State which, without the degradation of being governed by foreigners, has a much greater command of ability than might be expected from her population. She has drawn to herself the ablest men from all the small States round her. Gneisenau, Scharnhorst, Niebuhr, all felt no doubt that they had gained a step of promotion when they had reached Berlin. And yet in this respect Prussia had no advantage over Austria. To serve the Emperor seemed to most Germans a greater honour than to serve the King of Prussia, and foreigners rose at Vienna even more easily than at Berlin, so that even the founder of modern Austria, the great Eugene, was a foreigner. How then did it happen that such a galaxy of fame shone at Berlin in the period of the distress of Prussia, and that nothing similar was to be seen at Vienna? Austria could indeed boast during those years of the most eminent publicist of Germany, a Prussian by birth, Friedrich Gentz, and she acquired in Clemens Wenzel Lothar Metternich-Winneburg, born at Coblenz and belonging by education to the Rhine district, a dignified and adroit diplomatist, who rose to great renown. But even these compare unfavourably with the Prussians, for Gentz was painfully wanting in manliness and dignity of character, nor could Metternich ever gain credit for the more solid qualities of the statesman; and besides these two and Count Stadion, an Imperial Knight with more than Stein's pride but with none of his ideas or enlightenment, and therefore with none of his success, Austria attracted no men of marked ability to her service.

The fact seems to be that while Prussia could offer a larger field and a better prospect of distinction than the smaller States, over Austria her service had some considerable advantages; for example Fichte, driven away from his Saxon University by a charge of heterodoxy, thought more naturally of taking refuge in Prussia than in Austria; Scharnhorst, a peasant's son, could not probably have risen in Austria to be War Minister; while others, particularly Stein and Gneisenau, were attracted to Prussia by the glory with which Frederick had invested her name. It is the more important to notice these advantages, because the more obvious advantages were conspicuously wanting to Prussia. That she should come out of the conflict at last with more triumphant success than any other State, was hardly expected by the best observers of the age. A year after his own retirement, when so many reforms had already been made in Prussia and when Austria had just suffered the crushing defeat of 1809, which was her Jena, Stein wrote the following curious comparison between the spirit of the two populations:

In this land (Austria) reigns good humour, sound good sense, piety: this with well-being, natural wealth and a mild climate, makes it pleasant to live here. People mean still perseveringly to continue the fight for independence and freedom, and their exertions are very great and energetic. It is a pleasure to see the noble and honourable views, the willingness, which reigns in this fine nation, to endure everything and sacrifice everything, in order to save itself from ruin.

With you (*i.e.* in Prussia) the path of irresolution, the path of the wavering will is trodden, which leads to ignominious destruction. It is a sad sight when so much that is great and good, which the exigency of the time demands, is left undone, and languor, selfishness and contentment under a degrading yoke, make progress. In North Germany nothing is to be expected except from the peasantry and the middle class: the rich noble wants to enjoy his property, and the poor noble wants a place and a livelihood; the official is possessed by a hireling spirit. If these classes are not roused by some stimulus they will remain inactive and do mischief by their example.

CHAPTER III.

IT is not generally the spirit of progress, as is often imagined, which brings about great reforms in a country, but the pressure of need. Reforms are not undertaken because people have come to conceive of a higher degree of well-being than before, but because some trial has overtaken them under which their institutions break down. It was the bankruptcy and disgrace of the old régime in France that ripened the spirit of innovation there; in England the reform party was called into existence by the burdens which the great war left behind it; still more pressing and overwhelming was the need which opened the door to reform in Prussia.

Nevertheless great reforms, though seldom brought about simply by the spirit of progress, can hardly take place in a community in which the spirit of progress is not active. The pressure of suffering will find the community helpless unless it contains a sufficient number of active and vivid minds which are ready with the necessary suggestions, and have

conviction and courage enough to take the responsibility of executing them. We have seen
that Prussia was not ill furnished with men, and
that adversity speedily produced its effect of bringing these men into power. It remains to consider what were their views and what they were
prepared to recommend. What Stein had in his
mind when he took the reins into his hands we
have ascertained. On some great points we have
seen his views clear and strong, but on other
points we have seen reason to think that he had
been outstripped by others who had had an opportunity of looking more closely at affairs since the
beginning of the year, and who had taken a
deeper impression of the public exigency.

Prussia was by no means in the condition of many
despotically governed countries, which, owing to the
jealousy and repressiveness of the government, are
entirely devoid of political culture. While in Austria
during the same period no one appeared who can
be called a political thinker, in Prussia there was
scarcely less political thought, though it was less
widely diffused and was of a somewhat different
type, than in free countries. Among the officials a
great fund of reflexion on public affairs had been
accumulated, and the mass had been quickened by
ideas thrown into it by writers and University Professors. Mirabeau had nearly twenty years before
elaborately criticised Prussian institutions and stated
the case of political economy against Frederick;
Kant's influence had extended to politics, and Kraus
closed his career in this very summer. In 1797
Kraus wrote, 'For the last six years, and latterly

without any concealment, I have not only expounded the only true, great, noble, just and beneficent system, but have succeeded in possessing some excellent heads with it, for instance, a certain v. Schön, whom our Minister v. Schrötter has sent to travel, and my favourite Dohna Wundlacken;' and again in 1796, 'Scheffner has a perfect right to say that the world has never yet seen a more important book than that of Adam Smith; assuredly since the time of the New Testament no work has had more beneficial effects than this will have if it should be more widely diffused, and more deeply impressed upon the minds of all who have to do with public affairs.' In the July of this summer he wrote a memoir on 'the means of procuring the money necessary for paying the French indemnity,' and then on August 28th he departed this life.

Since the end of April, some of the most intelligent of these highly educated officials had been formed into a Council to deliberate on public affairs, under the name of the Immediate Commission. These at the beginning had been Schön, Niebuhr, Stägemann and Altenstein, but a considerable alteration took place when Hardenberg retired early in July. Niebuhr and Altenstein departed with him to Riga, and did not return when the Commission was erected into a sort of provisional government pending the arrival of Stein.

Although no report of the deliberations of this Commission is preserved, yet we are able to form some conception of the boldness and comprehensiveness of the suggestions which were laid before it. There exist two memoirs, both written at Riga and

dated September 12th, 1807. The one is by Altenstein and is entitled, 'On the Direction of the Government after the Peace;' the other bears the title,
which however was not given it by the author himself, 'On the Reorganisation of the Prussian State,
written at the command of His Majesty the King;'
it is by Hardenberg, and may be considered his
political testament. The latter memoir, which has
been printed at length, is founded upon the former,
of which we have only extracts, and refers to it constantly; thus, as Altenstein acknowledges himself
indebted for many of his suggestions to his friends
Schön and Niebuhr, we may fairly regard Hardenberg's testament as the fruit of the Immediate Commission in its earlier form.

The first reflexion which this document suggests
is that Prussia was not likely to perish for want of
intelligence or breadth of view. Familiarity has not
made these politicians blind to the faults of the State,
nor details concealed principles from their view.
They judge of the institutions among which they
live with all the impartiality of historians, and recognize without hesitation the necessity of a comprehensive reform.

Hardenberg begins with a few prefatory sentences, of which the following is the most important.
'The principal question of all is to what chief the
execution (of the plan) is committed, and that unlimited scope both with respect to design and means
should be given to such a leading mind, if only it is
equal to the great task.'

He then lays down some general principles, such
as that there must be progress without violence or

breach of continuity, that revolution is only hastened by blind resistance, that Napoleon's strength depends upon his connexion with the Revolution. Accordingly he declares the true guiding principle to be, Democratical principles in a monarchical government. To attain this object a league of good men must be formed, which must be like the Jacobin Club in all but its criminality, and in which Prussia must take the lead. The Great Elector took a similar course in his time, and no season can be more opportune than the present, when the State has suffered so great a change and must undergo a complete regeneration.

He then treats of the different departments of government, beginning naturally with Foreign Affairs. The country, he says, has lost its independence and is in serious danger of being annexed. He recommends a diligent preparation of strength and husbanding of resources, and a decisive abandonment of the policy of neutrality. The first object must be to relieve the country from the French troops. But the greatest circumspection must be used in dealing with Napoleon. We must not dispute with him, but on the other hand we must beware of cringing to him. And here Hardenberg has the courage to add, 'I have it from a very sure hand that the King's letters to Napoleon were spoken of in Paris as '*les Elégies de Frédéric Guillaume.*' Prussia must never join the Confederation of the Rhine; that would be to assume the badge of slavery. We must recognize that we have been scandalously deserted by Russia, but we must remember the circumstances and influences which determined the Czar's conduct and not

throw away her good will.   Austria refused to help
us, but unfortunately in 1805 we treated her in the
same way or rather much worse.   England did not
help us promptly or energetically, but this was
chiefly by our own fault.   No Power but England
can help us with money in time of war.   A union
with England, Austria and the minor Powers may
again save Europe from bondage.

When Hardenberg passes to treat of internal
affairs, he begins at once to lean upon the support of
Altenstein.   He speaks of social reform under the
heads of the Noblesse, the Citizens and the Peasants.   The Nobles must lose all monopoly of office,
all exemption from taxation, precedence in eligi-
bility to posts in Foundations, Knighthoods, &c.
Here let the reader note particularly the following
sentence.   'The exclusive right of the Noblesse to
the possession of so-called knightly estates is, as
H. v. Altenstein has justly argued, so mischievous
and so little adapted now to our times and institutions, that the abolition of it is absolutely necessary,
as well as that of all other privileges which the laws
grant to the noble as a landed proprietor.'   Of the
citizens he says only the following : 'The citizen
class will gain by obtaining admission to all posts,
trades and occupations, and it must in return renounce all privileges from which other classes have
hitherto been excluded.'   What does he say of the
peasantry ?   'The abolition of serfdom must be
decreed by a law briefly and at once.   At the same
time the laws which prevent the peasant from passing out of the peasant class must be repealed.
Our military system will not suffer by this if proper

arrangements are adopted with respect to it. Their
acquisition of property must also be facilitated either
in respect of new purchases or buying up the rights
of the landlord. To abolish the system of corvées
is not necessary. Often it is not only not burdensome, but even more advantageous to the person
who is subject to it than a money payment, according to the local circumstances....It is further most
necessary in order to raise the peasant class that the
State should favour by an improved legislation the
abolition of commonalties, of detrimental servitudes,
of tithes in kind....A precedent established in the
peasantry of the Domains will have the greatest
effect in the Prussian State, where there are so
many Domains.'

In these rapid sentences Hardenberg travels
over the whole ground which was soon to be occupied by the Emancipating Edict of Stein. He
suggests all that the Edict actually did, and in some
places dictates the very form it should assume.
When for instance he says that 'the abolition of
serfdom must be decreed briefly and at once' he
points to just such a declaration as will be found
below in the Emancipating Edict. It would however be very erroneous to say that the original
contriver of the Edict was not Stein but Hardenberg. The memoir before us contains no doubt
some original suggestions of Hardenberg's, but in
this particular section he seems to follow Altenstein,
for he prefaces it with the remark, 'As H. v.
Altenstein has treated of this important subject in
a particularly noble manner, I assent to him with
full conviction, and may be the more summary

myself.' Altenstein, as a Member of the Immediate Commission, which had examined the internal condition of the country while Hardenberg guided its foreign affairs, and as being fresh from its deliberations, naturally laid before him an inchoate form of that Edict which as soon as Stein arrived became law.

To us therefore, with that Edict in view, this section of Hardenberg's memoir is much more important than the rest of it. Nevertheless we must not overlook what follows, that we may not fail to realise how bold, free, and comprehensive were the plans of reform which at this crisis found favour even with veteran politicians.

The next section is entitled, 'Restoration of the connexion between the nation and the government.' It refers to a scheme of a National Representation which has been proposed by Altenstein and which it pronounces to be 'good and appropriate, and not of the nature of a dangerous National Assembly.' We learn that Altenstein had proposed the amalgamation of a certain number of representatives with the different administrative Departments. In this way the advantages of the representative principle were to be obtained without incurring its dangers, for the government would obtain the support of a popular vote, yet would not have to contend with an organised popular body. This is perhaps the first proposal of representative government that was made in modern Prussia, and it becomes particularly interesting here when we inquire with whom it originated. Was it suggested to Altenstein at the Immediate Commission by Niebuhr or Schön? Altenstein tells

us expressly that he derived the idea from the
Minister vom Stein.   We may have noticed Stein's
significant opening of his 'Representation of the
Faulty Organisation' &c. (p. 268).   'The Prussian
State has no constitution; the supreme power is not
divided between the Sovereign and the representatives of the nation...as it has no political constitution
it is all the more important that its governmental
constitution should be formed on correct principles.'
Through these words may be discerned a yearning
after constitutionalism, which, considering that the
words were Stein's, is much to be noted.   What
should lead an official of Frederick the Great to hint
at a constitution, unless indeed he were infected
with the doctrines and language of the French
Revolution?   No one was less so than Stein, and
it appears that these expressions are really, as we
should guess, not mere loose allusions, but point to a
definite opinion and plan which Stein holds in reserve.   As a financier he had been struck with the
complete inelasticity of the revenue, which indeed
had been set in a strong light by the recent war.
Why had the fortresses been found so deplorably
unprepared?   Simply because the revenue had for
some years yielded no supplies which could be
applied to the fortresses, and however great the
necessity might be, there was no resource.   What
the State evidently wanted was a budget founded
upon the actual wants of the country, not merely
upon the traditional rights of the crown.   It was in
studying how to introduce such a financial system
that Stein had convinced himself of the necessity
of appealing to the representative principle.   The

kings of Prussia could no more raise taxes arbitrarily than the kings of England; their absolutism was
complete so long as their domain lands and recognized dues furnished them with money; but if they
were to cope with a Napoleon and rival his scale of
enterprise and expenditure the first requisite was an
elastic revenue, and for this purpose it would be
necessary to take the subject into counsel, though it
was still thought possible to dispense with a formal
Parliament.

The next section is entitled, 'Restoration of the
freest possible use of their powers to all classes of
the subjects.' Under this head is included Abolition
of the Guilds—' perhaps not at once but by degrees,
as H. v. Altenstein describes it'—and of Mono-
polies as far as possible.

Then comes a short section entitled, 'Abolition
of all cushions for idleness.'

Hardenberg then declares that though uniformity is not to be pushed too far and violence is
not to be done to the peculiarities of the different
provinces, yet he would not retain the administration by provinces. 'Let the whole State be
called Prussia. In this name let the Prussian proper,
the Pomeranian, and the Brandenburger be merged.'
He closes his remarks on Internal Reform with
an emphatic declaration that he agrees with H. v.
Altenstein in thinking that only a radical cure of
our constitution can give and secure new life to
our State. There must be no half measures. The
execution must not be committed to great compli-
cated Commissions. A few men of insight must
conduct the whole. There follow elaborate chapters

on Military Affairs, on Internal Government, on Finance, on Religion, on Justice, on the Mode of Conducting Business. From these it will not be desirable to transcribe extracts here.

On Sept. 12th Hardenberg wrote in his diary,

Terminé l'ouvrage auquel j'ai travaillé tout le temps depuis que je suis ici, pour donner au Roi mon avis sur la réorganisation de la monarchie. Altenstein a donné son avis systématiquement et d'une manière très circonstanciée après que nous fûmes convenus des principes. Niebuhr a dit le sien sur les objets de grande finance. J'ai mis la plume à la main les premiers jours du mois d'août.

In sending his memoir to the King he accompanied it with a letter, from which I extract one paragraph.

The Minister v. Stein has, as I expected from his patriotism, obeyed unconditionally your Majesty's summons. Be pleased to give him your confidence completely and express it warmly. It will be absolutely necessary to him if he is to attain that high goal which your Majesty has set before him. With the character he has it will enable him to do his part to you and will secure his attachment, and your Majesty will thereby the better paralyse the cabals against him. Listen to all that is said of him, but let nothing come between him and you ; speak to him always directly and immediately and give him to understand your opinion, your will, ay, your displeasure. That has the best effect upon a man of uprightness, of frank spirit, and high sense of duty and honour, and it strengthens confidence.

He then mentions the names of other public men whom, 'without forestalling the judgment and proposals of the Minister v. Stein,' he desires to recommend to the King from personal knowledge. These are first Altenstein, who continues always

Hardenberg's chief personal adherent; next Schön, of whom he says that 'he possesses the noblest economical acquirements, both theoretical and practical, trained by travel and careful study of foreign countries, and also strict morality.' 'He is rough in appearance,' he adds, 'but has delicate feelings, and devotes himself to what is good without personal regards; he is very active, and works easily and quickly.' Then he speaks of Stägemann, and next of Niebuhr, as 'a man of the rarest and most extensive learning, and with a very deep and practical knowledge of trade and currency. He is in every respect one of the purest and noblest characters; pity that his health is so weak! He may be thoroughly trusted with everything which he will undertake, remuneration must be pressed upon him.'

Surely a very noble political testament! If indeed we supposed its chief suggestions original, it would entitle Hardenberg to be considered the inspirer of almost the whole legislation to which Stein's name was soon to be attached. The evidence however is clear that he was not this, but only the first statesman who welcomed and approved the scheme of reform designed in the Immediate Commission. But to welcome and approve so warmly so daring a plan was in itself no inconsiderable public service; and at the same time that he gave so advantageous an introduction to the reform, he performed the same service still more signally to the reformer. All along we have found Frederick William hampered by his want of the sense which discerns great capacity, perhaps also by his want of the courage to trust himself to great capacity.

In the midst of his disasters, however, he had had the good luck by the help of the Czar to discern in Hardenberg a minister not wanting in intelligence or trustworthiness or courage. But Hardenberg was obliged to withdraw just at the moment when tasks awaited the Government to which it is doubtful whether even he would have been equal. At this crisis therefore nothing could save the State but a greater effort of self-control and docility on the part of the King than he had yet been required to make. Either he must commit himself again to the fatal guidance of the Lombards and the Beymes, or he must confide in one who was not even, what Hardenberg was, a courtier, in a man of imperious manners, inexorable firmness, and indefatigable energy. Yet this person seemed in himself better fitted than Hardenberg for the work of reform which Hardenberg himself saw to be necessary. It was one thing to acknowledge its necessity, to discern the course it should take, and another thing to have the courage to attempt it and the spirit and ascendancy to accomplish it. For such a task there was needed a man of the type of the old Hohenzollerns, and no one questioned that Stein had this type. But the King had already shown how much it cost him to submit to Stein's masterful bearing ; he had struggled with a mixture of anger and terror against the yoke, and Stein might have quoted to himself—only he had not yet read Faust —' er fühlt dass ich ganz sicher ein Genie, vielleicht wohl gar der Teufel bin.' If this difficulty was overcome, if Frederick William for once in his reign admitted a Minister not merely able but great, if a new chapter in the great destiny of Prussia began at this point, it is fair to attribute the result in great part to the generous and impressive appeal to the King's best feelings with which Hardenberg smoothed his successor's way to office.

It is now time to trace the steps by which large views of reform such as Hardenberg's memoir displays became converted into definite acts of legislation.

We have traced these plans very clearly to the Immediate Commission in the form which it had before Hardenberg's retirement. This would lead us to give the credit of them to four men, Altenstein, Schön, Stägemann and Niebuhr; were it not that another fact here claims our attention. We discover that there was dissension on this Board. Niebuhr was much discontented with the Commission. Writing to Schön from Riga, July 17, 1809, he says: 'Towards the Commission too I feel no inclination, no confidence that anything clever will come out of it; and I am sure your feeling is the same. A number of voices is only good where they are in harmony; the devil take the concert where two or three bagpipes drown the flutes.' And he goes on in language already quoted to insist on the necessity of a dictatorship. But so far it seems to be only as an administrative, not as a legislative Board that his criticisms apply to it. In a letter to Stein, also quoted above, there drops out, in the midst of similar language, a hint of a different kind of difficulty, which, as we shall soon see, he was not likely to mention to Schön. He says: 'Innovations are in contemplation, with regard to some of which I do not feel myself sufficiently acquainted with the particular case, while on others I am entirely unable to form a judgment ;' and he adds that he could not sit longer on the Commission without quarrelling with friends, 'since their principles are often really too monstrous, and the consistency with which they apply them more appalling still.' The reference to 'monstrous principles' leads us to think that the scheme of legislative reform which found favour with the majority was disapproved by Niebuhr, and the expressions he uses indicate in some degree the nature of his disapprobation. He objects to the ruthless application of theoretic principles, which in themselves he thinks of as not exactly erroneous, but rather too terrible to be true. When this tone is taken it is easy to guess that political economy is pointed at, and the conjecture is confirmed when we remember that of the three men Niebuhr may have in view, one, Schön, was a fanatical disciple of the economist Kraus.

But what was the particular economical discussion which had been raised at the Board? I imagine that within the time during which Niebuhr attended its meetings the controversy had not actually broken out; he himself speaks of it rather as one which he expects than as one which has already commenced, and Schön, who has left reminiscences of those meetings and dwells particularly on the impression made on him by Niebuhr, knows nothing of any controversy between Niebuhr and himself. Indeed we can understand that plans of legislative reform would not begin to be seriously or formally discussed until the Treaty was signed, though they

might be ventilated earlier, and when this had
happened Niebuhr and Altenstein had already been
separated from their colleagues of the Commission.
It is in fact on the morrow of the Treaty of Tilsit,
at the beginning of that interregnum between Hardenberg and Stein, when the Immediate Commission
was reconstituted as a kind of Provisional Government, that such large legislative views as we have
found in the memoirs of Hardenberg and Altenstein
begin to make way for a definite legislative project,
and that the outline of a law begins to appear. It
is evident that when the conqueror was gone
again and the King and his officials were left alone
with their ruin and with their Treaty which was
no Treaty, reforms would begin to seem ten times
as urgent as they had seemed while there was still
a war to be conducted. It was not merely that the
disasters of the war had opened the eyes of public
men to abuses which had grown up among them;
it was not that they hastened to take measures by
which such disasters might be prevented from occurring again. Not so much foresight as this was
needed. The question was at once simpler and
more urgently pressing; it was how to assist the
landowners, over whose fields the war had raged
and who now found themselves ruined by its de-
vastations; or, if they could not be assisted, how to
prevent the cultivation of the country from falling
into a condition of permanent decay like that which
had been witnessed in Poland. For a moment the
Government thought only of exceptional measures
of relief—subsidies, exemptions, indulgences—such
as may be employed in a province suffering from a

bad harvest or a cattle-plague. But very speedily it was perceived that more than this was called for, and further that even if such exceptional relief would have been sufficient it could not be given, since the disaster had not fallen upon some districts only, though some districts had suffered more than others, but upon the whole country, and the Government, impoverished itself, was in no condition to help individuals. As soon as this was perceived, not only did it become necessary to inquire of political economy what means there are of increasing the wealth of a whole nation at once, but other reforms, less obviously adapted to the immediate need, were now, because they had already ripened before the disasters began and were only awaiting their season, eagerly carried into effect. Free trade in land belonged to the first class; the emancipation of the serfs to the second.

It is said that a definite proposal for the abolition of hereditary serfdom was laid before the Commission by Privy Councillor Wilken as early as July 11th, only a week after the signing of the Treaty; and on the 20th the Minister for the Province of Prussia, v. Schrötter, made an application which brought the true problem of the hour immediately under the consideration of the Government: it was an application for help towards the restoration of ruined buildings and of the supply of horses and stock within his province. He seems to have proposed to meet the immediate need by the purchase of two or three hundred cows in Courland. The report of the Commission on this application was not sent in till August 17th, but in the mean time other voices, in particular that of Morgenbesser, a friend of Kant's, then President of the Provincial Court of Law, were raised for the abolition of serfdom.

The Report of August 17th is now before us; as the composition of Schön, it has been printed among his Remains, and I insert here an abstract of it.

It begins by mentioning that the King had resorted to a subsidy of 50,000 thalers for the distressed province, besides granting to some of the inhabitants the liberty of gathering wood in the Royal Forests. It then points out that there are two ways of restoring a distressed district, viz. to help individuals, or to apply general remedies; that the first method, which the Government has adopted, would certainly increase pauperism if it were adopted in a workhouse, and can only be approved as a momentary expedient. It should be limited to the bare preservation of life; for instance, meal might be given, but not stock; to give wood was still worse, for it would foster a belief already too prevalent that it is the part of Government to make grants of wood. Measures of this sort can only lead to disappointment and discontent, and they will impair the energy of self-help, which is weak enough among us already. All that Government can do is to remove hindrances to self-help, or in other words to repeal earlier regulations, and it is fortunate that the province of Prussia has suffered less than other provinces from the mercantile system, that it is not full of artificial industries and has actually not more persons engaged in manufactures and trade than the state of production requires.

It is agriculture, not trade or manufacture, that is seriously distressed. The landowner has lost the greater part of his capital, his stock, and in many cases his buildings. It is therefore the business of Government to remove any hindrances that may prevent the landowner from replacing his lost capital. Are there such hindrances? There are two standing hindrances, (1) limitation of the right of owning land, (2) limitation of the right of alienating it.

The first limitation may have had its political use in past

times, but evidently at the present moment it injures, instead of supporting, the noblesse. A landowner who cannot restore his estate for want of capital and credit must wish to sell it. This particular province has a larger middle class than any other province of the Monarchy, and in the middle class there is plenty of capital. But they cannot purchase because they have not the right of owning noble land. Meanwhile those who *have* this right, *i.e.* the nobles, cannot purchase because they want all their surplus capital for the restoration of their own estates. Drop this limitation, and the estate that its owner cannot restore will be restored by some one else; production will be as great as before; and all estates will retain their value and their credit. Frederick the Great saw the truth of this principle when he occupied West Prussia. There too capital was wanting, and he dropped the limitation. But now he who has an estate has no capital, and he who has capital is not allowed to have an estate.

Limitations on the power of alienation operate of course in the same way. They lower the value and credit of estates. The possessor of an estate under settlement or a fief cannot alienate, and can only mortgage with the consent of other interested parties. Cultivation is reduced to a low level and, whatever compensations individuals may receive, the State suffers in diminished production.

A third hindrance, continues the Report, is the regulation which interferes with the internal management of an estate by providing that the number of peasant holdings upon it shall never be diminished. It is supposed that the maintenance of our army requires this regulation. But it would not be so if serfdom did not exist. As the Government allows its subjects to become subjects of subjects, it is obliged, in order to compensate for this deviation from rule, to make itself guardian of these deserted ones. At any rate, the value of estates is now lowered by the obligation which lies upon the owners to work them on a system which is not the most profitable, and practically it will now be found impossible to restore all the peasant holdings.

Another hindrance—and this is the most important point of all, were not the discussion already exhausted—is hereditary serfdom. The present moment is peculiarly favourable for laying down the rule that all serfdom be abolished within four or six

years at furthest. It is so, first, because the change will not at
this moment leave any landowners without labourers except those
who are bad masters and therefore deserve to be without labourers,
since at this moment the supply of labour exceeds the demand;
secondly, because we can compensate the owners for the loss of
services by giving them unlimited freedom in the management of
their property : thirdly, because in this particular province serfdom excites more discontent than elsewhere, since the serfs here
compare themselves with a large population of free peasants, *e.g.*
on the Royal Domains, where serfdom has been abolished in this
province since the time of Frederick William I., and also because
serfdom has just been abolished in the Duchy of Warsaw, which
is contiguous to the province on two sides. Thus policy as well
as morality demands the change, that the loyal may not be worse
off than the disloyal.

So far the Report has pointed out hindrances to restoration
inherent in the existing constitution of the country. In addition
it remarks that a new hindrance may be created in a hasty attempt to remedy the evil. A General Indulgence had been promulgated, by which the landowners who had suffered from the
war were protected from their creditors. It might be supposed
that it was intended to apply only to such debts as had been
contracted before its publication ; but this was not clear ; and the
Report points out that while such an Indulgence was in force no
man who had money to spare would lend it to a landowner, and
that the State by its well-meant interference had actually destroyed
the credit of the class it intended to protect. The General
Indulgence might be admissible during the war, but ought to be
abolished as soon as possible after the return of peace.

The general recommendations of the Report are therefore,
besides the speediest possible withdrawal of the Indulgence, as
follows :

Abolition of what may be called the *status* of noble land, and
along with this equality of rights to every landowner without
regard to his birth.

Discouragement of all restrictions of the right of alienation
by *majorats*, feudal tenures, &c.

Abolition of the regulation making the number of peasant
holdings incapable of diminution.

Abolition of the menial services rendered by serfs. These are distinguished from the agricultural services which are the consequences of the possession of a holding or a house, and have nothing to do with serfdom.

In this important report, sent in six weeks before Stein's arrival, we have the substance of the Edict of October.

On the very same day the Minister v. Schrötter also reported. His recommendations were to the same effect, and seem to have gone even further in the direction of Free-trade. He fixes Martinmas, 1810, as the moment of the ceasing of serfdom, a date which we find adopted in the Edict; he recommends that an attempt should be made to raise a foreign loan, and accompanies this recommendation with a paper on the subject by Professor Kraus; and he gives it as his opinion that the Province will scarcely bear more taxation.

On August 23rd the King commissioned Minister v. Schrötter and his brother to make the draught of a law founded on these proposals. The draught was sent in early in September, and was again discussed in the Immediate Commission. Here it was completely remodelled, and at the end of the month it was laid before the King in its new form accompanied with remarks by Beyme.

Not till this point does Stein appear among the legislators. On reading the draught he wrote the following observations, which bear date the fourth day after he had received his powers.

This Edict grants to the Landowner the free use of his territorial property and to the cultivator (Landbauer) competence to use his power in freedom. It is very beneficial, *and must be extended as soon as possible to the whole Monarchy.*

There is but one legal limitation of free disposition of landed property which must be allowed to remain; it is that which restrains the covetousness of the rich and educated class and hinders the absorption of peasant land in manorial farms. This will be the more necessary because the free-trade in land allowed in § 1 [1] will multiply alterations with the change in ownership and the rise of the value of land will more and more tempt the new proprietor to seek his advantage.

The inconvenience arising from keeping up too small peasant holdings is avoided by the permission given in § vi. to consolidate holdings; the limitation in favour of the peasant class will therefore work for good only, and all inconvenient consequences from it are done away.

It is feared that the limitation in favour of the peasant holdings will hinder the restoration of the peasant holdings ruined in the last war; to prevent this it will be necessary to insert in § vi. of the Law the provisions suggested by Privy Councillor Stägemann August 15th, and thus to encourage the putting to use the holdings devastated in the last war.

STEIN, October 8th.

On the same day he had audience of the King, and sent the following instructions to the Commission :

The King's Majesty has been pleased in to-day's audience to decree that

The Edict be extended to all provinces of the Monarchy, since the principle of the free use of person and property is equally applicable to all provinces and beneficial to all alike ;

That the consolidation of peasant holdings with manorial farms is indeed admissible with the sanction of the Chambers, but that each Provincial Department must draw up and deliver to them an instruction, enumerating the cases in which such a consolidation may take place.

[1] See the Edict given below, p. 442.

I gather that this last provision (see Edict § VI, last clause) is that which Stein refers to above as having been suggested by Stägemann.

Thus was prepared a Legislative Edict which accomplished a great social and industrial revolution. On the next day it was signed by the King and delivered to the two Schrötters for publication. And now let us turn our attention to the document itself.

CHAPTER IV.

THE EMANCIPATING EDICT.

I CALL by this name the great Edict which was signed on the 9th of October, *i.e.* only five days after Stein had received his powers, not solely because it contains the provision that from a certain date there shall be only free persons in the States of the King of Prussia. It is indeed to be remarked that the principal authors of the measure are so intoxicated with the pride of being the bestowers of freedom upon bondsmen, that they forget to remark how much more and how many other emancipations they accomplished by the same act. Stein's own account of the Edict of October runs as follows :—

The measures adopted to reach the above-mentioned general object were :

(1) Abolition of personal serfdom in the Prussian Monarchy : by an Edict of October, 1807, it was decreed that from October 8th, 1809 (*sic;* it should be 1810), personal serfdom with its consequences, especially the very oppressive obligation of menial service, should be abolished ; but the obligations of the peasant, as far as they flowed from his possession of property, remained unaltered. It was reserved for the Chancellor Hardenberg's love

of innovation (on the advice of a H. Scharrenweber, a dreamer who died in a madhouse at Eberbach in 1820) to transform in 1811 the relations of the landlord to the peasant class, and its inner family relations in a manner pernicious to it; in this I had no share.

(2) The transformation of the peasants on the Domain in East and West Prussia into free proprietors.

Here not a word is said of any changes made by the Edict of October except those which affected the peasant. It is the same aspect of the Edict which interests Schön. This Edict, he says, 'has made the figure of the king stand higher, since he is henceforth no longer a king of slaves, but of free men.' And again :—

Thus came into existence the law of October 9th, 1807, that Habeas Corpus Act of our State. The idea of freedom had begun to live. With ninety-nine hundredths of the people it made a deep and elevating impression; the few friends of slavery intrigued and murmured no doubt a good deal, so that according to Rhediger's story a prejudiced man said at the Berlin Casino after reading the law, 'Rather three Battles of Auerstädt than such a law !' But the King stood firm, and God maintained the right.

In stating pretty strongly his claims to be considered the real author of the law, Schön uses language which shows that he is thinking almost exclusively of this part of it. 'All else that I did in life,' he says, 'was as nothing compared to calling into life the idea of freedom.' Only from one casual expression do we learn that he even knew that the measure had another side, where he says, 'I represented that hereditary serfdom, that scourge of our country, must be brought to an end, and that a proclamation of free trade in landed property would be sufficient to promote material interests.'

Here we are suddenly introduced to something quite new and very different from the abolition of serfdom, namely, free trade in landed property.

Up to a certain point it is true that these two things coincide. One part of the burden of serfdom lay in the incapacity of the serf to alienate his land; but this is a small matter. The proclamation of free trade in land affected all classes of society at once, and the upper and middle classes much more than the peasantry. When therefore we observe that the Edict of the 9th of October, at the same time that it abolished personal serfdom, removed all the principal restrictions that interfered with traffic in land, we see that it is in fact not a single law but two laws in one, and two laws of such magnitude that each by itself might be considered equivalent to a social revolution.

But when we look closer still we discover that the Edict goes even further, and should be rather described as threefold than as twofold. Englishmen are only too familiar with the notion of a depressed class of agricultural labourers, but such depression may be of two kinds and may spring from two very different causes. We are not to suppose that the peasantry of Prussia were in a condition resembling that of our own labourers any further than as it was bad. The evils afflicting the Prussian peasantry were those arising out of *status;* those which afflict English labourers arise mainly out of contract. The English labourer is nominally free, and at liberty to carry his industry to the best market; he is reduced to real dependence by his inability to make a favourable bargain for himself. The Prussian peasant was nominally a serf, but in reality some very important rights were secured to him. We are not to suppose, for instance, that cruel punishments were allowed, or that he was subject to the caprice of the landlord. He was far more of a proprietor than the English labourer, for, though on a degrading tenure, he did for practical purposes own land. Nor were his interests neglected as those of a freeman, who is supposed able to take care of himself, may be neglected. Not only was he a member of an ancient and organized village community, but the Government also took and was obliged to take the greatest possible interest in his class, for these serfs were neither more nor less than the Prussian army.

Now it might very plausibly be maintained that the proclamation of free trade in land would not create a happy peasant class, but would simply substitute for a peasantry labouring under certain evils that class of famished drudges whom we know in England, and who if they cannot be called serfs can still less be called peasants, for a peasant properly so called must have a personal interest in the land. Hence the conservative opponents of Stein, such as Marwitz, actually declare that there existed no slavery or serfdom in the land when he professed to abolish it, but 'that it then for the first time began to appear, namely, the serfdom of the small holder towards the creditor, of the poor and sick towards the police and the workhouses;' and again, 'that with the proclamation of free trade disappeared the previous security of the peasantry in their holdings; every rich landowner could now buy them

out and send them off—fortunately, scarcely any-
body was rich any longer!'

These were the criticisms of the conservative
party, which might have been very truly applicable
to a simple measure of free trade in land. But the
Edict of October had in fact taken account of the
danger and contained an express provision to meet
it. Hence, as I have said, it was actually a threefold enactment, for not only did it first abolish serfdom and secondly establish free trade in land, but
thirdly it endeavoured to guard the peasantry
against the danger, which in so many countries
has proved serious, of being gradually driven out
or turned from proprietors into wages-receivers by
the effects of the unequal competition to which
they are exposed.

At the same time that we carefully distinguish
these different enactments all included in one Legislative Edict, let us be as careful to remark what
was not included in it. Englishmen are apt to
attribute to the legislation of Stein all the innovations introduced in this period. In particular it has
been supposed that he created the peasant-proprietorship of modern Prussia. But this he did not do,
except, as he says in the passage quoted above,
on the Domain Lands of West and East Prussia.
Proprietors in a certain sense the peasantry were
before this Edict, that is, they cultivated land for
themselves and with a considerable sense of security; proprietors in the full sense they were not,
because they held of a landlord to whom they owed
various dues and services. Now Stein's Edict
altered the nature of these services and abolished

the most oppressive, but it did not destroy the rights of the landlord or leave the peasant sole master of the land he cultivated. It was reserved for Hardenberg to do this by an Edict issued on September 14th, 1811, and it should be noticed that Stein expressly declines to accept any responsibility for this innovation. Again, it is not to be supposed that the provision just mentioned, by which Stein tried to prevent the absorption of the small holdings by the great proprietors, has actually proved the means of preserving the peasant class in Prussia; for all this passed away with the legislation of Hardenberg, and it has been by its own vitality and not by State interference that peasant-proprietorship has maintained itself.

Further, it is to be remarked that Stein is quite accurate when he describes his Land Reform as not consisting solely in the Edict of October, but as including also another quite distinct act of legislation which applied only to the provinces of East and West Prussia. This act belongs to July, 1808, and is confined not simply to the peasants of these two provinces, but to a particular class of peasants, viz. those sometimes called *immediate* peasants, or in other words those who living on the Royal Domains had no other landlord but the King. It is evident that the Government could deal with these more easily than with those peasants whose condition it could not improve without meddling with the rights of another class. The extreme distress in which these two provinces lay, and which the Government was in no condition to relieve directly, was the justification for granting privi-

28—2

leges to these particular immediate peasants which
for the moment were not extended to those of the
other provinces.

Such then, defined in general terms, was the
extent of this reform. It needs, however, a much
closer description. In the first place the reader
must guard against a misapprehension of the phrase
'free trade in land,' into which he is likely to be
led by his English experience. Free trade in land
is also a cry of our own reformers, but we must
beware of supposing that what they call for is the
same thing that was granted in Prussia by Stein's
Edict. The complaint in England is that a number of practical obstructions prevent land from being
the object of such free purchase and sale as other
commodities. Much of the land of the country, it
is said, is in the hands of persons who in family
settlements have given up the right to alienate it;
the system under which landed property is conveyed is so cumbrous and expensive as to deter
people from transactions of the kind; and lastly,
by recognizing the principle of primogeniture with
respect to land and not with respect to personal
property in cases of intestacy, the law itself countenances the notion that landed property stands in
a class by itself and is not to be dealt with or
transferred as if it were purely a commodity. Now
it is an instance of the confusing and misleading
inaccuracy of our party cries, when the removal
of these restrictions is called free trade in land.
Free trade in other cases means the removal of
restrictions imposed by the law or by the government, but these restrictions are of quite another

kind. Only the last mentioned is the work of the law, and it cannot in any proper sense be called a restriction, for the only way in which it operates restrictingly is by lending the moral influence of the law to the support of a restrictive system. The cumbrousness of our conveyancing is merely the result of the gradual way in which our land system has been formed, and as to the system of settlements, so far from being a restriction of freedom it is the direct result of freedom of contract, so much so that the reformers themselves demand an interference of the law to prevent it, in other words, wish to promote what they call free trade by a new legal prohibition.

Now when Stein is said to have established free trade in land, the expression is to be understood literally. The hindrances to the sale and purchase of land which he removed were not accidental practical obstacles but formal legal prohibitions. In the old law of Prussia, and in the Code of Frederick or Allgemeines Landrecht, which came into force in 1794, it is laid down that noble estates (adelige Güter) can only be held by nobles, and that persons of civic origin (bürgerlicher Herkunft) can only acquire them by express permission of the sovereign. In the same way peasant-land could, as a rule, only be held by peasants, and land belonging to towns only by citizens. We are familiar with the idea of caste as applied to human beings, that is, of an unalterable *status* stamped upon a man from his birth; in Prussia it may be said that caste extended actually to the land, so that every rood of soil in the country was of a definite and unalterable rank and, however it might change its owners, always remained either noble or citizen or peasant land. Now the first innovation contained in Stein's Edict consisted in cancelling in the fewest and simplest words all the regulations which established caste in land.

When the Edict is examined more closely it will be seen to be much more comprehensive even than it was represented above, when I pointed out how much more comprehensive it was than was commonly supposed or than Stein himself described it. For at the same time that it abolishes caste in land, it accomplishes another act of emancipation which is in no way expressed in the phrase free trade in land; it removes another quite distinct set of restrictions and abolishes caste in persons. The Code of Frederick prohibited the nobleman from engaging in any occupation properly belonging to the citizen, and only allowed under certain conditions the citizen to pass into the class of peasants or the peasant into the class of citizens. The Nobles, the Citizens, the Peasants; these were the three castes into which the Prussian population, outside the professions, was divided; into one or other of them each person was born and in the same, as a rule, he died. To each caste was assigned its special pursuit. The Noble cultivated his estate and exercised jurisdiction over the peasantry who held under him, though he could not himself hold or cultivate peasant land; he also served the king in civil or military office. The Peasant cultivated his plot of ground, rendering fixed services to the lord and subject to his jurisdiction, and belonged at the same time to the rank and file of the army.   Between them stood the Citizen, holding a monopoly of trades and industries which by law were confined, with few exceptions, to the towns.   It is remarkable that the military profession was for the most part closed to him.   This must be borne in mind when we compare the Seven Years War with the War of Liberation. We have read of the fearful consumption of men caused by the Seven Years War, and of the desperate shifts of Frederick to procure recruits; but we must understand that no *levée en masse* took place then and that the citizen class had scarcely any share in what was going forward.   This is the more to be noted because the connexion between the citizen class and the learned class was closer than in other countries.   The learning, literature and philosophy which flourished so remarkably in that age took the tone of the middle class, and a curious result followed: In the most military of all modern States, literature, because it sprang from a class which enjoyed an exemption from military service, and as a consequence the tone of public feeling which is determined by literature, was in an especial degree wanting in the military spirit—Scharnhorst describes the army as being generally hated and despised and Kant speaks with contempt of a man of education who had embraced a military life—and this fact goes some way to explain that phenomenon of a military State fighting exceptionally ill which we have so long had before us.

This state of society is very foreign to our ideas,

and may perhaps, because we have no experience
of it, fascinate some imaginations. No Laissez
faire here; every man's place is assigned to him
from his birth; his occupations are prescribed, and
a great Taskmaster or earthly Providence stands
at the head of the whole society, which may be
called army or nation at pleasure, since even the
unmilitary citizens were regarded by the State
principally as a sort of commissariat department.
And for the immediate purpose of Frederick William
I. and Frederick the Great the system was well
adapted, for that purpose was simply military. A
place for every man and every man in his place; the
'productive forces of the country perfectly inventoried
and a debtor and creditor account of its resources
kept[1];' by such a system the rulers could wield the
whole force of the country most easily and certainly.
Nevertheless, the destruction of this whole system
by a stroke of Stein's pen, was now regarded as
the greatest of reforms and the commencement of
the restoration of Prussia. For it will be evident
that the same system which concentrated so powerfully and measured so exactly the forces of the
country at the same time entirely prevented them
from growing, not to mention the intellectual stag-
nation, outside the University world, which was produced by such rigid uniformity of life. A country
in which no man can follow his natural bent, take
to agriculture if he does not like trade or to trade if
he does not succeed in agriculture, is evidently not
an industrial country; its material resources under
such a system will remain undeveloped, and if it

[1] Morier.

be a poor country, as Prussia was, the system will actually in the end defeat its own object, for such a country from mere poverty will be weak in war.

As the first section of the Edict abolished what I have called 'caste in land,' so the second, consisting of about three lines, abolished caste in persons. And here it may perhaps be observed that I omitted above one principal circumstance which made such sweeping changes so easy to Stein. Before the Peace of Tilsit it would have been scarcely possible to carry out such reforms however much the rulers might have been convinced of their necessity. Frederick had shrunk from the emancipation of the serfs because he felt that it would introduce disorder into his army, and for the same reason these reforms also would have been scarcely practicable so long as the army existed. The disasters brought with them the compensation that they destroyed for a moment this incubus; the necessity of maintaining a great position in Europe, the necessity even of defending the country, ceased when the country actually fell into French occupation, and thus, as we may say, the building being down, it was for the first time possible to mend a defect in the foundations.

These reforms, favoured as they were by circumstances and requiring but few lines in the Edict, were yet much more fundamental and pregnant with consequences than any such practical reforms as may be called for in England to make the purchase of land more easy. They were a sort of Magna Charta to the Prussians, and Schön might well have applied to them the enthusiastic expressions which

LIFE AND TIMES OF STEIN. [PART III.

he keeps for the sections which emancipated the serf. In v. Rönne's standard text-book of Prussian Constitutional Law, I find in the chapter on Rights under the first Title, Freedom or Security of the Person, that this freedom is composed of three rights, (1) the right of movement and free choice of abode (Freizügigkeit), (2) the right of emigration (Auswanderungsrecht), (3) *the right of choosing a calling or trade* (Freie Wahl von Beruf und Gewerbe); and this third right we are informed was given to the Prussians by the Edict of October 1807. The same is said of the first of the rights which go to make up the second Title, viz. free right to the acquisition and possession of property (Freies Recht zum Erwerbe und Besitze des Eigenthums).

I proceed to give the text of this Edict, the vast importance of which will have by this time become clear. The less important sections are printed in a smaller type, and of §§ III. and v., as purely technical, only the heading is given.

Edict concerning the facilitation of possession and the free use of landed property, as well as the personal relations of the inhabitants of the country.

WE, Frederick William, by the grace of God King of Prussia, &c., &c.,

Make known hereby and give to understand. Since the beginning of the peace We have been before all things occupied with the care for the depressed condition of our faithful subjects, and the speediest restoration and greatest improvement of it. We have herein considered that in the universal need it passes the means at Our command to furnish help to each individual, and yet We could not attain the object; and it accords equally with the imperative demands of justice and with the principles of a proper national economy, to remove all the hindrances which hitherto prevented the individual from attaining the prosperity which, according to the measure of his powers, he was capable of reaching; further, We have considered that the existing restrictions, partly on the possession and enjoyment of landed property, partly on the personal condition of the agricultural labourer, specially thwart Our benevolent purpose and disable a great force which might be applied to the restoration of cultivation, the former by their prejudicial influence on the value of landed property and the credit of the proprietor, the latter by diminishing the value of labour. We purpose, therefore, to reduce both within the limits required by the common well-being, and accordingly ordain as follows :

§ I.   Freedom of Exchange in Land.

Every inhabitant of our States is competent, without any limitation on the part of the State, to possess either as property or pledge landed estates of every kind : the nobleman therefore to possess not only noble but also non-noble, citizen and peasant lands of every kind, and the citizen and peasant to possess not only citizen, peasant, and other non-noble but also noble, pieces of land, without either the one or the other needing any special permission for any acquisition of land whatever, although, henceforward as before, each change of possession must be announced to the authorities.

§ II.   Free Choice of Occupation.

Every noble is henceforth permitted without any derogation from his position, to exercise citizen occupations ; and every citizen or peasant is allowed to pass from the peasant into the citizen class, or from the citizen into the peasant class.

§ III.   How far a legal Right of Preemption and a First Claim still exist.

§ IV.   Division of Lands.

Owners of Estates and Lands of all kinds, in themselves alienable either in Town or Country, are allowed after due notice given to the provincial authority, with reservation of the rights of Direct Creditors and of those who have the right of preemption (§ III.), to separate the principal estate and its parts, and in general to alienate piecemeal. In the same way Co-proprietors may divide among them property owned in common.

§ V.   Granting of Estates under Leases for a Long Term.

§ VI.   Extinction and Consolidation of Peasant Holdings.

When a landed Proprietor believes himself unable to restore or keep up the several peasant holdings existing on an estate which are not held by a hereditary tenure, whether of a long lease or of copyhold, he is required to give information to the government of the province, with the sanction of which the consolidation, either of several holdings into a single peasant estate or with demesne land, may be allowed as soon as hereditary serfdom shall have ceased to exist on the estate.   The provincial Authorities will be provided with a special instruction to meet these cases.

§ VII.   If on the other hand the peasant tenures are hereditary, whether of long lease or of copyhold, the consolidation or other alteration of the condition of the lands in question, is not admissible until the right of the actual possessor is extinguished, whether by the purchase of it by the lord or in some other legal way.   In this case the regulations of § VI. also apply.

§ VIII.   Indebtedness of Feudal and Entailed Estates in consequence of the Ravages of War.

Every possessor of feudal or entailed property is empowered to raise the sums required to replace the losses caused by war, by mortgaging the substance of the Estates themselves as well as the revenues of them, provided the application of the money is attested by the Administrator (Landrath) of the Circle or the

Direction of the Department. At the end of three years from the contracting of the debt, the possessor and his successor are bound to pay off at least the fifteenth part of the capital itself.

§ IX. Extinction of Feudal Relations, Family Settlements, and Entails, by Family Resolution.

Every feudal connexion not subject to a Chief Proprietor, every family settlement and entail may be altered at pleasure or entirely abolished by a Family Resolution, as is already enacted with reference to the East Prussian Fiefs (except those of Erme-land) in the East Prussian Provincial Law, Appendix 36.

§ X. Abolition of Villainage.

From the date of this Ordinance no new relation of villainage, whether by birth, or marriage, or acquisition of a villain holding, or by contract, can come into existence.

§ XI. With the publication of the present Ordinance the existing condition of villainage of those villains with their wives and children who possess their peasant-holdings by hereditary tenures of whatever kind ceases entirely both with its rights and duties.

§ XII. From Martinmas, 1810, ceases all villainage in Our entire States. From Martinmas, 1810, there shall be only free persons, as this is already the case upon the Domains in all Our provinces; free persons, however, still subject, as a matter of course, to all the obligations which bind them as free persons by virtue of the possession of an estate or by virtue of a special contract.

To this declaration of Our royal Will every man whom it may concern, and in particular Our provincial and other governments, are exactly and loyally to conform themselves, and the present Ordinance is to be made universally known.

Authentically, under Our royal Signature. Given at Memel, October 9th, 1807.

FRIEDRICH WILHELM,
Schrötter, Stein, Schrötter II.

The elder Schrötter was at this time Minister for the province of Prussia, and he with his brother was intrusted with the task of publishing the Ordinance in the province where it had received the King's signature. It is for this reason that their names are affixed to it along with Stein's.

That threefold character of the Edict which was pointed out above, will appear very visibly by observing the three groups of sections, which on account of their especial importance have been printed in large type. The abolition of caste, both in land and in persons, is accomplished in the first two sections; the abolition of villainage in the last three, which, it is evident, might as well have composed a separate edict. Sections 6 and 7 are introduced to prevent the system of free trade in land from bearing too hard on the peasant and making the proprietorship of land a monopoly of the richer classes.

Having traced the history of the preparation of this Edict, and examined its nature and the changes it introduced, we are in a condition to inquire who are the persons to whom the Prussians may consider themselves chiefly indebted for it.

In such cases the popular mind invariably makes a misapprehension which it is almost in vain to attempt to correct. It attributes to the unassisted intelligence and will of a single author what was necessarily the joint work of many. In this instance Stein has obtained a popular fame to which he has little right, and which partly compensates for much unjust neglect. While his real life and actions have been little known, he has gained a sort of legendary reputation, such as has gathered round many other legislators, and has been credited with all the judgment, technical skill and wisdom implied in the framing of a law which has revolutionised a country. His admirers need not hesitate for a moment to disown for him all such ungrounded pretensions. In the construction of the Emancipating Edict Stein had no great share. Before it reached his hands it was almost complete, and we may distinguish two agents by whom it had been made such as it then was. The first agent was what we call the Spirit of the Age, that is, the sum of influence proceeding partly from the humanitarian writers partly from the economists of the 18th century, by which the majority of those who guided public affairs had been convinced of the necessity of certain great changes. When a man like Hardenberg, who had no special or professional learning, confidently sanctioned such sweeping proposals as those which Altenstein laid before him, he proclaimed in effect that the work of the Zeitgeist was done. From that moment the matter of the law existed, and the question of the form came under consideration. Then began the work of the second agent, that is the Immediate Commission. We have seen who the men were from whose deliberations the law came forth clothed in form. But perhaps the question may be asked which member, or members, of the Commission deserved best of the law, and this question can only be answered partially and doubtfully, many of the documents being missing in the archives. We have the fact that Niebuhr separated himself deliberately from his colleagues because he

would not take the responsibility of their plans.
For the rest we have Schön's Report, of which an
abstract has been given above, and we have some
reminiscences of Schön, which were written down at
a much later period and not published till 1875.
The latter indeed give us many statements, but we
are embarrassed when we find that their drift is to
claim the whole credit of the Edict for Schön. It
seems hardly fair to the other members of the Commission to accept a representation which is made at
their expense and published after their death. When
we test it in the only way open to us, that is by
comparing it with Schön's Report, which for what
it asserts is far better testimony, we find the suspicions decidedly strengthened, which the claim
itself by its exorbitant and egotistic character suggests. That Schön deserved a great share of the
credit we are quite prepared, from what we hear
of the influence he exerted, to believe; nay, after
a reasonable deduction for evident self-conceit, we
might be willing to think that perhaps his claim to
have been the guiding spirit of the Commission was
substantially well-founded. But when we compare
his late reminiscences with his own Report written
at the time, as well as with other evidence, we discover that his self-conceit was of an unusual intensity
and that it certainly clouded and corrupted his
remembrances. His statement is not merely exaggerated; it is certainly untrue, and gives an
incorrect impression of the nature as well as of the
degree of the influence he exerted.

We have gathered from Niebuhr's hints that
he had friends on the Commission who applied

certain doctrinaire theories with a consistency which appalled him, and in fact frightened him away. It is scarcely possible to doubt who is pointed at. Schön was just such a doctrinaire and such inexorable consistency was just in his character, while nothing similar seems to be true of Altenstein or Stäge-mann. It seems also unquestionable what rigorous applications of theory are pointed at. The introduction of free trade in land created so manifest a danger of the absorption of the peasant-holdings by the rich that it was found in the end necessary to protect those holdings by a special limitation. Now the theory of free trade was precisely that which at the moment possessed the heads of the Prussian doctrinaires under the influence of Kraus, and it was precisely that of which Schön was the mouth-piece on the Immediate Commission. 'Kraus,' says Schön himself, 'was my great teacher; he mastered me entirely and I followed him without reserve.' The theory was still so new, that it is not likely that the Prussian legislators could have adopted it with such courageous completeness as they did in the Emancipating Edict unless there had been among them some strongly convinced free-trader, whose arguments were heard at the Immediate Commission. Schön's influence is necessary to account for the result, and we can fancy how hard and ruthless his language must sometimes have sounded, particularly to one so timid by tempe-rament as Niebuhr. Thus Niebuhr's evidence and the nature and known facts of the case concur to show us Schön advocating with all his in-fluence and with more energy than any one else that part of the Edict which introduces free trade in land.

On the other hand we do not expect to be told that Schön had much influence in deciding the Commission to propose the abolition of serfdom, not because he did not feel strongly on the question, but because there was no difference of opinion about it. How did we find Hardenberg treating this subject? 'The abolition of serfdom,' he wrote, 'must be decreed by a law briefly, and at once.' In other words, it is a matter on which argument has long been exhausted. That this was really the case, that, to use the vigorous words of—what writer? —of Schön himself,

The great majority of the nation, a few weak and wicked persons only excepted, have long been agreed upon the principle that there is no greater injustice than that a reasonable being should be prevented from using his energies for his own welfare in a way not prejudicial to the State by a fellow-subject, simply because he was born on this or that clod,

all evidence concurs to show. To abolish serfdom had been a favourite object of Frederick William III. since his accession, ' towards which,' as he himself said in his Cabinet Order of August 23rd, 'he had undeviatingly striven.' The question had been agitated in every way, in the Estates of West Prussia as early as 1799, .in writings by Kraus, Leopold Krug, and others; Stein himself, as has been remarked above, had been busy with it in Westphalia. A good notion of the general state of public opinion on the subject may be formed from the following statement given in Bassewitz' 'State of the Electoral Mark of Brandenburg in 1806.'

Though the peasant, used to routine, had in his fettered condition little industry and did not yet appreciate the advantages which were offered him for the future in a perfectly free proprietorship, yet he felt keenly enough the pressure of the service-payments, and of the compulsory service. This, and the views of the rights of man that were diffused among the people, created among the peasantry the wish to be relieved from their services, from their dependence on the landlords, and from the compulsory menial service, as it subsisted under the Servants Ordinance (Gesindeordnung) for the country districts of the Electoral Mark of February 11, 1769, and the later interpretations of it.

Now what startles us in Schön's reminiscences and excites the suspicion that he does not merely exaggerate, but deliberately distorts and misrepresents the truth, is this, that he describes himself as having carried the abolition of serfdom in spite of general opposition, while he is not only silent about his exertions in the cause of free trade, but endeavours by studied turns of language to convey the impression that he took no interest in that question. What curious freak of vanity can have actuated him we can only guess ; I suppose he thought the glory of a liberator of bondsmen more desirable than a mere reputation for enlightened views of political economy. It is however the fact that he, the enthusiastic disciple of Kraus, describes one of the most memorable triumphs of the free trade theory in such a way that it can only be discovered from a single casual expression that free trade triumphed at all. Meanwhile he describes his zeal for the abolition of serfdom as resembling that of a martyr or apostle, and has a pathetic picture of his own devotedness, when, as he was engaged in composing

29—2

his Report, he received intelligence that his wife
was at the point of death, if he would see her again
alive he must leave his work and hurry to her side,
but 'though deeply afflicted he felt he must not
betray the great idea, and with violent self-mastery
wrote on till his task was ended, and then setting
out, found his wife, the angel that hovered over him,
no longer living.' And he repeats several times that
this had been 'his sole and single object in public
life,' that 'he had desired only this,' which assertions
of course imply, and seem intended to imply, that he
had never taken the smallest interest in free trade.
Equally strong are his assertions that the abolition
of serfdom was owing to his own efforts. The
reform is described, not as one about the desirable-
ness of which all were agreed, not as one which
had long been agitated and over every part of the
Monarchy, which the King had always had at
heart, and the peasantry themselves were eagerly
looking forward to, but in a strain which might have
suited the Abolition of the Slave Trade by Clark-
son and Wilberforce. It is a grand philanthropic
idea conceived by a few Königsberg philosophers
and diffused from them to a band of faithful disciples, but remaining for a long time a doctrine
peculiar to the Prussian province, so that it 'seemed
a mere brain-cobweb to Westphalians and Markers.'
This idea he personally has the glory of representing in the Immediate Commission. Stägemann
is the first convert, then Beyme raises himself to
the level of the Idea, his conversion being helped
by the authority of another Königsberger, Morgenbesser; Klewitz is the last to come in. While the

abolition of serfdom required so much preaching,
the doctrines of free trade, we are asked to believe,
were received as a matter of course. But in the
moment of his triumph this Prussian Wilberforce
sank down exhausted; no sooner was the struggle
over than the sense of his bereavement overcame
him. Accordingly he could not draught the law—
here at least is an important statement—and Stägemann, 'faithful companion on the great journey,'
undertook this task. 'All else that I have done in
the world is nothing compared to calling into life
the idea of freedom.' And this hymn to himself
Schön introduces with the mock-modest heading,
*What did I do? Answer: Nothing worth speaking
of.*

The Report which cost Schön such 'violent self-
mastery' is now before us, and we cannot read it
without feeling that the Frau v. Schön was somewhat hardly used. It is from this very Report that
I have just extracted the statement that 'the great
majority of the nation had long been agreed on the
principle of the abolition of serfdom.' So far from
arguing strongly and eloquently against serfdom,
so far from directing his argument principally to
this point, he puts serfdom last among six causes
to which he refers the impoverishment of the
country. He does indeed describe it as the most
important of the six, but he refrains from treating
it with the same fulness as the others, because, as
he says, 'on the necessity and safety of abolishing
it your Majesty has heard so much that it would tire
you to hear more.' And in the short preface which
he has prefixed to the Report he says expressly,

This matter (*i.e.* the abolition of serfdom) had occupied all good heads and hearts in Prussia many years before the war. The number of those who were slavishly disposed was small, but they were powerful.

At the same time it refutes the reminiscences not less completely on the subject of free trade in land. It shows, as we should expect, that Schön's mind is fully occupied with this question, and that he gives it precedence over the question of the abolition of serfdom. We find in this Report just those hard and cruel-sounding statements of economic principle which Niebuhr had led us to expect. We find him attacking as a mischievous prejudice the accepted rule that the number of peasant-holdings on an estate should never be diminished, and declaring that 'there is no reason why the landowner should not have an unlimited right to dispose at pleasure of his land and soil,' and that 'as a matter of fact it would be found impossible to keep up as many peasant-holdings as before the war,' and throwing out hard assertions that 'the Government can never have an interest in securing A or B in the possession of his property[1].'

It is however a mistake to suppose that Stein's reputation is in any way concerned in the question of the trustworthiness of Schön's account. Schön's

---

[1] I have carefully avoided depending upon the narrative given in Pertz of the party-contest at the Immediate Commission, which I agree with the anonymous author of *Zu Schutz und Trutz am Grabe Schöns* in regarding as somewhat legendary. I trust I have made it appear that the statements of Schön's Autobiography can be disproved without assuming the truth of a narrative equally unsatisfactory that has unfortunately crept into Pertz, and in any case that Stein is not at all concerned in the controversy.

sphere was the Immediate Commission, while Stein's
sphere was altogether outside it. What Schön has
snatched at is not any reputation belonging to Stein,
but that which ought to fall to his colleagues, Stägemann, Klewitz, and in some degree also Altenstein
and Niebuhr. An achievement which officially belonged to the whole Commission jointly he has
tried to appropriate in the main to himself. Fortunately evidence enough remains to defeat this
attempt, and to show that the only statement in his
whole narrative which we can safely accept is the
statement that the draughting of the Edict was the
work of Stägemann. As to Stein, his share in the
achievement is altogether distinct from that of the
Commission, and therefore from that of any member
of the Commission. It is to be divided into two
parts, of which the one can be precisely stated, and
the other is essentially indefinable, though not
necessarily the smaller on that account.

The first consists in any alterations he may
have made in the Edict after it was laid before
him. Of these the principal was the extension of
the Edict to all the provinces of the Monarchy.
That the credit of this belongs to Stein we find
Schön himself, who when he wrote his Autobiography had formed the habit of denying him all share
in the Edict beyond that of putting his name to it,
fully acknowledging while the facts were still fresh
in memory. In a diary written about the time of
Stein's fall Schön writes of him, 'He made his
début with the Edict of October which he found
ready, and which it is his merit only to have made
universal.' Besides this, as we have seen, the in-

corporation of Stägemann's suggestion into Art. 6 is due to Stein.

But it is strangely perverse to limit Stein's share in the Edict to those alterations in the text of it which are known to be due to him. It is not thus that the merit of an act of legislation ought to be, or commonly is, awarded. When Lord Grey is called the author of the Reform Bill, is it intended that he first thought of reforming Parliament or that he devised and draughted all or most of the provisions of the Bill? Plainly his title to the achievement would be entirely unaffected if it could be shown that no single word of the Bill was suggested or determined by him. It is not draughting a Bill, but passing it, that is the difficulty. What we say of Lord Grey is that he gained that ascendancy both in his own party and in the nation by the height and firmness of his character, that he was able to guide them safely through a legislative enterprise which with an inferior leader they would either have feared to attempt, or in attempting would have stumbled into revolution and civil bloodshed. When we call the Edict of October Stein's Edict we mean something similar. But it may be thought that the cases were not parallel, because in Prussia there was no Parliament to guide, no turbulent public opinion to control. And indeed I imagine that no one would pretend to equal this single act of Stein's to the passing of the Reform Bill. Still between the draughting of the Emancipating Edict and the making it law in Prussia there was a space to be traversed, though not so wide a space as that over which Lord Grey carried the Reform Bill. Not a Parliament or a people, but officials and the King had to be inspired with courage. No noisy parliamentary opposition indeed, but tenacious interests exceedingly strong in the court and in the army had to be defied. When Hardenberg and Altenstein and the Commission recommended these reforms, they did so with the knowledge that Stein was at hand to carry them out. Would they have made the same suggestions if Voss or Schulenburg or Struensee had been at the head of affairs? Hardenberg's recommendations proceed avowedly upon the assumption that Stein is to be Minister, and we cannot even be sure that he would himself have had courage to attempt what he felt sure Stein would not shrink from. Much more may we doubt whether the King would have borne the weight of such responsibility unsupported, or supported only by a common Minister.

In one word, we must not confound the reforming legislator with the jurist and parliamentary draughtsman. It is not inventiveness, or originality, or technical skill, that we honour in those who have presided over the transitions of States. It is chiefly the massive courage that moves freely under responsibility and lightens the burden of responsibility to all around; it is the 'Atlantean shoulders.'

On these principles we ought perhaps to regard the rapidity with which Stein hurried the reform through as an essential and principal part of the reform itself. It was most material that the nation should feel the stay and sway of a powerful hand. Stein always acted with an almost Napoleonic swift-

ness, but in this instance we are particularly struck
with his promptitude. It was perhaps rather instinctive than calculated, and yet he may have been
aware of the importance of justifying without a
moment's delay the great expectations that had
been formed of him. He receives his powers on
October 4th, and on the 9th the most comprehensive measure ever passed in Prussia, affecting
every class and the whole framework of society,
appears, not as a proposal, but as an accomplished
act with the King's signature, as a part of the law
of the country.

CHAPTER V.

STEIN'S POSITION.

IT thus appears that the Emancipating Edict, though the greatest single achievement of Stein's Ministry, was yet that which was least of all originated by him and least bears the marks of his mind. I have argued that his strong will and character entered into the calculations of those who designed and prepared it in his absence; still it is not so much one of the achievements of his dictatorship as a kind of sign, or announcement by a thunderclap, that he had become dictator. At the time the Edict was issued his mind was preoccupied with quite other schemes of reform and the country had other needs more pressing even than any reform of its institutions could be. What these needs were and what means Stein had to deal with them, we must consider now that we have left the Emancipating Edict, for the present at least, behind us.

In the first place let us consider for a moment the nature of the power which Stein wielded. It was exceedingly precarious, and probably Stein may have felt this at the moment when he laid the Emancipating Edict before the King. His power was neither committed to him for any fixed term nor was he the representative of any powerful interest. In Prussia indeed Ministers had not for a long time been in the habit of looking to any support but that of the King; but Stein, though not at all resembling a leader of opposition in England, such as Lord Rockingham or Fox, who forces himself into power against the royal will, had yet humbled the King and was the first Minister in Prussia of whom it might be thought that he was more important than the King. By the King therefore he could not expect to be supported very enthusiastically or much longer than his services were found absolutely indispensable. Could he then look to any other quarter for help? There was one whose word could no doubt at any moment have driven him from office, and whose support probably could have long secured him in office— Napoleon. We have seen that he had Napoleon's good will at the outset and there was nothing in the sample he had just given in the Emancipating Edict to deprive him of this. On the contrary, Napoleon might point to this Edict as a proof of the awakening effect of those rude blows he dealt to kings and as a victory of the principles of the French Revolution. In other respects he might regard Stein's energy with satisfaction, for Stein would know how to raise money from Prussia, and so long as Napoleon retained the power of appropriating this money Stein was working most effectually for him. It is

true that this was not Stein's object.   He meant—
at least after a few months he resolved—to strike
a desperate blow for freedom; and if by any chance
Napoleon should discover this resolution and should
come to regard him as more dangerous than useful,
Stein's power would be at an end, unless he should
have succeeded by that time in hurrying his country
into a new war, in which case no doubt a splendid
opportunity would present itself to him of winning
renown as a war-minister.

Besides Napoleon there was another power
which could do much towards making or marring
Stein by its influence over the King. The Prussian
aristocracy could not indeed resist Stein as effectually
as the French aristocracy resisted Turgot. In their
submission to the Government, and at the same
time in the large share they took in the administration of the State, the Prussian aristocracy offered
no doubt a strong contrast to the French. The
King was their master, and so long as Stein had
his confidence he could defy the aristocracy; and
even if his measures struck at them and diminished their privileges, he might hope to be
supported by a Hohenzollern, who knew well that
his interest was quite distinct from that of the aristocracy. At the same time the King lived in the
midst of the noblesse, who formed not only his
court but also his official service, for almost all the
higher administrators as well as the officers belonged to this class. Its influence, if it could avail
nothing against the power of the King, was none
the less great in itself and most formidable to a
minister who was not firmly established in the

royal favour. Stein, as I have said, was no king's man; the sweeping measures he proposed might even, and ultimately did, seem dangerous to the court. In these circumstances he could not defy the noblesse after the fashion of a Richelieu. But still less was he in a condition to conciliate them. After the 9th of October, that is, after his first week of power, he must have known that he could not expect their support, for of all classes the Edict struck the noblesse much the hardest.

It is true that the policy of Stein, when it is viewed as a whole, appears such as might well have been supported by all classes of the nation alike. By patriots, for if Napoleon had some share in appointing him, it very soon appeared that he was by no means less patriotic than Hardenberg. Nor need the King have been seriously alarmed, for if a despotic monarch cannot without risk enter on the path of reform the time was past when the Prussian Monarchy could be saved without risk, and Stein was the man to save it by daring. Even the aristocracy had the security that Stein himself belonged to them, and that he had never dallied with revolution nor shown a disposition to break, like Mirabeau, with the order into which he was born. But at the time Stein's policy *could* not be viewed as a whole, and public opinion might easily misunderstand the scope of it. 'All he did,' says Marwitz, 'was to bring the Revolution upon us.' The Emancipating Edict might easily be regarded as the beginning of a course which would end in adhesion to the Confederation of the Rhine. Or again, since the Emancipating Edict was certainly Prussia's Fourth

of August, it might seem the beginning of that
process of substituting the local official for the
local magnate by which bureaucracy had been
introduced in all lands that had fallen under the
influence of France. Stein might seem to be
Prussia's Montgelas. That he was strongly Anti-
Gallican, profoundly patriotic, and had a particularly
strong conviction of the value of self-government
could not as yet be generally known.

For throughout this narrative of Stein's ministry
the reader must bear in mind that the changes we
describe, though vast and memorable, were accomplished in silence, almost in secrecy, amid a people
ignorant of everything beyond the actual ordinances
that were published, for the most part completely
indifferent to what they knew, and accustomed, if
any enactment drew their attention, to attribute it to
the King rather than to the Minister. Stein had
few means of taking the people into his confidence.
He defended his measures in no Parliaments, at no
public meetings, he published no letters to consti-
tuents, no pamphlets. Those who had opportunities
of conversing with him knew what he aimed at ; a
few officials knew ; the official class generally had
an impression, but the public at large neither knew,
until it was announced to the world by Napoleon's
edict of proscription, nor' for the most part cared.
The excitement which Stein's acts caused was confined to a very small circle, and to the people at
large his name perhaps almost unknown.

Our own Chatham affords an example of a man
rising above the character of a party leader and
born to lead a whole nation, yet labouring under

the want of a proper machinery for acting on the nation. He made up for it as well as he could by theatrical manners and oratory. Stein had certainly the same grandeur of views, but he was divided from the nation still more completely. The indifference of the middle class to politics was such as we can scarcely imagine, and there were no parliamentary debates even so imperfectly reported as those through which Chatham strove to address his countrymen. Stein had not even the Tapestry to talk to. And thus the utmost he could do was to inspire some half-dozen officials with his views and to found something like a political school whose manifesto was signed by him on leaving office and called his Political Testament.

It appears then that Stein's power had no basis which could be expected to remain firm under his feet for any length of time, and this was shown to be so by the event. The King learnt gradually to regard him with much esteem and parted from him at last unwillingly; the ablest officials and, still more, officers rallied round him with enthusiasm; even a large section of the middle class became aware of his merit before he retired; but he was thwarted by a *fronde* among the nobles, and he became after a time an object of suspicion to the leaders of the French invasion and at last to Napoleon himself. We are induced to ask, Was he aware of the instability of his position, and did he take any measures to strengthen the foundation he stood on, or did he neglect to do so either from recklessness or from a deliberate conviction of the impossibility of holding office long?

It was not, after all, quite impossible for him to establish a solid and lasting power, supposing him to have desired it. For Hardenberg later had much the same difficulties to contend with and overcame them all. In 1810 he recommences the work of Stein, if not with the same mastery yet with equal courage, striking at all interests and again eclipsing the King. And yet his power proves to be durable. He holds it for twelve years, and only loses it with his life. The explanation of this seems to be, first the extreme and abject need of the country, then the war. When the war was over his position, like that of Lord Liverpool in England, was secured to him for life by the glory which had been won. Now Stein might have had the same good luck; and if he thought at all about securing his power, it was perhaps in this way that he expected to do it. For the moment the country could not do without him, and he foresaw a period when it would be able to dispense with him still less. For when he came to see the condition of the country and to conjecture what Napoleon's purposes were with respect to Prussia, when he saw that the Treaty of Tilsit was no Treaty, how could he doubt that there would be another war? In sheer self-defence and to save herself from destruction, Prussia must, it seemed, join the first Power that should venture to challenge Napoleon; and when once a war should begin, his power would be safe, as that of Hardenberg afterwards proved to be. Perhaps indeed he expected much more, for great as were Stein's actual achievements, it seems probable that he missed the great oppor-

tunity of his life. He had already, as we have
seen, had much experience in war finance, and it
was only in war that the great side of his nature
could display itself, his fire, his constancy, and his
large national views. His proper place was evidently that of Prime Minister in a German War of
Liberation. The King spoilt this destiny in 1809
and Hardenberg intercepted it in 1813.

Indeed we shall be much mistaken if we regard
Stein's actual achievements as in any way answering
either to what he designed, or to what was expected
of him, or to what he seemed naturally fitted to
accomplish. Great legislative measures were not
what Prussia wanted most urgently, although she
did want them. If Stein passed such measures, it
was not because he had a special genius for legislation, or because with German profundity he chose
rather to lay a deep foundation of national well-being
than simply to do what the exigency of the moment
demanded. The truth is that short as his term of
power was and great as were the legislative changes
he made, yet he was not mainly occupied with
these changes during that term of office. It will
be remarked that the first and greatest of them cost
him scarcely any time or trouble, for he found it
ready to his hand, so that in fact for legislative
purposes his ministry may be reckoned as three
months longer than the time he actually held it,
and as beginning immediately after the Peace of
Tilsit. Schön writes at the moment of his fall,
'He accomplished much, but only at the first beginning and at the end of his administration.' How
far this is true we shall see, but it points to the

truth that he had much else on his hands besides legislation and that he did not in any way neglect this more urgent work or postpone it to legislation. The reason why this has been overlooked is simply that in all but legislation he failed, and that not from any want of skill but from the inherent difficulties of the situation. To understand his administration properly, we must take note of this and observe that the tasks which occupied him most intensely were not those in which he succeeded and by which he won his fame. The greatest of these I have already mentioned ; it belongs to the final months, and consists in the attempt to hurry Prussia into the war which broke out in 1809. But before this, and in the earlier part of his administration, he had been principally occupied in bargaining with the French in order to rid the territory of them, and in devising ways and means to satisfy their demands out of a ruined country.

In all this he may be said to have failed. If the French did leave the country, it was not owing to his efforts ; if great sums of money were raised, they merely profited Napoleon without in any way satisfying him, and when Stein left office no real progress had been made towards removing the French incubus. More than all, the great chance was lost of bringing Prussia's humiliation to an end in 1809. As it proved, the campaign of Wagram was the last of Napoleon's triumphs ; but for Stein's failure to carry the King with him, it might perhaps have proved the beginning of his disasters. This fact then, that Stein was mainly occupied with urgent tasks in which he failed, is the explanation of what Schön

remarks, that he only accomplished great things at
the beginning and end of his term of office.   It may
seem out of keeping with the portentous rapidity of
his first and greatest innovation, that he does not
earnestly take up his second, the Municipal Reform,
till the summer, and still more that that Administrative Reform to which he had given most thought and
which he had most at heart was undertaken even
later, and was left imperfect at his retirement.   It is
true that the Emancipating Edict, effecting such
vast changes, could not but involve much supple-
mentary legislation and also much administrative
work, which partly occupied the interval; but the
main cause of interruption was a long negotiation with France, having for its object to prevail
upon Napoleon to take less money, a negotiation
which, as Napoleon preferred to receive more
money and as he was all-powerful, proved necessarily abortive.   This negotiation not only occupied
Stein but, as it was found desirable that he should
conduct it in person, forced him to leave the King,
that is to leave the centre of business, and go to
Berlin, where Daru, the French Intendant General,
resided.   This absence of Stein lasted from February 29th till May 31st, and forms a great landmark in his ministry, dividing its two periods of
legislative activity from each other.   After his return, though reform recommences, yet a new pre-
occupation takes possession of him and involves
him in enterprises which not only distract him but
speedily lead to his fall.   This is the result of a
great European event, which forms the turning
point of the whole drama of that age and the com-

mencement of what is called in this book the Anti-Napoleonic Revolution, I mean the insurrection of Spain in the latter half of May, 1808, followed by the capitulation of Baylen on July 22nd. This great occurrence not only determined the whole character of the period of war which followed, and filled the minds of German patriots with new hopes and ideas, but by forcing Napoleon to withdraw his troops from Prussia it occupied the Prussian statesmen with the absorbing question, whether they should continue in submission to Napoleon or take advantage of his first perplexities to throw off his yoke. September 1808 is the critical month for Stein. An intercepted letter discovers his plans to Napoleon, and at the same time the King rejects his warlike policy. As he could only stand either by the favour of Napoleon or by war with him, his fall is henceforth decided, but his resignation does not actually take place till November 24th, 1808. This is the outline of the first of the two most memorable periods of Stein's life, which it becomes now our part to clothe with detail.

Such detail however as the biographer desires is not very abundant just at this memorable part of his life. Stein is not yet surrounded by admirers making mental notes of his conversation, such as Arndt was to him at times in his later years, and he is too busy to write letters of general interest. On the whole Stein, like Samuel Johnson, can only be known at all intimately in his old age.

I find a few sentences which show us what he was thinking of on the memorable 9th October, the day of the Emancipating Edict. A certain

Scheffner, who had been in the War Department and was now passing his old age in retirement at Königsberg known and valued by the intellectual circle of which Kant had been the centre, (the philosopher had died in 1804,) was one of his warmest admirers. He had greeted him on his arrival at Memel with a poem; and Stein replies as follows:

The feelings towards me expressed by a man of your high worth in the poem you have sent, and the estimate you form of me, help to remove many misgivings which plague me about my powers and their proportion to the tasks I have undertaken. In this respect I find the resolution I took in my fever—not when the fit was on me—rather *feverish*, and console myself with the reflexion, que le cœur d'un honnête homme est un puits de lumière. We are all craving for Königsberg, in order to return to the society of educated men, and have plans of establishing the royal family in Krüger's house and turning you out of it. Not very friendly on our part unless it were true what is said about the Dame de votre pensée.

Against the last sentence is written in Scheffner's hand, 'What am I to make of this?' and against the sentence before, 'A joke, I suppose!'

The exigencies of the war had compelled the King to fix his court at Memel. So long as the French occupation continued, that is till the autumn of 1808, he could not return to Berlin; he did not, as a matter of fact, return thither till the end of 1809. It is said that in these circumstances he was himself glad of the seclusion of Memel, but, as Stein hints in this letter, there were strong reasons for fixing the head quarters of Government in a more important town, such as the capital of the Prussian province, Königsberg. These reasons, perceived by Stein as soon as he entered upon the administration, prevailed after a time, and the Court arrived in Königsberg on January 16th, 1808. Thus it was first Memel and then Königsberg that was the scene of Stein's labours; throughout his ministry Berlin is no longer the seat of Government, but on the contrary it is the head quarters of the French with Daru at their head and of the French party among the Prussian noblesse who cabal against Stein and at last triumph in his overthrow.

Stein's family had been left at Nassau in the summer of 1807. He did not see them again till his time of greatness was over, though his sister Louise was much with him during those months. We find the Frau vom Stein passing the winter at Frankfurt; in May she is again at Nassau, where she receives the visit of her sister, the Countess v. Kielmansegge. She is still there in June, when he writes thus to her :

Does Marianne think of visiting you ? The society of my good excellent sister, who is good sense and gentleness itself, will do you good. I beg you, dearest, to make Wieler give you a daily report of the affairs of the estate, since you will have to burden yourself sooner or later with these details and this is the way to learn them.

And again with a clear presentiment of what was at hand :

Who knows what is still reserved for us, and when the appointed cup will be drunk out? let us be prepared for everything, and look the future bravely in the face—it may still put us to hard trials. We must take care that Henriette's sensibility does not sink into weakness, and try rather to calm her both physically and morally, and accustom her to govern herself and not abandon herself to her feelings, since probably in her future condition her strength and courage will be more wanted than her feelings. I am charmed that you like Frücht; the lands are well farmed, the wood is fine and well kept, and I am particularly fond of this property; my parents are buried there. Pray write me whether Wieler has had a little enclosure made there near the churchyard; I want to put the coffin of my parents there and make a place for myself beside them, and surround it all with the red cedar, arbor vitae, Babylonian willows and a few cypresses.

In July :

Professor Heinrich's German History is well written, and less voluminous than Schmidt's. As to children's parties, we must avoid those that do not suit our children, especially those of the people that I have chiefly to see. There are private theatricals here in which young girls act. I don't approve of making children into play-actors.

In this month his mother-in-law is at Ems again and so close to her daughter; we note that Stein admires her still as much as we remember that he did fourteen years before.

On the 14th he writes :

In the uncertainty in which we continue to live I have taken a house for the time; one that you will like—here is the plan of it: the rooms have double windows and are good; there is a large garden which can even be used in winter.

This house, I suppose, is in Berlin, since the family are living in Berlin when Stein arrived there in December after resigning his office. There they were reunited, though only for a few days, after a separation of fifteen months.

I give here extracts from a letter to Stein written by Niebuhr on January 4th, 1808, from Berlin, because it gives us an early glimpse into the *fronde* which set the fashion in the capital.

While *we* know that everything remains unaltered and that a settlement cannot take place at best for a considerable time, the well-disposed part of the public consoles itself with alternate rumours about the speedy departure of the French army and favourable expressions of the Emperor Napoleon about our preservation. But as the well-disposed make only a part and perhaps a minority of the actual public—I do not count the people—they are uncorrupted—it is commoner to hear views of the most utter hopelessness expressed with a definiteness that one is tempted in the spirit of these people to call actual certainty. It may indeed be true that very many in Berlin have gained by the general calamity, and are so deeply corrupted as not at all to desire the end of the present state of things; perhaps are even at once perverted and corrupted so deeply as to dread that moment. Still these can hardly be the persons one meets in society; these latter seem merely actuated by the unhappy ruling passion of the Germans for lazy slander, one of the most detestable traits that can disfigure a national character and one which assuredly the Germans cannot be acquitted of. It seems as if these people, without feeling for general well-being and the private happiness that flows from it, if they can only anyhow vegetate on, even without any lively desire for personal comfort and enjoyment such as in other nations rouses so many so often to action and exertion, are comfortable enough if they can only drag down everything superior, disturb all confidence, dissolve all allegiance. According to this set not only will our yoke never be broken, but it does not even matter whether it is or not: the condition of the people would only become more painful, for it is clear that the army will be retained at the highest point to which it can be forced by overstraining the resources of what remains to the monarchy and by utterly defrauding the public creditor; that the War Department will waste money and the civil service starve. This set gauges our political incapacity by the fact that the King has not yet joined the Confederation of the Rhine at all hazards; and each man selects according to his fancy a different measure of the Government, from which he draws the foregone conclusion of a wavering and blundering administration. Many bewail the unhappy frustration of those beneficial systems—first that of Haugwitz, then that of Zastrow. I do not know whether such a spirit is diffused through Germany; it seems to me deeply rooted here. It will

take great rigour and a very decided tone on the part of
Government to root it out. May we hope to shame and rebuke
flippancy and malice by a firm and impartial sentence of banishment, not to be remitted in consideration of any connexions, both
from the court and the higher internal administration? that it may
be made a rule without any mistaken hesitation to trample out
the spirit of discontent by imperious resolution, and paralyse it by
an open declaration and definite detailed statement, in consideration of the extreme shallowness of the public, of the principles
which are to be regarded as the spirit of the future administration.
For example, it would certainly be necessary that the resolution
of keeping up a small army should be announced in a credible
manner to the public in some sort of official document. For
scarcely any one is free from apprehensions of fantastic and
unpractical overstraining on this side, and the most sensible find a
strong confirmation of this in the retention of all officers from the
ceded German provinces, with the complete sacrifice of the civil
service. People ask with an excusable hatred against the officers,
whether they ought not rather to have been all dismissed, so that
readmission into the service should be only earned by proved
fitness and acquittal from well-grounded accusations general and
particular.

He goes on to argue that the Government
should publicly announce that it did not intend to
keep on foot an army of more than 20,000 men;
and then adds:

It is not to be doubted that our officers still dream ('think'
would be too strong a word) of a great army on the old footing;
the landowner, tradesman and peasant are to pay and suffer.
Every limitation is a crime. This was the tone of Kalkreuth.

He then speaks of the learned world:

That our savants with the exception of Ancillon, Klaproth, and
a few others (of those that are eminent) are not the best citizens or
subjects, has been long shown. It does not surprise me, but yet
it is sad for my science, philology, that Wolf too is now showing that his residence at Berlin, his wish for an appointment

in an Academy to be founded here, were only shifts, while he thought his position at Halle at an end. He will write to your Excellency or has already written, about the offer that is now made him. It seems the worthy Müller wants to draw him away: their friendship is not surprising, since there can be no rivalry *of any sort* between them. Still, it is a great pity that we should lose the only thoroughly learned philologer now living in Germany. I recommend to your Excellency his treatise on the Knowledge of Antiquity as the most interesting thing, in the way of peaceful literature, that has appeared for a long time. I think we must determine not to see his blemishes, however black they may be, so as not to wish less to keep him. For one that he may infect morally by his conversation and utterances he will certainly advance many on the way to the higher life, *which leads only through antiquity*. I hope that will be considered, and that he absolutely cannot be replaced; moreover it does not look well to foreign countries if we let him be taken from us when it is possible to keep him. Even as to Müller's dismissal it were much to be wished that the whole course of the affair could be made known.

He adds that he has not been introduced to Daru :

For I thought it scarcely proper to let myself be introduced by Wolf, who visits him as a man of letters and is much courted by him, especially as I suspect Wolf of having had a share in the notorious creeping review of his Horace. If I had read it and wanted to flatter M. Daru, I might perhaps have won his favour.

Napoleon at Paris had not as yet reason to think Stein a dangerous Minister, and I find that Stein believed himself not to have forfeited his favour in January. But his immediate dependence was upon the King, who fortunately was not surrounded solely by the French party, but conversed with many, such as Scharnhorst, who were in every respect like-minded with the Minister. The student of history often has in his mind the proverb that 'the heart of a king is unsearchable'; if it is difficult to form a trustworthy conception of any historical character, it is doubly difficult when the character is a king, for kings are alternately the subject of fond pane- gyric and spiteful abuse, but are scarcely ever judged fairly. It seems that we should be mistaken in supposing that the King had completely forgotten his contest with Stein at the beginning of the year, or that Stein's magnanimous conduct in the summer had been met with corresponding magnanimity. The least the King could do, we should think, was to concede the point about which Stein had de- clared himself so strongly and to dismiss Beyme from his counsels. This would seem more necessary than ever, for it was not to be supposed that Beyme's disposition towards Stein was made more favourable by the quarrel that had taken place, or that his dismissal was now a less essential point than it had been. It is indeed scarcely possible to imagine how Stein can have brought himself to concede the point, or to allow a minister to remain close to the sovereign's ear who might be supposed to be a sort of agent for the discontented party. Yet we find that though the King at the beginning pro- posed to send Beyme to Berlin as President of the Kammergericht, yet he retained him temporarily, and that as a matter of fact his departure did not take place till the beginning of June. Now Stein was himself absent in Berlin from the end of Febru- ary to the end of May, and all this time his personal opponent remained at the King's side. This is a remarkable state of affairs, and seems to show several things; for instance, that Stein was after all not so very obstinate, that the King *was*, and perhaps that there was not very much harm in Beyme.

Nevertheless Stein did not think Beyme harmless and the old quarrel sometimes broke out again. Pertz gives the following letter from Queen Louise, undated, which preserves a trace of these quarrels.

> I conjure you, have but patience in these first months. The King will certainly keep his word; Beyme will go, but not till we are in Berlin. Let him have his way till then. For heaven's sake do not let the good cause be lost for want of three months' patience. I conjure you for the sake of the King, of the country, of my children, for my own sake! Patience!
>
> LOUISE.

So Beyme was to go to Berlin, but not till the King went to Berlin also! We do not gather from all this that Stein was likely to be protected from the attacks of the French party by any very cordial feelings towards him in the mind of the King himself. Still as the King was perhaps in practical matters a good deal in the hands of those about him, it is important to notice that Queen Louise evidently supported him warmly at the time when this letter was written. His position had still some strength so long as the Queen's voice echoed the voices of Scharnhorst, Schön, Gneisenau and the rest.

Queen Louise was as good as she was charming. But her virtues and graces were purely womanly; there was no touch in her of Queen Isabella or Queen Elizabeth. Her favour therefore was somewhat precarious. In the end, as Beyme between Stein and the King, so there came a certain Nagler between him and the Queen. Stein advised against accepting an invitation to St Petersburg, which he considered likely to be too expensive in the circumstances of the country.   But the Queen had set her heart upon it and this difference artfully used by Nagler is thought to have cost Stein the Queen's favour.

It was not till near the end of the year that this happened, but I have thought it well to collect here all that throws light upon the basis on which Stein's power stood.   It will be seen at once how unsafe it was so long as the State was not absolutely in extremity.   At the same time the respect felt for his energy and capacity was great enough to support him in extreme public need.   Had the King broken with Napoleon in the autumn Stein's power would have been firm enough.

CHAPTER VI.

NEGOTIATIONS.

PIERRE Antoine Bruno Daru, at this time Intendant General of the Grand Army, was one of the
few men of the Napoleonic régime who made a name
in literature. He was known principally as a poet,
having published in 1800 his 'Traduction en vers
des poésies d'Horace,' and also his 'Cléopédie, ou
la théorie des réputations en littérature.' It was not
till the period of the Restoration that his great historical works were published. The 'Histoire de la
République de Venise' appeared in 1819—21, and
the 'Histoire de la Bretagne' in 1826. He became
a Peer in 1818, and died in 1829, at the age of 62.

This person now represented Napoleon at Berlin.
A commission had been appointed to negotiate with
him on the pecuniary claims of France and the
evacuation of the territory left to Prussia by the
French army, which consisted of 157,000 men.   On
Sept. 26th, 1807, that is, about a week before Stein's
arrival, Napoleon wrote at Fontainebleau the following letter to Daru.   (Corr. de Nap. I., 13186.)

M. Daru,—I am in receipt of your letter of September 18th. I beg you not to sign the definitive treaty about the contributions till you have submitted it to me. My *sine qua non* is, first, a hundred and fifty millions; secondly, payment in valuable commercial goods; and if that is impossible and I must content myself with the King's bills it is my intention to hold the places Stettin, Glogau and Küstrin with 6,000 men as a garrison in each of them, until these bills are fully met, and as these 18,000 men would occasion me additional expense, it is my intention that the expenses of pay, provision, dress and board of these 18,000 men should be charged to the King.

You must speak strongly to the Ministers of the King of Prussia. What is going on at Memel seems to me a bad joke, and certainly this is no occasion for it. You must declare that if they wish to pay they can find the means. The King of Prussia has no need to keep up an army; he is not at war with any one...

I think I have already[1] instructed you to notify that if these conditions are not accepted you will declare null the article of the treaty which relates to the convention of evacuation, and put distraint on the revenues of the months of September and October for the use of the army; in fact, it is my intention in this case to take possession of all the revenues.

NAPOLÉON.

This letter throws a flash of light upon the relations of Napoleon and Prussia. The question which Daru and the Commission were to examine together, namely, what was the sum due to France under the Convention, is here settled by Napoleon beforehand without any examination, and he proposes to enforce his claim by naked force. The sum he names is a hundred and fifty million francs, and if he had named ten or a hundred times as much the effect would have been the same. One sum was as good as another so long as it was more than Prussia could pay, and therefore kept her permanently in the con-

[1] See Corr. de Nap. I., 13147.

dition of an insolvent debtor. It was left to Daru
to supply the calculations of which his master had
thus dictated the result, and he was found equal to
the task. At the end of October arrived in Memel
a proposal that the French army should evacuate
the territory, reserving five fortresses with garrisons
amounting to 40,000 to be supported entirely by
Prussia, on payment of 120,000,000 fr., half in money
and half in domain lands. An excited letter from
Queen Louise comes to Stein on the receipt of this
proposal, begging him to come and comfort her
and concluding, 'God! where are we? what will be
the end? Our sentence of death is pronounced.'
Thus was the problem presented to Stein which
occupied him throughout his term, a problem which,
be it always observed, was entirely new and was not
contemplated by him when he took office.

Daru's proposal seemed to leave no prospect to
Prussia but that of remaining a conquered country,
whether it were accepted or rejected. In the latter
case the occupation would continue and the current
revenues would be appropriated to the army; this
was a condition much worse than that of most conquered countries, for in what conquered country is a
hostile army of 157,000 men supported out of the
resources of a population of less than 5,000,000? In
the former case not only was a hostile army of 40,000
to be kept up, but a large part of the land of Prussia
was to pass into the proprietorship of the French
Government, which would involve the introduction
into the country of a colony of French officials.

That Napoleon was by no means content with
humbling Prussia, but meant to reduce her still

further, if not entirely to annex the country, will appear, I think, to the reader, if he will consider the above letter and compare it with the following, written on November 7, to Savary, his representative at St Petersburg :

M. Tolstoi (the Czar's Ambassador newly-arrived in Paris) spoke much to me of the evacuation of Prussia. I told him I desired it too, but the Prussians brought nothing to an end, that I was waiting till the arrangements should finally take place, and that that would happen soon. I added that it was no doubt part of the policy of Russia to keep Wallachia and Moldavia, and that if that was Russia's plan, as a matter of compensation I should keep some provinces of Prussia. (Corr. de Nap. I., 13339.)

Thus it is evident that Prussia was in these months on the very verge of destruction, for, diminished as she had been by the treaty, the loss of more provinces would have been equivalent to destruction. Stein did not see the letter just quoted, but he must have seen enough to enable him to form his conclusions. In these circumstances nothing was left for the Prussian Government but on the one hand to endeavour by every means to shake Napoleon's purpose and induce him to abate something of his cruelty, and on the other hand to strain all the resources of the country to the utmost in order to satisfy his pecuniary demands. This was Stein's task, this and not legislative reform. How he performed it we are now to consider, under the two heads of his negotiations with Daru and Napoleon and his financial expedients. We shall be summary in this part of the subject because, as has been said, Stein's efforts were all in vain, except so far as they involved or were closely connected with measures of permanent reform.

In studying this diplomatic and financial struggle of Stein's, it is difficult not to yield to the suspicion that it ought to have been recognized as hopeless from the very beginning, and rather avoided than energetically undertaken. How could they hope to change Napoleon's purpose? Could they prove to him by arguments that he would not gain by the annexation of Prussia? Or could they convince him that it was better for him to take less money than it was possible to extort? On these heads they could tell him nothing that was likely to move him, nothing that he did not know before. It seems as if the Prussian statesmen considered that his course would not be determined by a mere calculation, but that sentimental or moral considerations would influence his mind, that something might be gained by showing that he demanded more than was really due, or by pleading the distress of the country and appealing to his compassion. They seem to have dreamed that Napoleon may have been like those old warriors described by Homer, who

$$\delta\omega\rho\eta\tau o\iota \; \tau\epsilon \; \pi\epsilon\lambda o\nu\tau o \; \pi\alpha\rho\alpha\rho\rho\eta\tau o\iota \; \tau' \; \epsilon\pi\epsilon\epsilon\sigma\sigma\iota\nu.$$

They had not yet learned to appreciate his thoroughness or to understand that he would have reproached himself with the most contemptible weakness if he had yielded to any such feelings. To us his object seems to have been to absorb the country into the Confederation of the Rhine as soon as the Czar would permit him, and in the mean time to draw the largest possible sum of money from it; the only arguments therefore to which he was accessible were those drawn from the dispositions of the Czar and—had it been possible, which it was not, to urge such an argument—the likelihood of provoking a formidable rebellion in Prussia, if oppression were carried beyond a certain point.

If this were so, and Napoleon would certainly go in any case as far as his fear of Russia or of the other enemies of his empire would allow him, it seems to follow that it was the interest of Prussia to pay him as little rather than as much as possible. Every penny paid to Napoleon went to strengthen the enemy of Prussia, and therefore ought to be withheld unless it contributed to extinguish Napoleon's claim. The sequel seems to show that it had no such effect. Up to 1812 he went on making demands, and it seems likely that it was his plan to make an end of the whole relation in that year by the annexation of Prussia. It follows that all the money paid to Napoleon between 1807 and 1812, beyond the sum absolutely necessary to appease his anger, was thrown away. This is as much as to say that the only redemption of Prussia lay in a new war with France, and that it was so became before long the conviction of Stein.

The measures adopted in order to propitiate France were, first—and perhaps this was the only effective measure—to procure the intervention of the Czar. The language used by Alexander in December to Caulaincourt, the new ambassador at St Petersburg, was firm and strong, and could not fail to impress Napoleon. He said:

The Emperor Napoleon has spoken to Tolstoi of Prussia ; that has given me pain... I cannot consent to share the spoils of an unhappy prince whom the Emperor Napoleon has displayed to France and to Europe as restored out of consideration for me. King Frederick William cannot in honour cease to be my ally till he has been put in possession of all that the Peace restores to him.

The next course was, proceeding on the false supposition that it was Daru himself rather than his master who was so pitiless, to appeal to Napoleon against him and seek the help of Daru's enemies. It is apparently under this mistaken impression that Stein, writing in December to Hardenberg, speaks of 'this monster of a Daru.'

One difficulty which arose from the necessary refusal of the Government to accept Daru's proposal of October came from the inconceivable French party at Berlin. As Kalkreuth had signed without hesitation in the summer that convention from which Napoleon had drawn such enormous consequences, so now Zastrow was indignant that there should be any hesitation in accepting the terms offered. He charged the Commission with conducting the negotiations with Daru in a too legal spirit, and if this meant that it was absurd to expect France to limit her claims by her rights, there was some ground for the charge. It was in fact a servile repetition of Daru's own declaration: 'Il s'agit ici d'un calcul de politique et point d'arithmétique.' Stein however was obliged to send in a refutation of Zastrow's arguments, and he here offered, if his Majesty thought that a person of greater rank and knowledge of language should be added to the Berlin Commission, to go himself to Berlin and conclude an arrangement.

Meanwhile it had been determined to appeal to
Napoleon himself, by sending the King's youngest
brother, Prince Wilhelm, on a special mission to
Paris.   These two negotiations then took place in
succession: that of Prince Wilhelm in January and
February, that of Stein with Daru in March, April
and May.

The mission of Prince Wilhelm had so little
success and produced so little impression that we
must not linger upon it.   The object of it was to
dissipate the prejudices Napoleon had conceived
against the King and Queen, to procure a re-
duction of the contribution to 40,000,000 francs to
be paid in a year, and to offer in return an alliance,
and, under certain conditions, military assistance.
The Prince was twenty-five years old, and Stein
proposed to give him more importance by nomi-
nating him War Minister, but this suggestion was
not adopted by the King.   Another proposal, that
the daughter of Joseph Bonaparte, then King of
Naples, should be asked in marriage for the young
Crown Prince, afterwards Frederick William IV., was
condemned by Stein as immoral and degrading.

The Prince took his departure, and was joined
at Frankfurt by Alexander v. Humboldt, who accompanied the embassy and gave it the lustre of
his renown, then in its first freshness.   Napoleon was
absent in Italy, and did not return till the new year
had begun.   He then gave him audience but refused to enter upon business, referring him to the
foreign minister Champagny, while Champagny for
his part declared that he must await the conclusion
of the Berlin negotiations with Daru.   Thus the

mission failed completely, and in such a manner as
to make it pretty evident how firmly fixed were
Napoleon's intentions with respect to Prussia.   An
innocent flight in which the Prince indulged, and
which it appears had been meditated between him
and his young wife even before they left Memel,
of offering himself and his Princess as hostages
until the debt was paid, may have caused Napoleon
a momentary embarrassment.   He refrained however from asking what advantage he should derive
from the detention of the Prince, or how it would
compensate the pecuniary sacrifice involved in withdrawing his army from a country where they were
supported at the expense of the inhabitants ; and
escaped from the difficulty with a very tolerable
grace by embracing the Prince and saying, 'This
is very noble, but it is impossible.'

Stein had heard from the Princess of the plan
which the young couple had formed, and wrote the
Prince a letter of advice with respect to it.

Napoleon (he says) will admire your conduct very much and
so far it will do good, but he will not evacuate the fortresses, for
they afford him a basis of operations against Russia and Austria.
In the nature of things a security that the weaker shall perform
his engagements to the stronger is not necessary; accordingly
something else must be in view when securities are required,
and this will not be attained by pledging one's person or the like,
and accordingly it is not to be expected that such an offer will be
accepted.

This letter came too late ; it doubtless gives the
common sense of the matter, but the Prince and
Princess were much consoled for the failure of their
mission by the consciousness of their heroism.   For

the Princess Stein seems to have conceived a warm admiration ; and she for her part writes to him as one 'whom she prizes and loves infinitely.'

In the same letter, dated February 19th, Stein mentions that the King has sanctioned his plan for going in person to Berlin to conduct the negotiation with Daru, and that he is to start in the next week. His reasons for resolving on this step lie before us. He does not think it likely that Napoleon will abate much of his claims, for he remarks :

The Emperor Napoleon treats his brothers' States with no more forbearance than Prussia. Holland has had to pay 10,000,000 livres for East Friesland... He takes to himself half the domains of King Jerome. Is it likely that he will withdraw either wholly or partially his claims on Prussia for con- tribution or domain lands ? that he will deprive himself of the means of increasing by grants of land his influence in Germany, and the number of his adherents ?

He then quotes instances to show that it is not impossible Napoleon may content himself with draw- ing revenues from the country, and may not insist on possessing domain lands. However, he continues,

Should he insist on appropriating domains to the value of 50,000,000 livres, even then it will be wiser to allow the claim than allow the State to continue longer in its present condition of dissolution... As to my journey to Berlin, I should not like to appear as a negotiator without a clearer knowledge of the state of things there. If it proves impossible to come to an arrangement on account of the hardness of the terms offered, my participation will be useless. My journey will be useful, because by residence in Berlin and conversation with the persons busy there I shall get a new and livelier view of things, because the public will see in it a new step to relieve their sufferings, and perhaps during our intercourse means will present themselves of influencing M. Daru.

but was supported at the expense of the country ?
Accordingly for some time Napoleon returns no
answer.   He then declares the security insufficient
and demands more.   This claim is admitted at the
end of April, and then he relapses into a silence
which is not broken till August 20th, at which date
all the circumstances have been altered by the Spanish Insurrection and the Capitulation of Baylen.
In other words, Stein's mission, successful as it
seemed and indeed was so far as he could make it so,
is in the end completely frustrated by the difficulty
which he had been aware of from the beginning.

Meanwhile let us ask ourselves from what resources Stein had drawn the sum he had been able
to offer Daru.

It is a notable peculiarity of Stein's career that
he meets immediate necessities by measures which
have lasting and far-reaching effects.   In the case of
the Emancipating Edict this has been pointed out ;
personal liberty, free trade, freedom of vocation, are
there used to relieve the temporary distress which
had been brought upon the country by the war.
We have occasion to remark it again when we
consider the financial expedients he has recourse
to in order to pay Napoleon.   The enemy himself had called his attention to the royal domains
by proposing that if the Prussian Government could
not find money it should make a cession of the
lands at its disposal.   Considering the extent of
the domains and the great revenues which the
State drew from them, the occupation of them
by France would have been nothing less than a
commencement of annexation.   But it was true that

If the arrangement is concluded during my stay my presence
will be useful, since the measures to be adopted in fulfilment of
our engagements will then be more promptly carried into effect...
In case, however, M. Daru should prefer concluding the arrangement with me rather than the Commission, it is desirable that I
should be furnished with full powers to settle, which I might use
in the circumstances described.

In short he went to Berlin, as he himself tells
us, 'in order not to leave untried any way of alleviating the condition of the Prussian Monarchy.'
It was important to satisfy public opinion, but
that anything could be accomplished at Berlin he
does not himself seem clearly to believe.   What
was the use, it may be asked, of influencing Daru?
The man whom it was important to influence was
Napoleon.   And again we may ask with great confidence after the event, What would be the value
of any arrangement concluded with Daru?   If it
was not such as to satisfy Napoleon, or in other
words as unfavourable as possible to Prussia, it
would be null and void as a matter of course.

Meanwhile did Stein consider the risk he ran
in leaving Königsberg?   That he says nothing of
it in the paper just quoted is no proof that he did
not, for that paper was addressed to the King and
therefore could not deal with such a question as
the possibility of losing ascendancy over the King
by absence.   But as Stein's power depended entirely on the King, it seems surprising that he
should have thought it judicious to leave him for
several months together, and so allow him to fall
under the influence of his old antagonist, Beyme,
or of the courtiers.   But perhaps he hoped on the
other hand to overawe the French party in Berlin

by his presence; or perhaps he judged that his ascendancy over the King actually gained by not being obtruded, and that the King would grow used to it the more easily by being relieved for a time from his too commanding presence. At any rate, we cannot trace that any ill effects did actually follow from Stein's absence; when he returns to Königsberg at the end of May his influence appears to be as great as ever.

No doubt it was worth while to procure the good will of Daru, even at some sacrifice. It was perhaps doubtful whether his influence with Napoleon would be of any positive use to Prussia, but it might, no doubt, if actuated by ill-will, do her much harm. And he was now greatly incensed. The most important member of the Berlin Commission with whom he had hitherto negotiated was the Privy Councillor Sack, and he was not even an Excellency! During the last two months Daru had been passed by altogether, and a vain attempt had been made to appeal from him to Caesar. In itself, therefore, and for the immediate purpose of propitiating Daru, the measure now adopted was excellent, and it proved fully successful. It was a most complete atonement to him, that the Chief Minister of the State should actually abandon the Court and come to live for three months as a kind of Ambassador in Berlin, now a French town under the government of Daru.

It was not believed at Berlin that Stein would shine in diplomacy. He, so famous for angularity and irritability, and who seemed to have been named in some foresight of his immovable obstinacy! If

there was another man in the country as obstina as himself it was probably Daru, who, they marked, was also named Pierre. What was to expected from the encounter of the two Rocks!

Stehen wie Felsen doch zwei Männer gegen einander.

But these forebodings were not realised. S was remarkably and easily successful, so much that though he only reached Berlin on March the treaty was signed and in the hands of a cou for Paris on the 9th. It was a treaty which sa Prussia from the necessity of yielding domain l to France, and provided for the evacuation of territory at the end of April.

Not, we may be sure, without concessions, concessions, the degradation of which Stein feel more bitterly than most men, was this gained. He had to emulate the tameness Haugwitz, to witness daily wrongs done to his try, and at times himself to obey Daru's o and this not only without complaint, but wh lavished marks of distinction upon Daru. instance, it is said, the Berlin Academy nam translator of Horace along with Laplace and others an Honorary Member. Even Stei proudest of men, was forced to recognize t the time the national pride was humbled.

But when Daru's jealousy had been sooth a tolerable arrangement made with him, Stei in sight for the first time of the real difficulty. Napoleon ratify the arrangement? Nay, why he consent to remove his army from Prussia, not only served there to overawe Austria and

in these domains the Prussian Government had value more than sufficient to meet the French demands, for they were estimated to be worth 60,000,000 thalers. Now there were other ways in which this wealth could be applied to the payment of the French debt besides that of simply handing it over to the foreign creditor. It was possible, in the first place, to raise money on it by way of mortgage. This was somewhat more easy than such an operation might be expected to be in a country where credit was still in its infancy. For the distress which had fallen on the landowners after the Seven Years War had brought into existence Mortgage Societies, which had first commenced in Silesia, where they were suggested by a man named Büring, and had afterwards spread to the other provinces of the Monarchy. They had for their object to facilitate by means of the principle of association the raising of money by the landowners on the security of their land. This machinery could now be used by the Government; in each Province the Royal Domain might enter the Mortgage Society. Objections were made, particularly by Schön, to this course, but they did not convince Stein, and he succeeded in raising more than 70,000,000 francs in this manner. Fifty-three millions more he raised by bills, which he prevailed on merchants at Breslau, Stettin, Elbing, Königsberg, Memel, and bankers at Berlin to accept; and it was thus that he was enabled to make the arrangement just described with Daru.

But there was another use to which the domains might be put. To part with them to a foreign

Government would no doubt be fatal, but parting with them for a price to Prussian citizens, or even to Germans outside Prussia, was not open to the same objection. What was lost by the Government would in that case not be lost by the nation. The revenues of these lands would no longer flow into the coffers of the State, but neither would they flow out of the country. They would pass into the pockets of the citizens, from which, if necessary, it was possible for the Government to recover them by taxation. And was it not in itself desirable that this change should take place? Even if no foreign creditor pressed, would it not be a step in advance for the Prussian Government to give up this old-fashioned method of raising a revenue? The innovation would no doubt be great, it would be such as in quiet times no Minister would readily propose; but on the other hand, was it not one which when adopted in a moment of necessity, would not only be sufficient for the immediate purpose, but would continue permanently so beneficial that the necessity itself might be blessed which led to its adoption? This was Stein's opinion. He held that the national wealth would be increased by giving up the domains to private industry on the economical principle that the sense of property is a spur to industry, and he also considered that the domains did positive harm by confusing the arrangement of administrative affairs, and by corrupting the officials. He writes, that 'the results of experience have everywhere confirmed the conclusions of theory, and agriculture flourishes most in the countries where there are no domains....'

It will be evident, however, that the scheme of selling the domains, though likely to be permanently useful, would not furnish any great supply for the immediate wants of the State. For not only did the legal arrangements which were necessary before anything so serious as the alienation of the ancient estate of the Hohenzollerns could be commenced require time, but it was evident that the sale itself when commenced must be slow and gradual if the land sold was not to sink in value. To throw so much land into the market at once was the surest way to depreciate it, and indeed it was not judicious to sell at all at a moment when there was so little money in the country. Accordingly the sale of the domains, though it was fairly initiated by Stein and occupied him throughout his Ministry, yet did not and could not make much progress in his time. Only the indispensable preliminary step, namely, the enactment of a so-called Domestic Law, which should be signed not only by the King but by all the descendants of Frederick William I. who were capable of succession, and which should sanction in certain defined circumstances the alienation of the domains, was brought to an advanced stage before Stein retired. The draught of this law was sent in by the Chancellor v. Schrötter on November 4th, 1808. In the last days of his Ministry Stein was occupied in mending this draught so as to avert the danger of such waste of the Crown Lands in capricious royal grants as he had no doubt read of in his favourite English history; but the Domestic Law was not actually completed and signed until Nov. 6th, 1809, that is, a year after his retirement.

It may be supposed that attempts were made to raise money by foreign loans. In more modern days Governments much less respectable and hardly less distressed have found the means to possess themselves of some part of the vast accumulation of capital waiting investment, particularly in England. But the time of foreign loans had then hardly arrived, and the fear of Napoleon would not allow London to be thought of. Niebuhr, however, was sent to see what he could do at Amsterdam. He left Memel in November, 1807, and after a journey which, in his description of it, seems to have been almost as dangerous as his father's travels in the Arabian desert, reached Berlin. How he found matters there the reader already knows. He arrived at Amsterdam early in March, and remained there till after the fall of the Minister who had sent him. King Louis received him well and inspired him with high admiration, but he made little way among the capitalists. While the world changed so much from year to year, and no one could guess at Napoleon's plans, it seemed no time for lending money to Governments. Just as he was on the point of departing, indeed, the bankers changed their tone and began to encourage him. He attributed this to the influence of Napoleon, whose interest, as we have remarked all along, was to preserve Prussia from absolute bankruptcy until he was ready to absorb her. Niebuhr now made progress and soon wanted nothing but the King's consent, which at that time was necessary in Holland in such a case. But this was refused on the ground that money could not be allowed in such times to go out of Holland; and in the spring of

1809, just while the campaign of the Danube was proceeding, Niebuhr was on his way back to Berlin. This mission of Niebuhr's is but a specimen of many similar attempts which the Prussian Government made at this time, always with the same ill-success, at Altona, at Frankfurt, at Paris.

There remained the method of increased taxation, which in the exhaustion of the country the Government resorted to most unwillingly. We have seen how little it had hitherto been the practice in Prussia to depend upon taxation for the means of meeting extraordinary needs. Since 1667—when the Great Elector after twenty years of perpetual quarrelling with the Estates succeeded in imposing a permanent Excise upon the towns, and so laid the foundation of Prussia's military greatness— taxation had existed, but it had been little developed, and the financial science of the Hohenzollerns had always occupied itself by preference with increasing the revenue of the domains. Their instinct, no doubt, showed them that this was the proper path of despotism, and that increased taxation led by a direct road to constitutional government. But in the present crisis all such scruples were vain. The King could no longer save the country, the nation must be called on to save itself; and what, when the crisis was over, the nation might demand of its sovereigns in return must be left to chance. The close connexion between new taxes and deliberative assemblies was visible from the first. Taxes were not imposed upon the whole country by arbitrary edict, but a separate arrangement was made for each province, and wherever

Estates still existed the arrangement was made through them. The financiers of that time would be likely to look to Pitt for lessons in war-taxation. His income tax had been proposed in 1798 in a speech which had attracted the attention of foreigners. Mallet du Pan wrote of it thus : ' From the time that deliberative assemblies have existed I doubt whether any man ever heard a display of this nature equally astonishing for its extent, its precision, and the talents of its author. It is not a speech spoken by the Minister; it is a complete course of public economy : a work, and one of the finest works upon practical and theoretical finance that ever distinguished the pen of a philosopher and statesman.' Mr Gladstone has pointed out that ' if there had been resolution enough to submit to the Income Tax at an earlier period our Debt need not at this moment have existed.' In 1806, the very year of Prussia's disasters, when Stein's financial studies must have been most anxious, the arrangements of the English Income Tax were revised and made much more effective. We may therefore be prepared to find an Income Tax now introduced in Prussia; in discussing the mode of raising it Stein expressly refers to the experience of England. On February 13th appeared an Edict imposing it in the Provinces of East Prussia and Lithuania, and establishing the machinery necessary for raising it. It was also introduced in West Prussia. Silesia took a course of its own under the active guidance of a certain v. Massow. A Property Tax was there established, and Stein recommended the same course to the Marks and Pomerania.

It may seem surprising that the provinces of a country ruled despotically should act with so much independence. The truth is that the pressure of French tyranny threw them back upon themselves, and made it impossible for them to wait for orders from head-quarters. In this temporary abeyance of the central authority, in this liberty introduced for the moment as a kind of provisional arrangement, and still more in the necessity of financial innovations, lay an opportunity which Stein was not likely to let slip of wiping away from Prussia the reproach that she 'had no Constitution.' In his brief summary of the policy of his Administration we find him noting that 'the King was already inclined to the formation of Estates General and took counsel in many cases of the existing Provincial Estates.'

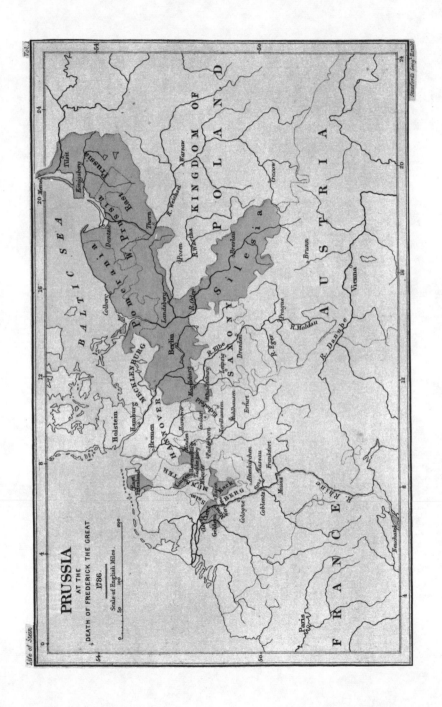

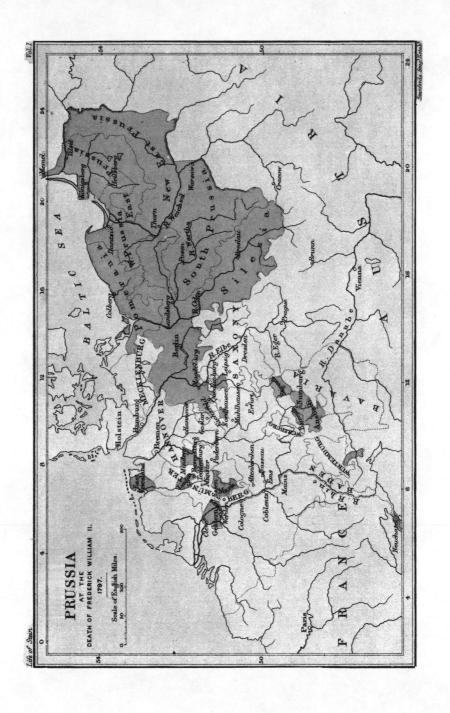

PRUSSIA
AT THE
DEATH OF FREDERICK WILLIAM II.
1797.

Scale of English Miles.

BALTIC SEA

East Prussia

New East Prussia

West Prussia

South Prussia

Silesia

Pomerania

MECKLENBURG

Berlin

HANOVER

SAXONY

BAVARIA

BADEN

WÜRTEMBERG

FRANCE

A U S T R I A

Memel
Königsberg
Tilsit
Thorn
Posen
Breslau
Danzig
Colberg
Landsberg
R. Oder
R. Warthe
R. Weichsel
Warsaw
Cracow
Brünn
Vienna
Prague
R. Eger
R. Danube
Holstein
Hamburg
Bremen
Magdeburg
R. Elbe
Dresden
Leipzig
Erfurt
Mülhausen
Paderborn
Münster
Altenkirchen
Nassau
Ems
Mainz
Coblentz
Cologne
Nürnberg
Würzburg
Paris
Neuchâtel

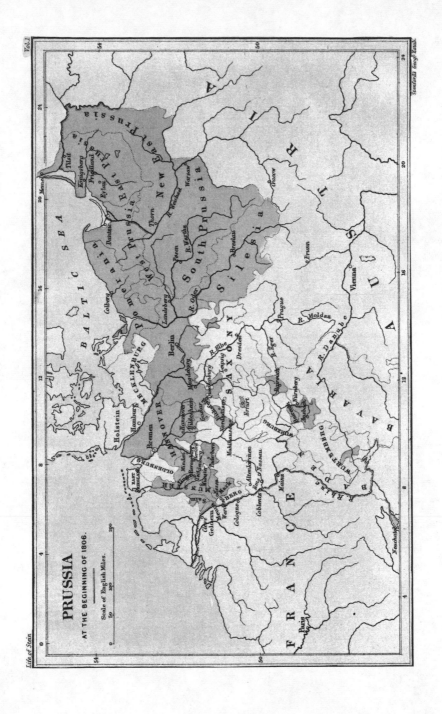

PRUSSIA
AT THE BEGINNING OF 1806.

Scale of English Miles.
0   50   100   150

Stanford's Geog.l Estab.t

INDEX TO VOL. I.